Mathematics
Today

Mathematics Today

 Harcourt Brace Jovanovich, Publishers

Orlando   New York   Chicago   Atlanta   Dallas

PHOTO CREDITS
Key: Top(t); Center(c); Bottom(b); Left(l); Right(r).

Ken Karp: Cover

Page 1, Chesebrough-Pond's. 4, Roy Morsch. 5(t), The Bettmann Archive, (b) Shostal. 6, © ASP Science Source/Photo Researchers. 7(r), Rowan/Photo Researchers. 8, Standard Oil Co. (N.J.). 9, Photo Researchers. 15(l), © David R. Frazier/Photo Researchers, (r) © Catherine Ursillo/Photo Researchers. 17(tl), The Bettmann Archive, (tc) © Marc Bernheim/Woodfin Camp & Assoc., (tr) The Bettmann Archive, (b) The Bettmann Archive. 21, both Ingbert Grüttner; 23, © Michal Heron. 26(t), Shostal, (b) © Michal Heron. 29, © Roy Morsch. 30(t), © William Bacon/Photo Researchers, (b) Woodfin Camp & Assoc. 31, Bob Glander/Shostal. 32, Carleton Ray/Photo Researchers. 35, from (l) to (r), Loren McIntyre/Woodfin Camp & Assoc., © James H. Carmichael, Jr./The Image Bank, © Tom and Pat Leeson/Photo Researchers, © James H. Carmichael, Jr./The Image Bank. 37, Harvey Barad/Photo Researchers. 41(l), © Karl Hentz/The Image Bank, (r) © Stephanie Stokes/Stock Market. 44, Michael Philip Manheim/Photo Researchers. 49, © Michal Heron. 50, Shostal. 51, © B. Krueger/Photo Researchers. 52, © Michal Heron. 53, © Michal Heron. 55(r), Bernard Pierre Wolff/Photo Researchers, (l) Shostal. 58(t), Ray Ellis/Photo Researchers, (b) Dennis Brack/Black Star. 59, © Nick Nicholson/The Image Bank. 63, © Michal Heron. 65, Shostal. 71, © Michal Heron. 75(t), Timothy Eagan/Woodfin Camp & Assoc., (b) © Treat Davidson/Photo Researchers. 81, © Roy Morsch. 82, Tom McHuch/Photo Researchers. 83, © Roy Morsch. 93, © Michal Heron. 96, Sepp Seitz/Woodfin Camp & Assoc. 97(l) Shostal, (r) Bell Jetranger/Shostal. 99, © Michal Heron. 102, Ingbert Grüttner. 101, © Michal Heron. 105, Halley Ganges. 109, The Bettmann Archive. 111, Shostal. 116, Barnsley Park/The Image Bank. 121, Shostal. 125, Halley Ganges. 129, © Michal Heron. 132, Shostal. 133, Carl E. Krupp/Shostal. 137, © Roy Morsch. 144, Catherine Ursillo/Photo Researchers. 151, Shostal. 153(t), © Manley Photo, Shostal, (b) Hirmer Photo Archive, Munich. 159, © Michal Heron. 166, Joe Munroe/Photo Researchers. 167, Cliff Feulner/The Image Bank. 168, Lee Bataglia/Photo Researchers. 169, © John Blaustein/Woodfin Camp & Assoc. 177, © Sepp Seitz/Woodfin Camp & Assoc. 178, © Peter Menzel/Stock. 180, Shostal. 183, Halley Ganges. 185, NASA. 188, © Michal Heron. 194, Shostal. 195, W. Rivelli/The Image Bank. 197, © Roy Morsch. 201, © Michal Heron. 204, © Ingbert Grüttner. 207, Walley McNamee/Woodfin Camp & Assoc. 215, © Peter Miller/The Image Bank. 218, Shostal. 220, HBJ Photos. 221, Shostal. 222, Jerry Cooke/Photo Researchers. 223, © Howard Hall, Living Ocean Soc./Photo Researchers. 225, © Roy Morsch. 233, Halley Ganges. 241, Catherine Ursillo/Photo Researchers. 243, © Roy Morsh. 245, D. Forbert/Shostal. 246, © Michal Heron. 247, © Peter Arnold. 249, © Junebug Clark/Photo Researchers. 250, Van Bucher/Photo Researchers. 252, Bob Glander/Shostal. 253, © Ingbert Grüttner. 255, © Roy Morsch. 259, The Stock Market. 260, Shostal. 256, George Hausman/The Image Bank. 263, Halley Ganges. 266, © Michal Heron. 281, Shostal. 291, Raymond Ng. 288(l) © Roy Morsch, (r) Martha Swope. 289, © Roy Morsch. 305, Halley Ganges. 310, Shostal. 312(t), from (l) to (r), George E. Jones III/Photo Researchers, Eric Carle/Shostal, © H. Wendler/The Image Bank, Shostal; (b) from (l) to (r) © Al Satterwhite/The Image Bank, © Don Carl Steffen/Photo Researchers, © Margot Granitses/Photo Researchers, © Lou Jones/The Image Bank. 314, Richard Weiss/ © Peter Arnold. 323, Bob Glander/Shostal. 324-325, Peter Shames. © Black Star. 333, © Michal Heron. 334-339 © Roy Morsch. 344, Shostal. 347-349, © Roy Morsch. 351, © John Marmaras/Woodfin Camp & Assoc. 353, © Tom Burnside. 355, Joe Munroe/Photo Researchers. 361, John Meany. 363, © Roy Morsch. 369, Van Bucher/Photo Researchers. 373, © Roy Morsch/Stock Market. 374, © Timothy White/Shostal. 375, © Carl Frank/Photo Researchers. 380(t) © Michal Heron, (b) © Ed Bohon/The Stock Market. 390, Ingbert Grüttner.

ART CREDITS
Key: Top(t); Center(c); Bottom(b); Left(l); Right(r).

Susan Banta: 77, 110, 111, 217, 296, 354; Wendy Biggins: 74, 113, 121, 130, 142, 148, 171, 176, 192, 251, 294 (b); Jan Brett: 34, 117, 258, 301, 324, 359; Penny Carter: 38, 39, 94, 106, 134, 174, 203, 272, 321, 334; Ric Del Rossi: 181, 268; Len Ebert: 12, 13, 72, 73, 86, 87, 117, 135, 173, 267; Konrad Hack: 24, 25, 60, 127, 145, 172, 227, 365, 384, 385; Thomas Hamilton, Jr.: 19, 281, 282, 283, 284, 285, 286, 322, 323; Dave Hannum: 68, 69; Meryl Henderson: 119, 269, 286; John Killgrew: 138, 335, 367; Verlin Miller: 264, 291, 318, 337, 356; Michael O'Reilly: 2, 9, 10, 11, 45, 89, 112, 114, 126, 160, 193, 237, 239, 244, 257, 268, 336, 378; Ondre Pettingill: 356; John Rice: 74, 80, 92, 93, 191, 236; Gail Roth: 107, 161, 190, 238, 297, 361; Nancy Schill: 14, 36, 162, 242, 299; Dennis Schofield: 62, 84, 91, 95, 220, 241, 340; Ruth Soffer: 150, 187; Jim Spence: 42, 61, 91, 149, 175, 254, 297; Judy Sutton: 40, 198, 209, 234, 235, 291, 296; Gary Undercuffler: 33, 59, 88, 141, 186, 214, 219, 376; Lane Yerkes: 8, 28, 76, 78, 79, 122, 128, 170, 341, 372; Sara Mintz Zwicker: 62 (b), 67, 68, 85, 211, 294 (t) and (c), 350, 352.

Technical art, charts, graphs, and maps: Blaise Zito Associates, Inc.
Glossary art: Vantage Art, Inc.

Printed in the United States of America
ISBN: 0-15-350708-X

CONTENTS

chapter 13 Ratio and Percent

chapter 14 Integers

Numeration

Expanded Form • Place Value • Millions and
Billions • Comparing, Ordering, and Rounding
Numbers • Powers and Exponents • Problem
Solving: Using a Table • Roman Numerals
• Time Line

Expanded Form

We use ten **digits** to name numbers.

0 1 2 3 4 5 6 7 8 9

We use only ten digits because we group by tens.
This system is called the **decimal** numeration system.

thousand	hundred	ten	one
(10 × 100)	(10 × 10)	(10 × 1)	1
1,000	100	10	1

We can show the number two thousand three hundred forty-nine in **expanded form.**

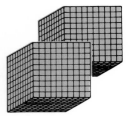 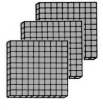 

2 thousands		3 hundreds		4 tens		9 ones
(2 × 1,000)	+	(3 × 100)	+	(4 × 10)	+	(9 × 1)

Expanded form
→ 2,000   +   300   +   40   +   9

Number → 2,349

A comma separates the hundreds from the thousands.

Practice • Write the numbers.

1.

2.

3. eight thousand seven hundred sixty-five

4. 2,000 + 500 + 40

5. 7,000 + 20 + 9

Write the expanded forms.

6. 672   **7.** 807   **8.** 3,459   **9.** 1,923   **10.** 2,006

Mixed Practice • Write the numbers.

11. four thousand, six hundred forty-eight
12. nine thousand, three hundred seven
13. seven thousand, ninety-five
14. 5,000 + 400 + 30 + 8   **15.** 3,000 + 600 + 60 + 2
16. 1,000 + 900 + 70 + 6   **17.** 6,000 + 800 + 50 + 4
18. 2,000 + 10 + 8   **19.** 9,000 + 100 + 80 + 9

Write the expanded forms.

20. 357   **21.** 841   **22.** 6,044   **23.** 3,340   **24.** 7,058

25. 1,960   **26.** 3,456   **27.** 2,123   **28.** 2,738   **29.** 8,621

Write the numbers in words.

30. 396   **31.** 760   **32.** 1,037   **33.** 8,986   **34.** 3,002

35. 4,619   **36.** 7,345   **37.** 8,090   **38.** 5,153   **39.** 1,096

PROBLEM SOLVING • APPLICATIONS

The following airline distances are expressed in words.
Write the numbers.

40. The distance from New York to Cairo is eight thousand, nine hundred ninety kilometers.

41. The distance from New York to Paris is five thousand, eight hundred seventeen kilometers.

42. The distance from Peking to New York is ten thousand, nine hundred fifty kilometers.

Skills Maintenance

1. 5
$+3$

2. 9
$+2$

3. 8
$+5$

4. 7
$+4$

5. 9
$+9$

6. 9
-4

7. 6
-2

8. 5
-3

9. 18
-9

10. 17
-9

3

Place Value

hundred thousands 10 × 10,000 100,000	ten thousands 10 × 1,000 10,000	thousands 10 × 100 1,000	hundreds 10 × 10 100	tens 10 × 1 10	ones 1
					3
				3	0
			3	0	0
		3	0	0	0
	3	0	0	0	0
3	0	0	0	0	0

In the ones place, the digit 3 names the number 3.
In the tens place, the 3 names the number 30.
In the hundreds place, the 3 names the number 300.
What number does the 3 name
    in the thousands place?
    in the ten-thousands place?
    in the hundred-thousands place?

*Each place in a number has a value
ten times the value of the place to its right.*

Practice • What number does the 7 name?

	hundred thousands	ten thousands	thousands	hundreds	tens	ones
1.			3	7	5	8
2.	4	7	6	0	3	2
3.		1	8	4	7	6
4.	2	5	7	3	9	4
5.	7	9	8	6	0	2

In what place is each blue digit?

6. 11,130 **7.** 268,272 **8.** 7,136 **9.** 86,205 **10.** 266,479

4

Mixed Practice • In what place is each blue digit?

11. 234

12. 3,219

13. 174,057

14. 35,276

15. 312,407

16. 659,807

17. 324,962

18. 920,703

19. 462,503

20. 864,217

21. 143,067

22. 309,216

What number does each blue digit name?

23. 234

24. 3,219

25. 174,057

26. 35,276

27. 312,407

28. 659,807

29. 324,962

30. 920,703

31. 545,378

32. 694,132

33. 135,629

34. 387,569

Look at each pair of numbers. In which one does the 7 name the greater number?

35. 7,286 or 2,786

36. 11,974 or 12,715

37. 34,720 or 67,543

38. 1,742 or 3,907

39. 27,892 or 24,765

40. 86,017 or 18,711

41. 567,920 or 576,920

42. 407,643 or 740,529

43. 173,296 or 837,492

Use all the digits in each exercise. Write the greatest number possible.

★ **44.** 8, 7, 9 and 0

★ **45.** 0, 2, 7, 8 and 1

★ **46.** 2, 6, 0, 4, 6 and 3

Use all the digits in each exercise. Write the least number possible.

★ **47.** 6, 2, 7 and 5

★ **48.** 5, 2, 6, 0 and 0

★ **49.** 5, 3, 1, 5, 2 and 0

PROBLEM SOLVING • APPLICATIONS

Use the table to answer the questions.

50. In which year was the population eight thousand?

51. In which year was the population two hundred seventy-eight thousand, seven hundred eighteen?

★ **52.** In which year was the population between ten thousand and fifty thousand?

★ **53.** In which years was the population greater than two hundred thousand?

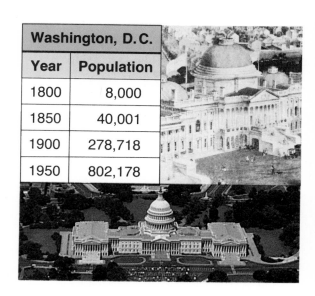

Washington, D.C.	
Year	Population
1800	8,000
1850	40,001
1900	278,718
1950	802,178

5

Millions and Billions

The distance between the sun and Uranus is about two billion, eight hundred seventy-two million, seven hundred thousand kilometers.

Billions Period			Millions Period			Thousands Period			Ones Period		
hundred billions $10 \times 10,000,000,000$	ten billions $10 \times 1,000,000,000$	billions $10 \times 100,000,000$	hundred millions $10 \times 10,000,000$	ten millions $10 \times 1,000,000$	millions $10 \times 100,000$	hundred thousands $10 \times 10,000$	ten thousands $10 \times 1,000$	thousands 10×100	hundreds 10×10	tens 10×1	ones 1
		2	8	7	2	7	0	0	0	0	0

1,000 thousand is 1 million.   1,000 million is 1 billion.

Large numbers are separated into **periods** by commas.
The commas make the numbers easier to read.

Read: → 2 billion, 872 million, 700 thousand
Write: → 2,872,700,000

Here is another large number.

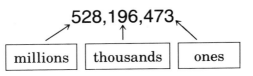

Read: → 528 million, 196 thousand, 473

Practice • Write the numbers.

1. 7 million, 602 thousand, 567

2. 86 billion, 127 million, 400 thousand, 265

3. 550 billion, 336 million, 942 thousand, 466

Write the digits that are in the millions period.

4. 62,480,172

5. 164,327,430

6. 8,372,197,806

Write the digits that are in the billions period.

7. 155,674,000,162

8. 9,205,372,428

9. 42,567,332,531

6

Mixed Practice • Write the numbers.

10. 5 million, 364 thousand, 298
11. 2 billion, 900 thousand
12. 68 billion, 435 million, 703 thousand, 264
13. 15 billion, 502

Write the digits that are in the millions period.

14. 2,496,158,370   15. 3,012,798,654   16. 46,269,800,355

17. 8,086,908,726   18. 6,967,444,210   19. 77,100,264,993

Write the digits that are in the billions period.

20. 45,301,276,489   21. 3,012,798,654   22. 2,496,158,370

23. 6,500,000,362   24. 9,605,867,300   25. 316,249,527,348

Name 1,000,000 more.

26. 2,674,385   27. 3,496,582,718   ★ 28. 49,999,562,180

Name 1,000,000,000 more.

29. 4,325,694,126   30. 164,533,600,217   ★ 31. 999,000,000,000

PROBLEM SOLVING • APPLICATIONS

Use the table to answer the questions.

32. Which planet is about one hundred eight million, two hundred thirty thousand kilometers from the sun?

★ 33. Which planet is less than one hundred million kilometers from the sun?

Planet	Average Distance from the Sun in Kilometers
Earth	149,590,000
Mars	227,270,000
Mercury	57,900,000
Venus	108,230,000

Midchapter Review

Write the expanded forms.

1. 845   2. 6,072   3. 7,105   4. 8,690   5. 4,227

Write the numbers.

6. 4,000 + 500 + 80 + 1   7. 3 billion, 6 million, 900 thousand

Write the digits that are in the millions period.

8. 3,178,405,619   9. 72,500,316,004   10. 412,907,683,010

Comparing and Ordering Numbers

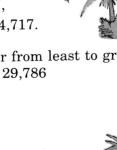

The railroad is an important means of transportation. There are 34,717 kilometers of track in one country and 34,817 kilometers of track in another.

Compare: 34,717 and 34,817.

Think:
Same number of ten thousands.
Same number of thousands.
Compare the hundreds.

$$7 < 8$$

So 34,717 is less than 34,817,
and 34,817 is greater than 34,717.

Write these lengths of track in order from least to greatest.

40,753   70,716   29,786

Think: 29,786 < 40,753
40,753 < 70,716

So 29,786 < 40,753 < 70,716.

Practice • Write >, <, or =.

1. 8,234 ● 8,324
2. 9,301 ● 8,469
3. 5,468 ● 5,468
4. 42,697 ● 42,679
5. 86,014 ● 87,601
6. 38,824 ● 38,284

Write in order from least to greatest.

7. 672; 736; 689
8. 2,061; 2,601; 2,016
9. 56,172; 56,672; 56,217; 56,127
10. 496,784; 496,748; 469,874; 469,784

Mixed Practice • Write >, <, or =.

11. 6,024 ● 6,204
12. 5,196 ● 5,196
13. 4,926 ● 4,962
14. 21,825 ● 22,824
15. 330,467 ● 303,764
16. 273,461 ● 274,641
17. 566,723 ● 566,723
18. 666,562 ● 559,999
19. 1,141,014 ● 1,114,114
20. 1,000,000 ● 1,999,999
21. 9,908,800 ● 9,909,900
22. 4,670,900 ● 4,670,900

8

Write in order from least to greatest.

23. 4,826; 4,286; 4,682

24. 1,255; 5,125; 1,552

25. 34,622; 43,632; 24,262

26. 478,002; 474,200; 784,400

★ **27.** 500,000; 600,000; 650,000; 560,500

★ **28.** 1,264,563; 1,246,634; 1,264,536; 1,426,346

PROBLEM SOLVING • APPLICATIONS

Use the table to answer questions 29 through 33.

29. Which country has the most railroad track?

30. Which country has the least railroad track?

31. Write a true sentence to compare the lengths of track in the United States and in Argentina.

32. Write a true sentence to compare the lengths of track in Australia, Brazil, and China.

33. Write the lengths of track from the chart in order from least to greatest.

Railroad Track	
Country	Length of Track in Kilometers
Argentina	39,782
Australia	40,753
Brazil	29,786
Canada	70,716
China	48,000
India	60,357
Soviet Union	138,500
United States	560,052

Skills Maintenance

Write the numbers.

1. 6 thousands, 9 hundreds, 3 ones

2. 7 thousands, 9 ones

3. 9 million, 653 thousand

4. 109 million, 370

6. 73 billion, 16 thousand

6. 567 billion, 3 thousand, 24

Rounding Numbers

In a local election Tanya Brooks received 6,328 votes. To the nearest thousand, about how many votes did she receive?

$$6,328 \quad 6,500 \quad 6,875$$
$$6,000 \quad\quad 6,500 \quad\quad 7,000$$

6,328 is between 6,000 and 7,000.
It is nearer to 6,000.
6,328 rounded to the nearest thousand is 6,000.

Tanya Brooks received about 6,000 votes.

John Forester received 6,875 votes.
6,875 is between 6,000 and 7,000.
It is nearer to 7,000.
6,875 rounded to the nearest thousand is 7,000.

Sabrina Bates received 6,500 votes.
6,500 is halfway between 6,000 and 7,000.
Round 6,500 up to 7,000.
6,500 rounded to the nearest thousand is 7,000.

You can round numbers without using a number line.

Round 23,535 to the nearest ten thousand.
The digit in the ten-thousands place is 2.
The digit to the right of the 2 is less than 5.
Keep the digit in the ten-thousands place the same.

ten thousands
↓
23,535
↑

23,535 rounded to the nearest ten thousand is 20,000.

Round 784,500 to the nearest hundred thousand.
The digit in the hundred-thousands place is 7.
The digit to the right of the 7 is 5 or greater.
Increase the digit in the hundred-thousands place by 1.

hundred thousands
↓
784,500
↑

784,500 rounded to the nearest hundred thousand is 800,000.

Practice • Round to the nearest ten.

1. 57 **2.** 32 **3.** 89 **4.** 75

Round to the nearest hundred.

5. 3,247 **6.** 4,596 **7.** 2,351 **8.** 7,449

Round to the nearest thousand.

9. 6,896 **10.** 14,261 **11.** 17,500 **12.** 52,733

Mixed Practice • Round to the nearest ten.

13. 63 **14.** 186 **15.** 732 **16.** 3,455

Round to the nearest hundred.

17. 8,639   **18.** 7,555   **19.** 52,649   **20.** 13,614

Round to the nearest thousand.

21. 4,875   **22.** 3,900   **23.** 856,104   **24.** 977,648

Round to the nearest ten thousand.

25. 64,372   **26.** 58,512   **27.** 27,350   **28.** 411,469

Round to the nearest hundred thousand.

29. 764,372   **30.** 458,512   **31.** 6,327,350   **32.** 2,858,295

Round to the nearest million.

33. 4,434,433   **34.** 4,444,976   **35.** 6,906,421   **36.** 15,569,200

Round to the nearest billion.

★ **37.** 7,896,050,321   ★ **38.** 14,095,621,484   ★ **39.** 46,724,641,312   ★ **40.** 816,432,151,029

PROBLEM SOLVING • APPLICATIONS

Pretend that you are a newspaper reporter. You are writing a story about some presidential election results. You need to round to the nearest hundred thousand. What numbers will you use?

41. In the election of 1928, Alfred E. Smith received 15,016,443 votes.

42. Franklin D. Roosevelt won the election in 1932 with 22,821,857 votes.

43. Herbert Hoover received 15,761,841 votes when he ran against Franklin D. Roosevelt.

Copy and complete the table.

Presidential Election Results of 1912

	Candidate	Votes	Round to the nearest			
			thousand	ten thousand	hundred thousand	million
★ **44.**	Woodrow Wilson	6,286,214				
★ **45.**	Theodore Roosevelt	4,126,020				
★ **46.**	William H. Taft	3,483,922				

Powers and Exponents

Look at the number sentence.
  Each 10 is a **factor.**
  1,000 is the **product.**
  1,000 is a **power** of 10.

$$10 \times 10 \times 10 = 1,000$$

You can use an **exponent** to tell how many times 10 is used as a factor.

$$\overset{\text{exponent}}{10^3} = 10 \times 10 \times 10 = 1,000$$

Read 10^3 as ten to the third power.

Look for a pattern in the chart. Compare the number of zeros in the number with the exponent in the exponent form.

Number	Factor Form	Exponent Form	Read
100	10×10	10^2	ten to the second power or ten squared
1,000	$10 \times 10 \times 10$	10^3	ten to the third power or ten cubed
10,000	$10 \times 10 \times 10 \times 10$	10^4	ten to the fourth power

These all name five thousand.

5,000 $5 \times 1,000$ $5 \times 10 \times 10 \times 10$ 5×10^3

In the expression 2^4, the 4 is the exponent and the 2 is the base.

$$2^4$$
$$\downarrow$$
$$2 \times 2 \times 2 \times 2 = 16$$

Read 2^4 as two to the fourth power.

Practice • Write the exponent forms.

1. 10×10

2. $10 \times 10 \times 10$

3. $10 \times 10 \times 10 \times 10$

4. $2 \times 2 \times 2$

5. 5×5

6. $3 \times 3 \times 3 \times 3 \times 3$

Multiply to find the numbers.

7. 10^5

8. 10^6

9. 10^7

10. 2^5

11. 6^2

12. 3^4

Write the numbers.

13. $6 \times 10 \times 10$

14. $9 \times 1,000$

15. 3×10^4

Mixed Practice • Write the exponent forms.

16. $10 \times 10 \times 10$

17. $10 \times 10 \times 10 \times 10$

18. $10 \times 10 \times 10 \times 10 \times 10$

19. $3 \times 3 \times 3 \times 3 \times 3 \times 3$

20. $9 \times 9 \times 9$

21. $7 \times 7 \times 7 \times 7$

Write the numbers.

22. $10 \times 10 \times 10$

23. $10 \times 10 \times 10 \times 10$

24. $10 \times 10 \times 10 \times 10 \times 10$

25. 10^3

26. 10^4

27. 10^5

28. 8^2

29. 4^3

30. 2^5

31. 3^2

32. 7^2

33. 5^3

34. 5×100

35. $8 \times 1,000$

36. $6 \times 10,000$

37. $5 \times 10 \times 10$

38. $8 \times 10 \times 10 \times 10$

39. $6 \times 10 \times 10 \times 10 \times 10$

40. 5×10^2

41. 8×10^3

42. 6×10^4

Write the powers of ten in exponent form.

★ **43.** $(2 \times 10,000) + (5 \times 1,000) + (6 \times 100) + (8 \times 10) + (7 \times 1)$

★ **44.** $(6 \times 100,000) + (4 \times 10,000) + (3 \times 1,000) + (9 \times 100) + (8 \times 10) + (3 \times 1)$

Write the numbers.

★ **45.** $(9 \times 10^6) + (3 \times 10^4) + (5 \times 10^3) + (1 \times 10^2) + (8 \times 1)$

★ **46.** $(7 \times 10^8) + (4 \times 10^7) + (2 \times 10^5) + (6 \times 10^3) + (3 \times 10^2) + (4 \times 10)$

PROBLEM SOLVING • APPLICATIONS

Rewrite the sentences using a number.

47. There are 6×10 minutes in an hour.

48. There are 10^2 years in a century.

Archeologists study ancient buildings, tools, and other objects to learn about the past. They use exponents to date objects many millions of years old.

Copy and complete the table.

	Object	Number of Years Old	Exponent Form
★ **49.**	earthen bowl	5,000	?
★ **50.**	rock	?	6×10^6
★ **51.**	gold mask	700	?
★ **52.**	bone	?	3×10^4

PROBLEM SOLVING · STRATEGIES

Using a Table

Sometimes you must locate information in a table in order to solve a problem. Use the headings to help you find the information you need.

During one census, these populations were reported for twelve states.

State	Population
Alaska	400,481
California	23,668,562
Colorado	2,888,834
Iowa	2,913,387
Maryland	4,216,446
Michigan	9,258,344
New York	17,700,000
North Dakota	652,695
Tennessee	4,590,750
Texas	14,228,383
Vermont	511,456
Wyoming	470,816

Which state had the largest population?

Use these steps to help you solve the problem.

Step 1 Read the problem. What does it ask? Find the state with the largest population.

Step 2 Make a plan. Use the headings to find the state and its population.

Step 3 Find the answer. Find the largest population in the table. Then find the state.

Step 4 Check the answer. Read the question again. Does the information answer the question?

California had the largest population.
California is the correct answer.

Use the table to answer the questions.

1. Was the number of people in California closer to 23,000,000 or 24,000,000?

A table organizes information clearly.

---

2. Which state had a population between 10 million and 15 million?

3. Which state had the smallest population?

4. Was the number of people in Texas closer to 15,000,000 or 14,000,000?

5. Which state had a population of about 9 million?

Use the heading at the top of each column to find the correct information.

---

6. Which state had the smaller population, Vermont or Wyoming?

7. Round each number in the table to the nearest hundred thousand.

8. Which two states had a population of 500,000 when rounded to the nearest hundred thousand?

9. Which 2 states had a population of 2,900,000 when rounded to the nearest hundred thousand?

10. Which state had the larger population, Maryland or Tennessee?

⋆ 11. New York had about 5 million fewer people than Canada. What was the population of Canada?

⋆ 12. New York had about 10,000,000 more people than New Jersey. What was the population of New Jersey?

⋆ 13. List the states in order from the least to the greatest number of people.

REVIEW

Write the numbers. (pages 2–3)
1. four thousand, two hundred ninety-one
2. 1,000 + 70 + 5

Write the expanded forms. (pages 2–3)
3. 317   4. 5,069   5. 4,800   6. 6,660   7. 5,385

In what place is the blue digit? (pages 4–5)
8. 923,008   9. 265,891   10. 847,203   11. 658,349

Write the numbers. (pages 6–7)
12. 15 million, 168 thousand, 214
13. 309 billion, 516 million, 55 thousand, 428

Use 409,212,676,885. Write the digits that are in the
(pages 6–7)
14. thousands period.   15. billions period.   16. millions period.

Write >, <, or =. (pages 8–9)
17. 6,972 ● 6,472   18. 10,025 ● 10,225   19. 6,638 ● 6,638

Write in order from least to greatest. (pages 8–9)
20. 2,784; 3,206; 1,295   21. 4,389; 4,983; 4,893; 4,398

Round 9,218 to the nearest
(pages 10–11)
22. ten.
23. hundred.
24. thousand.

Round 54,273,596 to the nearest
(pages 10–11)
25. ten thousand.
26. hundred thousand.
27. million.

Write the exponent forms. (pages 12–13)
28. $10 \times 10 \times 10 \times 10$ 29. $3 \times 3 \times 3 \times 3 \times 3$ 30. 5×5

Write the numbers. (pages 12–13)
31. $10 \times 10 \times 10 \times 10 \times 10$ 32. 6^3 33. 2×10^2

Solve.
34. The 1980 Census recorded the population of Maryland as 4,216,446 and the population of Louisiana as 4,203,972. Which had the greater population? (p. 14)

35. According to the 1980 Census, the population of Massachusetts was 5,737,037. What is the population rounded to the nearest ten thousand? (p. 14)

PROJECT

Roman Numerals

The ancient Romans used these symbols to name numbers.

I	V	X	L	C	D	M
1	5	10	50	100	500	1,000

The Roman system was not a place-value system. The values of the symbols are added or subtracted.

When the symbols are the same or decrease in value from left to right, the values are added.

When a symbol with a smaller value is written before a symbol with a larger value, the values are subtracted.

Symbol	Operation	Decimal Number
VII	5 + 1 + 1	7
XXVI	10 + 10 + 5 + 1	26
MDLX	1,000 + 500 + 50 + 10	1,560
IV	5 − 1	4
XC	100 − 10	90
MCMXL	1,000 + (1,000 − 100) + (50 − 10)	1,940

Write the decimal numbers.

1. MCCXV

2. DCCXXXI

3. MCDXL

Write the Roman numeral for each year.

4. 1543

5. 1752

6. 1945

Roman numerals are still used today. You may see them on clocks and buildings. Find ten places where Roman numerals are used. Make a poster. Show a picture of the place, the Roman numeral, and the equivalent decimal number for each.

TEST

Write the numbers.

1. seven thousand, four hundred fifty-nine

2. $3,000 + 400 + 8$

Write the expanded forms.

3. 503   **4.** 6,745   **5.** 9,487   **6.** 3,040   **7.** 4,209

In what place is each blue digit?

8. 153,206   **9.** 700,591   **10.** 548,197   **11.** 759,842

Write the numbers.

12. 9 million, 478 thousand, 74

13. 27 billion, 891 million, 43 thousand, 604

Use 769,455,298,009. Write the digits that are in the

14. thousands period.   **15.** millions period.   **16.** billions period.

Write $>$, $<$, or $=$.

17. 17,358 ● 17,385   **18.** 741,668 ● 741,668   **19.** 54,623 ● 54,603

Write in order from least to greatest.

20. 6,039; 5,477; 5,747; 6,903

21. 5,601,927; 859,266; 1,470,700; 86,295

Round 8,595 to the nearest

22. ten.
23. hundred.
24. thousand.

Round 5,316,089 to the nearest

25. ten thousand.
26. hundred thousand.
27. million.

Write the exponent forms.

28. $10 \times 10 \times 10 \times 10 \times 10$ **29.** $2 \times 2 \times 2$ **30.** $8 \times 8 \times 8 \times 8$

Write the numbers.

31. 7^3 **32.** $6 \times 1,000$ **33.** 7×10^7

Solve.

34. During one week the post office delivered $8,000 + 700 + 60 + 4$ letters to the town of Maple Grove. How many letters is that?

35. On Monday the post office delivered 16,084 letters. On Tuesday 16,123 letters were delivered. On which day was more mail delivered?

ENRICHMENT

Time Line

Many inventions have changed the way people live. These are some of the inventions introduced between 1800 and 1900.

  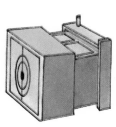 

A **time line** shows dates on a number line.
Copy the time line.
Make a mark on the time line to show approximately when each event listed below occurred.
Write the letter of the event above the mark.
Then list the letters of the events in order.
Start with the event that happened first.

| 1800 | 1820 | 1840 | 1860 | 1880 | 1900 |

A. Jean Joseph Étienne Lenoir built a one-cylinder internal-combustion engine in 1860.

B. The first safety match was invented in 1844.

C. Whitcomb L. Judson of Chicago patented the first zipper in 1893.

D. Elias Howe invented the first sewing machine for home use in 1846.

E. In 1876 Alexander Graham Bell invented the telephone.

F. In 1826 Joseph Nicéphore Niépce made the first permanent photograph with a camera.

G. The first steam locomotive was invented in 1804.

H. In 1895 Guglielmo Marconi invented the wireless telegraph.

I. Thomas A. Edison invented an incandescent lamp in 1879.

J. In 1867 three inventors designed the first typewriter.

COMPUTER

Computer Basics

A *computer* is a machine that works with numbers and letters.

Computer hardware is the metal and plastic machinery of the computer itself.

A *computer system* includes input, output, hardware, and software.

A *programmer* is a person who writes a program of instructions to a computer.

A *program* is a list of step-by-step input to a computer.

Computer software includes all the programs and data used by the computer.

Data are the numbers, letters, and instructions with which the computer works.

A computer can get *input* from a keyboard, punched cards, tape, or disks. A *keyboard* is a typewriter that is attached to a computer. Punched cards, tape, and disks can hold much data. Data that are input to one program may have been output from another program.

A computer can place *output* on any or all of these types of output devices:
A *cathode-ray tube (CRT)* displays output on a television screen.
A *printer* can print output on paper to make a permanent document.
Punched cards can save output for years.
Magnetic tapes hold output data in a very condensed form.
Diskettes, sometimes called *floppy disks,* are very portable.
Hard disks can hold millions of letters or numbers.

Computers use binary numbers.
Binary numbers have only zeros and ones.
Each 0 or 1 is called a *bit*.
A group of *four* bits is called a *nibble*. A group of *eight* bits is called a *byte*.
A byte can have one of 256 different decimal values.
Each value of a byte can be translated into a different character.
A *character* can be a number, a letter, a command, or
a special symbol such as a question mark or a dollar sign or a parenthesis.

A computer can use a cathode-ray tube (CRT) for display.
The smallest square of light on a CRT is called a *pixel.*
All digits, letters, and special symbols can be made from groups of pixels.

Computer *storage* is measured in *K.* K stands for a storage of 1,024 bytes. A 32K computer can hold about as much information as 16 pages like this one.

Hard disks contain *megabytes,* millions of bytes, of storage. A 12-megabyte hard disk can hold as much information as 6,000 pages like this one.

In the near future, storage devices such as floppy disks will be storing more characters. Today a $5\frac{1}{4}$-inch floppy disk stores 850,000 characters. The surface of the disk is like a long spiral of 850,000 tiny magnets linked up end to end. Its surface is similar to the surface of a phonograph record. Soon a process of *vertical recording* will stand the magnets on end. These new disks will be able to store 5,000,000 characters.

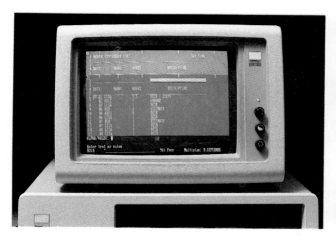 

Choose the correct answers.

1. A group of eight bits is

    A. a bit.
    B. a nibble.
    C. a byte.
    D. none of the above.

2. K stands for a storage of

    A. 1,000 bytes.
    B. 1,024 bytes.
    C. 6,000 bytes.
    D. none of the above.

3. A character can be

    A. a number.
    B. a letter.
    C. a special symbol.
    D. all of the above.

4. Megabytes are

    A. 1,024 bytes.
    B. 6,000 bytes.
    C. millions of bytes.
    D. none of the above.

5. A 12-megabyte hard disk holds

    A. 16 pages like this one.
    B. 6,000 pages like this one.
    C. 850,000 pages like this one.
    D. 5,000,000 pages like this one.

6. The surface of a floppy disk is

    A. like a phonograph record.
    B. like a spiral of magnets.
    C. both of the above.
    D. neither A nor B.

SKILLS MAINTENANCE

Chapter 1

Choose the correct answers.

1. Write the number.

$$4,000 + 600 + 3$$

A. 463
B. 4,603
C. 4,630
D. not here

2. Write 782 in expanded form.

A. $70 + 80 + 2$
B. $700 + 80 + 2$
C. $7,000 + 800 + 20$
D. not here

3. In what place is the blue digit?

845,690

A. ten thousands
B. millions
C. hundred thousands
D. not here

4. What number does the blue digit name?

53,941

A. 3
B. 30
C. 3,000
D. not here

5. What digits are in the billions period?

789,401,362,895

A. 789
B. 401
C. 362
D. not here

6. Compare.

4,872 ● 4,787

A. >
B. <
C. =
D. not here

7. Write the numbers in order from least to greatest.

3,264 3,642 3,462

A. 3,642 3,462 3,264
B. 3,264 3,462 3,642
C. 3,462 3,642 3,264
D. not here

8. Round 8,484,070 to the nearest hundred thousand.

A. 8,400,000
B. 8,500,000
C. 8,480,000
D. not here

9. Write the number.

4×10^5

A. 400
B. 4,000
C. 400,000
D. not here

10. The population of Ellis City is 45,867. What is the population to the nearest thousand?

A. 45,000
B. 45,900
C. 40,000
D. not here

11. Clarksville has a population of 269,051. Johnson City has one million more people. What is the population of Johnson City?

A. 369,051
B. 10,269,051
C. 1,269,051
D. not here

Addition and Subtraction

Addition and Subtraction Facts • Estimating Answers • Addition and Subtraction with Regrouping • Zero in Subtraction • Problem Solving: Adding and Subtracting Money • Equal to, Greater Than, Less Than • Problem Solving: Using Equations • Logic

Addition Facts

Miguel Elias is a public health nurse.
He visits patients in their homes.
On Monday he saw 4 patients in the
morning and 5 patients in the afternoon.
How many patients did Miguel see on
Monday?

When groups are joined, use **addition**.

$$
\begin{array}{r}
\text{addend} \longrightarrow 4 \\
\text{addend} \longrightarrow +5 \\
\hline
\end{array}
$$

$4 + 5 = 9 \longleftarrow \text{sum} \longrightarrow 9$

Miguel saw 9 patients on Monday.

These properties of addition will help you.

Commutative Property of Addition	
You can add two numbers in either order. The sum is always the same.	$9 + 8 = 17$ $8 + 9 = 17$

Associative Property of Addition	
You can group addends differently. The sum is always the same.	$(3 + 4) + 6 = 3 + (4 + 6)$ $7 + 6 = 3 + 10$ $13 = 13$

Property of Zero for Addition	
When you add zero to any addend, the sum equals the addend.	$0 + 18 = 18$ $0 + 0 = 0$ $18 + 0 = 18$

Practice • Add.

1. $\begin{array}{r} 9 \\ +3 \\ \hline \end{array}$	**2.** $\begin{array}{r} 3 \\ +9 \\ \hline \end{array}$	**3.** $\begin{array}{r} 9 \\ +7 \\ \hline \end{array}$	**4.** $\begin{array}{r} 8 \\ +9 \\ \hline \end{array}$	**5.** $\begin{array}{r} 4 \\ +0 \\ \hline \end{array}$	**6.** $\begin{array}{r} 3 \\ +5 \\ \hline \end{array}$	**7.** $\begin{array}{r} 8 \\ +6 \\ \hline \end{array}$
8. $\begin{array}{r} 2 \\ +9 \\ \hline \end{array}$	**9.** $\begin{array}{r} 6 \\ +4 \\ \hline \end{array}$	**10.** $\begin{array}{r} 5 \\ +3 \\ \hline \end{array}$	**11.** $\begin{array}{r} 6 \\ +5 \\ \hline \end{array}$	**12.** $\begin{array}{r} 4 \\ +7 \\ \hline \end{array}$	**13.** $\begin{array}{r} 9 \\ +8 \\ \hline \end{array}$	**14.** $\begin{array}{r} 2 \\ +4 \\ \hline \end{array}$

15. $4 + 6 = \underline{?}$ **16.** $5 + 7 = \underline{?}$ **17.** $3 + 4 = \underline{?}$

Mixed Practice • Add.

18.	1 +2	19.	7 +3	20.	8 +6	21.	6 +7	22.	5 +8	23.	0 +8	24.	4 +8
25.	4 +5	26.	7 +2	27.	2 +1	28.	1 +7	29.	2 +0	30.	6 +3	31.	5 +7
32.	5 +6	33.	5 +5	34.	0 +0	35.	2 +2	36.	6 +1	37.	8 +7	38.	0 +8

39. $2 + 5 = $ __?__

40. $8 + 9 = $ __?__

41. $8 + 3 = $ __?__

42. $5 + 2 = $ __?__

43. $8 + 1 = $ __?__

44. $6 + 9 = $ __?__

45. $(3 + 2) + 8 = $ __?__

46. $3 + (2 + 8) = $ __?__

47. $2 + (7 + 7) = $ __?__

Use the numbers in the INPUT column. Follow the rules. List the OUTPUTS.

★ **48.** Add 6.

INPUT	OUTPUT
7	13
3	?
0	?
9	?

★ **49.** Add 8.

INPUT	OUTPUT
8	?
6	?
2	?
7	?

★ **50.** Add 4.

INPUT	OUTPUT
9	?
7	?
8	?
5	?

PROBLEM SOLVING • APPLICATIONS

51. On Wednesday Miguel saw 3 patients in the morning and 3 patients in the afternoon. How many patients did Miguel see on Wednesday?

★ **52.** Miguel visited 3 adult patients another morning. He visited 8 young patients that afternoon and 7 in the evening. How many patients did Miguel see in all?

53. On Friday morning Miguel saw 4 patients. He saw 6 patients in all on Friday. How many did he see in the afternoon?

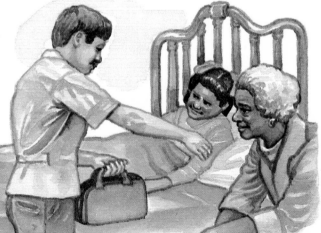

Subtraction Facts

Thelma has enough film to take 12 pictures. She takes 7 pictures at Lake Sunapaw. How many more pictures can she take?

When groups are separated, use **subtraction**.

$$12 - 7 = 5 \quad \begin{array}{r} 12 \\ -\ 7 \\ \hline 5 \end{array} \text{ difference}$$

She can take 5 more pictures.

> **Inverse Operation**
> Addition and subtraction are **inverse operations**. Use one to check the other.
>
> | Subtraction | Addition |
> |---|---|
> | $\begin{array}{r} 12 \\ -\ 7 \\ \hline 5 \end{array}$ | $\begin{array}{r} 5 \\ +7 \\ \hline 12 \end{array}$ |

Practice • Subtract.

1. $\begin{array}{r} 9 \\ -9 \\ \hline \end{array}$
2. $\begin{array}{r} 16 \\ -\ 8 \\ \hline \end{array}$
3. $\begin{array}{r} 6 \\ -5 \\ \hline \end{array}$
4. $\begin{array}{r} 7 \\ -2 \\ \hline \end{array}$
5. $\begin{array}{r} 16 \\ -\ 9 \\ \hline \end{array}$
6. $\begin{array}{r} 14 \\ -\ 5 \\ \hline \end{array}$
7. $\begin{array}{r} 12 \\ -\ 6 \\ \hline \end{array}$

8. $\begin{array}{r} 7 \\ -4 \\ \hline \end{array}$
9. $\begin{array}{r} 1 \\ -1 \\ \hline \end{array}$
10. $\begin{array}{r} 13 \\ -\ 7 \\ \hline \end{array}$
11. $\begin{array}{r} 9 \\ -0 \\ \hline \end{array}$
12. $\begin{array}{r} 10 \\ -\ 6 \\ \hline \end{array}$
13. $\begin{array}{r} 9 \\ -7 \\ \hline \end{array}$
14. $\begin{array}{r} 11 \\ -\ 8 \\ \hline \end{array}$

Mixed Practice • Subtract.

15. $\begin{array}{r} 12 \\ -\ 3 \\ \hline \end{array}$
16. $\begin{array}{r} 5 \\ -2 \\ \hline \end{array}$
17. $\begin{array}{r} 10 \\ -\ 4 \\ \hline \end{array}$
18. $\begin{array}{r} 6 \\ -1 \\ \hline \end{array}$
19. $\begin{array}{r} 6 \\ -6 \\ \hline \end{array}$
20. $\begin{array}{r} 2 \\ -2 \\ \hline \end{array}$
21. $\begin{array}{r} 13 \\ -\ 4 \\ \hline \end{array}$

22. $\begin{array}{r} 7 \\ -1 \\ \hline \end{array}$
23. $\begin{array}{r} 8 \\ -7 \\ \hline \end{array}$
24. $\begin{array}{r} 14 \\ -\ 9 \\ \hline \end{array}$
25. $\begin{array}{r} 3 \\ -1 \\ \hline \end{array}$
26. $\begin{array}{r} 5 \\ -3 \\ \hline \end{array}$
27. $\begin{array}{r} 12 \\ -\ 7 \\ \hline \end{array}$
28. $\begin{array}{r} 15 \\ -\ 7 \\ \hline \end{array}$

29. $\begin{array}{r} 9 \\ -4 \\ \hline \end{array}$
30. $\begin{array}{r} 4 \\ -3 \\ \hline \end{array}$
31. $\begin{array}{r} 11 \\ -\ 7 \\ \hline \end{array}$
32. $\begin{array}{r} 7 \\ -0 \\ \hline \end{array}$
33. $\begin{array}{r} 17 \\ -\ 9 \\ \hline \end{array}$
34. $\begin{array}{r} 4 \\ -4 \\ \hline \end{array}$
35. $\begin{array}{r} 15 \\ -\ 6 \\ \hline \end{array}$

36. $\begin{array}{r} 10 \\ -\ 8 \\ \hline \end{array}$
37. $\begin{array}{r} 8 \\ -0 \\ \hline \end{array}$
38. $\begin{array}{r} 12 \\ -\ 4 \\ \hline \end{array}$
39. $\begin{array}{r} 10 \\ -\ 9 \\ \hline \end{array}$
40. $\begin{array}{r} 13 \\ -\ 5 \\ \hline \end{array}$
41. $\begin{array}{r} 11 \\ -\ 2 \\ \hline \end{array}$
42. $\begin{array}{r} 13 \\ -\ 9 \\ \hline \end{array}$

43. $18 - 9 = $ ___?___

44. $16 - 7 = $ ___?___

45. $6 - 4 = $ ___?___

46. $7 - 3 = $ ___?___

47. $2 - 0 = $ ___?___

48. $9 - 2 = $ ___?___

49. $5 - 4 = $ ___?___

50. $5 - 1 = $ ___?___

51. $8 - 3 = $ ___?___

Find the missing numbers.

52. $8 + $ ___?___ $= 12$

53. $9 + $ ___?___ $= 18$

54. ___?___ $+ 3 = 12$

55. $9 + $ ___?___ $= 15$

56. $2 + $ ___?___ $= 11$

57. ___?___ $+ 6 = 11$

When parentheses are used with addition and subtraction, do the operation inside the parentheses first.

58. $(3 - 3) + 8 = $ ___?___

★ **59.** $(6 + 3) - 5 = $ ___?___

★ **60.** $4 + (11 - 2) = $ ___?___

★ **61.** $(14 - 7) + 6 = $ ___?___

★ **62.** $(13 - 4) - 1 = $ ___?___

★ **63.** $8 + (15 - 7) = $ ___?___

Use the numbers in the INPUT and OUTPUT columns.
Use the rules to find the missing numbers.

★ **64.** Subtract 6.

INPUT	OUTPUT
14	8
?	4
13	?
?	9

★ **65.** Subtract 5.

INPUT	OUTPUT
8	?
?	7
10	?
?	0

★ **66.** Subtract 8.

INPUT	OUTPUT
11	?
?	2
8	?
?	5

PROBLEM SOLVING • APPLICATIONS

67. Challene has 18 photos from her trip along Skyline Drive. She sends 9 to a friend. How many photos does Challene have left?

★ **68.** On June 8, Tara sent film by mail to be developed and printed. On June 17, she received the prints. How many days did she wait for her prints?

Skills Maintenance

What number does each blue digit name?

1. 752

2. 8,469

3. 4,560

4. 356

5. 25,712

Write $>$, $<$, or $=$.

6. 72,324 ⬤ 72,715

7. 9,281 ⬤ 9,812

8. 46,259 ⬤ 46,259

9. 61,433 ⬤ 61,403

10. 8,347 ⬤ 8,743

11. 903,810 ⬤ 908,103

Estimating Answers

Tamara orders 288 white candles for her gift shops. She also orders 432 red candles. About how many candles does she order in all?

Estimate the answer.

Nearest Hundred

Round each number to the nearest hundred. Add.

$$288 \longrightarrow 300$$
$$+432 \longrightarrow +400$$
$$\overline{ \quad 700}$$

She orders about 700 candles.

During the past year Tamara bought 3,780 hand-dipped candles for her gift shops. Her records show that 2,546 hand-dipped candles were sold. About how many hand-dipped candles are left?

Estimate the answer.

Nearest Thousand

Round each number to the nearest thousand. Subtract.

$$3,780 \longrightarrow 4,000$$
$$-2,546 \longrightarrow -3,000$$
$$\overline{ \quad 1,000}$$

About 1,000 hand-dipped candles are left.

Practice • Estimate. Round to the nearest ten. Then add or subtract.

1. 42	2. 17	3. 39	4. 75	5. 89	6. 17
+39	+68	+21	+33	+43	+52

7. 59	8. 76	9. 32	10. 88	11. 91	12. 63
−14	−22	−19	−49	−27	−37

Mixed Practice • Estimate. Round to the nearest hundred. Then add or subtract.

13. 645	14. 237	15. 839	16. 587	17. 348
+178	+593	+478	+785	+279

18. 463	19. 643	20. 391	21. 835	22. 709
−267	−196	−293	−189	−123

Estimate. Round to the nearest thousand. Then add or subtract.

23. 3,909 +1,855	**24.** 4,366 +8,585	**25.** 2,782 +1,354	**26.** 7,087 +1,219	**27.** 1,174 +8,809
28. 5,981 −2,653	**29.** 7,319 −2,986	**30.** 4,793 −2,081	**31.** 8,172 −2,887	**32.** 3,041 −1,119

Estimate. Round to the nearest ten thousand. Then add or subtract.

33. 84,929 +19,076	**34.** 52,741 +25,559	**35.** 20,596 +33,971	**36.** 46,358 +12,977	**37.** 27,835 +58,987
38. 52,891 −19,246	**39.** 69,877 −34,959	**40.** 31,649 −19,762	**41.** 84,006 −17,188	**42.** 49,736 −16,918

Estimate. Round to the nearest hundred thousand. Then add or subtract.

★ **43.** 675,091 +229,634	★ **44.** 425,099 +259,683	★ **45.** 631,492 +187,406	★ **46.** 709,874 −354,012	★ **47.** 850,092 −329,684

PROBLEM SOLVING • APPLICATIONS

Estimate the answers. Round to the nearest hundred. Then add or subtract.

48. In six months Tamara sold 872 animal-shaped candles. During the next six months, she sold 649 of them. About how many of these candles did she sell that year?

49. Tamara had 746 candlesticks in her stockroom in January. By the end of April there were 362 left. About how many candlesticks were sold in those four months?

50. The manager of a restaurant needs 780 blue candles. Tamara has 552 blue candles in stock. About how many more blue candles does she need to order for this customer?

★ **51.** Tamara places an order for scented candles. She orders 168 bayberry candles, 420 strawberry candles, and 312 lemon candles. About how many scented candles does she order?

29

Addition with Regrouping

Alaska and Hawaii have coastlines along the Pacific Ocean. The length of Alaska's coastline is 8,978 kilometers. The length of Hawaii's coastline is 1,207 kilometers. What is the total length of these coastlines?

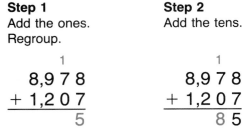

$8,978 + 1,207 =$

Step 1
Add the ones.
Regroup.

```
  1
  8,9 7 8
+ 1,2 0 7
─────────
        5
```

Step 2
Add the tens.

```
    1
  8,9 7 8
+ 1,2 0 7
─────────
      8 5
```

Step 3
Add the hundreds.
Regroup.

```
  1   1
  8,9 7 8
+ 1,2 0 7
─────────
    1 8 5
```

Step 4
Add the thousands.

```
  1   1
  8,9 7 8
+ 1,2 0 7
──────────
1 0,1 8 5
```

The total length is 10,185 kilometers.

More Examples

```
  2 1 1 1
  6 9,6 4 9
  3 8,0 2 7
+ 4 6,3 3 2
───────────
1 5 4,0 0 8
```

```
  1 1 2 1
      6 2 5
    8,4 8 7
  6 5,7 9 3
+       1 4
───────────
  7 4,9 1 9
```

Practice • Add.

1. 69
    +40

2. 44
    +78

3. 932
    + 43

4. 197
    +204

5. 56
    +987

6. 876
    +392

7. 2,406
    + 729

8. 674
    +1,467

9. 6,982
    +3,706

10. 7,067
    +9,245

Mixed Practice • Add.

11. 21
    +83

12. 86
    +25

13. 21
    +357

14. 824
    + 56

15. 375
    +386

16. 6,082
    +5,359

17. 7,443
    + 545

18. 838
    +6,443

19. 4,927
    +8,405

20. 6,143
    +9,817

21. 61
    32
    +14

22. 73
    28
    + 6

23. 217
    406
    +994

24. 7,188
    4,856
    + 773

25. 4,927
    1,989
    +8,405

26. 176,239	27. 332,896	28. 92,503	29. 53,024	30. 27,543
341,950	62,328	431,887	662,987	867
255,464	768,015	29,171	16	55,985
+ 6,133	+864,234	+ 827	+ 4,927	+ 2,100

31. 3,692 + 756 = _?_ **32.** 63 + 78 + 91 + 6 = _?_ **33.** 859 + 16 + 249 = _?_

34. 167 + 8,249 = _?_ **35.** 9 + 36 + 40 + 18 = _?_ **36.** 204 + 156 + 4 = _?_

What are the next two numbers in each pattern?

★ **37.**

4	37	70	?	?

★ **38.**

56	199	342	?	?

PROBLEM SOLVING • APPLICATIONS

Five states in the United States have coastlines along the Gulf of Mexico.

39. What is the total length of these coastlines?

★
40. Name the two states with the longest coastlines. What is the total length of their coastlines?

State	Kilometers
Alabama	85
Florida	1,239
Louisiana	639
Mississippi	71
Texas	591

Midchapter Review

Estimate. Round to the nearest hundred.

1. 345	2. 471	3. 257	4. 845	5. 939
+291	+545	+409	−361	−481

Add.

6. 47	7. 594	8. 4,175	9. 8,145	10. 53,914
+25	+269	+4,967	3,702	4,261
			+ 546	182,046
				+ 21,005

Subtraction with Regrouping

The average depth of the Atlantic Ocean is 3,677 meters. The greatest known depth in the Atlantic Ocean is in the Puerto Rico Trench. It is 8,648 meters below the ocean's surface. How much deeper is the Puerto Rico Trench than the average depth of the Atlantic Ocean?

$8,648 - 3,677 = ?$

Step 1
Subtract the ones.
Regroup.
Subtract the tens.

```
   5 14
 8,6 4 8
-3,6 7 7
     7 1
```

Step 2
Regroup.
Subtract the hundreds.

```
      15
   7 5 14
 8,6 4 8
-3,6 7 7
   9 7 1
```

Step 3
Subtract the thousands.

```
      15
   7 5 14
 8,6 4 8
-3,6 7 7
 4,9 7 1
```

The Puerto Rico Trench is 4,971 meters deeper than the average depth of the Atlantic Ocean.

More Examples

```
   6 13
   7 3
 - 1 9
   5 4
```

```
      14
   3 4 12
   4 5 2
 -3 8 7
   6 5
```

```
         11
   5 1 14 6 15
   6 2,4 7 5
 -   9,8 2 8
   5 2,6 4 7
```

Practice • Subtract.

1. 96
   −27

2. 75
   −28

3. 815
   − 72

4. 710
   −268

5. 217
   −196

6. 5,531
   − 264

7. 4,284
   − 693

8. 3,924
   −1,897

9. 2,176
   −1,998

10. 9,642
    −3,906

Mixed Practice • Subtract.

11. 87
    −29

12. 93
    −64

13. 813
    − 77

14. 719
    − 94

15. 476
    − 43

16. 813
    −626

17. 914
    −518

18. 665
    −280

19. 352
    −141

20. 857
    −781

21. 5,918 − 653	22. 3,884 −1,907	23. 5,420 −2,816	24. 4,375 −1,264	25. 8,276 −4,987

26. 36,527
  − 982
	27. 46,151
	  − 9,806
		28. 59,837
		−18,125
			29. 81,643
			−26,898
				30. 40,572
				  − 5,851

31. 444,870
  − 98,980
	32. 897,394
	−294,100
		33. 59,813
		−18,125
			34. 382,132
			−190,756
				35. 135,764
				  − 78,349

36. $532 - 78 = \underline{?}$ **37.** $5,980 - 987 = \underline{?}$ **38.** $2,254 - 865 = \underline{?}$

39. $33,474 - 8,765 = \underline{?}$ **40.** $62,473 - 996 = \underline{?}$ **41.** $458,767 - 32,989 = \underline{?}$

42. $597,680 - 46,982 = \underline{?}$ **43.** $971,324 - 615,817 = \underline{?}$ **44.** $682,414 - 309,985 = \underline{?}$

Write the digit for each □.

★ 45. □ 3 6
   − □ 8
   4 7 □
	★ 46. 7,□ 4 2
	   − 3 □ □
	   □,7 4 4
		★ 47. 8,□ □ 4
		  −1,2 9 □
		   □,9 5 8
			★ 48. 4 6,3 □ 1
			   −□ 8,□ 2 7
			   2 □,7 9 □

PROBLEM SOLVING • APPLICATIONS

49. The average depth of the Pacific Ocean is 4,122 meters. The average depth of the Atlantic Ocean is 3,677 meters. What is the difference between these average depths?

50. The Arctic Ocean has an average depth of 1,330 meters. Its greatest depth is 5,450 meters. What is the difference between the greatest depth and the average depth?

★ **51.** The difference between the average depths of the Indian Ocean and Arctic Ocean is 2,630 meters. The average depth of the Arctic Ocean is 1,330 meters. What is the average depth of the Indian Ocean?

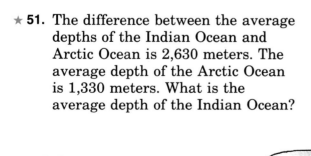

Zeros in Subtraction

Hakalou Greenhouse sends orchids all over the world. One distributor orders 4,004 orchids. 3,746 orchids are packaged and ready for shipment. How many more orchids need to be packaged?

$4,004 - 3,746 = ?$

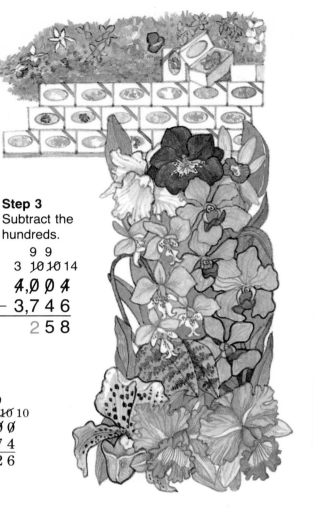

Step 1
Regroup.
Subtract the ones.

```
    9  9
  3 10 10 14
  4,0 0 4
- 3,7 4 6
        8
```

Step 2
Subtract the tens.

```
    9  9
  3 10 10 14
  4,0 0 4
- 3,7 4 6
      5 8
```

Step 3
Subtract the hundreds.

```
    9  9
  3 10 10 14
  4,0 0 4
- 3,7 4 6
    2 5 8
```

258 more orchids need to be packaged.

More Examples

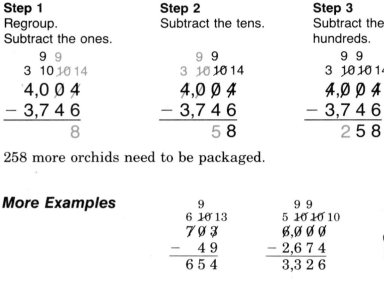

```
      9
    6 10 13
    7 0 3
  -   4 9
    6 5 4
```

```
      9  9
    5 10 10 10
    6,0 0 0
  - 2,6 7 4
    3,3 2 6
```

Practice • Subtract.

1. 460 −381	**2.** 800 −372	**3.** 470 − 93	**4.** 900 −518	**5.** 506 −159
6. 2,091 − 936	**7.** 8,009 − 705	**8.** 4,000 −2,176	**9.** 9,082 − 765	**10.** 6,040 −1,858

Mixed Practice • Subtract.

11. 590 − 77	**12.** 400 −164	**13.** 860 − 41	**14.** 300 −295	**15.** 702 −576
16. 1,000 − 68	**17.** 7,002 − 756	**18.** 2,010 − 865	**19.** 3,046 −1,096	**20.** 6,091 −1,824

21. 5,000
$-$1,354

22. 8,000
$-$2,674

23. 4,060
$-$ 995

24. 3,704
$-$ 92

25. 3,011
$-$1,763

26. 25,090
$-$ 8,164

27. 30,946
$-$26,295

28. 65,006
$-$ 642

29. 99,400
$-$64,500

30. 80,149
$-$70,032

31. 333,007
$-$297,457

32. 904,209
$-$ 62,194

33. 500,000
$-$386,593

34. 406,921
$-$ 4,734

35. 900,000
$-$826,542

36. $600 - 456 = \underline{\ ?\ }$

37. $4,000 - 2,645 = \underline{\ ?\ }$

38. $2,060 - 995 = \underline{\ ?\ }$

39. $94,002 - 3,670 = \underline{\ ?\ }$

40. $26,000 - 998 = \underline{\ ?\ }$

41. $447,006 - 38,695 = \underline{\ ?\ }$

42. $396,001 - 48,762 = \underline{\ ?\ }$ ★ **43.** $1,000,000 - 82,683 = \underline{\ ?\ }$ ★ **44.** $1,000,000,000 -$
$987,654,321 = \underline{\ ?\ }$

PROBLEM SOLVING • APPLICATIONS

45. Hakalou Greenhouse also prepares centerpieces. A distributor orders 600 centerpieces. 258 centerpieces are ready. How many more centerpieces still need to be prepared?

46. The greenhouse has 967 planters in stock. 2,010 are needed to complete several new orders. How many more planters are needed?

47. Yolanda Joffries orders 800 orchids for her florist shops. She receives 375 orchids in one shipment. How many more orchids should she receive to complete the order?

★ **48.** Hakalou Greenhouse packages 3,000 star orchids and 5,080 boat orchids. 2,090 packaged orchids are sent to one distributor. How many packaged orchids are left?

PROBLEM SOLVING • STRATEGIES

Adding and Subtracting Money

Add or subtract money as if you were adding or subtracting whole
numbers. Remember to write the dollar sign and cents point in the
answer.

Vanya is a member of a baseball team.
She buys a uniform for $12.75 and a
baseball cap for $4.59. How much does
she spend in all?

Use these steps to help you solve the problem.

Step 1
Read the problem.
What does it ask? How much in all?

Step 2
Make a plan.
To find how much in all, add.
$12.75 + $4.59 = ?

Step 3.
Find the answer.

Think:

```
  1275
+  459
```

Write:

```
  $12.75
+   4.59
  $17.34
```

Step 4
Check the answer.
Add the other way to check.

```
  $17.34 ←
  $12.75
+   4.59      These should
  $17.34 ←    be the same.
```
Vanya spends $17.34.

Vanya gives the clerk $20.
How much change does she get?
To find out much left, subtract.

Solve.

Think:

```
  2000
- 1734
   266
```

Write:

```
  $20.00
- $17.34
  $ 2.66
```

Check:

```
  $ 2.66
+  17.34
  $20.00
```

Vanya gets $2.66 change.

Which operation should you use to solve the problem? Write
ADDITION or SUBTRACTION.

1. The team purchased caps for $36.75,
   shirts for $56.85, and gloves for
   $82.56. How much did the team
   spend in all?

2. The team spent $328.68 for bats and $125 for baseballs. How much more did the team spend for bats than for baseballs?

Think: What information do I need?

Solve.

3. The Talls Basketball Team collected $820.50 in tickets to their first game. They collected $518.75 in tickets to their second game. How much less did they collect for the second game?

4. A soccer team spent $415.00 for uniforms, $76.50 for soccer balls, and $145.98 for shin guards. How much did the team spend in all?

5. A baseball fan took his two children to a baseball game. He spent $18.00 for tickets. During the game he bought food for $6.85 and a banner for $2.15. How much did he spend in all?

Read the questions carefully. What operations should you use?

6. A ticket to a football game costs $12.75. A ticket to a hockey game costs $7.98. How much more does the football ticket cost than the hockey ticket?

7. At a major league baseball game, the fans spent $527.35 on score cards. They spent $840.50 on souvenirs, and $2,457.96 on food. How much money did the fans spend at the game?

8. A ticket to a baseball game costs $9.25. A ticket to a football game costs $12.75. A ticket to a basketball game costs $9.35. How much would it cost a sports fan to attend all three games?

9. The manager of a hockey team spends $57.87 on hockey sticks. How much change does he receive from a $100 bill?

10. At a tennis match, the winner received a trophy that cost $125.00. The second-place player received a tennis racquet that cost $75.65. How much money was spent on the two prizes?

★ **11.** A bowler spends $43.50 for a bowling ball and $29.75 for shoes. A tennis player spends $58.90 for a racquet and $17.77 for shoes. Who spends more? How much more?

★ **12.** A soccer team has $1,286 to spend on new equipment. The team spends $214.27 on cleats, $87.50 on shin guards, and $575.85 on uniforms. How much money does the team have left?

Equal to, Greater Than, or Less Than

There are 38 cans of tomato soup and 41 cans of vegetable soup on the top shelf. There are 86 cans of bean soup on the bottom shelf. Are there more, fewer, or the same number of cans on the top shelf as on the bottom shelf?

Find whether $=$, $>$, or $<$ makes this a true sentence.

$$38 + 41 \bullet 86$$

Which of these sentences is true?

$38 + 41 = 86$	$38 + 41 > 86$	$38 + 41 < 86$
Since 79 is not equal to 86, the sentence is FALSE.	Since 79 is not greater than 86, the sentence is FALSE.	Since 79 is less than 86, the sentence is TRUE.

Since $38 + 41 < 86$, there are fewer cans of soup on the top shelf.

If two numbers are not equal, then we can write two sentences showing how they are related.

86 is greater than **79**.　　　　**79** is less than **86**.

　　　$86 > 79$　　　　　　　　$79 < 86$

Practice • Write $>$, $<$, or $=$.

1. $32 + 61 \bullet 93$ 　　　　**2.** $46 + 71 \bullet 120$ 　　　　**3.** $148 + 375 \bullet 520$

4. $43 - 14 \bullet 41$ 　　　　**5.** $92 - 54 \bullet 38$ 　　　　**6.** $680 - 326 \bullet 194$

More Practice • Write $>$, $<$, or $=$.

7. $26 + 43 \bullet 65$ 　　　　**8.** $42 + 91 \bullet 133$ 　　　　**9.** $54 + 18 \bullet 71$

10. $46 + 42 \bullet 90$ 　　　　**11.** $841 + 131 \bullet 976$ 　　　　**12.** $640 + 130 \bullet 768$

13. $763 + 144 \bullet 911$ 　　　**14.** $327 + 432 \bullet 750$ 　　　**15.** $84 - 16 \bullet 68$

16. 76 − 38 ⬤ 34   **17.** 32 − 15 ⬤ 16   **18.** 81 − 29 ⬤ 52

19. 236 − 147 ⬤ 89   **20.** 916 − 420 ⬤ 200   **21.** 742 − 416 ⬤ 326

22. 546 − 192 ⬤ 355   **23.** 653 + 139 ⬤ 792   **24.** 246 − 178 ⬤ 86

25. 95 − 26 ⬤ 87 − 19   **26.** 539 − 216 ⬤ 487 − 164

★ **27.** 116 + 211 + 47 ⬤ 463 − 98   ★ **28.** 3,482 − 987 ⬤ 1,554 + 187 + 763

PROBLEM SOLVING • APPLICATIONS

Write a true sentence for each.

29. A grocer has 216 frozen fish dinners and 178 frozen beef dinners on the top shelf of the frozen-food section. There are 364 frozen chicken dinners on the bottom shelf. Are there more, fewer, or the same number of frozen dinners on the top shelf as on the bottom shelf?

★ **30.** There are 87 cans of sardines and 68 cans of salmon on the top shelf of the canned-goods section. There are 54 cans of tuna and 79 cans of shrimp on the bottom shelf. Are there more, fewer, or the same number of cans on the top shelf as on the bottom shelf?

Skills Maintenance

Round to the nearest ten.

1. 94   **2.** 135   **3.** 198   **4.** 9,991   **5.** 5,362

Round to the nearest hundred.

6. 415   **7.** 4,326   **8.** 7,868   **9.** 16,422   **10.** 82,554

Round to the nearest thousand.

11. 7,758   **12.** 3,987   **13.** 5,500   **14.** 18,871   **15.** 19,099

PROBLEM SOLVING · STRATEGIES

Using Equations

A jumping course is being set up for a horse show. The horses will jump over 9 obstacles. 6 of them are ready. How many more obstacles need to be set up to complete the course?

You can write an **equation** to solve the problem.

Think: 6 plus some number is 9.

Write: $6 + n = 9$

To solve the equation, find the number that makes it true. The sum is 9. One addend is 6. Subtract to find the other addend.

$$\begin{array}{r} 9 \\ -6 \\ \hline 3 \end{array}$$

3 makes the equation true. $6 + 3 = 9$
3 more obstacles are needed.

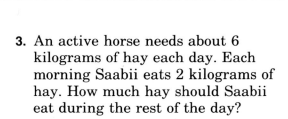

Write the equations. Then solve.

1. On Monday tickets go on sale for the horse show. 1,235 tickets are available. By Friday 198 are left. How many tickets have been sold?

2. In one event each horse must perform a series of movements. The score for this event is the sum of the scores given by the judges. Gretchen and her horse, Windfall, receive 8, 6, 9, 8, and 8 points from the judges. What is Gretchen's total score?

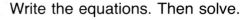

What are you asked to find?

3. An active horse needs about 6 kilograms of hay each day. Each morning Saabii eats 2 kilograms of hay. How much hay should Saabii eat during the rest of the day?

4. The steeplechase event is about 4 kilometers long. The time allowed for this event is 5 minutes. Neils has been riding for 3 minutes. How many minutes does he have left to complete the event in the allowed time?

5. Alexi won an event with 77 points. She lost 4 points for making a mistake. How many points did she have before she made the mistake?

6. Kip traveled 326 kilometers to the horse show. Paul traveled 298 kilometers to the horse show. How much farther did Kip travel than Paul?

Find the number that makes the equation true.

---

7. A truck holds 900 kilograms of bagged oats. 405 kilograms of bagged oats are already on the truck. How many more kilograms of bagged oats can be put on the truck?

8. One type of horseshoe weighs 280 grams. A lighter type of horseshoe weighs 56 grams less. How much does the lighter horseshoe weigh?

9. An American Saddle Horse is about 16 hands high. A Shetland Pony is 9 hands high. How many hands higher is the American Saddle Horse?

10. The horse show was presented on Saturday and Sunday. 73 people saw the horse show on Saturday. 206 people saw the horse show in all. How many people saw the horse show on Sunday?

11. At the horse show 62 red ribbons were awarded. 38 fewer blue ribbons were awarded. How many blue ribbons were awarded?

12. Ella wins an event with 40 points. She lost 2 points for tapping a fence. How many points did she have before she tapped the fence?

★ 13. Tara buys 2 tickets for the horse show. Each ticket costs $8.56. How much change does she get from a $20 bill?

★ 14. There are 8 saddles on display at the horse show. On Sunday 2 are sold. On Friday there are 3 left. How many saddles were sold during the week?

REVIEW

Add or subtract. (pages 24–27)

1. 5 +7	**2.** 13 – 9	**3.** 15 – 6	**4.** 8 +8	**5.** 9 +5
6. 9 +8	**7.** 10 – 1	**8.** 8 –6	**9.** 7 +9	**10.** 13 – 6

Estimate. Round to the nearest hundred. (pages 28–29)

11. 215 +476	**12.** 759 +148	**13.** 697 +236	**14.** 409 +351	**15.** 378 +462
16. 619 –428	**17.** 759 –281	**18.** 827 –336	**19.** 553 –384	**20.** 695 –459

Add. (pages 30–31)

21. 249 +538	**22.** 9,283 +3,897	**23.** 20,598 + 6,507	**24.** 282,795 + 17,648	**25.** 739,163 15,194 + 56,888

Subtract. (pages 32–35)

26. 722 –496	**27.** 3,574 – 985	**28.** 40,209 – 9,678	**29.** 210,424 –182,688	**30.** 700,000 – 98,546

Write >, <, or =. (pages 38–39)

31. 50 − 16 ⬤ 30   **32.** 138 + 138 ⬤ 400   **33.** 764 − 243 ⬤ 521

Solve.

34. Mr. Bluehouse drove his car 18,375 kilometers during one year. The next year he drove 17,898 kilometers. How far did he drive the car in two years? (p. 30)

35. When Ms. Nakai bought her used car, the odometer read 43,245 kilometers. It now reads 86,000 kilometers. How far has she driven the car? (p. 34)

Triplets for Fifty

Look at the number grid below. There are more than 20 triplets that add up to 50. A triplet is any three boxes that touch at some point, either horizontally, vertically, or diagonally. Two triplets are shown. Find the others. You can use a number more than once.

Copy the grid. Use colored lines to show triplets.

5	15	16	22	13	14	18	10
14	15	3	17	23	17	12	19
20	22	30	12	13	28	21	13
15	11	22	8	20	14	27	18
13	17	15	4	29	9	8	5
28	27	19	7	17	25	6	29
16	6	11	25	18	8	26	5
25	7	18	8	24	14	16	10

How do you rate?
   10 triplets—Try again!
   15 triplets—Very good.
   20 triplets—Outstanding.
   25 triplets—Genius material.

43

TEST

Add or subtract.

| 1. | 4
 +9 | 2. | 14
 − 6 | 3. | 18
 − 9 | 4. | 8
 +5 | 5. | 7
 +6 |

| 6. | 3
 +8 | 7. | 12
 − 5 | 8. | 10
 − 4 | 9. | 8
 +7 | 10. | 11
 − 6 |

Estimate. Round to the nearest hundred.

11. 169
+214

12. 439
+181

13. 561
+348

14. 672
+208

15. 345
+255

16. 727
−329

17. 545
−224

18. 971
−283

19. 738
−183

20. 808
−567

Add.

21. 568
+327

22. 5,634
+939

23. 52,961
+67,925

24. 355,192
+ 29,816

25. 397,789
209,403
+ 26,587

Subtract.

26. 678
−299

27. 2,375
−1,986

28. 10,760
− 9,949

29. 209,400
− 28,736

30. 625,008
−426,569

Write >, <, or =.

31. 121 − 56 ⬤ 65

32. 70 + 483 ⬤ 530

33. 600 − 343 ⬤ 280

Solve.

34. On Monday 3,750 bricks were delivered to a construction site. On Thursday 1,075 bricks were delivered to the site. How many bricks were delivered in the two days?

35. In the morning there were 4,753 bricks. At the end of the day, there were 2,879 bricks. How many bricks were used?

ENRICHMENT

Thinking Logically

There are 136 cartons of eggs.
24 cartons are Grade A large.
36 cartons are Grade A medium.
How many cartons are *neither*
Grade A large *nor* Grade A medium?

First find how many are Grade A
large and Grade A medium.

$$24 + 36 = 60$$

Then find how many are not
large or medium.

$$136 - 60 = 76$$

76 cartons are neither Grade A large nor Grade A medium.

Solve.

1. There are 864 cans of soup.
   148 cans are tomato soup.
   120 cans are chicken soup.
   How many cans are neither
   tomato soup nor chicken soup?

2. There are 108 cartons of milk.
   12 cartons are buttermilk.
   36 cartons are skimmed milk.
   How many cartons are neither
   buttermilk nor skimmed milk?

3. There are 48 bottles of juice.
   12 bottles are apple.
   10 bottles are orange.
   9 bottles are grape.
   How many bottles are neither
   apple, grape, nor orange?

4. There are 156 cans of vegetables.
   39 cans are peas.
   24 cans are corn.
   48 cans are string beans.
   How many cans are neither
   peas, corn, nor string beans?

5. There are 75 kilograms of fruit.
   23 kilograms are apples.
   15 kilograms are pears.
   30 kilograms are oranges.
   How many kilograms are neither
   apples, pears, nor oranges?

6. In the supermarket there are 15
   checkout counters.
   2 take ten items or less.
   3 take fifteen items or less.
   There is no limit at the other
   counters. You have twelve items.
   How many of the checkout counters
   will take your items?

CALCULATOR

Calculator Review

A calculator has *number buttons*   and   *command buttons.*

7	8	9
4	5	6
1	2	3
	0	

÷ Divide

× Times

− Minus

+ Plus

= Equals

First turn the calculator on.

To subtract 7 from 15, push [1] [5] [−] [7] [=].   Look at the screen: [8.]

The answer is 8.

Addition and Subtraction Facts Drill

1. $8 + 3 =$ __?__   **2.** $7 + 0 =$ __?__   **3.** $8 - 1 =$ __?__   **4.** $6 - 6 =$ __?__

5. $7 - 5 =$ __?__   **6.** $4 + 6 =$ __?__   **7.** $9 - 4 =$ ____   **8.** $5 + 2 =$ __?__

To divide 72 by 6, push [7] [2] [÷] [6] [=].   Look at the screen: [12.]

The answer is 12.

You may know the answer without using your calculator.

Multiplication and Division Facts Drill

9. $16 \div 2 =$ __?__   **10.** $8 \times 9 =$ __?__   **11.** $1 \times 7 =$ __?__

12. $24 \div 6 =$ __?__   **13.** $40 \div 5 =$ __?__   **14.** $15 \div 3 =$ __?__

15. $6 \times 5 =$ __?__   **16.** $27 \div 3 =$ __?__   **17.** $4 \times 2 =$ __?__

Push [CE]   if you make a mistake in your last entry.

Push [C]   if you make a mistake and want to start the problem over.

For the rest of the book, you will see "push [6] [5] [2] [−] [4] [3] [=]"

written "push 6 5 2 − 4 3 =."

The calculator has no commas and no dollar signs.

$\begin{array}{r} \$8,459 \\ -\ 6,273 \end{array}$ Push 8 4 5 9 − 6 2 7 3 = . Screen: ⌜ 2186 ⌝

Write the dollar sign and the comma in the proper places. The correct answer is $2,186.

Calculate. Remember to write the dollar signs and commas.

18. $\begin{array}{r} \$7,469 \\ +\ 2,045 \end{array}$ **19.** $\begin{array}{r} \$8,034 \\ -\ 5,985 \end{array}$ **20.** $7\overline{)\$9,457}$ **21.** $\begin{array}{r} \$6,081 \\ \times\quad 32 \end{array}$

Repeated operations can be done using only the equals button.

$8 \times 8 \times 8 \times 8 = ?$ Push 8 × = = = . The answer is 4,096.

Note that you use *the same number* of equals signs as there are multiplication signs.

Multiply.

22. $4 \times 4 \times 4 \times 4 \times 4 \times 4 = \underline{\ ?\ }$ **23.** $7 \times 7 \times 7 \times 7 \times 7 = \underline{\ ?\ }$

You must use *one more* equals sign than the number of plus signs for repeated addition.

$6 + 6 + 6 + 6 = ?$ Push 6 + = = = = . The answer is 24.

Add.

24. $5 + 5 + 5 + 5 + 5 = \underline{\ ?\ }$ **25.** $9 + 9 + 9 + 9 = \underline{\ ?\ }$

You use *the same number* of equals signs as minus signs for repeated subtraction.

$81 - 3 - 3 - 3 - 3 - 3 = ?$ Push 8 1 − 3 = = = = = . The answer is 66.

Subtract.

26. $48 - 13 - 13 - 13 = \underline{\ ?\ }$ **27.** $23 - 2 - 2 - 2 - 2 - 2 - 2 - 2 = \underline{\ ?\ }$

You use *the same number* of equals signs as division signs for repeated division.

$1000 \div 10 \div 10 \div 10 = ?$ Push 1 0 0 0 ÷ 1 0 = = = . The answer is 1.

Divide.

28. $72 \div 2 \div 2 \div 2 = \underline{\ ?\ }$ **29.** $6561 \div 9 \div 9 \div 9 \div 9 = \underline{\ ?\ }$

Always remember to turn the calculator off.

Choose the correct answers.

1. In what place is the blue digit?

709,514

- **A.** ten thousands
- **B.** hundred thousands
- **C.** thousands
- **D.** not here

2. What digits are in the millions period?

896,402,498,357

- **A.** 896
- **B.** 402
- **C.** 498
- **D.** not here

3. Compare.

69,487 ⬤ 69,874

- **A.** >
- **B.** <
- **C.** =
- **D.** not here

4. Round 54,997 to the nearest thousand.

- **A.** 54,000
- **B.** 50,000
- **C.** 55,000
- **D.** not here

5. Add.

$(7 + 3) + 6 = \underline{\ ?\ }$

- **A.** 10
- **B.** 9
- **C.** 14
- **D.** not here

6. Complete.

$8 + (15 - 9) = \underline{\ ?\ }$

- **A.** 32
- **B.** 6
- **C.** 14
- **D.** not here

7. Estimate. Round to the nearest thousand.

7,909
−3,487

- **A.** 5,000
- **B.** 3,000
- **C.** 4,000
- **D.** not here

8. Add.

67,912
4,031
+295,619

- **A.** 367,552
- **B.** 366,552
- **C.** 367,562
- **D.** not here

9. Subtract.

54,020
− 6,154

- **A.** 47,866
- **B.** 48,866
- **C.** 47,876
- **D.** not here

10. Hena buys a pair of sandals for $14.39. She gives the clerk $20.00. How much change does she get?

- **A.** $6.61
- **B.** $5.71
- **C.** $5.61
- **D.** not here

11. On Monday 1,874 people shopped at Packard's Grocery Store. On Tuesday 2,095 people shopped, and on Wednesday 1,765 people shopped. How many customers did Packard's have in three days?

- **A.** 5,724
- **B.** 5,734
- **C.** 5,634
- **D.** not here

Multiplication

Multiplication Facts and Properties • Multiplying by
One-Digit Numbers • Multiplying by Multiples of 10,
100, and 1,000 • Multiplying by Two-Digit Numbers
• Problem Solving: Multiplying Money • Multiplying
by Three-Digit Numbers • Problem Solving: Do You
Have Enough Money? • Combinations

Multiplication

People are buying tickets to the state fair.
There are 3 lines, and 7 people are in each line.
How many people are in line?

When groups of the same size
are joined, use **multiplication.**

$$\begin{array}{r} \text{factor} \longrightarrow \quad 7 \\ \text{factor} \longrightarrow \times 3 \\ \hline \end{array}$$

$3 \times 7 = 21 \longleftarrow \text{product} \longrightarrow \quad 21$

There are 21 people in line.

These properties of multiplication will help you.

Commutative Property of Multiplication You can multiply two numbers in either order. The product is always the same.	$2 \times 5 = 10$ $5 \times 2 = 10$
Associative Property of Multiplication You can group factors differently. The product is always the same.	$(4 \times 2) \times 3 = 4 \times (2 \times 3)$ $8 \times 3 = 4 \times 6$ $24 = 24$
Property of One for Multiplication When one of two factors is 1, the product equals the other factor.	$1 \times 9 = 9$ $9 \times 1 = 9$
Property of Zero for Multiplication When a factor is 0, the product is 0.	$0 \times 7 = 0$ $7 \times 0 = 0$ $0 \times 0 = 0$

Practice • Multiply.

1. $\begin{array}{r} 5 \\ \times 3 \\ \hline \end{array}$
2. $\begin{array}{r} 3 \\ \times 5 \\ \hline \end{array}$
3. $\begin{array}{r} 4 \\ \times 0 \\ \hline \end{array}$
4. $\begin{array}{r} 8 \\ \times 1 \\ \hline \end{array}$
5. $\begin{array}{r} 2 \\ \times 4 \\ \hline \end{array}$
6. $\begin{array}{r} 4 \\ \times 2 \\ \hline \end{array}$
7. $\begin{array}{r} 5 \\ \times 4 \\ \hline \end{array}$

8. $6 \times 8 =$ __?__

9. $8 \times 6 =$ __?__

10. $7 \times 1 =$ __?__

11. $6 \times 5 =$ __?__

12. $7 \times 6 =$ __?__

13. $9 \times 4 =$ __?__

Mixed Practice • Multiply.

| 14. 3
×3 | 15. 6
×1 | 16. 6
×3 | 17. 2
×9 | 18. 4
×3 | 19. 7
×4 | 20. 6
×7 |

| 21. 9
×9 | 22. 7
×8 | 23. 8
×9 | 24. 6
×6 | 25. 7
×5 | 26. 4
×8 | 27. 8
×5 |

28. $5 \times 9 = $ ___?___ 29. $3 \times 8 = $ ___?___ 30. $5 \times 5 = $ ___?___

31. $4 \times 1 = $ ___?___ 32. $3 \times 7 = $ ___?___ 33. $7 \times 3 = $ ___?___

34. $(3 \times 3) \times 2 = $ ___?___ 35. $3 \times (3 \times 2) = $ ___?___ 36. $(8 \times 0) \times 4 = $ ___?___

37. $(5 \times 6) \times 1 = $ ___?___ 38. $5 \times (6 \times 1) = $ ___?___ 39. $(2 \times 2) \times 4 = $ ___?___

Find the missing factors.

40. $7 \times $ ___?___ $= 42$ 41. $8 \times $ ___?___ $= 16$ 42. $9 \times $ ___?___ $= 54$

43. ___?___ $\times 6 = 0$ 44. ___?___ $\times 9 = 63$ 45. ___?___ $\times 3 = 27$

Complete. Multiply inside the parentheses first.

★ 46. $(8 \times 7) + 6 = $ ___?___ ★ 47. $(9 \times 6) - 8 = $ ___?___ ★ 48. $9 + (4 \times 9) = $ ___?___

★ 49. $(5 \times 4) + 35 = $ ___?___ ★ 50. $(4 \times 7) - 12 = $ ___?___ ★ 51. $86 + (7 \times 2) = $ ___?___

PROBLEM SOLVING • APPLICATIONS

52. 6 people bring pies to sell at the fair. Each person brings an apple pie, a blueberry pie, a peach pie, and a cherry pie. How many pies are for sale?

53. 5 groups take part in the animal exhibit at the fair. Each group can enter 8 small animals. How many small animals can be entered in the exhibit?

54. There are 7 divisions for the art exhibit. 4 prize ribbons will be awarded in each division. How many ribbons will be awarded at the art exhibit?

★ 55. Everyone in line buys 8 tickets. They buy 64 tickets altogether. How many people are in line?

Multiplying by One-Digit Numbers

A stamp dealer sells a set of 249 stamps to each of 7 customers. How many stamps does she sell in all?

You can use the **distributive property** to think about the product.

$$7 \times 249 = 7 \times (200 + 40 + 9)$$
$$= (7 \times 200) + (7 \times 40) + (7 \times 9)$$
$$= 1,400 + 280 + 63$$
$$= 1,743$$

Here is how you show the work.

Step 1
Multiply the ones by 7. Regroup 63 as 6 tens 3 ones.

```
    6
  2 4 9
×     7
──────
      3
```

Step 2
Multiply the tens by 7. Add 6 tens. Regroup 34 as 3 hundreds 4 tens.

```
  3 6
  2 4 9
×     7
──────
    4 3
```

Step 3
Multiply the hundreds by 7. Add 3 hundreds.

```
  3 6
  2 4 9
×     7
──────
1,7 4 3
```

She sells 1,743 stamps in all.

More Examples

```
   48      1,065      4 3 2       2 1 1 2
 × 3      ×    7    7,8 6 4      2 5,3 4 6
────      ──────    ×     5     ×       4
  144      7,455    3 9,3 2 0   1 0 1,3 8 4
```

Practice • Multiply.

1. 86
× 8

2. 34
× 2

3. 836
× 6

4. 9,312
× 6

5. 2,478
× 9

Mixed Practice • Multiply.

6. 63
× 5

7. 77
× 4

8. 702
× 4

9. 200
× 5

10. 401
× 8

11. 4,623
× 9

12. 1,982
× 6

13. 3,746
× 7

14. 5,924
× 3

15. 3,874
× 5

16. 40,865
× 8

17. 45,360
× 3

18. 65,635
× 9

19. 64,502
× 4

20. 73,201
× 3

21. 406,395
× 6

22. 578,900
× 8

23. 120,000
× 7

24. 131,402
× 2

25. 942,347
× 3

26. 5 × 23 = _?_

27. 6 × 42 = _?_

28. 2 × 346 = _?_

29. 5 × 608 = _?_

30. 9 × 8,607 = _?_

31. 8 × 4,529 = _?_

32. 3 × 53,084 = _?_

33. 7 × 64,876 = _?_

34. 6 × 79,084 = _?_

Write >, <, or =.

35. 6 × 79 ⬤ 474

36. 3 × 67 ⬤ 271

37. 3 × 789 ⬤ 2,367

38. 4 × 265 ⬤ 1,040

39. 9 × 244 ⬤ 6 × 132

40. 8 × 2,067 ⬤ 4 × 4,136

Complete the tables.

★ **41.**

Multiply by 9.

INPUT	OUTPUT
18	162
54	?
73	?
89	?
62	?

★ **42.**

Multiply by 6.

INPUT	OUTPUT
21	126
27	?
65	?
38	?
94	?

★ **43.**

Multiply by 7.

INPUT	OUTPUT
434	3,038
656	?
283	?
2,967	?
8,595	?

PROBLEM SOLVING • APPLICATIONS

44. Lita has 275 foreign stamps in her collection. Maria has 4 times as many. How many stamps does Maria have in her collection?

★ **45.** Maria buys 3 new stamp albums. Each album has 3 pages for British stamps. Each of these pages holds 28 stamps. How many British stamps can the albums hold?

Multiplying by Tens, Hundreds, Thousands

Look for a pattern.

$$\begin{array}{r} 23 \\ \times 10 \\ \hline 230 \end{array} \qquad \begin{array}{r} 23 \\ \times 20 \\ \hline 460 \end{array} \qquad \begin{array}{r} 23 \\ \times 30 \\ \hline 690 \end{array} \qquad \begin{array}{r} 23 \\ \times 40 \\ \hline 920 \end{array}$$

When multiplying by tens, write 0 in the ones place.
Then multiply the number of tens.

Look for a pattern.

$$\begin{array}{r} 23 \\ \times 100 \\ \hline 2{,}300 \end{array} \qquad \begin{array}{r} 23 \\ \times 200 \\ \hline 4{,}600 \end{array} \qquad \begin{array}{r} 23 \\ \times 300 \\ \hline 6{,}900 \end{array} \qquad \begin{array}{r} 23 \\ \times 400 \\ \hline 9{,}200 \end{array}$$

When multiplying by hundreds, write a 0 in the ones place and a 0
in the tens place. Then multiply by the number of hundreds.

Look for a pattern.

$$\begin{array}{r} 23 \\ \times 1{,}000 \\ \hline 23{,}000 \end{array} \qquad \begin{array}{r} 23 \\ \times 2{,}000 \\ \hline 46{,}000 \end{array} \qquad \begin{array}{r} 23 \\ \times 3{,}000 \\ \hline 69{,}000 \end{array} \qquad \begin{array}{r} 23 \\ \times 4{,}000 \\ \hline 92{,}000 \end{array}$$

When multiplying by thousands, write a 0 in the ones place, the tens
place, and the hundreds place. Then multiply by the number of thousands.

Practice • Multiply the numbers by 10.

1. 84   2. 73   3. 27   4. 432   5. 607

Multiply the numbers by 100.

6. 62   7. 29   8. 54   9. 793   10. 865

Multiply the numbers by 1,000.

11. 25   12. 69   13. 52   14. 906   15. 332

Mixed Practice • Multiply.

16. $\begin{array}{r} 46 \\ \times 70 \\ \hline \end{array}$
17. $\begin{array}{r} 73 \\ \times 30 \\ \hline \end{array}$
18. $\begin{array}{r} 24 \\ \times 50 \\ \hline \end{array}$
19. $\begin{array}{r} 838 \\ \times 90 \\ \hline \end{array}$
20. $\begin{array}{r} 68 \\ \times 400 \\ \hline \end{array}$
21. $\begin{array}{r} 20 \\ \times 800 \\ \hline \end{array}$

22. $\begin{array}{r} 416 \\ \times 700 \\ \hline \end{array}$
23. $\begin{array}{r} 594 \\ \times 600 \\ \hline \end{array}$
24. $\begin{array}{r} 53 \\ \times 5{,}000 \\ \hline \end{array}$
25. $\begin{array}{r} 62 \\ \times 6{,}000 \\ \hline \end{array}$
26. $\begin{array}{r} 420 \\ \times 3{,}000 \\ \hline \end{array}$
27. $\begin{array}{r} 751 \\ \times 2{,}000 \\ \hline \end{array}$

28. $20 \times 45 = \underline{}$ 29. $40 \times 65 = \underline{}$ 30. $800 \times 92 = \underline{}$

31. $300 \times 647 = \underline{}$ 32. $4{,}000 \times 86 = \underline{}$ 33. $9{,}000 \times 256 = \underline{}$

Study the pairs of INPUTS and OUTPUTS.
Then write the rules.

★ **34.** **Rule?**

INPUT	OUTPUT
3	90
27	810
65	1,950
358	10,740

★ **35.** **Rule?**

INPUT	OUTPUT
520	520,000
865	865,000
1,430	1,430,000
4,760	4,760,000

PROBLEM SOLVING • APPLICATIONS

36. One worker who picks tea can harvest 40 pounds of tea leaves a day. At this rate, how many pounds will one worker harvest in 45 days?

★ **37.** 2,900 tea plants grow on an acre of land. At this rate, how many tea plants grow on 268 acres of land?

Skills Maintenance

1. 56
   +98

2. 75
   +94

3. 978
   +981

4. 856
   +979

5. 1,423
   + 857

6. 2,709
   +3,156

7. 14,987
   +12,368

8. 51,472
   + 8,698

9. 14,807
   2,186
   +   957

10. 66,192
      78
   + 4,057

Multiplying by Two-Digit Numbers

Cardiss Burke is a buyer for a
department store. She received
a shipment of 59 cartons from
a knitting mill. Each carton contained
42 sweaters. How many sweaters
were in the shipment?

Estimate the answer.

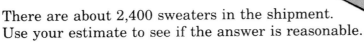

Nearest Tens

Round 42 to 40. $42 \longrightarrow 40$

Round 59 to 60. $59 \longrightarrow \times 60$

Multiply. $ \underline{2,400}$

There are about 2,400 sweaters in the shipment.
Use your estimate to see if the answer is reasonable.

$59 \times 42 = ?$

Step 1	Step 2	Step 3
Multiply by 9.	Multiply by 50.	Add. Compare the answer with your estimate.

$$
\begin{array}{r} 42 \\ \times 59 \\ \hline 378 \end{array}
\qquad
\begin{array}{r} 42 \\ \times 59 \\ \hline 378 \\ 2100 \end{array}
\qquad
\begin{array}{r} 42 \\ \times 59 \\ \hline 378 \\ \underline{2\,100} \\ 2,478 \end{array}
$$

There are 2,478 sweaters in the shipment.

More Examples
$$
\begin{array}{r} 196 \\ \times\ 48 \\ \hline 1\,568 \\ 7\,840 \\ \hline 9,408 \end{array}
\qquad
\begin{array}{r} 607 \\ \times\ 35 \\ \hline 3\,033 \\ 18\,210 \\ \hline 21,245 \end{array}
\qquad
\begin{array}{r} 65,483 \\ \times\ \ \ \ \ 47 \\ \hline 458\,381 \\ 2\,619\,320 \\ \hline 3,077,701 \end{array}
$$

Practice • Estimate, and then multiply. Compare the answers with your estimates.

1. $\begin{array}{r}82\\\times 19\end{array}$	2. $\begin{array}{r}38\\\times 72\end{array}$	3. $\begin{array}{r}677\\\times\ 29\end{array}$	4. $\begin{array}{r}548\\\times\ 56\end{array}$	5. $\begin{array}{r}62\\\times 46\end{array}$
6. $\begin{array}{r}312\\\times\ 45\end{array}$	7. $\begin{array}{r}34,497\\\times\ \ \ \ \ 21\end{array}$	8. $\begin{array}{r}7,335\\\times\ \ \ \ 66\end{array}$	9. $\begin{array}{r}42,107\\\times\ \ \ \ \ 86\end{array}$	10. $\begin{array}{r}3,290\\\times\ \ \ \ 37\end{array}$

Mixed Practice • Multiply.

11. $\begin{array}{r}28\\\times 38\end{array}$	12. $\begin{array}{r}39\\\times 49\end{array}$	13. $\begin{array}{r}257\\\times\ 18\end{array}$	14. $\begin{array}{r}47\\\times 53\end{array}$	15. $\begin{array}{r}452\\\times\ 89\end{array}$

16. 366 $\times\ 57$	17. 1,841 $\times\ \ \ 26$	18, 673 $\times\ \ 45$	19. 2,759 $\times\ \ \ 34$	20. 6,117 $\times\ \ \ 68$
21. 32,783 $\times\ \ \ \ 32$	22. 53,619 $\times\ \ \ \ 57$	23. 618,578 $\times\ \ \ \ \ \ 74$	24, 74,306 $\times\ \ \ \ 45$	25. 391,234 $\times\ \ \ \ \ \ 21$

26. $66 \times 18 =$ __?__

27. $24 \times 98 =$ __?__

28. $37 \times 45 =$ __?__

29. $52 \times 564 =$ __?__

30. $37 \times 2,061 =$ __?__

31. $82 \times 5,169 =$ __?__

32. $38 \times 32,409 =$ __?__

33. $44 \times 68,224 =$ __?__

34. $59 \times 785,436 =$ __?__

Write the factor forms and the numbers.

★ 35. 5^3 ★ 36. 3^5 ★ 37. 2^6 ★ 38. 6^2 ★ 39. 9^3 ★ 40. 7^2

★ 41. Complete the table.

Exponent Form	10^3	2^3	4^3	3^4	5^4	2^8
Factor Form	$10 \times 10 \times 10$	$2 \times 2 \times 2$	$4 \times 4 \times 4$	?	?	?
Number	1,000	8	?	?	?	?

PROBLEM SOLVING • APPLICATIONS

42. Cardiss orders 72 cartons of umbrellas. There are 12 umbrellas in each carton. How many umbrellas does Cardiss order?

★ 43. Cardiss bought 20 boxes of stuffed toy bears and 25 boxes of stuffed toy rabbits. Each box held 24 stuffed animals. How many stuffed animals did Cardiss buy?

Midchapter Review

1. 47 $\times\ 8$	2. 435 $\times\ \ 6$	3. 2,923 $\times\ \ \ \ 5$	4. 41,378 $\times\ \ \ \ \ 3$	5. 215,976 $\times\ \ \ \ \ \ \ 7$
6. 837 $\times\ 40$	7. 451 $\times 700$	8. 321 $\times 3,000$	9. 972 $\times\ 51$	10. 4,536 $\times\ \ \ \ 27$

Write >, <, or =.

11. 5×72 ⬤ 355

12. 3×250 ⬤ 760

13. 6×894 ⬤ 5,364

PROBLEM SOLVING · STRATEGIES

Multiplying Money

Multiply money as if you were
multiplying whole numbers.

A class of 32 students is going on
a trip to the Natural History Museum.
A student admission to the museum is
$1.25. What is the total cost of
admission for all the students?

To find the total cost, multiply 32 × $1.25.

Step 1
Multiply.

$$
\begin{array}{r}
\$1.25 \\
\times \quad 32 \\
\hline
2\ 50 \\
37\ 50 \\
\hline
40\ 00
\end{array}
$$

Step 2
Write the dollar sign
and the cents point.

$$
\begin{array}{r}
\$1.25 \\
\times \quad 32 \\
\hline
2\ 50 \\
37\ 50 \\
\hline
\$40.00
\end{array}
$$

Admission for 32 students costs $40.00.

Solve.

1. Two teachers and three parents are
   going on the trip to the museum.
   Admission for an adult is $2.75.
   How much does it cost for the 5
   adults to enter the museum?

   Read the questions carefully.
   Find the facts you need.

2. A movie about prehistoric people is
   being shown at the museum. One
   student ticket to the movie costs
   $1.35. How much does it cost for
   18 students to see the movie?

3. Bus fare to the museum is $2.25 for
   each student. What is the total cost
   for 32 students?

4. Each poster in the gift shop costs
   $4.85. Mrs. Jenkins, the science
   teacher, buys 3 posters for the
   classroom. How much do the 3
   posters cost?

5. Small dinosaur models are big sellers in the museum gift shop. The shop spends $2.57 for each model. How much does it cost the shop to buy a carton of 24 dinosaur models?

6. The museum has located 3 dinosaur skeletons. The total cost of shipping each skeleton is $1,259.00. How much will it cost the museum to ship all 3 skeletons?

7. It cost the museum an average of $827.57 to create each display of early mammals. There are 12 displays in the early mammal room. How much does the museum spend on this exhibit?

Remember to place the dollar sign and cents point in the answer.

---

8. The museum charges $2.50 for a headphone set that a visitor can use to hear a talk at each exhibit. If 98 people use these headphones, how much does the museum collect?

9. The museum buys display racks at $2.48 each for the research laboratory. How much do 48 display racks cost?

10. The children in the sixth grade at the Mark Twain School sold popcorn to raise money for the Native American exhibit at the museum. They sold 84 packages for $1.25 each. How much money did they collect for the museum?

★ 11. Mrs. Brown, their principal, told the class that she would contribute 15¢ for each of the 84 packages of popcorn the class sold. She gave the students a $20 bill. How much change did she get?

★ 12. Mr. and Mrs. Gumbs and their 3 children are going to the museum. Admission costs $2.75 for each adult and $1.25 for each child. The entire family is going to see the museum movie. Tickets for the movie cost $1.35 each. How much does the Gumbs family spend at the museum?

Multiplying by Three-Digit Numbers

A book company sends out 678 science kits. There are 235 activity cards in each kit. How many cards are in the kits?

$678 \times 235 = ?$

Step 1 Multiply by 5.	**Step 2** Multiply by 30.	**Step 3** Multiply by 200.	**Step 4** Add.
678 ×235 3 390	678 ×235 3 390 20 340	678 ×235 3 390 20 340 135,600	678 ×235 3 390 20 340 135 600 159,330

There are 159,330 cards.

More Examples

```
    3,657          23,945          $4.89
 ×   248        ×     874        ×    607
   29256           95780           3423
  146280         1676150         293400
  731400        19156000       $2,968.23
  906,936      20,927,930
```

Practice • Multiply.

1. 265
×337

2. 803
×376

3. 985
×504

4. 961
×340

5. 897
×562

6. 4,514
× 662

7. 6,134
× 475

8. 9,843
× 162

9. 2,621
× 734

10. 3,501
× 660

Mixed Practice • Multiply.

11. 473 ×542	**12.** 850 ×162	**13.** 929 ×273	**14.** 7,243 × 254
15. 6,474 × 309	**16.** 5,143 × 523	**17.** 82,913 × 641	**18.** 26,198 × 423
19. 13,672 × 608	**20.** $13.48 × 174	**21.** $574.92 × 283	**22.** $263.75 × 502
23. $179.95 × 459	★ **24.** 634,604 × 206	★ **25.** 292,763 × 913	★ **26.** 915,768 × 4,235

27. 212 × 586 = __?__   **28.** 633 × 702 = __?__   **29.** 297 × 5,752 = __?__

30. 305 × 2,460 = __?__   **31.** 219 × 43,762 = __?__   **32.** 349 × 92,562 = __?__

PROBLEM SOLVING • APPLICATIONS

33. An English book costs $12.17. There are 185 books on order. What is the total cost of these books?

★ **34.** A dictionary costs $7.50. The workbook that goes with the dictionary costs $2.69. A school principal orders 485 of each. What is the total cost of the books?

★ **35.** The math department has $2,000 to spend on books. An order is placed for 240 math books. Each book costs $6.98. Is there enough money left over to buy 240 workbooks that cost $2.47 each? If not, how much more money is needed?

Skills Maintenance

1. 80 −36	**2.** 57 −49	**3.** 415 − 89	**4.** 901 −576	**5.** 2,715 −1,586
6. 7,541 −3,487	**7.** 6,438 −5,549	**8.** 5,000 − 678	**9.** 19,047 −16,395	**10.** 67,005 − 9,576

Do You Have Enough Money?

Estimating can help you decide if you have enough money for a purchase.

The Arts and Crafts Club has saved $110 for a project. Each member plans to make a bottle figure. The club needs to order all these art supplies. Does the club have enough money?

Round each amount to the nearest ten dollars. Add to estimate the sum.

Price List	
Plastic bottles	$13
Assorted buttons	7
Paint (20 bottles)	22
Paintbrushes	16
Fabric (per bolt)	26
Plaster gauze (7.5 kg)	13

Estimate. Then add.

$13 → $10
$ 7 → $10
$22 → $20
$16 → $20
$26 → $30
$13 → $10
        $100

Yes, the club has enough money.

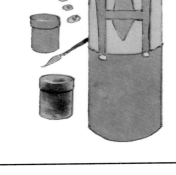

Suppose you must order supplies for your club. Do you have enough money? Write YES or NO.

1. You have $45.
You want paintbrushes, paint, and plaster gauze.

2. You have $38.
You want 2 boxes of plaster gauze.

Round up when a number ends in a 5.

3. You have $75.
You want buttons, paint, plastic bottles, and 1 bolt of fabric.

4. You have $97.
You want 4 bolts of fabric and a box of buttons.

You are the treasurer of the Arts and Crafts Club. You buy the supplies.
Do you have enough money? Write YES or NO.

5. You have $30.
You want to buy buttons and
paintbrushes.

6. You have $40.
You want to buy 1 bolt of fabric,
paintbrushes, and buttons.

Remember the dollar sign and
the cents point when writing
amounts of money.

---

7. You have $90.
You want to buy plaster gauze,
2 bolts of fabric, and plastic bottles.

8. You have $80.
You want to buy plastic bottles,
buttons, paintbrushes, and plaster
gauze.

9. You have $50.
You want to buy plastic bottles,
buttons, and paint.

10. You have $70.
You want to buy plastic bottles,
assorted buttons, paint, and
paintbrushes.

11. You have $60.
You want to buy plastic bottles,
40 bottles of paint, and
paintbrushes. If the answer is no,
about how much more money do
you need?

★**12.** You have $50.
You want to buy paint,
paintbrushes, buttons, and plastic
bottles. If the answer is no, about
how much more money do you
need?

Multiply. (pages 50–57, 60–61)

1. 2
  ×6

2. 3
  ×9

3. 5
  ×4

4. 7
  ×6

5. 8
  ×8

6. $7 \times 0 =$ ___?___

7. $8 \times 1 =$ ___?___

8. $(3 \times 2) \times 2 =$ ___?___

9. 25
  × 6

10. 684
  × 7

11. 3,089
  × 5

12. 24,652
  × 8

13. 684,764
  × 9

14. 61
  ×10

15. 245
  × 50

16. 458
  ×200

17. 196
  ×600

18. 712
  ×5,000

19. 41
  ×23

20. 687
  × 39

21. 3,151
  × 78

22. 12,562
  × 44

23. 416,273
  × 62

24. 810
  ×379

25. 700
  ×415

26. 970
  ×253

27. 863
  ×794

28. $6.78
  × 144

29. 722
  ×191

30. 806
  ×254

31. 2,519
  × 302

32. 63,959
  × 780

33. $308.28
  × 459

Solve.

34. A tire company makes 345 tires each day. How many tires are made in 42 days? (p. 56)

35. Each tire inspector can inspect 116 tires each day. There are 24 inspectors. How many tires can be inspected daily? (p. 56)

36. One tire that the company makes costs $87.95. A bus company orders 850 of these tires. What is the total cost of the tires? (p. 60)

37. The tire company employs 360 people in its plant. Each employee is paid $248.00 per week. How much money in total does the company pay weekly to its employees? (p. 60)

PROJECT

Peasant Multiplication

This is a very old method of multiplication.

Step 1 Write two factors side by side.

Step 2 Multiply the left-hand number by 2. Write the product under the number.

Step 3 Divide the right-hand number by 2. Drop any remainder. Write the quotient under the number.

Step 4 Repeat steps 2 and 3 until the right-hand quotient is 1.

Step 5 Find all the odd numbers in the right-hand column. Circle the numbers opposite them in the left-hand column.

Step 6 Add the circled numbers. The sum is the product.

Multiply 31 × 72 using this method.

31	×	72
31 × 2		72 ÷ 2
62 × 2		36 ÷ 2
124 × 2		18 ÷ 2
(248) × 2		9 ÷ 2
496 × 2		4 ÷ 2
992 × 2		2 ÷ 2
(1,984)		1

9 and 1 are odd.
Circle 248 and 1,984.
Add.

$$248$$
$$+1,984$$
$$2,232$$

The product of 31 and 72 is 2,232.

More Examples

27	×	64
27 × 2		64 ÷ 2
54 × 2		32 ÷ 2
108 × 2		16 ÷ 2
216 × 2		8 ÷ 2
432 × 2		4 ÷ 2
864 × 2		2 ÷ 2
(1,728)		1

27 × 64 = 1,728

42	×	146
42 × 2		146 ÷ 2
(84) × 2		73 ÷ 2
168 × 2		36 ÷ 2
336 × 2		18 ÷ 2
(672) × 2		9 ÷ 2
1,344 × 2		4 ÷ 2
2,688 × 2		2 ÷ 2
(5,376)		1

42 × 146 = 6,132

$$84$$
$$672$$
$$+5,376$$
$$6,132$$

Use this method to multiply.

1. 41 × 32 = __?__

2. 72 × 86 = __?__

3. 21 × 132 = __?__

4. 246 × 67 = __?__

5. 964 × 89 = __?__

6. 780 × 405 = __?__

TEST

Multiply.

1. 7
$\times 4$

2. 8
$\times 9$

3. 3
$\times 8$

4. 5
$\times 7$

5. 2
$\times 9$

6. $5 \times 0 =$ ___?___

7. $1 \times 3 =$ ___?___

8. $4 \times (2 \times 2) =$ ___?___

9. 53
$\times\ 3$

10. 701
$\times\ \ 7$

11. 2,166
$\times\ \ \ \ 9$

12. 48,174
$\times\ \ \ \ \ 6$

13. 327,016
$\times\ \ \ \ \ \ \ 4$

14. 84
$\times 10$

15. 863
$\times\ 40$

16. 275
$\times 600$

17. 319
$\times 800$

18. 529
$\times 4,000$

19. 73
$\times 21$

20. 409
$\times\ 38$

21. 3,050
$\times\ \ \ 49$

22. 27,859
$\times\ \ \ \ \ 43$

23. 822,597
$\times\ \ \ \ \ \ 28$

24. 363
$\times 126$

25. 511
$\times 264$

26. 747
$\times 278$

27. 922
$\times 356$

28. $7.95
$\times\ \ 192$

29. 278
$\times 155$

30. 603
$\times 419$

31. 5,297
$\times\ \ \ 426$

32. 46,601
$\times\ \ \ \ 923$

33. $412.59
$\times\ \ \ \ \ 624$

Solve.

34. Some students are making decorations for a school carnival. They have 15 rolls of crepe paper. There are 12 yards of paper in each roll. How many yards of crepe paper do they have?

35. The students have 18 boxes of school banners. There are 24 banners in each box. How many banners do they have in all?

36. Each roll of crepe paper costs $1.39. The students use all 15 rolls for the carnival. What is the total cost for the crepe paper?

37. Tickets to the carnival cost $1.50 each. 175 people attend the carnival. How much money is collected from ticket sales?

Combinations

Felicia and Devin are buying an automobile. They can buy a two-door or a four-door automobile. Each comes in 5 colors: red, blue, green, yellow, or white.

How many choices are there?

First they have 2 choices: a two-door or a four-door car.
Then they have 5 color choices. In all there are 2 × 5, or 10, choices.

Solve.

1. Hathleen is going to a baseball game. She can enter the stadium through any one of 4 gates. She can leave by any one of 9 gates. How many ways can Hathleen get in and out of the stadium?

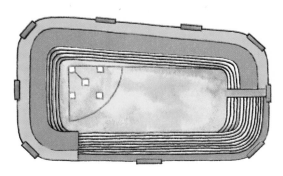

2. Cora wants to buy a bicycle. It can be three-speed, five-speed, or ten-speed. It can be blue, red, green, yellow, or white. How many choices does she have?

3. These buttons are on a jukebox. You push them to play a record. First you push a letter. Then you push a digit. How many choices can you make?

4. Each place on the counter can show any one of the ten digits. How many numbers can be named?

67

5. Melita goes shopping for new clothes. She buys 2 vests, 5 blouses, 4 skirts, and 3 pairs of shoes. How many different outfits can she make?

6. This is a license plate. It has 6 places for letters or digits. The first 3 places show letters. (There are 26 different letters.) The last 3 places show digits. (There are 10 different digits.) How many different license plates can there be?

7. A combination lock has 36 numbers. First you turn right, then left, and then right again. How many different combinations are possible?

8. This is a Social Security card. There are nine places for digits. How many Social Security cards can be issued using only the digits 1 through 5?

9. A town uses 345, 346, or 347 for the first three digits in all of its telephone numbers. How many telephone numbers can there be?

10. A local beach sells season beach badges. Each has a different code. The first two places show digits. The second two places show letters. How many different badges are possible?

COMPUTER

Computer Software

The lesson in Chapter 1 was mostly about computer hardware.
Computer software is any program that contains information or instructions for
the computer.
In this lesson and the next computer lesson, we examine two types of computer
software: controlling programs and programming languages.
Remember, any set of instructions to the computer, for whatever purpose, is
called a *program.*
A person, the programmer, types instructions onto an input keyboard.
A controlling program, the *interpreter,* translates the instructions into bits.
A computer, the hardware, processes the bits to get the instructions in a form
it can use.
The computer then processes the instructions. It executes, in a step-by-step
manner, the job the programmer wants done.
Output programs produce results on any output device described before.

A *controlling program* handles the specific operations of a specific computer.

    a. It contains the bootstrap program. A *bootstrap program* readies a
computer for operation after power has been turned on.

    b. It handles input devices, memory storage, and output devices.

    c. It keeps track of time, and it controls all the other programs.

CPM, Z–80, and DOS are names of controlling programs for computers.
    CPM (or CP/M) means Control Program/Microprocessor. It is widely used.
    Z–80 is a controller for a specific class of smaller microcomputers.
    DOS means Disk-Operating System. It is used in larger microcomputers.

Match the letter with the correct phrase.

1. Computer software is

A. a program that readies a computer for operation after power has been turned on.

2. The interpreter is

B. a program used in larger microcomputers.

3. A bootstrap program is

C. a program that translates instructions into bits.

4. Z–80 is

D. a program that informs or instructs the computer.

5. DOS is

E. a controller for a specific class of smaller microcomputers.

6. Clip advertisements from magazines and newspapers and circle the words and
phrases that you learned in this lesson.

Choose the correct answers.

1. Round 19,409 to the nearest ten thousand.

    A. 20,000
    B. 18,000
    C. 19,000
    D. not here

2. Choose the number forty thousand, four hundred six.

    A. 4,406
    B. 40,406
    C. 44,406
    D. not here

3. Add.

$$97 + 8 + 284 = \underline{\ ?\ }$$

    A. 379
    B. 461
    C. 289
    D. not here

4. Add.

$$\begin{array}{r} \$47.59 \\ 18.35 \\ +527.18 \\ \hline \end{array}$$

    A. $593.12
    B. $592.02
    C. $582.12
    D. not here

5. Subtract.

$$\begin{array}{r} 50,402 \\ -\ 3,928 \\ \hline \end{array}$$

    A. 54,330
    B. 47,484
    C. 46,474
    D. not here

6. Subtract.

$$\begin{array}{r} \$24.50 \\ -\ 9.79 \\ \hline \end{array}$$

    A. $34.29
    B. $15.81
    C. $14.71
    D. not here

7. Multiply.

$$\begin{array}{r} 783 \\ \times\ \ \ 6 \\ \hline \end{array}$$

    A. 4,298
    B. 4,698
    C. 4,648
    D. not here

8. Multiply.

$$\begin{array}{r} 4,892 \\ \times\ \ \ \ \ 8 \\ \hline \end{array}$$

    A. 32,136
    B. 39,426
    C. 39,136
    D. not here

9. Multiply.

$$\begin{array}{r} 369 \\ \times\ \ 48 \\ \hline \end{array}$$

    A. 17,712
    B. 17,212
    C. 4,528
    D. not here

10. A grocery store has 7 shelves of cereal boxes. Each shelf can hold 254 boxes. How many boxes can the shelves hold in all?

    A. 1,738
    B. 1,778
    C. 1,478
    D. not here

11. The store received a shipment of 125 cartons of canned soup. Each carton contained 24 cans. How many cans of soup were shipped to the store?

    A. 3,000
    B. 2,880
    C. 2,900
    D. not here

CHAPTER 4

Division

Dividing by One-Digit Numbers • Zero in the Quotient • Averages • Dividing by Multiples of Ten • Dividing by Two-Digit Numbers • Correcting Estimates • Problem Solving: Dividing with Money • Dividing by Three-Digit Numbers • Problem Solving: Thinking About the Remainder • Collecting Data • Mean, Median, and Mode

Division

Lillian is preparing 3 baskets of fruit. She uses 27 oranges. She puts the same number of oranges in each basket. How many oranges does she put in each basket?

$27 \div 3 = ?$

When a group is separated into smaller groups of the same size, use **division**.

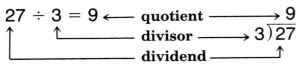

Lillian puts 9 oranges in each basket.

Divide: $14 \div 3$.

Step 1
How many threes in 14?
$3 \times 3 = 9$
$3 \times 4 = 12$
$3 \times 5 = 15$
Write 4 above 14.

Step 2
Multiply:
$4 \times 3 = 12$.

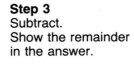

Step 3
Subtract.
Show the remainder in the answer.

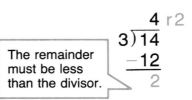

The remainder must be less than the divisor.

Practice • Find the quotients and the remainders.

1. $2\overline{)19}$
2. $6\overline{)36}$
3. $5\overline{)29}$
4. $8\overline{)34}$
5. $9\overline{)68}$
6. $3\overline{)16}$

7. $4\overline{)10}$
8. $7\overline{)51}$
9. $2\overline{)5}$
10. $4\overline{)19}$
11. $6\overline{)34}$
12. $5\overline{)33}$

Mixed Practice • Divide.

13. $9\overline{)50}$
14. $8\overline{)46}$
15. $3\overline{)25}$
16. $7\overline{)49}$
17. $2\overline{)7}$
18. $5\overline{)49}$

19. $3\overline{)28}$
20. $6\overline{)46}$
21. $9\overline{)26}$
22. $5\overline{)45}$
23. $7\overline{)66}$
24. $8\overline{)60}$

25. $8\overline{)52}$
26. $3\overline{)20}$
27. $6\overline{)53}$
28. $4\overline{)35}$
29. $9\overline{)35}$
30. $7\overline{)44}$

31. $9\overline{)61}$
32. $3\overline{)22}$
33. $7\overline{)25}$
34. $5\overline{)36}$
35. $8\overline{)65}$
36. $4\overline{)25}$

37. $3\overline{)11}$ **38.** $7\overline{)53}$ **39.** $4\overline{)30}$ **40.** $9\overline{)75}$ **41.** $5\overline{)24}$ **42.** $8\overline{)39}$

43. $2\overline{)9}$ **44.** $6\overline{)44}$ **45.** $4\overline{)23}$ **46.** $6\overline{)50}$ **47.** $9\overline{)84}$ **48.** $8\overline{)18}$

49. $80 \div 9 =$ ___?___

50. $17 \div 9 =$ ___?___

51. $50 \div 8 =$ ___?___

52. $61 \div 8 =$ ___?___

53. $47 \div 9 =$ ___?___

54. $19 \div 4 =$ ___?___

Multiplication and division are
inverse operations.
Use one to check the other.

$$5\overline{)45}^{\,9} \qquad \begin{array}{r} 9 \\ \times 5 \\ \hline 45 \end{array}$$

Divide. Use the inverse operation to check your answers.

55. $7\overline{)21}$ **56.** $4\overline{)32}$ **57.** $9\overline{)63}$ **58.** $3\overline{)24}$ **59.** $2\overline{)18}$

60. $9\overline{)45}$ **61.** $8\overline{)56}$ **62.** $5\overline{)35}$ **63.** $6\overline{)54}$ **64.** $5\overline{)25}$

Do the operation inside the parentheses first.

★ **65.** $(48 \div 6) \times 3 =$ ___?___ ★ **66.** $(72 \div 9) \div 4 =$ ___?___ ★ **67.** $6 + (35 \div 7) =$ ___?___

★ **68.** $(18 \times 3) \div 6 =$ ___?___ ★ **69.** $107 \times (28 \div 7) =$ ___?___ ★ **70.** $9 \times (63 \div 7) =$ ___?___

PROBLEM SOLVING • APPLICATIONS

71. Lillian uses 3 meters of ribbon to make one bow for a fruit basket. How many bows can she make using 29 meters of ribbon? How much ribbon does she have left over?

★ **72.** Odessa needs 18 packages of cheese to fill 2 cheese baskets. How many packages of cheese does Odessa need to fill 6 cheese baskets?

Two-Digit Quotients

Latrice has 7 cartons. She has 320 jars of honey. She wants to pack the cartons with the same number of jars in each. How many jars can she pack in each carton? How many jars are left over?

$320 \div 7 = ?$

$7\overline{)320}$ There are not enough hundreds to divide.

$7\overline{)320}$ There are enough tens to divide.

The first digit of the quotient is in the tens place.

Step 1
Divide the tens.
Think: $7\overline{)32}$. Multiply. Subtract.

$$\begin{array}{r} 4 \\ 7\overline{)320} \\ -28 \\ \hline 4 \end{array}$$

Step 2
Divide the ones.
Think: $7\overline{)40}$. Multiply. Subtract. Show the remainder.

$$\begin{array}{r} 45\ r5 \\ 7\overline{)320} \\ -28 \\ \hline 40 \\ -35 \\ \hline 5 \end{array}$$

Check your answer.
Multiply the quotient by the divisor. $\longrightarrow$
Add the remainder. $\longrightarrow$
Should equal the dividend. $\longrightarrow$

$$\begin{array}{r} 45 \\ \times\ 7 \\ \hline 315 \\ +\ \ 5 \\ \hline 320 \end{array}$$

Latrice can pack 45 jars in each carton. There are 5 jars left over.

More Examples

$$\begin{array}{r} 12\ r2 \\ 5\overline{)62} \\ -5 \\ \hline 12 \\ -10 \\ \hline 2 \end{array} \qquad \begin{array}{r} 71 \\ 6\overline{)426} \\ -42 \\ \hline 6 \\ -6 \\ \hline 0 \end{array} \qquad \begin{array}{r} 29\ r3 \\ 9\overline{)264} \\ -18 \\ \hline 84 \\ -81 \\ \hline 3 \end{array}$$

Practice • Divide. Check your answers.

1. $7\overline{)150}$ 2. $5\overline{)274}$ 3. $4\overline{)178}$ 4. $5\overline{)225}$ 5. $3\overline{)112}$

6. $4\overline{)84}$ 7. $3\overline{)96}$ 8. $8\overline{)616}$ 9. $9\overline{)714}$ 10. $7\overline{)503}$

Mixed Practice • Divide.

11. $9\overline{)225}$ 12. $9\overline{)273}$ 13. $3\overline{)229}$ 14. $9\overline{)412}$ 15. $6\overline{)324}$

16. $9\overline{)327}$ 17. $5\overline{)450}$ 18. $4\overline{)147}$ 19. $6\overline{)104}$ 20. $9\overline{)620}$

21. $2\overline{)183}$ 22. $8\overline{)111}$ 23. $7\overline{)506}$ 24. $8\overline{)89}$ 25. $6\overline{)518}$

26. $3\overline{)29}$ 27. $7\overline{)93}$ 28. $7\overline{)427}$ 29. $5\overline{)27}$ 30. $9\overline{)265}$

31. $9\overline{)381}$ **32.** $4\overline{)107}$ **33.** $2\overline{)157}$ **34.** $4\overline{)153}$ **35.** $5\overline{)40}$

36. $84 \div 7 =$ __?__ **37.** $218 \div 9 =$ __?__ **38.** $313 \div 5 =$ __?__

39. $92 \div 8 =$ __?__ **40.** $402 \div 6 =$ __?__ **41.** $191 \div 4 =$ __?__

42. $69 \div 5 =$ __?__ **43.** $196 \div 3 =$ __?__ **44.** $137 \div 2 =$ __?__

Do the operation inside the parentheses first.

★**45.** $648 \div (3 \times 3) =$ __?__ ★**46.** $(525 - 169) \div 4 =$ __?__ ★**47.** $(264 \div 8) + 49 =$ __?__

★**48.** $576 \div (4 \times 2) =$ __?__ ★**49.** $(349 + 295) \div 7 =$ __?__ ★**50.** $(35 \times 6) \div 5 =$ __?__

Is it possible to divide by zero?
Problem: $6 \div 0 = ?$ **Think:** $? \times 0 = 6$ There is no number that will make the sentence true.

You cannot divide by zero.

Divide. Write NO ANSWER for division by zero.

51. $0\overline{)8}$ **52.** $3\overline{)0}$ **53.** $9\overline{)0}$ **54.** $0\overline{)4}$ **55.** $0\overline{)7}$

PROBLEM SOLVING • APPLICATIONS

56. It takes 6 bees a lifetime to collect enough nectar to make 270 grams of honey. If each bee collects the same amount of nectar, how many grams of honey does each bee make?

57. There are 774 bumblebees in 9 colonies. There are the same number of bees in each colony. How many bumblebees are in one colony?

★ **58.** In one week 8 colonies of honeybees gather 504 kilograms of nectar. Each colony gathers the same amount of nectar. How much nectar is gathered by one colony in one day?

★ **59.** A honeycomb measuring 78 square centimeters has 300 cells. Each cell is about the same size. How many cells are in a 13-square-centimeter section of the honeycomb?

75

Dividing Greater Numbers

Sam Jericho has 3,247 logs at his logging camp.
His loggers are to store them in 5 equal piles.
How many logs are in each pile?
How many logs are left over?

$3,427 \div 5 = ?$

$5\overline{)3{,}247}$ There are not enough thousands to divide.

$5\overline{)3{,}2\,47}$ There are enough hundreds to divide.

The first digit of the quotient is in the hundreds place.

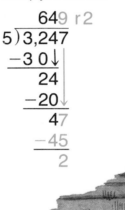

Step 1
Divide the hundreds.
Think: $5\overline{)32}$.
Multiply. Subtract.

$$
\begin{array}{r}
6 \\
5\overline{)3{,}247} \\
-3\,0 \\
\hline
2
\end{array}
$$

Step 2
Divide the tens.
Think: $5\overline{)24}$.
Multiply. Subtract.

$$
\begin{array}{r}
64 \\
5\overline{)3{,}247} \\
-3\,0\downarrow \\
\hline
24 \\
-20 \\
\hline
4
\end{array}
$$

Step 3
Divide the ones.
Think: $5\overline{)47}$.
Multiply. Subtract.

$$
\begin{array}{r}
649\ r2 \\
5\overline{)3{,}247} \\
-3\,0\downarrow \\
\hline
24 \\
-20\downarrow \\
\hline
47 \\
-45 \\
\hline
2
\end{array}
$$

There are 649 logs in each pile.
There are 2 logs left over.

Divide: $9,107 \div 4$.

Sometimes there are
thousands in the quotient.

$$
\begin{array}{r}
2{,}276\ r3 \\
4\overline{)9{,}107} \\
-8 \\
\hline
1\,1 \\
-\ 8 \\
\hline
30 \\
-28 \\
\hline
27 \\
-24 \\
\hline
3
\end{array}
$$

Practice • Divide.

1. $4\overline{)2{,}536}$ 2. $6\overline{)3{,}175}$ 3. $9\overline{)1{,}903}$ 4. $5\overline{)9{,}721}$ 5. $8\overline{)3{,}563}$

6. $3\overline{)963}$ 7. $2\overline{)842}$ 8. $9\overline{)2{,}263}$ 9. $8\overline{)9{,}873}$ 10. $6\overline{)7{,}630}$

Mixed Practice • Divide.

11. $6\overline{)5{,}935}$ 12. $4\overline{)3{,}811}$ 13. $7\overline{)1{,}599}$ 14. $6\overline{)7{,}036}$ 15. $4\overline{)9{,}089}$

16. $9\overline{)1{,}760}$ 17. $5\overline{)8{,}321}$ 18. $5\overline{)2{,}555}$ 19. $8\overline{)3{,}376}$ 20. $4\overline{)3{,}502}$

21. $8\overline{)3{,}956}$ 22. $7\overline{)988}$ 23. $6\overline{)2{,}888}$ 24. $3\overline{)399}$ 25. $7\overline{)5{,}500}$

26. $8\overline{)649}$ 27. $7\overline{)5{,}007}$ 28. $7\overline{)23{,}394}$ 29. $9\overline{)13{,}600}$ 30. $6\overline{)49{,}307}$

31. $166 \div 4 =$ ___?___

32. $2{,}853 \div 8 =$ ___?___

33. $2{,}714 \div 7 =$ ___?___

34. $2{,}209 \div 5 =$ ___?___

35. $12{,}316 \div 5 =$ ___?___

36. $21{,}478 \div 9 =$ ___?___

Use the digits 1, 2, 3, 4, and 5.

★ 37. Arrange the digits to get the largest quotient possible. Use each digit only once.

★ 38. Arrange the digits to get the smallest quotient possible. Use each digit only once.   □$\overline{)\square\square\square\square}$

PROBLEM SOLVING • APPLICATIONS

39. It takes 4 truckloads to fill a regular order for the Johnson Lumber Company. In one year Sam Jericho's drivers make 2,512 trips. How many orders for Johnson Lumber did they fill?

40. The cook at Jericho's camp puts 4,453 potatoes in 3 storage bins. He puts the same number of potatoes in each bin. How many potatoes are in each storage bin? How many potatoes are left over?

41. The drivers for Jericho's logging camp make many trips with different-sized loads. In one year his drivers moved 1,972 logs with 2 logs on each truck and 1,965 logs with 3 logs on each truck. How many trips did these drivers make?

Skills Maintenance

Write >, <, or =.

1. 145 ⬤ 154

2. 329 ⬤ 239

3. 859 ⬤ 995

4. 1,001 ⬤ 999

5. 4,368 ⬤ 4,386

6. 5,174 ⬤ 5,174

7. 2,928 ⬤ 2,982

8. 37,561 ⬤ 37,651

9. 42,646 ⬤ 42,549

Zero in the Quotient

GVN Oil Refinery can process
5,430 barrels of oil in 6 days.
The refinery processes the same
number of barrels each day.
How many barrels of oil does
it process in one day?

$5,430 \div 6 = ?$

Step 1
Divide the hundreds.
Think: 6)‾54.
Multiply. Subtract.

```
     9
6)5,430
 -5 4
```

Step 2
Divide the tens.
Think: 6)‾3.
Multiply. Subtract.

```
     90
6)5,430
 -5 4↓
     3
    -0
     3
```

Step 3
Divide the ones.
Think: 6)‾30.
Multiply. Subtract.

```
     905
6)5,430
 -5 4↓
     3↓
    -0↓
     30
    -30
      0
```

GVN Oil Refinery processes 905 barrels of oil in one day.

More Examples

```
   370 r3
8)2,963
 -2 4
   56
  -56
    3
   -0
    3
```

```
    4,058 r3
7)28,409
 -28
    4
   -0
   40
  -35
   59
  -56
    3
```

```
   2,006 r2
4)8,026
 -8
   0
  -0
   2
  -0
   26
  -24
    2
```

Practice • Divide.

1. 2)‾1,618
2. 8)‾883
3. 9)‾1,807
4. 7)‾7,700
5. 4)‾1,840

6. 3)‾1,202
7. 6)‾1,922
8. 5)‾1,504
9. 2)‾1,816
10. 3)‾9,270

Mixed Practice • Divide.

11. 3)‾1,050
12. 6)‾6,240
13. 5)‾3,000
14. 8)‾3,272
15. 6)‾624

16. 7)‾4,928
17. 5)‾2,854
18. 8)‾3,247
19. 9)‾810
20. 6)‾1,239

21. 7)‾1,542
22. 8)‾3,720
23. 3)‾7,042
24. 5)‾2,250
25. 7)‾6,048

26. $9\overline{)2,886}$ **27.** $8\overline{)4,885}$ **28.** $2\overline{)2,012}$ **29.** $8\overline{)5,624}$ **30.** $9\overline{)9,850}$

31. $6\overline{)12,537}$ **32.** $5\overline{)26,340}$ **33.** $8\overline{)24,000}$ **34.** $9\overline{)18,279}$ **35.** $3\overline{)19,491}$

36. $5\overline{)10,376}$ **37.** $3\overline{)16,211}$ **38.** $7\overline{)35,638}$ ★ **39.** $8\overline{)320,720}$ ★ **40.** $4\overline{)2,243,604}$

41. $2,882 \div 8 = $ __?__   **42.** $3,039 \div 5 = $ __?__   **43.** $63,128 \div 9 = $ __?__

44. $1,265 \div 6 = $ __?__   **45.** $1,855 \div 7 = $ __?__   **46.** $10,010 \div 2 = $ __?__

47. $1,808 \div 2 = $ __?__   ★ **48.** $303,300 \div 5 = $ __?__   ★ **49.** $39,204 \div 3 = $ __?__

When you divide by 5, the remainder can be 0. It can also be 1, 2, 3, or 4. It cannot be 5. Why?

What remainders can you get when you divide by

★ **50.** 2?   ★ **51.** 3?   ★ **52.** 4?   ★ **53.** 6?   ★ **54.** 7?   ★ **55.** 8?   ★ **56.** 9?

PROBLEM SOLVING • APPLICATIONS

57. The PNO Refinery can process 30,048 barrels of oil in 6 days. This large refinery processes the same number of barrels each day. In one day how many barrels does it process?

58. An oil well produces 4,690 gallons of oil in 7 days. It produces the same number of gallons each day. How many gallons of oil does this well produce in one day?

★ **59.** One of the deepest oil wells in the world is 9,583 meters deep. Workers used 9-meter lengths of pipe when drilling the well. How many lengths of pipe did they need for this well?

★ **60.** A barge carrying 15,000 barrels of oil makes 5 stops along the way. The same number of barrels are removed at each stop. At the end of the trip, 5,000 barrels remain on the barge. How many barrels were removed at each stop?

Averages

Vivette usually has a bowling score of around 90. This is an **average** number. This does not mean that her score is 90 each time she bowls.

Vivette bowls 5 games.
These are her scores.

  80, 95, 85, 100, 90

Find the **average**, or **mean**, of her scores.

Step 1
Find the sum of the scores.

80 + 95 + 85 + 100 + 90 = 450

Step 2
Divide the sum by the number of scores.

$$90 \longleftarrow \text{average}$$
$$\text{number of} \longrightarrow 5\overline{)450} \longleftarrow \text{sum of scores}$$
$$\text{scores}$$

Vivette's average score is 90.

Althea earns these bowling scores in 6 games.

  75, 96, 98, 88, 100, 83

Find the average.

  75 + 96 + 98 + 88 + 100 + 83 = 540 $6\overline{)540}$ (=90)

Althea's average score is 90.

Practice • Find the averages.

1. 55, 30, 80, 60, 75

2. 93, 70, 85, 80, 82

3. 95, 100, 164, 88, 123

4. 117, 92, 75, 100, 91

Mixed Practice • Find the averages.

5. 83, 43, 63, 33, 53

6. 13, 27, 79, 85, 46

7. 91, 80, 34, 67, 13

8. 78, 97, 93, 84, 98

9. 82, 78, 62, 80, 71, 83

10. 79, 95, 80, 66, 77, 77

11. 93, 82, 100, 77, 100, 100

12. 86, 95, 59, 74, 58, 83, 70

13. 76, 93, 100, 84, 60, 57, 97

14. 80, 84, 76, 90, 94, 100, 99

15. 62, 74, 56, 47, 64, 82, 86, 73

16. 72, 64, 36, 57, 88, 97, 65, 57

17. 73, 100, 90, 98, 100, 80, 99, 96

18. 63, 56, 44, 17, 32, 50, 60, 76, 70

19. 93, 80, 92, 100, 74, 64, 86, 80, 87

20. 73, 72, 71, 40, 48, 64, 70, 80, 76

Here is a shorter way to divide.

Divide. $6\overline{)1{,}582}$

Step 1
Divide the hundreds.

$$
\begin{array}{r}
2 \\
6\overline{)1{,}5\,^38\ 2}
\end{array}
$$

$6\overline{)15}$ is about 2.
$2 \times 6 = 12$
$15 - 12 = 3$

Step 2
Divide the tens.

$$
\begin{array}{r}
2\ 6 \\
6\overline{)1{,}5^38\,^22}
\end{array}
$$

$6\overline{)38}$ is about 6.
$6 \times 6 = 36$
$38 - 36 = 2$

Step 3
Divide the ones.

$$
\begin{array}{r}
2\ 6\ 3\ \text{r}4 \\
6\overline{)1{,}5^38^22}
\end{array}
$$

$6\overline{)22}$ is about 3.
$6 \times 3 = 18$
$22 - 18 = 4$

$1{,}582 \div 6 = 263\ \text{r}4$

Divide. Use the shorter way.

21. $5\overline{)1{,}690}$

22. $8\overline{)2{,}508}$

23. $9\overline{)4{,}563}$

24. $4\overline{)6{,}029}$

PROBLEM SOLVING • APPLICATIONS

25. What is Iola's average score after six games?

26. What is Cora's average score after six games?

27. What is Althea's average score after six games?

★ **28.** Pat's average was 96 after six games. What was her score for the sixth game?

★ **29.** Ezell has an average of 104 after six games. What was his score for the first game?

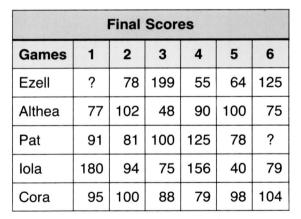

Final Scores						
Games	**1**	**2**	**3**	**4**	**5**	**6**
Ezell	?	78	199	55	64	125
Althea	77	102	48	90	100	75
Pat	91	81	100	125	78	?
Iola	180	94	75	156	40	79
Cora	95	100	88	79	98	104

Dividing by Multiples of Ten

A new shopping mall is opening. There are 30 stores in the mall. 180 people will be working in the stores. What is the average number of employees in each store?

$180 \div 30 = ?$

You can use a basic fact to divide by tens.

$$3\overline{)18} \quad = 6 \qquad 30\overline{)180} = 6$$

There is an average of 6 employees in each store.

Divide: $165 \div 20$.

Step 1
Think: $2\overline{)16}$.
Write 8 in the ones place.

$$20\overline{)165} \quad 8$$

Step 2
Multiply.
$8 \times 20 = 160$

$$20\overline{)165} \quad 8$$
$$160$$

Step 3
Subtract.
Show the remainder.

The remainder must be less than 20.

$$20\overline{)165} \quad 8\,r5$$
$$-160$$
$$5$$

Check your answer.

Multiply the divisor ⟶ by the quotient.

$$20$$
$$\times\ 8$$
$$160$$

Add the remainder. ⟶

$$+\quad 5$$
$$165 \longleftarrow \text{Should equal the dividend.}$$

$165 \div 20 = 8\,r5$

Practice • Divide.

1. $30\overline{)60}$
2. $40\overline{)200}$
3. $20\overline{)80}$
4. $30\overline{)120}$
5. $90\overline{)270}$

6. $90\overline{)571}$
7. $80\overline{)321}$
8. $10\overline{)460}$
9. $50\overline{)161}$
10. $30\overline{)132}$

Mixed Practice • Divide.

11. $60\overline{)420}$
12. $80\overline{)347}$
13. $80\overline{)240}$
14. $90\overline{)810}$
15. $90\overline{)104}$

16. $60\overline{)376}$
17. $50\overline{)200}$
18. $30\overline{)168}$
19. $40\overline{)295}$
20. $50\overline{)250}$

21. $60\overline{)280}$
22. $80\overline{)493}$
23. $20\overline{)40}$
24. $60\overline{)191}$
25. $60\overline{)540}$

26. $90\overline{)754}$ **27.** $50\overline{)378}$ **28.** $10\overline{)80}$ **29.** $20\overline{)199}$ **30.** $70\overline{)639}$

31. $70\overline{)350}$ **32.** $10\overline{)650}$ **33.** $80\overline{)745}$ **34.** $60\overline{)483}$ **35.** $30\overline{)90}$

36. $346 \div 40 =$ ___?___   **37.** $168 \div 70 =$ ___?___   **38.** $591 \div 60 =$ ___?___

39. $95 \div 30 =$ ___?___   **40.** $254 \div 30 =$ ___?___   **41.** $258 \div 50 =$ ___?___

★ **42.** $1,400 \div 70 =$ ___?___   ★ **43.** $1,500 \div 30 =$ ___?___   ★ **44.** $1,600 \div 20 =$ ___?___

PROBLEM SOLVING • APPLICATIONS

45. The movie theater in the shopping mall has seating for 560 people. There are 80 seats in each section. How many sections are there?

46. In parking lot A there are spaces for 450 cars. There are 50 spaces in each row of the lot. How many rows are there?

47. The shopping mall receives a shipment of 210 banners. Each of the 30 stores will receive the same number of banners. How many banners does each store receive?

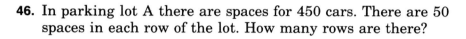
OPENING DAY SALE

★ **48.** Each of the 30 stores receives at least one banner of each color. What color banner will not appear more than once in any store?

GRAND OPENING

Number of Banners	Color
30	Orange
35	Green
50	Red
50	White
45	Blue

Midchapter Review

1. $9\overline{)75}$ **2.** $4\overline{)92}$ **3.** $8\overline{)612}$ **4.** $7\overline{)458}$ **5.** $5\overline{)2,739}$

6. $3\overline{)9,863}$ **7.** $8\overline{)6,432}$ **8.** $9\overline{)5,584}$ **9.** $6\overline{)17,429}$ **10.** $90\overline{)810}$

Find the averages.

11. 68, 71, 60, 84, 92   **12.** 26, 24, 31, 30, 29, 28

Dividing by Two-Digit Numbers

Radio Hut receives a shipment of 138 pocket calculators. They arrive in 23 cartons. Each carton contains the same number of calculators. How many calculators are in each carton?

$138 \div 23 = ?$

You can estimate to help you find the quotient. Round the divisor to the nearest ten.

$$\begin{array}{r} 20 \\ 23\overline{)138} \end{array}$$

Step 1
Think: $2\overline{)13}$.
Try 6.

$$\begin{array}{r} 6 \\ 23\overline{)138} \end{array}$$

Step 2
Multiply:
$6 \times 23 = 138$.

$$\begin{array}{r} 6 \\ 23\overline{)138} \\ 138 \end{array}$$

Step 3
Subtract.

$$\begin{array}{r} 6 \\ 23\overline{)138} \\ -138 \\ \hline 0 \end{array}$$

There are 6 calculators in each carton.

Divide: $240 \div 36$.
Estimate the quotient.

$$\begin{array}{r} 40 \\ 36\overline{)240} \end{array}$$

Step 1
Think: $4\overline{)24}$.
Try 6.

$$\begin{array}{r} 6 \\ 36\overline{)240} \end{array}$$

Step 2
Multiply.

$$\begin{array}{r} 6 \\ 36\overline{)240} \\ 216 \end{array}$$

Step 3
Subtract.
Show the remainder.

$$\begin{array}{r} 6 \text{ r}24 \\ 36\overline{)240} \\ -216 \\ \hline 24 \end{array}$$

$240 \div 36 = 6 \text{ r}24$

Practice • Divide.

1. $83\overline{)332}$ 2. $62\overline{)256}$ 3. $71\overline{)440}$ 4. $32\overline{)97}$ 5. $53\overline{)283}$

6. $58\overline{)420}$ 7. $67\overline{)386}$ 8. $25\overline{)92}$ 9. $38\overline{)175}$ 10. $88\overline{)633}$

Mixed Practice • Divide.

11. $53\overline{)384}$ 12. $31\overline{)291}$ 13. $64\overline{)273}$ 14. $51\overline{)112}$ 15. $43\overline{)301}$

16. $76\overline{)446}$ 17. $46\overline{)350}$ 18. $68\overline{)300}$ 19. $48\overline{)221}$ 20. $29\overline{)275}$

21. $39\overline{)170}$ **22.** $42\overline{)136}$ **23.** $50\overline{)487}$ **24.** $54\overline{)171}$ **25.** $36\overline{)168}$

26. $29\overline{)245}$ **27.** $52\overline{)277}$ **28.** $87\overline{)434}$ **29.** $74\overline{)450}$ **30.** $58\overline{)367}$

31. $77\overline{)500}$ **32.** $60\overline{)444}$ **33.** $38\overline{)173}$ **34.** $54\overline{)270}$ **35.** $90\overline{)312}$

36. $94\overline{)395}$ **37.** $56\overline{)213}$ **38.** $21\overline{)136}$ **39.** $93\overline{)237}$ **40.** $52\overline{)233}$

41. $124 \div 35 = \underline{\quad?\quad}$ **42.** $449 \div 70 = \underline{\quad?\quad}$ **43.** $295 \div 41 = \underline{\quad?\quad}$

44. $171 \div 32 = \underline{\quad?\quad}$ **45.** $163 \div 29 = \underline{\quad?\quad}$ **46.** $467 \div 92 = \underline{\quad?\quad}$

47. $285 \div 91 = \underline{\quad?\quad}$ **48.** $185 \div 23 = \underline{\quad?\quad}$ **49.** $237 \div 33 = \underline{\quad?\quad}$

Use the digits 5, 6, 7, 8, and 9.

★**50.** Arrange the digits to get the largest quotient possible. Use each digit only once. $\square\square\overline{)\square\square\square}$

★**51.** Arrange the digits to get the smallest quotient possible. Use each digit only once. $\square\square\overline{)\square\square\square}$

PROBLEM SOLVING • APPLICATIONS

52. There are 178 radios. 21 fit on each shelf. How many shelves can be filled? How many radios are left over?

★**53.** Eila has 120 old tapes and 348 new tapes. He wants to display them on racks. 52 fit on each rack. How many racks does he need?

★**54.** Complete the table. Find the number of cartons delivered to Radio Hut.

Radio Hut Order			
Item	Number of Cartons	Number of Items	Number in Each Carton
Pocket calculator	?	144	24
Headsets	?	84	12
Radios	?	432	48
Computer tennis	?	36	36
Tape recorders	?	144	18

Correcting Estimates

Divide: 148 ÷ 24.
Sometimes your first estimate
for the quotient is too much.

Step 1
Round 24 to 20.
Think: 2)‾14‾.

20

$$24\overline{)148}$$

Step 2
Try 7.

7 is
too much.

$$\begin{array}{r} 7 \\ 24\overline{)148} \\ -168 \end{array}$$

Step 3
Try 6.
Multiply. Subtract.

$$\begin{array}{r} 6\ r4 \\ 24\overline{)148} \\ -144 \\ \hline 4 \end{array}$$

The quotient is 6 r 4.

Divide: 192 ÷ 38.
Sometimes your first estimate
for the quotient is not enough.

Step 1
Round 38 to 40.
Think: 4)‾19‾

40

$$38\overline{)192}$$

Step 2
Try 4.

4 is not
enough.

$$\begin{array}{r} 4 \\ 38\overline{)192} \\ -152 \\ \hline 40 \end{array}$$

Step 3
Try 5.
Multiply. Subtract.

$$\begin{array}{r} 5\ r2 \\ 38\overline{)192} \\ -190 \\ \hline 2 \end{array}$$

The quotient is 5 r 2.

Practice • Divide.

1. 22)‾183‾   2. 12)‾78‾   3. 53)‾401‾   4. 91)‾541‾   5. 42)‾205‾

6. 48)‾243‾   7. 94)‾729‾   8. 18)‾115‾   9. 47)‾282‾   10. 28)‾58‾

Mixed Practice • Divide.

11. $93\overline{)361}$ **12.** $28\overline{)196}$ **13.** $61\overline{)226}$ **14.** $85\overline{)446}$ **15.** $24\overline{)99}$

16. $94\overline{)279}$ **17.** $25\overline{)224}$ **18.** $14\overline{)112}$ **19.** $69\overline{)403}$ **20.** $72\overline{)565}$

21. $62\overline{)492}$ **22.** $77\overline{)702}$ **23.** $64\overline{)597}$ **24.** $36\overline{)161}$ **25.** $11\overline{)108}$

26. $44\overline{)214}$ **27.** $16\overline{)105}$ **28.** $21\overline{)96}$ **29.** $46\overline{)322}$ **30.** $41\overline{)365}$

31. $19\overline{)100}$ **32.** $51\overline{)441}$ **33.** $23\overline{)181}$ **34.** $57\overline{)478}$ **35.** $32\overline{)235}$

36. $27\overline{)262}$ **37.** $84\overline{)403}$ **38.** $22\overline{)178}$ **39.** $39\overline{)355}$ **40.** $63\overline{)482}$

41. $68\overline{)553}$ **42.** $23\overline{)160}$ **43.** $39\overline{)238}$ **44.** $35\overline{)296}$ **45.** $71\overline{)565}$

46. $431 \div 74 = \underline{\ ?\ }$ **47.** $369 \div 46 = \underline{\ ?\ }$ **48.** $161 \div 34 = \underline{\ ?\ }$

49. $358 \div 86 = \underline{\ ?\ }$ **50.** $145 \div 21 = \underline{\ ?\ }$ **51.** $528 \div 75 = \underline{\ ?\ }$

52. $356 \div 59 = \underline{\ ?\ }$ **53.** $564 \div 72 = \underline{\ ?\ }$ **54.** $456 \div 57 = \underline{\ ?\ }$

★ **55.** $542 \div \underline{\ ?\ } = 67 \text{ r}\underline{\ ?\ }$ ★ **56.** $806 \div \underline{\ ?\ } = 89 \text{ r}\underline{\ ?\ }$ ★ **57.** $487 \div \underline{\ ?\ } = 81 \text{ r}\underline{\ ?\ }$

★ **58.** $397 \div \underline{\ ?\ } = 79 \text{ r}\underline{\ ?\ }$ ★ **59.** $672 \div \underline{\ ?\ } = 96 \text{ r}\underline{\ ?\ }$ ★ **60.** $203 \div \underline{\ ?\ } = 33 \text{ r}\underline{\ ?\ }$

★ **61.** $579 \div \underline{\ ?\ } = 72 \text{ r}\underline{\ ?\ }$ ★ **62.** $783 \div \underline{\ ?\ } = 97 \text{ r}\underline{\ ?\ }$ ★ **63.** $508 \div \underline{\ ?\ } = 84 \text{ r}\underline{\ ?\ }$

PROBLEM SOLVING • APPLICATIONS

64. Alecca Samuels runs a tree farm. She has 148 pine seedlings to plant. 24 fit in one row. How many rows can she fill? How many seedlings are left over?

65. It takes 18 workers to plant 162 small maple trees in one day. What is the average number of trees each worker plants in one day?

★ **66.** There are 276 spruce trees to plant. Workers plant 6 rows with 32 trees in each row. The remaining trees are planted with 28 trees in each row. How many rows of 28 can be made?

★ **67.** Alecca orders 315 hemlocks. She usually plants 45 in each row. How many more rows will she fill if she plants 35 in each row?

More Two-Digit Quotients

A wagon train on the Western frontier traveled 21 kilometers a day. At this rate, how many days did it take to go 1,155 kilometers?

$1,155 \div 21 = ?$

21)1,155   There are not enough thousands to divide.

21)1,155   There are not enough hundreds to divide.

21)1,155   There are enough tens to divide.

The first digit of the quotient is in the tens place.

Step 1
Divide the tens.
Think: 2)11. Multiply. Subtract.

$$\begin{array}{r} 5 \\ 21\overline{)1,155} \\ -1\ 05 \\ \hline 10 \end{array}$$

Step 2
Divide the ones.
Think: 2)10. Multiply. Subtract.

$$\begin{array}{r} 55 \\ 21\overline{)1,155} \\ -1\ 05\downarrow \\ \hline 105 \\ -105 \\ \hline 0 \end{array}$$

It took 55 days to go 1,155 kilometers.

More Examples

$$\begin{array}{r} 75 \\ 24\overline{)1,800} \\ -1\ 68 \\ \hline 120 \\ -120 \\ \hline 0 \end{array} \qquad \begin{array}{r} 18\ r14 \\ 37\overline{)680} \\ -37 \\ \hline 310 \\ -296 \\ \hline 14 \end{array} \qquad \begin{array}{r} 40 \\ 56\overline{)2,240} \\ -2\ 24 \\ \hline 00 \\ -\ 0 \\ \hline 0 \end{array}$$

Practice • Divide.

1. 32)544

2. 21)882

3. 70)5,809

4. 48)2,688

5. 27)2,615

6. 62)4,922

7. 29)2,630

8. 75)4,688

Mixed Practice • Divide.

9. 83)1,771

10. 39)2,450

11. 67)2,909

12. 32)2,616

13. 21)455

14. 67)914

15. 48)3,120

16. 38)1,978

17. 42)3,321

18. 86)5,493

19. 74)5,000

20. 12)115

21. $12\overline{)756}$ 22. $48\overline{)2,496}$ 23. $58\overline{)1,914}$ 24. $64\overline{)5,561}$

25. $16\overline{)99}$ 26. $37\overline{)162}$ 27. $25\overline{)1,775}$ 28. $83\overline{)2,454}$

29. $25\overline{)1,500}$ 30. $90\overline{)3,460}$ 31. $54\overline{)4,032}$ 32. $93\overline{)4,185}$

33. $654 \div 87 =$ ___?___   34. $2,443 \div 62 =$ ___?___

35. $6,300 \div 84 =$ ___?___   36. $1,530 \div 50 =$ ___?___

37. $7,660 \div 92 =$ ___?___   38. $3,689 \div 46 =$ ___?___

Each letter in the exercises below represents a digit. Each time a letter
is used, it represents the same digit. Find the missing digits.

★ 39.
```
        C7
   8B)C39A
    - 8B
      57A
     -57A
        0
```

★ 40.
```
         5F
   E7)DE91
    -DF5
     1E1
    -1E1
       0
```

★ 41.
```
         9K r3
   G3)K98G
    -K77
     HLG
    -HLH
       3
```

PROBLEM SOLVING • APPLICATIONS

42. A wagon train traveled 25 kilometers a day. At this rate, how many days did it take to go 1,650 kilometers?

43. One pony-express route was 432 kilometers long. The rider changed horses every 18 kilometers. How many horses were used on this route?

★ 44. A pioneer family moved west. The first trail they followed was 779 kilometers long. The second trail was 985 kilometers long. They traveled 18 kilometers a day. A this rate, how many days did the trip take?

★ 45. It took a wagon train 45 days to complete its trip. It traveled 650 kilometers along one trail and 362 kilometers along another trail. It stopped for one day between trails. How many kilometers did the wagon train cover each day that it traveled?

More Dividing of Greater Numbers

A local newspaper prints 25,210 papers each day. An equal number of these papers is put into 48 vans. How many newspapers are put into each van? How many newspapers are left over?

$25,210 \div 48 = ?$

$48\overline{)25,210}$ There are not enough ten thousands to divide.

$48\overline{)25,210}$ There are not enough thousands to divide.

$48\overline{)25,210}$ There are enough hundreds to divide.

The first digit of the quotient is in the hundreds place.

Step 1
Divide the hundreds.
Think: $5\overline{)25}$.
Multiply. Subtract.

$$
\begin{array}{r}
5 \\
48\overline{)25,210} \\
-24\ 0 \\
\hline
1\ 2
\end{array}
$$

Step 2
Divide the tens.
Think: $5\overline{)12}$.
Multiply. Subtract.

$$
\begin{array}{r}
52 \\
48\overline{)25,210} \\
-24\ 0 \\
\hline
1\ 21 \\
-\ \ 96 \\
\hline
25
\end{array}
$$

Step 3
Divide the ones.
Think: $5\overline{)25}$.
Multiply. Subtract.

$$
\begin{array}{r}
525\ \text{r}10 \\
48\overline{)25,210} \\
-24\ 0 \\
\hline
1\ 21 \\
-\ \ 96 \\
\hline
250 \\
-240 \\
\hline
10
\end{array}
$$

525 newspapers are put into each van. There are 10 left over.

Divide: $96,434 \div 26$.

Sometimes there are thousands in the quotient.

$$
\begin{array}{r}
3,709 \\
26\overline{)96,434} \\
-78 \\
\hline
18\ 4 \\
-18\ 2 \\
\hline
23 \\
-\ 0 \\
\hline
234 \\
-234 \\
\hline
0
\end{array}
$$

Practice • Divide.

1. $75\overline{)23,550}$

2. $43\overline{)7,654}$

3. $24\overline{)7,865}$

4. $42\overline{)54,364}$

5. $62\overline{)60,202}$

6. $67\overline{)32,688}$

7. $89\overline{)95,720}$

8. $55\overline{)64,450}$

Mixed Practice • Divide.

9. $92\overline{)77,777}$ 10. $94\overline{)27,434}$ 11. $47\overline{)81,688}$ 12. $40\overline{)7,516}$

13. $67\overline{)7,683}$ 14. $25\overline{)7,849}$ 15. $46\overline{)7,278}$ 16. $62\overline{)8,866}$

17. $18\overline{)6,250}$ 18. $28\overline{)14,448}$ 19. $42\overline{)8,728}$ 20. $82\overline{)47,810}$

21. $68\overline{)7,915}$ 22. $58\overline{)6,500}$ 23. $59\overline{)10,830}$ 24. $68\overline{)21,394}$

25. $82\overline{)16,762}$ 26. $85\overline{)15,603}$ 27. $57\overline{)5,249}$ 28. $89\overline{)82,173}$

29. $39\overline{)67,612}$ 30. $30\overline{)5,252}$ 31. $63\overline{)70,052}$ 32. $62\overline{)89,907}$

33. $38\overline{)43,300}$ 34. $23\overline{)2,254}$ ★ 35. $76\overline{)965,564}$ ★ 36. $72\overline{)848,840}$

37. $68,922 \div 81 = \underline{\quad?\quad}$ 38. $7,396 \div 86 = \underline{\quad?\quad}$

39. $11,710 \div 39 = \underline{\quad?\quad}$ 40. $53,262 \div 48 = \underline{\quad?\quad}$

41. $50,184 \div 23 = \underline{\quad?\quad}$ 42. $94,064 \div 91 = \underline{\quad?\quad}$

PROBLEM SOLVING • APPLICATIONS

43. A local newspaper reporter travels 20,712 kilometers in one year. What is the average distance she travels each month?

44. 17,100 meters of paper can pass through an offset press in one hour. At this rate, how many meters of paper can pass through the press in one minute?

★ 45. 46,475 copies of the *Sundown News* are printed daily. 9,485 are mailed. The workers put the remaining papers into bundles of 50 each. How many bundles do they make? How many papers are left over?

★ 46. In one year 2,053,220 copies of the *Sundown News* Sunday edition were sold. The next year 2,221,752 copies were sold. How many more copies per week were sold in the second year?

Skills Maintenance

1. $\begin{array}{r} 204 \\ \times\ \ 8 \\ \hline \end{array}$ 2. $\begin{array}{r} 678 \\ \times\ \ 5 \\ \hline \end{array}$ 3. $\begin{array}{r} 176 \\ \times\ \ 9 \\ \hline \end{array}$ 4. $\begin{array}{r} 2,834 \\ \times\ \ \ \ 6 \\ \hline \end{array}$ 5. $\begin{array}{r} 6,749 \\ \times\ \ \ \ 7 \\ \hline \end{array}$

6. $\begin{array}{r} 239 \\ \times\ 35 \\ \hline \end{array}$ 7. $\begin{array}{r} 608 \\ \times\ 68 \\ \hline \end{array}$ 8. $\begin{array}{r} 347 \\ \times\ 59 \\ \hline \end{array}$ 9. $\begin{array}{r} 4,196 \\ \times\ \ \ 25 \\ \hline \end{array}$ 10. $\begin{array}{r} 8,512 \\ \times\ \ \ 74 \\ \hline \end{array}$

PROBLEM SOLVING • STRATEGIES

Dividing with Money

Divide amounts of money as if you were dividing whole numbers.

A discount store sells items by the carton, box, and sack. 6 students decide to share a carton of felt-tip pens. The carton costs $7.38. How much does each student pay?

$7.38 ÷ 6 = ?

Step 1
Divide.

```
     1 23
6)$7.38
  6 ↓|
  1 3 |
  1 2↓
    18
    18
     0
```

Step 2
Write the dollar sign and the cents point in the answer.

```
    $1.23
6)$7.38
  6 ↓|
  1 3 |
  1 2↓
    18
    18
     0
```

Each student pays $1.23.

Solve.

1. Notebooks are packed 24 to a carton. If a carton costs $17.52, how much does each notebook cost?

Use multiplication to check division.

---

2. During a special sale, the price of a carton of 24 notebooks is reduced to $14.16. What is the sale price for each notebook?

3. A box of kites cost $20.80. There are 10 kites in the box. How much does each kite cost?

4. Baseballs come in boxes of 18. A box costs $23.22. How much does each baseball cost?

5. 5 students share a sack of marbles. The sack costs $10.25. How much does each student pay?

6. There are 72 pencils in a box that costs $12.96. What is the cost of 1 pencil?

7. There are 15 bars of soap in a sack. The sack costs $5.70. How much does each bar of soap cost?

Remember to place the dollar sign and the cents point in the answer.

---

8. There are 48 drawing pads in a carton. The carton costs $109.92. What is the price of each drawing pad?

9. A carton of 80 tea bags sells for $11.20. How much does each tea bag cost?

10. Cassette tapes are packed 30 to a carton. A carton costs $62.70. How much does each cassette tape cost?

11. Socks come in bags of 12 pairs. The bag costs $8.76. How much does each pair cost?

12. There are 84 small toy cars in a carton that sells for $23.52. What is the price of each car?

★ 13. The store has a special on whole wheat crackers. A carton of 24 boxes is reduced to $14.16. The new price of each box is $.10 less than the regular price. What is the regular price of each box of crackers?

★ 14. A carton of 36 whistles costs $18.00. A carton of 40 yo-yos costs $16.80. Does a whistle or a yo-yo cost more?

★ 15. A carton of 38 puzzles sells for $51.68. A carton of 16 puzzles sells for $22.88. Which carton contains puzzles that cost less?

Dividing by Three-Digit Numbers

In December 52,380 people saw a movie at the Crown Theater. At each showing all 388 seats were filled. How many times was the movie shown?

$52,380 \div 388 = ?$

$388\overline{)52,380}$ There are not enough ten thousands to divide.

$388\overline{)52,380}$ There are not enough thousands to divide.

$388\overline{)52,380}$ There are enough hundreds to divide.

The first digit of the quotient is in the hundreds place.

Step 1
Divide the hundreds.
Think: $4\overline{)5}$.
Multiply. Subtract.

```
        1
388)52,380
   -38 8
    13 5
```

Step 2
Divide the tens.
Think: $4\overline{)13}$.
Multiply. Subtract.

```
       13
388)52,380
   -38 8↓
    13 58
   -11 64
     1 94
```

Step 3
Divide the ones.
Think: $4\overline{)19}$. 4 is not enough. Try 5.
Multiply. Subtract.

```
       135
388)52,380
   -38 8↓
    13 58
   -11 64↓
     1 940
    -1 940
         0
```

The movie was shown 135 times.

More Examples

```
         15 r504
564)8,964
   -5 64
    3 324
   -2 820
      504
```

```
        607 r13
926)562,095
   -555 6
      6 49
   -    0
      6 495
     -6 482
         13
```

```
          2,247
439)986,433
   -878
    108 4
   - 87 8
     20 63
    -17 56
      3 073
     -3 073
          0
```

Practice • Divide.

1. $426\overline{)3,966}$ **2.** $236\overline{)3,317}$ **3.** $453\overline{)18,326}$ **4.** $341\overline{)79,560}$

5. $506\overline{)435,160}$ **6.** $768\overline{)321,024}$ **7.** $650\overline{)196,997}$ **8.** $246\overline{)123,000}$

Mixed Practice • Divide.

9. $515\overline{)3,671}$ 10. $302\overline{)19,552}$ 11. $913\overline{)13,865}$ 12. $800\overline{)81,600}$

13. $863\overline{)63,043}$ 14. $738\overline{)94,208}$ 15. $456\overline{)28,282}$ 16. $898\overline{)5,688}$

17. $643\overline{)8,949}$ 18. $523\overline{)10,992}$ 19. $904\overline{)75,000}$ 20. $259\overline{)98,841}$

21. $613\overline{)954,629}$ 22. $636\overline{)294,516}$ 23. $308\overline{)460,097}$ 24. $214\overline{)145,167}$

25. $197\overline{)128,151}$ 26. $216\overline{)712,536}$ 27. $375\overline{)200,695}$ 28. $363\overline{)854,216}$

29. $572\overline{)419,370}$ 30. $400\overline{)497,256}$ 31. $258\overline{)396,987}$ 32. $142\overline{)997,097}$

33. $742,398 \div 495 =$ ___?___   34. $496,273 \div 578 =$ ___?___

35. $516,784 \div 634 =$ ___?___   ★ 36. $295,068 \div 4,000 =$ ___?___

★ 37. $924,138 \div 3,000 =$ ___?___   ★ 38. $658,371 \div 6,000 =$ ___?___

PROBLEM SOLVING • APPLICATIONS

39. In one year (365 days) the Crown Theater sold a total of 359,890 tickets. What is the average number of tickets sold in one day?

40. The cashier collected a total of $2,541.50 after selling 598 adult tickets. What is the price of each ticket?

★ 41. Concession workers collected $897.95 for selling 862 small containers of popcorn and 527 cups of apple juice. Each cup of juice cost $.15. What was the price of each small container of popcorn?

★ 42. 254 adult tickets were sold for a total of $1,079.50. 167 children's tickets were sold for a total of $459.25. How much more does an adult ticket cost?

Thinking About the Remainder

When you divide, there is often a remainder in your answer. Many times, however, you may need a whole number for the answer. Sometimes the answer to the problem will be the quotient. At other times the answer will be the next greater whole number.

Delia is planning a ski trip to Windy Lodge. 84 people will make the trip by bus. Each of the buses she orders can carry 58 people. How many buses are needed?

$$\begin{array}{r} 1\ r26 \\ 58\overline{)84} \\ -58 \\ \hline 26 \end{array}$$

2 buses are needed.

Mavis is a ski instructor at Windy Lodge. She works 5 days each week. She has worked 97 days so far this year. How many full weeks is this?

$$\begin{array}{r} 19\ r2 \\ 5\overline{)97} \\ -5 \\ \hline 47 \\ -45 \\ \hline 2 \end{array}$$

She has worked 19 full weeks.

Is the answer 8 or is it 9?

1. 51 people want to take a side trip to Mt. Pilatus. They plan to take this trip by car. Each car can carry 6 people. How many cars are needed?

    Reread the question. Does your solution make sense?

2. Saturday night is Western Night at Windy Lodge. 67 people have signed up for the square dance. Each set in a square dance needs 8 people. How many full sets will there be?

Solve.

3. There are 317 guests at Windy Lodge. Each table in the dining room seats 8. How many tables are needed?

4. A printer prepares 1,780 brochures about Windy Lodge. She must pack them into bundles of 50 brochures each. How many full bundles can she pack?

5. The minibus leaves Windy Lodge for the ice-skating pond each morning. The bus can carry 18 people. 81 people want to go ice-skating. How many trips does the minibus make?

Think: Is the answer the next greater whole number?

---

6. A tailor is making special tablecloths for a holiday celebration at Windy Lodge. She has 740 square meters of fabric. 16 square meters of fabric are needed for each tablecloth. How many tablecloths can she complete?

7. 20 people are waiting to take a helicopter ride. The helicopter can carry 3 passengers on each trip. How many trips must the helicopter make?

8. The cook at the ski lodge makes 218 cups of hot chocolate. How many four-cup serving pitchers does he need?

9. The manager of the gift shop at Windy Lodge is ordering sweatshirts. Each sweatshirt costs $7. She has budgeted $500 for this purchase. How many sweatshirts can she order?

10. One weekend there are 466 guests at Windy Lodge. Each guest receives one ski badge. The badges come packed 24 to a package. How many packages are opened?

★ 11. A group of 187 people go on a ski weekend at Windy Lodge. 35 rooms sleep 4 people in each. The other rooms sleep 3 people in each. How many rooms does the group need in all?

★ 12. 154 people take a bus tour to a nearby village. Each bus can seat 32 people. How many buses do they need? 9 people want to join them for the return trip. Are there enough buses to take everyone back to the lodge?

Divide. (pages 72–79)

1. $4\overline{)39}$
2. $8\overline{)67}$
3. $7\overline{)341}$
4. $3\overline{)297}$

5. $4\overline{)1,731}$
6. $4\overline{)32,466}$
7. $9\overline{)9,659}$
8. $6\overline{)12,295}$

Find the averages. (pages 80–81)

9. 29, 67, 31, 20, 43
10. 112, 84, 65, 51
11. 12, 19, 50, 45, 36, 30
12. 141, 69, 98, 80, 102

Divide. (pages 82–95)

13. $20\overline{)160}$
14. $40\overline{)320}$
15. $70\overline{)493}$
16. $60\overline{)549}$

17. $59\overline{)311}$
18. $37\overline{)299}$
19. $63\overline{)554}$
20. $89\overline{)624}$

21. $32\overline{)1,792}$
22. $78\overline{)1,800}$
23. $41\overline{)2,255}$
24. $17\overline{)1,572}$

25. $56\overline{)23,576}$
26. $82\overline{)96,699}$
27. $37\overline{)31,090}$
28. $63\overline{)284,886}$

29. $56\overline{)\$182.00}$
30. $14\overline{)\$181.30}$
31. $198\overline{)28,161}$
32. $680\overline{)205,369}$

33. $540\overline{)270,482}$
34. $300\overline{)364,981}$
35. $498\overline{)698,112}$
36. $592\overline{)485,396}$

Solve.

37. 4,644 people saw the high school basketball team play this year. There were 18 games. What was the average number of people who saw each game? (p. 96)

38. The Pep Club ordered 5,000 team banners. The banners arrived in 20 cartons. How many banners were in each carton? (p. 96)

39. At one game cashiers collected $617.50 after selling 247 tickets. All the tickets cost the same amount. What was the price of each ticket? (p. 97)

40. The Pep Club collected $481.25 for banners at one game. 175 people bought banners. What was the price of each banner? (p. 97)

Collecting Data

Royale is taking a survey. She wants to find the **mean,** or **average,** height of the students in her class.

She makes a list of the names of the students in her class. She finds each student's height in centimeters and records it next to the student's name.

Royale finds the mean, or average, height. First, she finds the sum of the heights. Then she divides the sum by the number of heights.

Here are some surveys you can take on your own.

1. Find the mean, or average, height of the students in your class.

Jean	Mike	Liona	Katy	Patwin	Total	Average
132 cm	154 cm	150 cm	140 cm	155 cm	731 cm	$146\frac{2}{5}$ cm

2. Find the mean, or average, time it takes your classmates to travel to school each morning.

Jina	Liona	Stefan	Cam	Mike	Total	Average
0:35	0:45	0:30	0:15	0:20	145 minutes	29 minutes

3. Find the mean, or average, age in months of your classmates.

Jina	Patwin	Rochelle	Cam	Stefan	Total	Average
12 years	13 years	13 years	12 years	12 years	62 years	$12\frac{2}{5}$ years

TEST

Divide.

1. $8\overline{)57}$ 2. $6\overline{)39}$ 3. $4\overline{)385}$ 4. $5\overline{)415}$

5. $6\overline{)1,077}$ 6. $7\overline{)52,136}$ 7. $3\overline{)2,117}$ 8. $7\overline{)49,044}$

Find the averages.

9. 27, 35, 10, 41, 17   10. 107, 33, 67, 33

11. 60, 78, 44, 81, 115, 96   12. 54, 37, 66, 79, 24

Divide.

13. $50\overline{)450}$ 14. $30\overline{)240}$ 15. $30\overline{)216}$ 16. $60\overline{)448}$

17. $39\overline{)156}$ 18. $62\overline{)498}$ 19. $94\overline{)632}$ 20. $47\overline{)380}$

21. $48\overline{)1,069}$ 22. $77\overline{)2,323}$ 23. $16\overline{)1,360}$ 24. $26\overline{)2,094}$

25. $83\overline{)45,198}$ 26. $12\overline{)49,700}$ 27. $57\overline{)50,456}$ 28. $67\overline{)52,394}$

29. $34\overline{)\$142.46}$ 30. $42\overline{)\$112.98}$ 31. $314\overline{)91,100}$ 32. $626\overline{)493,926}$

33. $283\overline{)144,896}$ 34. $625\overline{)264,379}$ 35. $300\overline{)397,221}$ 36. $246\overline{)384,777}$

Solve.

37. Ms. Lenno's car averages 13 kilometers per liter of gasoline. How many liters does she use on a 1,664-kilometer trip?

38. It is 3,672 kilometers from Woodville to Newton. Mr. Dane's van averages 12 kilometers per liter of gasoline. How many liters will he use on the trip from Woodville to Newton?

39. Ms. Hototo's car used 153 liters of gasoline on a 1,836-kilometer trip. How many kilometers per liter of gasoline did her car travel?

40. Ms. Jacobs drove 4,284 kilometers on 306 liters of gasoline. How many kilometers per liter of gasoline did she average?

ENRICHMENT

Mean, Median, and Mode

Gwen earned these scores on 9 tests.

34, 99, 96, 100, 94, 96, 100, 94, 97.

What is Gwen's **mean**, or average, score?

Arrange her scores in order from least to greatest.

34, 94, 94, 96, 96, 97, 99, 100, 100

Which score is in the middle?
The middle score is the **median**.

All but one of Gwen's scores are very high. Find the mean of the 8 high scores. Compare it with the mean of the 9 scores How does one low score affect the mean? Did the low score affect her median score?

Marsha earned these scores on 9 tests.

65, 65, 75, 70, 90, 100, 100, 100, 100

Which score did Marsha have most often?
This score, 100, is the **mode**.

Look at Marsha's scores. What score do you think Marsha might earn on her next test? Why?

Find the mean, the median, and the mode.

1. 94, 86, 64, 73, 73

2. 91, 86, 75, 72, 91

3. 90, 82, 82, 80, 79, 79, 82

4. 77, 24, 52, 63, 24, 37, 24

5. 62, 81, 76, 85, 81, 84, 63

6. 39, 90, 95, 90, 92, 95, 90, 94, 98

Estimating Division

Always estimate before dividing with a calculator. Divide $42\overline{)8{,}988}$.

Estimate: 9,000 divided by 40 is more than 200.

First do the example correctly. Push 8 9 8 8 ÷ 4 2 = . The answer, 214, looks correct.

Suppose you had pushed 8 9 8 ÷ 4 2 = . The screen shows 21 and some decimal. That is much too low. Check your numbers. You left out an 8 in the dividend.

Divide. Be careful to write dollar signs where you need them.

1. $73\overline{)4{,}964}$ **2.** $37\overline{)\$8.88}$ **3.** $64\overline{)\$0.00}$ **4.** $25\overline{)975}$

5. $\$8{,}500 \div 50 =$ _____?_____ **6.** $1{,}936 \div 22 =$ _____?_____

You can find remainders with the calculator. Remember to check your numbers.

Divide $63\overline{)4{,}238}$.

Estimate: 4,000 divided by 60 is more than 60.

Push 4 2 3 8 ÷ 6 3 = .

Copy the quotient: 67. Now multiply 6 7 × 6 3 = .

Copy the product: 4221. Now subtract 4 2 3 8 − 4 2 2 1 = .

Copy the remainder: 17. The answer is 67 r 17.

Divide. Find the quotients and remainders.

7. $25\overline{)\$8{,}439}$ **8.** $19\overline{)9{,}201}$ **9.** $44\overline{)\$0.00}$ **10.** $92\overline{)4{,}738}$

11. $7{,}342 \div 65 =$ _____?_____ **12.** $8{,}154 \div 21 =$ _____?_____

13. $1{,}479 \div 99 =$ _____?_____ **14.** $\$4{,}120 \div 73 =$ _____?_____

15. $\$456 \div 36 =$ _____?_____ **16.** $\$00.00 \div 48 =$ _____?_____

SKILLS MAINTENANCE
Chapters 1 Through 4

1. Choose the expanded form of 3,094.

   A. 3,000 + 900 + 4
   B. 3,000 + 90 + 4
   C. 3,000 + 900 + 40
   D. not here

2. Complete.

   $(17 - 9) + 6 = \underline{\ ?\ }$

   A. 2
   B. 32
   C. 14
   D. not here

3. Estimate. Round to the nearest hundred.

   752
   +437

   A. 1,100
   B. 1,200
   C. 1,150
   D. not here

4. Add.

   4,897 + 396 + 21,043

   A. 26,336
   B. 25,336
   C. 25,236
   D. not here

5. Subtract.

   $845.00
   − 359.29

   A. $485.81
   B. $486.71
   C. $485.71
   D. not here

6. Find the missing factor.

   $8 \times \underline{\ ?\ } = 64$

   A. 9
   B. 7
   C. 6
   D. not here

7. Multiply.

   738
   × 40

   A. 2,952
   B. 29,520
   C. 28,520
   D. not here

8. Multiply.

   492
   ×367

   A. 179,954
   B. 175,564
   C. 180,564
   D. not here

9. Divide.

   7)59

   A. 8
   B. 8 r3
   C. 7 r10
   D. not here

10. Divide.

    4)383

    A. 95 r3
    B. 90 r3
    C. 95
    D. not here

11. Divide.

    6)12,539

    A. 2,089 r5
    B. 289 r5
    C. 2,089
    D. not here

12. Divide.

    38)2,739

    A. 61 r7
    B. 72 r3
    C. 74 r27
    D. not here

Skills Maintenance continued

Choose the correct answers.

13. Mount Everest reaches an altitude of 29,028 ft. What is the height to the nearest ten thousand?

   A. 29,000
   B. 28,000
   C. 30,000
   D. not here

14. Otis buys 2 video games for $27.95 each and a record album for $7.29. How much does he spend?

   A. $35.24
   B. $63.19
   C. $55.90
   D. not here

15. Baldwin's Bookstore had 7,542 books in stock in January. In March there were 3,785 books left. How many books were sold during the three months?

   A. 3,857
   B. 3,757
   C. 11,327
   D. not here

16. In one month Ms. Kline flew 2,987 kilometers on business trips. The next month she flew 3,495 kilometers. How many kilometers did she travel in the two months?

   A. 6,472
   B. 6,382
   C. 6,482
   D. not here

17. Thelma buys 7 blank cassette tapes for $3.29 each. How much does she spend?

   A. $23.03
   B. $22.43
   C. $21.03
   D. not here

18. A warehouse receives a shipment of 57 cartons packed with boxes of nails. Each carton contains 275 boxes. How many boxes of nails are in the cartons?

   A. 14,675
   B. 15,675
   C. 15,175
   D. not here

19. Mrs. Brooks orders 36 vinyl floor tiles for $106.92. How much does each tile cost?

   A. $3.24
   B. $2.97
   C. $2.90
   D. not here

20. Mrs. Gallo drove 11,604 miles in one year. What is the average number of miles driven per month?

   A. 967
   B. 907
   C. 968
   D. not here

Graphing

GAMES WON

	1	2	3	4	5	6	7	8	9	10
BILL										
MARY										
JIM										
CAROL										
BOB										
JOAN										

Pictographs • Bar Graphs • Reading and Making Line Graphs • Graphing Ordered Pairs • Problem Solving: Add, Subtract, Multiply, or Divide? • Graphing Data • Using Line Graphs to Solve Problems

Pictographs

Graphs are used to show and compare **data**, or facts.

Number of Periodicals in the United States
Each □ stands for 100 magazines.

Weekly	□ □ □ □ □ □ □ □ □ □ □ □ □ □ □ □ □
Semimonthly	□ □ □
Monthly	□ □
Bimonthly	□ □ □ □ □ □ □ □ □ □ □
Quarterly	□ □ □ □ □ □ □ □ □ □ □ □ □ □ ▢
Other	□ □ □ □ □ □ □ □ □ ▢

This **pictograph** shows the number of periodicals in the United States.
There are more monthly periodicals than weekly periodicals.
There are more weekly than quarterly.

What does the symbol □ represent?
Each □ stands for 100 periodicals.
The □ stands for half of 100, or 50, periodicals.
There are 17 symbols in the weekly row.
So there are 17 × 100, or 1,700, weekly periodicals.

Practice • Use the graph above to answer questions 1 through 7.

1. Which kind has the most periodicals?

2. Which kind has the fewest periodicals?

3. Are there more semimonthly or more bimonthly periodicals?

About how many periodicals are

4. monthly? **5.** quarterly? **6.** bimonthly? **7.** semimonthly?

More Practice • Use the graph below to answer questions 8 through 13.

Newspapers in the Middle Atlantic States
Each ☐ stands for 60 newspapers.

New Jersey	☐ ☐ ☐ ▢
New York	☐ ☐ ☐ ☐ ☐ ☐ ☐ ☐ ☐ ☐ ☐ ☐ ☐
Pennsylvania	☐ ☐ ☐ ☐ ☐ ☐ ☐

8. In which state are the most newspapers published?

9. In which state are the fewest newspapers published?

About how many newspapers are published in

10. Pennsylvania?   11. New Jersey?   12. New York?

13. About how many more newspapers are published in New York than in New Jersey and Pennsylvania together?

Use the graph below to answer questions 14 through 19.

Newspapers in the United States Each □ stands for 250 newspapers.	
Semiweekly	□ □
Weekly	□ □ □ □ □ □ □ □ □ □ □ □ □ □ □ □ □ □ □ □ □ □ □ □ □ □ [
Daily	□ □ □ □ □ □ □
Other	□

14. Which kind of newspaper is found most frequently?

15. What kind of newspaper is least common?

About how many newspapers are published

16. weekly?   17. daily?   18. semiweekly?

19. About how many more weekly than daily newspapers are there?

PROBLEM SOLVING • APPLICATIONS

★ 20. Make a pictograph from the data shown in the table. Round each number to the nearest billion. Use $ to stand for 1 billion dollars.

Advertising Money Spent in the United States in One Year	
Newspapers	$14,493,000,000
Magazines	$ 2,930,000,000
Television	$10,195,000,000
Radio	$ 3,385,000,000
Direct mail	$ 6,650,000,000
Other	$ 9,817,000,000

Skills Maintenance

In which place is each blue digit?

1. 46,197   2. 308,109   3. 87,453   4. 673,240   5. 534,721

Write the numbers.

6. 10^5 7. 4×10^3 8. 9×10^2 9. 3×10^4 10. 5×10^7

Bar Graphs

Each year the Thornwood School elects a mayor to lead the student government.

The table to the right shows the candidates and the number of votes each received.

The data from the table can be used to make a **bar graph**.

Candidate	Number of Votes	Rounded Number
Steven Boughs	205	210
Thelma Daven	178	180
Henry Nattle	143	140
Carl Sanders	162	160
Phyllis Warner	216	220

In the bar graph below, each bar shows the number of votes rounded to the nearest ten.

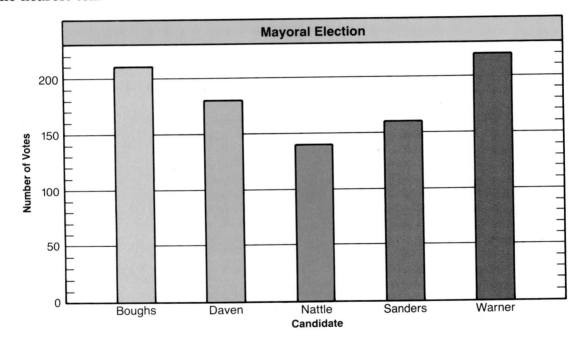

The tallest bar is for Phyllis Warner.
She received the greatest number of votes.

Practice • Use the bar graph above to answer questions 1 through 4.

1. Who received the greater number of votes, Thelma Daven or Carl Sanders?

2. Which candidates received more votes than Thelma Daven?

3. Which candidates received fewer votes than Steven Boughs?

4. About how many votes did Phyllis Warner receive?

More Practice • Use the bar graph below to answer questions 5 through 11.

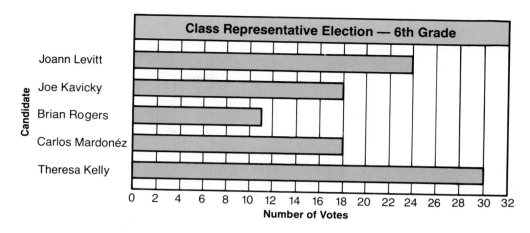

Class Representative Election — 6th Grade

Candidate / Number of Votes

Joann Levitt
Joe Kavicky
Brian Rogers
Carlos Mardonéz
Theresa Kelly

Which candidate received the greater number of votes?

5. Joann Levitt or Brian Rogers?

6. Joe Kavicky or Theresa Kelly?

Which candidate received

7. the greatest number of votes?

8. the least number of votes?

9. Which candidates received the same number of votes?

10. How many students voted for Carlos Mardonéz?

11. How many more students voted for Theresa Kelly than Joann Levitt?

PROBLEM SOLVING • APPLICATIONS

Use the bar graph below to answer questions 12 through 15.

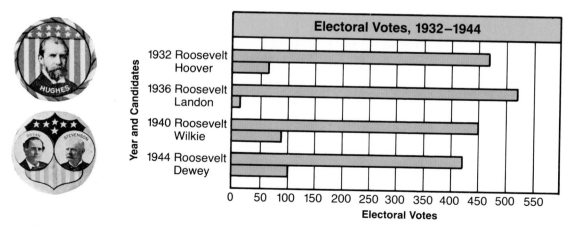

Electoral Votes, 1932–1944

Year and Candidates / Electoral Votes

1932 Roosevelt Hoover
1936 Roosevelt Landon
1940 Roosevelt Wilkie
1944 Roosevelt Dewey

★ **12.** In which year did Roosevelt receive the most electoral votes?

★ **13.** In which year did he receive the least?

★ **14.** Which opponent received the most electoral votes?

★ **15.** In which year were the candidates furthest apart?

Line Graphs

Mrs. Adams owns a small gift shop.
She is very busy on Saturdays.
She decides to hire a student to work part-time.
To see when she needs the student most,
she makes a **line graph**.

A line graph is used to show change.

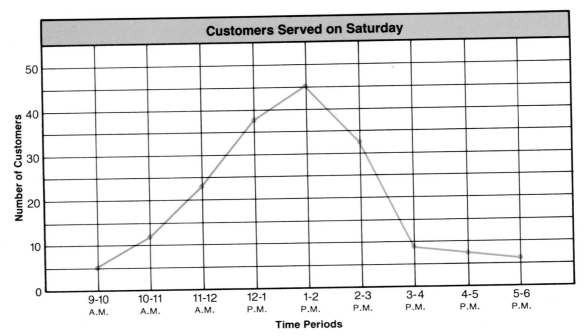

This line graph shows the number of customers served each hour.

The busiest hour is between 1:00 P.M. and 2:00 P.M.
Business increases from the time the shop opens until 2:00 P.M.
How does the graph show this?

Practice • Use the line graph above to answer questions 1 through 5.

1. During which hour are the fewest customers served?

2. At what hour does business begin to decrease?

3. During which hours are more than 25 customers served?

4. During which hours are fewer than 10 customers served?

5. Mrs. Adams hires a student to work from 11:00 A.M. to 3:00 P.M.
   Do you think this is a good decision?

110

More Practice • Use the line graph below to answer questions 6 through 12.

Mrs. Adams made another line graph.
It shows the number of sales she made each month for one year.

Sales for One Year

Number of Dollars (y-axis: 6,000 5,000 4,000 3,000 2,000 1,000 0)

Months: Jan. Feb. Mar. Apr. May June July Aug. Sept. Oct. Nov. Dec.

6. During which months did sales increase over the preceding month's sales?

7. During which months did sales decrease from the preceding month's sales?

8. In which month were the sales the greatest?

9. In which months were the sales the least?

10. In which months were sales greater than $4,000?

11. In which months were sales less than $3,000?

★12. Mrs. Adams subtracts her expenses from her sales. This tells her how much she has left over, or what her profit is. Her expenses average $2,500 a month. During which months was there no profit?

PROBLEM SOLVING • APPLICATIONS

Use the line graph below to answer questions 13 through 15.

Mrs. Adams keeps a record of her cash and charge sales. The red line shows her cash sales. The blue line shows her charge sales.

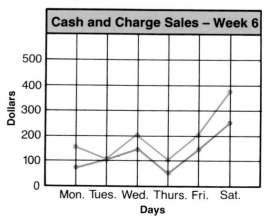

Cash and Charge Sales – Week 6

Dollars (y-axis: 500 400 300 200 100 0)

Days: Mon. Tues. Wed. Thurs. Fri. Sat.

★13. On which day were cash and charge sales the same?

★14. On which days did charge sales decrease from the preceding day's charge sales?

★15. Estimate Mrs. Adams's total cash and charge sales for this week.

111

Making Line Graphs

One day Erica and Eric recorded the temperature every two hours. Their table shows the time and the temperature in degrees Celsius.

Time	Temperature
7 A.M.	2°C
9 A.M.	5°C
11 A.M	10°C
1 P.M.	12°C
3 P.M.	12°C
5 P.M.	8°C
7 P.M.	4°C

They followed these steps to make a line graph.

Step 1 Write the intervals for degrees Celsius along the vertical scale on the left of the graph.

Step 2 Write the times along the horizontal scale at the bottom of the graph.

Step 3 Put a dot above the time to show the number of degrees Celsius.

Step 4 Connect the dots.

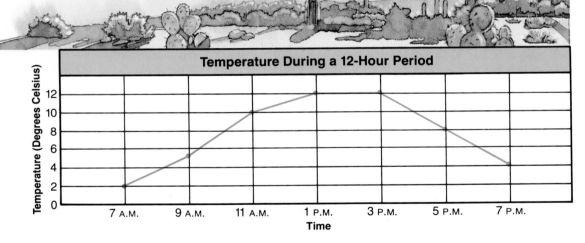

Practice

1. Use the table to the right to make a line graph. Give the graph a title.

2. How do you label the vertical scale at the left side of the graph?

3. How do you label the horizontal scale at the bottom of the graph?

Time	Temperature
9 A.M.	6°C
11 A.M.	10°C
1 P.M.	10°C
3 P.M.	8°C
5 P.M.	4°C

4. At what hour was the lowest temperature recorded?

5. At what hours was the highest temperature recorded?

More Practice

The table to the right shows the average monthly high temperatures for Phoenix, Arizona.

6. Use the table to make a line graph. Give the graph a title.

7. How do you label the vertical and the horizontal scales?

8. In which month does the average temperature begin to decrease?

Month	High Temperature	Month	High Temperature
Jan.	18°C	July	41°C
Feb.	21°C	Aug.	39°C
March	24°C	Sept.	37°C
April	29°C	Oct.	31°C
May	34°C	Nov.	24°C
June	39°C	Dec.	20°C

★9. Name two months in which the average temperature is the same.

PROBLEM SOLVING • APPLICATIONS

The table to the right shows the average monthly low temperatures for Phoenix, Arizona.

10. Use the table to make a line graph. Give the graph a title.

11. How do you label the vertical and the horizontal scales?

★12. What is the difference between the highest and the lowest temperatures shown on the graph?

Month	Low Temperature	Month	Low Temperature
Jan.	2°C	July	24°C
Feb.	4°C	Aug.	23°C
March	7°C	Sept.	19°C
April	10°C	Oct.	12°C
May	14°C	Nov.	5°C
June	19°C	Dec.	3°C

Midchapter Review

Use the bar graph to answer questions 1 through 4.

1. Who received the greatest number of votes?

2. Who received the least number of votes?

3. Who received more votes than Brian?

4. How many votes did Sara receive?

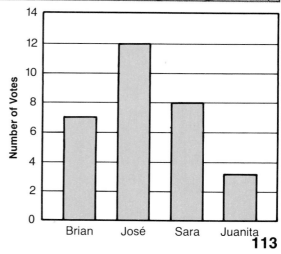

113

Graphing Ordered Pairs

You can use an **ordered pair** of numbers to locate points on a grid.

The ordered pair (6, 5) means move 6 spaces to the right and then move 5 spaces up.

The ordered pair (6, 5) locates point L.

Y is located by the ordered pair (0, 4).

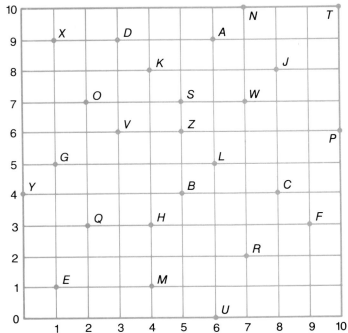

Practice • Use the grid to answer questions 1 through 40.

What letter is at each point?

1. (4, 1)   **2.** (7, 10)   **3.** (3, 9)   **4.** (4, 3)   **5.** (6, 9)

6. (9, 3)   **7.** (4, 8)   **8.** (2, 3)   **9.** (2, 7)   **10.** (10, 6)

11. (5, 4)   **12.** (7, 2)   **13.** (7, 7)   **14.** (8, 4)   **15.** (8, 8)

16. (5, 6)   **17.** (1, 1)   **18.** (3, 6)   **19.** (1, 5)   **20.** (10, 10)

What ordered pair tells the location of each point?

21. E   **22.** D   **23.** B   **24.** J   **25.** G

26. Q   **27.** A   **28.** M   **29.** H   **30.** R

31. X   **32.** C   **33.** K   **34.** U   **35.** T

36. Y   **37.** F   **38.** W   **39.** S   **40.** N

More Practice • Use the grid to answer questions 41 through 52.
What letter is at each point?

41. (1, 4)   **42.** (4, 0)   **43.** (4, 6)

44. (6, 3)   **45.** (3, 4)   **46.** (0, 1)

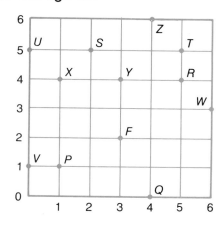

What ordered pair tells the location of each point?

47. F   **48.** Q   **49.** R

50. S   **51.** T   **52.** U

PROBLEM SOLVING • APPLICATIONS

Use a sheet of graph paper. Locate the ordered pairs.
Draw a dot at each point. Label the points.

53.

POINT	ORDERED PAIR
A	(4, 8)
B	(7, 2)
C	(3, 3)
D	(1, 10)
E	(5, 0)
F	(9, 3)
G	(10, 5)
H	(6, 1)

54.

POINT	ORDERED PAIR
S	(2, 3)
T	(3, 9)
U	(8, 7)
V	(6, 4)
W	(5, 9)
X	(5, 6)
Y	(10, 2)
Z	(9, 10)

★ **55.** Follow the rule. Complete the table. List the ordered pairs. Make a graph and locate the pairs.

★ **56.** Connect the points. What do you notice?

Point	Number	Add 2	Ordered Pair
A	1	3	(1, 3)
B	2	?	(2, ?)
C	3	?	(3, ?)
D	4	?	(4, ?)
E	5	?	(5, ?)
F	6	?	(6, ?)
G	7	?	(7, ?)

Skills Maintenance

1. 647
 ×386

2. 813
 ×950

3. 462
 ×309

4. 758
 ×119

5. 672
 ×295

6. 3,968
 × 539

7. 1,259
 × 249

8. 5,867
 × 134

9. 2,381
 × 472

10. 5,642
 × 356

PROBLEM SOLVING · STRATEGIES

Add, Subtract, Multiply, or Divide?

Sometimes you have to decide which operation to use. Key words can help you.

Archeologists are like detectives. They dig for facts to find out about people who lived long ago. When you solve problems, you look for facts to tell which operation to use.

Read the problem.

Some archeologists and students meet in Kampsville, Illinois. They meet for a dig. There are a number of high school students. They are joined by a number of college students. How many students are there in all?

Think:

The key words are **joined** and **in all**. Add to find how many students there are **in all**.

Which operation would you use? Write ADD, SUBTRACT,

MULTIPLY, or DIVIDE.

1. Each morning the students travel to the site of the dig. They go some kilometers by bus. They take a ferry some more kilometers across a river. Then they ride to a farm. How many kilometers do they travel in all?

   Read the question carefully.
   Find the key words.

2. The students dig pits to examine the soil. The soil samples are put into a number of large baskets. Some of the baskets are loaded into a car. These will be taken to a lab. How many baskets are not loaded into the car?

3. Archeologists' work is hard and exciting. It begins early in the day. They work a number of hours each week. One project goes on for some weeks. How many hours of work is that in all?

Which operation would you use? Write ADD, SUBTRACT, MULTIPLY, or DIVIDE. Then solve.

Write a number sentence to help you solve the problem.

4. There are 20 evening talks during the summer. The summer work lasts 10 weeks. How many talks is that each week?

5. 50 people work in the labs. There are 5 labs. How many people work in each lab?

6. Layers from before written history are called horizons. Horizon 1 is nearest the surface. Horizon 6 is about 2 meters below the surface. Horizon 7 is about 9 meters below the surface. How much deeper is Horizon 7 than Horizon 6?

7. Once archeologists have chosen a site, they dig test squares. At one site, they dug 130 test squares. Each is about 3 square meters in area. How many square meters did they dig in all?

8. Maude took 256 photographs while she was on the dig. She wants to put them in an album. Each page of the album holds 16 photographs. How many pages does she need for her photographs?

9. Recording information is as important as finding the artifacts. One student wrote 17 pages of notes. Another wrote 35 pages of notes. How many pages did they write in all?

10. On Tuesday Jeff spends 4 hours working at a test square. He spends 2 hours working on soil samples. Then he goes to the lab where he works 3 more hours. How many hours does he spend working in all?

★ **11.** One site is located 19 kilometers from the main camp. Another site is located three times as many kilometers from the camp. How much farther from camp is the second site than the first site?

★ **12.** A group of students travels to a site by bus. There are 9 buses. Each of 5 buses can hold 14 students. The other 4 buses can each hold 18 students. How many students can visit the site?

REVIEW

Use the pictograph to answer questions 1 through 5. (pages 106–107)

1. What is the most popular kind of bread?

2. What is the least popular kind of bread?

About how many children chose

3. white?   4. rye?   5. whole wheat?

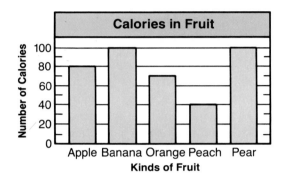

Favorite Breads
Each ⚊ stands for 20 children.

White	⚊⚊⚊⚊⚊⚊⚊
Whole Wheat	⚊⚊⚊⚊⚊
Rye	⚊⚊⚊
No Favorite	⚊⚊⚊

Use the bar graph to answer questions 6 through 12. (pages 108–109)

6. Which fruit has the fewest calories?

Which fruit has more calories

7. an apple or a peach?

8. a banana or an orange?

9. Which fruits have the same number of calories?

How many calories are in

10. a pear?   11. an apple?

12. How many more calories are in an orange than in a peach?

Use the line graph to answer questions 13 through 16. (pages 110–111)

13. During which months do the temperatures increase over the preceding month's temperature?

14. During which months do the temperatures decrease from the preceding month's temperature?

15. In which month is the temperature the highest?

16. In which months is the temperature higher than 20°C?

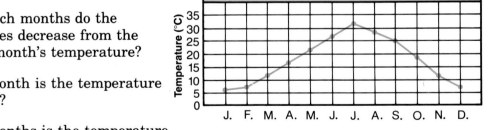

Use the grid to answer questions 17 through 24.
(pages 114–115)

What letter is at each point?

17. (3, 2)   18. (5, 5)   19. (1, 6)   20. (6, 4)

What ordered pair tells the location of each point?

21. A   22. F   23. E   24. B

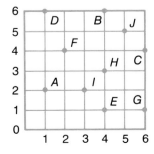

Graphing Data

Take a survey.
Ask 30 students to choose their favorite sport from this list.

Which sport has the greatest number of votes?

Which sport has the least number of votes?

Baseball
Bowling
Football
Golf
Hockey
Ice Skating
Soccer
Swimming
Tennis
Volleyball

Tally | Total

After you have collected the data, show the results on a bar graph like this.

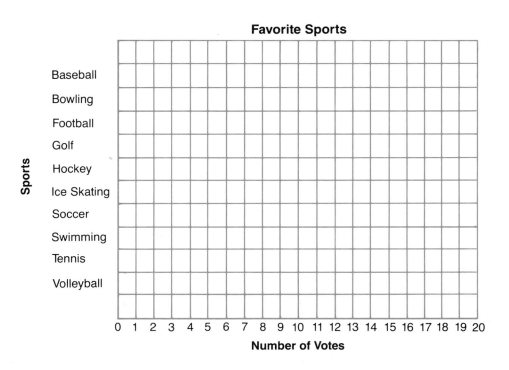

Favorite Sports

Sports: Baseball, Bowling, Football, Golf, Hockey, Ice Skating, Soccer, Swimming, Tennis, Volleyball

Number of Votes: 0 1 2 3 4 5 6 7 8 9 10 11 12 13 14 15 16 17 18 19 20

Now take another survey of your own. Graph your results.

Use the pictograph to answer questions 1 through 5.

1. Which category has the greatest number of books?

2. Which category has the fewest number of books?

About how many books are 3. fiction? 4. reference? 5. biography?

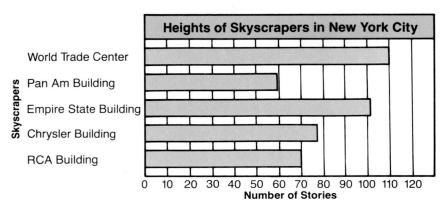

Kinds of Books in the School Library	
Reference	☐ ☐
Fiction	☐ ☐ ☐ ☐ ☐
Biography	☐ ☐ ☐
Nonfiction	☐ ☐ ☐ ☐

Each ☐ stands for 40 books.

Use the bar graph to answer questions 6 through 8.

6. Which skyscraper has the greatest number of stories?

Heights of Skyscrapers in New York City

Skyscrapers:
- World Trade Center
- Pan Am Building
- Empire State Building
- Chrysler Building
- RCA Building

Number of Stories (0 10 20 30 40 50 60 70 80 90 100 110 120)

7. Which skyscraper has more stories, the Pan Am Building or the RCA Building?

8. How many more stories does the World Trade Center have than the RCA Building?

Use the line graph to answer questions 9 through 13.

9. During which days did sales increase over the preceding day's sales?

10. During which day did sales decrease from the preceding day's sales?

11. On which day were the most cars sold?

12. On which day were no cars sold?

13. On which days were more than 15 cars sold?

Car Sales for One Week

Number of Cars (0, 10, 20, 30, 40, 50) vs. Mon. Wed. Fri.

Use the grid to answer questions 14 through 21.
What letter is at each point?

14. (4, 2) 15. (3, 6) 16. (5, 3) 17. (1, 5)

What ordered pair tells the location of each point?

18. C 19. B 20. F 21. D

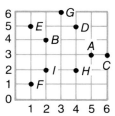

Using Line Graphs to Solve Problems

Teddy is driving to Mount Rushmore. He leaves home at 8:00 A.M. and drives at an average speed of 50 kilometers per hour. His sister, Jane, leaves one hour later and drives at an average speed of 75 kilometers per hour. About what time will Jane pass Teddy on the highway?

You can use tables and a graph to help you answer the questions.

Make a table for each driver. Show the time and the distance traveled. Use the data to make a line graph. Put both graphs on the same grid.

Teddy	
Time	Distance in Kilometers
8:00 A.M.	0
9:00 A.M.	50
10:00 A.M.	100
11:00 A.M.	150

Jane	
Time	Distance in Kilometers
9:00 A.M.	0
10:00 A.M.	75
11:00 A.M.	150

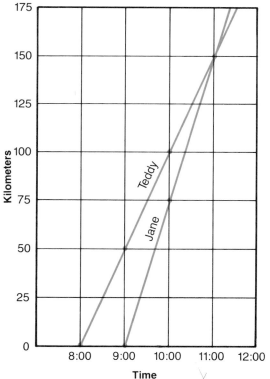

The two graphs intersect at the point (11:00, 150 km).
Jane will pass Teddy on the highway at about 11:00 A.M.
How far will they have traveled when they pass on the highway?
They will have traveled about 150 kilometers.

Enrichment continued

Complete the tables. Make a graph and solve.

1. Teddy starts walking on the forest trail at 1:00 P.M. He walks an average of 3 kilometers per hour. Jane starts walking on the forest trail one hour later. She walks at an average of 4 kilometers per hour. About what time will Jane meet Teddy?

Teddy	
Time	Distance in km
1:00	0
2:00	3
3:00	6
4:00	?
5:00	?

Jane	
Time	Distance in km
2:00	0
3:00	4
4:00	?
5:00	?
6:00	?

2. Bill is also driving to Mount Rushmore. He leaves at 11:00 A.M. and drives at an average speed of 60 kilometers per hour. His brother, Shaun, leaves at 12:00 noon and drives at an average speed of 90 kilometers per hour. About what time will Shaun pass Bill?

Bill	
Time	Distance in km
11:00	0
12:00	60
1:00	?
2:00	?

Shaun	
Time	Distance in km
12:00	0
1:00	90
2:00	?
3:00	?

Make tables and a graph to help you answer each problem.

3. Bill goes horseback riding on a mountain trail at 2:00 P.M. He rides an average of 6 kilometers per hour. Shaun starts riding on the trail two hours later. He rides about 12 kilometers per hour. At what time will Shaun catch up to Bill?

4. Bill and Shaun go hiking at 7:00 A.M. on a forest trail. They travel an average of 3 kilometers per hour. Teddy and Jane go hiking on the same trail at 9:00 A.M. They hike an average of 5 kilometers per hour. At what time will the four hikers meet?

5. That afternoon Teddy decides to go biking. He rides on the trail an average of 6 kilometers an hour starting at 1:00 P.M. Jane starts out an hour later. She rides an average of 8 kilometers an hour. About what time will Jane meet Teddy?

6. Teddy leaves Mount Rushmore the next day at 9:00 A.M. He averages 60 kilometers per hour. Jane leaves an hour later and averages 80 kilometers per hour. At what time will she pass Teddy?

★ 7. Bill and Shaun's sister, Darleen, meet them at Mount Rushmore. Darleen starts hiking on a nature trail at 10:00 A.M. She walks about 2 kilometers an hour. Bill starts hiking two hours later, walking about 3 kilometers per hour. Shaun begins on the nature trail an hour later than Bill, walking an average of 4 kilometers per hour. At what time will the three meet?

COMPUTER

Programming Languages

Programming languages help programmers give instructions to computers.
Programming languages use statements just as the natural languages of English
or mathematics do. Every programming language has a *grammar* that must
be followed exactly. Every programming language has a *compiler* that
translates programming-language statements into statements that tell the
computer what to do.

Here are the names of some programming languages.
BASIC means Beginner's All-purpose Symbolic Instruction Code. It is mainly
used in education and on computers for beginning programmers.
PASCAL is named for Blaise Pascal, who built the first digital adding machine.
PASCAL is mainly used in education and in computer-systems design.
FORTRAN means FORmula TRANslation and is used mainly in scientific work.
COBOL means COmmon Business-Oriented Language and is used mainly by businesses.
LISP means LISt Processor and is used in work on artificial intelligence.
PL/I means Programming Language I and is used in business and science.

Each programming language includes about one hundred kinds of statements.
Statements are used to specify data, input/output use, and calculations.

    a. Data must be defined according to quantity and type. Data may be
alphabetic data (letters) or *numeric data* (numbers).
    b. Input/output must be defined by quantity and type. Type refers to the use
and speed of keyboard, CRT, magnetic tape, and hard and floppy disks.
    c. Calculations process input data in order to get the required output data.

As an example, suppose that any number *X greater than 100* must be set equal
to 100. These are the statements used in each programming language to do this.
They give you an idea of what each language is like.

BASIC:	10 IF X =< 100 THEN 20 ELSE X = 100 =< means "is less than"
PASCAL:	IF X > 100 THEN X := 100 > means "is greater than"
FORTRAN:	IF X .GT. 100 THEN X = 100 .GT. means "is greater than"
COBOL:	IF X IS GREATER THAN 100 THEN SET X TO 100 GIVING X
LISP:	(SETQ X (MIN X (100))) SETQ X means "set X equal to"
PL/I:	X := MIN (X, 100) MIN (X, 100) means "the lesser of X and 100"

Write whether these statements are TRUE or FALSE.

1. BASIC means BASic Instructions for Compilers.

2. PASCAL is used in education and in computer-systems design.

3. FORTRAN means FORmula TRANslation and is used in business work.

4. COBOL means COmmercial Business-Oriented Language.

5. LISP means LISt Processor and is used in work with artificial intelligence.

6. PL/I means Programming Language I and is used in business and science.

Choose the correct answers.

1. What number does the blue digit name?

6,4**7**3,902,158

- **A.** 700 thousand
- **B.** 7 million
- **C.** 70 million
- **D.** not here

2. Add.

```
  7,342
    698
  4,025
+ 1,317
```

- **A.** 13,362
- **B.** 13,382
- **C.** 13,262
- **D.** not here

3. Subtract.

```
  52,040
 − 3,957
```

- **A.** 48,083
- **B.** 49,183
- **C.** 49,093
- **D.** not here

4. Multiply.

```
  684
× 37
```

- **A.** 25,308
- **B.** 24,808
- **C.** 24,288
- **D.** not here

5. Multiply.

```
  3,672
× 294
```

- **A.** 1,078,468
- **B.** 959,468
- **C.** 1,079,568
- **D.** not here

6. Find the average.

67, 49, 84, 32

- **A.** 58
- **B.** 53
- **C.** 59
- **D.** not here

7. Divide.

$5,600 \div 80 = \underline{\ ?\ }$

- **A.** 75
- **B.** 700
- **C.** 80
- **D.** not here

8. Divide.

$42\overline{)63,845}$

- **A.** 1,544 r37
- **B.** 1,520 r5
- **C.** 1,521 r8
- **D.** not here

9. How many baskets did Bill make?

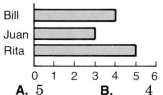

- **A.** 5
- **B.** 4
- **C.** 3
- **D.** not here

10. A hardware company packages 98 nails in a box. There are 4,410 nails to be packaged. How many boxes can be filled?

- **A.** 48
- **B.** 45
- **C.** 48 r6
- **D.** not here

11. The company packs 36 boxes of nails in a carton. There are 217 cartons. How many boxes of nails can be packaged?

- **A.** 7,772
- **B.** 7,712
- **C.** 7,812
- **D.** not here

Number Theory and Fractions

6

Divisibility • Factors, Primes, and Composites
• Prime Factors • Greatest Common Factor • Least
Common Multiple • Problem Solving: More Than One Step
• Fractions • Equivalent Fractions • Lowest Terms
• Comparing Fractions • Whole Numbers, Mixed Numbers,
and Fractions • Dividing to Find Mixed Numbers • Problem
Solving: Using a Schedule • Egyptian Numbers • Patterns

Divisibility

Divide one number by another.
If the remainder is 0, then the first number
is **divisible** by the second.

16 is divisible by 2.   17 is not divisible by 2.

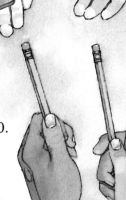

$$\begin{array}{r} 8 \\ 2\overline{)16} \\ 16 \\ \hline 0 \end{array}$$

$$\begin{array}{r} 8 \\ 2\overline{)17} \\ 16 \\ \hline 1 \end{array}$$

Here are rules for finding if a number is divisible by 2, 5, or 10.

Even numbers are divisible by 2.
Here are six even numbers. ⟶ 2, 4, 6, 8, 10, 12
Divide each by 2. There is no remainder.

Odd numbers are not divisible by 2.
Here are six odd numbers. ⟶ 3, 5, 7, 9, 11, 13
Divide each by 2. There is a remainder.

If there is a 0 or a 5 in the ones place, then the number is divisible by 5.

These numbers are divisible by 5. ⟶ 0, 5, 10, 15, 20, 25, 30

If there is a 0 in the ones place, the number is divisible by 10.

These numbers are divisible by 10. ⟶ 10, 20, 30, 40, 50

Practice • Is the first number divisible by the second? Write YES or NO.

1. 26, 4   2. 65, 5   3. 32, 8   4. 74, 10   5. 96, 12

6. 87, 3   7. 34, 17   8. 93, 8   9. 146, 5   10. 278, 2

More Practice • Is the first number of each divisible by the second?
Write YES or NO.

11. 57, 8   12. 15, 3   13. 27, 9   14. 26, 6   15. 37, 6

16. 147, 7   17. 85, 10   18. 101, 3   19. 104, 4   20. 250, 25

Is each number divisible by 2? Write YES or NO.

21. 20   22. 14   23. 23   24. 75   25. 180

26. 220   27. 233   28. 400   29. 450   30. 316

Is each number divisible by 5?

31. 20   **32.** 25   **33.** 36   **34.** 74   **35.** 180

36. 220   **37.** 225   **38.** 400   **39.** 450   **40.** 555

Is each number divisible by 10?

41. 20   **42.** 25   **43.** 90   **44.** 105   **45.** 180

46. 220   **47.** 250   **48.** 400   **49.** 450   **50.** 585

A number is divisible by 3 if the sum of its digits is divisible by 3.

$$15 \qquad 1 + 5 = 6$$

6 is divisible by 3, and so 15 is divisible by 3.

Is each number divisible by 3?

★ **51.** 25   ★ **52.** 36   ★ **53.** 738   ★ **54.** 571   ★ **55.** 3,996

A number is divisible by 9 if the sum of its digits is divisible by 9.

$$108 \qquad 1 + 0 + 8 = 9$$

9 is divisible by 9, and so 108 is divisible by 9.

Is each number divisible by 9?

★ **56.** 24   ★ **57.** 72   ★ **58.** 651   ★ **59.** 333   ★ **60.** 5,283

PROBLEM SOLVING • APPLICATIONS

61. Bob bought some rulers for $.06 each. He did not buy anything else. What could his bill have been?

$1.15 $1.26

★ **62.** Rulers cost $.06 each, and erasers are $.05 each. George spent $.23, Mary spent $.26, and Peter spent $.25. Which person bought only rulers or only erasers?

127

Factors, Primes, and Composites

Two factors of 20 are 4 and 5.

$4 \times 5 = 20$

A number is divisible by its **factors.**

$$4\overline{)20} \quad 5\overline{)20}$$

$$\begin{array}{r} 5 \\ 4\overline{)20} \\ \underline{20} \\ 0 \end{array} \quad \begin{array}{r} 4 \\ 5\overline{)20} \\ \underline{20} \\ 0 \end{array}$$

Find all the factors of 20. List them in order.

Step 1 Write 20 as the product of two whole numbers.

$$\begin{array}{ccc} 20 & 20 & 20 \\ \diagup\diagdown & \diagup\diagdown & \diagup\diagdown \\ 1 \times 20 & 2 \times 10 & 4 \times 5 \end{array}$$

Step 2 List the whole numbers in order. Show each whole number only once.

Factors of 20: **1, 2, 4, 5, 10, 20**

A **prime number** has exactly two factors: itself and 1.
The number 1 is not a prime number. It has only itself as a factor.

Factors of 5: 1, 5
5 is a prime number.

A **composite number** is greater than 1 and has more than two different factors.

Factors of 8: 1, 2, 4, 8
8 is a composite number.

Practice • Find all the factors for each. List them in order.

1. 9	**2.** 14	**3.** 18	**4.** 30	**5.** 28	**6.** 36

Write PRIME or COMPOSITE.

7. 31	**8.** 22	**9.** 48	**10.** 53	**11.** 64	**12.** 71

Mixed Practice • Find all the factors for each. List them in order.

13. 10	**14.** 25	**15.** 56	**16.** 63	**17.** 64	**18.** 144
19. 27	**20.** 42	**21.** 48	**22.** 81	**23.** 58	**24.** 225
25. 32	**26.** 40	**27.** 77	**28.** 39	**29.** 35	**30.** 100
31. 54	**32.** 72	**33.** 24	**34.** 96	**35.** 90	**36.** 150

Write PRIME or COMPOSITE.

37. 59	**38.** 43	**39.** 51	**40.** 21	**41.** 72	**42.** 35
43. 23	**44.** 96	**45.** 26	**46.** 17	**47.** 34	**48.** 54
49. 13	**50.** 46	**51.** 57	**52.** 25	**53.** 83	**54.** 100
55. 12	**56.** 67	**57.** 93	**58.** 76	**59.** 87	**60.** 117

PROBLEM SOLVING • APPLICATIONS

Copy the table. Then use it to find all the prime numbers between 1 and 50.

61. Cross out 1, since it is not a prime number.

62. Circle 2, since it is a prime number. Then cross out all the numbers in the table that are divisible by 2.

1	2	3	4	5	6	7	8	9	10
11	12	13	14	15	16	17	18	19	20
21	22	23	24	25	26	27	28	29	30
31	32	33	34	35	36	37	38	39	40
41	42	43	44	45	46	47	48	49	50

63. Repeat Exercise 62 for the numbers 3, 5, and 7.

64. Name the numbers in the table that have not been crossed out.

65. Are these numbers prime or composite?

★ **66.** Make a table for the numbers between 51 and 100. Repeat Exercises 62 through 65 using the new table.

51	52	53	54	55	56	57	58	59	60
61	62	63	64	65	66	67	68	69	70
71	72	73	74	75	76	77	78	79	80
81	82	83	84	85	86	87	88	89	90
91	92	93	94	95	96	97	98	99	100

Two prime numbers that have a difference of 2 are called **twin primes.** 3 and 5 are twin primes.

★ **67.** Name all the other twin primes less than 50.

129

Prime Factors

A composite number can be shown as a product of **prime factors.** This is called the **prime factorization** of the number. Use a **factor tree** to help you.

Write the prime factorization of 30.

A factor tree can be shown in different ways. The prime factors will always be the same. The order may be different. So always write the prime factors in order from least to greatest.

$$30 = 2 \times 3 \times 5$$

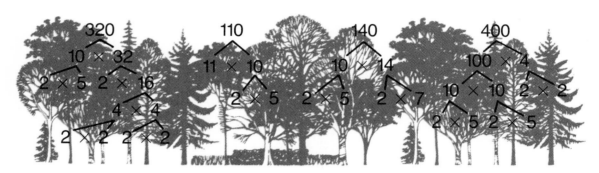

Practice • Complete the factor trees.

1.
18
2 × 9
2 × __?__ × __?__

2.
42
6 × __?__
__?__ × __?__ × __?__

3.
36
9 × __?__
__?__ × __?__ × __?__ × __?__

Write the prime factorization of each number. Use a factor tree. Write the factors in order from least to greatest.

4. 20   **5.** 63   **6.** 44   **7.** 95   **8.** 56   **9.** 38

Mixed Practice • Complete the factor trees.

10.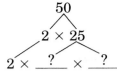

11.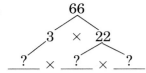

12.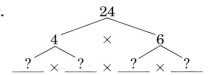

Write the prime factorization of each number. Use a factor tree.
Write the factors in order from least to greatest.

13. 12	**14.** 40	**15.** 28	**16.** 32	**17.** 35	**18.** 65
19. 16	**20.** 27	**21.** 88	**22.** 54	**23.** 48	**24.** 78
25. 72	**26.** 81	**27.** 64	**28.** 75	**29.** 99	**30.** 84
31. 80	**32.** 25	**33.** 33	**34.** 45	**35.** 52	**36.** 90

The prime factorization can be made easier to read by using exponents.

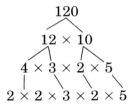

$120 = 2 \times 2 \times 2 \times 3 \times 5$
Since $2 \times 2 \times 2 = 2^3,$ **then**
$120 = 2^3 \times 3 \times 5.$

Write each prime factorization by using exponents.

⋆ **37.** 100   ⋆ **38.** 125   ⋆ **39.** 150   ⋆ **40.** 300   ⋆ **41.** 550   ⋆ **42.** 1,000

PROBLEM SOLVING • **APPLICATIONS**

43. Andrew is preparing a store window display. He has 6 boxes of stationery. He makes 3 stacks. 2 boxes are in each stack. Does this show the prime factors of 6?

⋆ **44.** Now Andrew is working with 9 rolls of masking tape. How would he stack them to show the prime factors of 9?

Skills Maintenance

1. $7\overline{)350}$ 2. $8\overline{)968}$ 3. $5\overline{)2,644}$ 4. $6\overline{)6,856}$ 5. $3\overline{)9,123}$

6. $4\overline{)2,864}$ 7. $9\overline{)7,920}$ 8. $6\overline{)30,362}$ 9. $5\overline{)82,692}$ 10. $8\overline{)65,193}$

Greatest Common Factor

1, 2, and 4 are factors of both 24 and 28.

Factors of 24 $\longrightarrow$ 1, 2, 3, 4, 6, 8, 12, 24
Factors of 28 $\longrightarrow$ 1, 2, 4, 7, 14, 28
Common Factors $\longrightarrow$ 1, 2, 4

These factors are **common factors**.
4 is the **greatest common factor (GCF)** of 24 and 28.

Find the greatest common factor of 12 and 30.

Step 1 List the factors of 12 in order. $\longrightarrow$ 1, 2, 3, 4, 6, 12

Step 2 List the factors of 30 in order. $\longrightarrow$ 1, 2, 3, 5, 6, 10, 15, 30

Step 3 List the common factors. $\longrightarrow$ 1, 2, 3, 6

Step 4 Write the greatest common factor. $\longrightarrow$ 6

Practice • List all the factors in order for each.

1. 21   **2.** 15   **3.** 18   **4.** 20   **5.** 32

List the common factors in order for each pair.

6. 21, 15   **7.** 15, 18   **8.** 18, 20   **9.** 20, 32   **10.** 15, 32

Find the greatest common factor for each pair.

11. 21, 15   **12.** 15, 18   **13.** 18, 20   **14.** 20, 32   **15.** 15, 32

Mixed Practice • List all the factors in order for each.

16. 8   **17.** 16   **18.** 36   **19.** 40   **20.** 25

21. 30   **22.** 48   **23.** 14   **24.** 27   **25.** 54

List the common factors in order for each.

26. 8, 16   **27.** 36, 27   **28.** 14, 40   **29.** 25, 30   **30.** 16, 48

31. 54, 27   **32.** 25, 40   **33.** 36, 16   **34.** 14, 30   **35.** 48, 54

Find the greatest common factor for each pair.

36. 8, 16   **37.** 36, 27   **38.** 14, 40   **39.** 25, 30   **40.** 16, 48

41. 54, 27   **42.** 25, 40   **43.** 36, 16   **44.** 14, 30   **45.** 48, 54

Here is another way to find the greatest common factor of 12 and 30.

Step 1 Write 12 and 30 as a number pair. Find a common factor. Try 2.

$$? \; \boxed{12, \; 30}$$

Step 2 Divide 12 and 30 by 2. Find a common factor for 6 and 15.

$$2 \; \boxed{12, \; 30}$$
$$? \; \boxed{6, \; 15}$$

Step 3 Divide 6 and 15 by 3. Do 2 and 5 have a common factor except 1?

$$2 \; \boxed{12, \; 30}$$
$$3 \; \boxed{6, \; 15}$$
$$? \; \boxed{2, \; 5}$$

The greatest common factor is the product of the divisors.
Since $2 \times 3 = 6$, the greatest common factor of 12 and 30 is 6.

Use this method to find the greatest common factor for each pair.

★ **46.** 24, 28   ★ **47.** 18, 36   ★ **48.** 32, 48   ★ **49.** 15, 40   ★ **50.** 20, 30

PROBLEM SOLVING • APPLICATIONS

The factors of 4 are inside the blue circle.
The factors of 6 are inside the green circle.
The factors of 8 are inside the yellow circle.
The common factors are inside all three circles.

Factors of 4   Factors of 6

3,6

1,2

4

8

Factors of 8

Draw circles that show the factors.

Show the common factors inside two circles.

51. 21, 45   **52.** 50, 60   **53.** 12, 32   **54.** 14, 49

Show the common factors inside three circles.

★ **55.** 10, 12, 16   ★ **56.** 3, 24, 15   ★ **57.** 15, 20, 35   ★ **58.** 16, 18, 24

Least Common Multiple

Multiply a number by 0, 1, 2, 3, and so on.
Each product is a **multiple** of that number.

0×6	1×6	2×6	3×6	4×6
↓	↓	↓	↓	↓

Here are five multiples of 6. ⟶ 0   6   12   18   24

Name the next two multiples of 6.

The **least common multiple (LCM)** is the smallest common multiple that is not zero.
Find the least common multiple of 4 and 6.

Step 1 List multiples of 4. ⟶ 0, 4, 8, 12, 16, 20, 24, 28, 32, 36 . . .

Step 2 List multiples of 6. ⟶ 0, 6, 12, 18, 24, 30, 36 . . .

Step 3 List the common multiples. ⟶ 0, 12, 24, 36 . . .

Step 4 Write the least common multiple. ⟶ 12

Here is another way to find the least common multiple of two numbers.
Begin by naming the multiples of the greater number in order. Each time
check to see if the multiple is also a multiple of the lesser number.

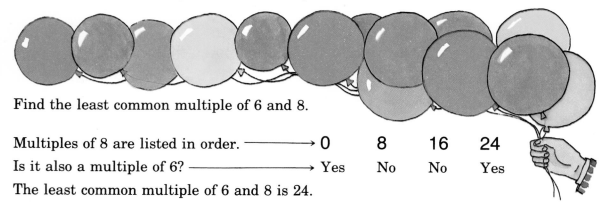

Find the least common multiple of 6 and 8.

Multiples of 8 are listed in order. ⟶ 0   8   16   24

Is it also a multiple of 6? ⟶ Yes   No   No   Yes

The least common multiple of 6 and 8 is 24.

Practice • List the first six multiples in order for each. Start with zero.

1. 8   **2.** 10   **3.** 7   **4.** 9   **5.** 12

Find the least common multiple for each pair.

6. 4, 8   **7.** 6, 10   **8.** 7, 8   **9.** 6, 9   **10.** 9, 12

Mixed Practice • List the first six multiples in order for each. Start with zero.

11. 2   **12.** 3   **13.** 5   **14.** 11   **15.** 13

16. 15   **17.** 20   **18.** 25   **19.** 50   **20.** 100

Find the least common multiple for each pair.

21. 2, 3   **22.** 10, 15   **23.** 5, 25   **24.** 6, 15   **25.** 3, 5

26. 2, 5   **27.** 15, 20   **28.** 4, 5   **29.** 25, 50   **30.** 20, 100

★**31.** 2, 3, 4   ★**32.** 3, 6, 9   ★**33.** 4, 5, 10   ★**34.** 5, 6, 10   ★**35.** 3, 9, 12

PROBLEM SOLVING • APPLICATIONS

36. Mike sells balloons at the Community Day Festival. He wants to have the same number of balloons and strings. There are 8 balloons in one package. There are 10 strings in one package. He must buy full packages. What is the smallest number of balloons he must buy? How many packages is this?

★**37.** Steve, Andrew, and Joellyn are hiking the Willow Trail. There are rest stops every kilometer. Steve stops every 3 kilometers. Andrew stops every 5 kilometers. Joellyn stops every 8 kilometers. What is the first rest stop they will all stop at together?

Midchapter Review

Is the number divisible by 2? Write YES or NO.
1. 81   **2.** 196

Is the number divisible by 5? Write YES or NO.
3. 75   **4.** 340

Find all the factors. List them in order.
5. 24   **6.** 50

Write PRIME or COMPOSITE.
7. 39   **8.** 47

Write the number as a product of prime factors. Use a factor tree.
9. 70   **10.** 54

Find the greatest common factors.
11. 45, 36

Find the least common multiple.
12. 6, 9

PROBLEM SOLVING · STRATEGIES

More Than One Step

To solve some problems, we must use more than one step.

Read the problem.

Mary uses 4 medium apples and 3 large oranges to make a fruit salad. How many calories are in Mary's fruit salad?

We must use two steps to solve this problem.

First multiply to find the number of calories in the apples and oranges.

$$
\begin{array}{r} 76 \\ \times\ 4 \\ \hline 304 \end{array}
\qquad
\begin{array}{r} 106 \\ \times\ \ 3 \\ \hline 318 \end{array}
$$

Then add to find the total number of calories in the fruit salad.

$$
\begin{array}{r} 304 \\ +318 \\ \hline 622 \end{array}
$$

There are 622 calories in Mary's fruit salad.

Vegetable-Fruit Group	
	Calories
1 medium apple	76
1 large orange	106
1 medium baked potato	97
1 medium carrot	21
Carbohydrate Group	
1 slice whole wheat bread	55
1 cup oatmeal	148
1 cup rice	170
1 medium corn muffin	125
Milk-Milk Products Group	
1 cup whole milk	165
1 slice Swiss cheese	105
1 cup skimmed milk	85
1 cup cottage cheese	215
Protein Group	
6 medium boiled shrimp	100
1 cup boiled navy beans	190
1 medium boiled egg	77
1 small piece chicken	210
Fats-Sweets Group	
1 pat margarine	35
1 dip sherbet	135

What steps must you take to solve the problems?

1. Mary uses 2 slices of whole wheat bread and 3 slices of Swiss cheese to make a sandwich. How many calories are in this sandwich?

   Read the problem carefully. Decide which operations you will use.

2. Brian prepares a salad to serve 6 people. The salad has 458 calories from the vegetable-fruit group. It also has 394 calories from the protein group. About how many calories are in each serving of salad?

Use the table. Decide which steps you will take to solve each problem. Then solve.

3. Wayne usually eats 2 slices of whole wheat bread at lunchtime. Today he has 2 corn muffins instead. How many more calories are in the 2 corn muffins?

4. A casserole serves 8 people. It has 340 calories from the carbohydrate group, 270 calories from the milk-milk products group, and 430 calories from the protein group. About how many calories are in each serving of this casserole?

5. Tracy makes breakfast for 4 people. She uses 4 boiled eggs, 2 cups of oatmeal, 2 cups of whole milk, and 4 slices of whole wheat bread. What is the total number of calories in this breakfast?

6. How many more calories are there in 4 cups of whole milk than in 4 cups of skimmed milk?

7. Marcella eats a 400-calorie breakfast, a 579-calorie lunch, and an 839-calorie dinner. What is the average number of calories for each meal?

Read the problem again. Does your answer make sense?

8. Nicole eats two foods listed in the protein group. She has 12 medium boiled shrimp and a boiled egg. What is the total number of calories Nicole has from the protein group?

9. How many fewer calories are in a package of 20 slices of whole wheat bread than in a package of 12 corn muffins?

10. Betty usually has 2 boiled eggs and 1 corn muffin for breakfast. Today she has 1 cup of cottage cheese and 1 large orange. How many fewer calories are in her usual breakfast?

★ 11. Rico has 1 cup skimmed milk, 1 slice whole wheat bread, 1 pat margarine, and 1 slice Swiss cheese for breakfast every day. What is the total number of breakfast calories for one week? If Rico had a boiled egg instead of Swiss cheese that week, how many fewer calories would that be?

★ 12. For breakfast Ginger has 1 cup of cottage cheese and 1 apple. For lunch she has 1 small piece of chicken, $\frac{1}{2}$ cup rice, and 1 cup whole milk. How many more calories are in her lunch? What food from the milk-cheese group could she change to bring the calorie difference to 89?

Fractions

A wild animal park is divided into 4 equal parts. 3 parts are filled with animals.

A **fraction** tells what part of the park is filled with animals.

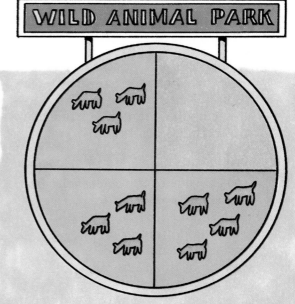

$\dfrac{3}{4}$ **numerator**   parts with animals
       denominator   parts in all

$\dfrac{3}{4}$ of the park is filled with animals.

There are 6 bears in a group. What part of the group are brown bears?

$\dfrac{4}{6} \longrightarrow$ brown bears
$\phantom{\dfrac{4}{6}} \longrightarrow$ bears in all

$\dfrac{4}{6}$ of the bears are brown.

There are 3 feeding stations for the bears. 2 are used by brown bears. What part of the feeding stations are used by brown bears?

$\dfrac{2}{3} \longrightarrow$ feeding stations used by brown bears
$\phantom{\dfrac{2}{3}} \longrightarrow$ feeding stations in all

$\dfrac{2}{3}$ of the feeding stations are used by brown bears.

Practice • Write the fraction that tells what part is blue for each.

1.

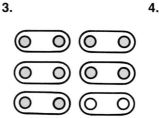

2.

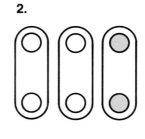

3.

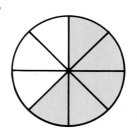

4.

138

Mixed Practice • Write the fraction that tells what part is blue for each.

5.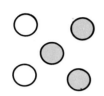

6.

7.

8.

9.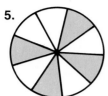

10.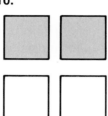

11.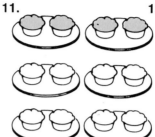

12.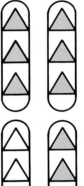

The number line between 0 and 1 is divided into 6 equal parts.

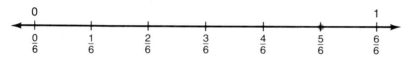

$\frac{5}{6}$ names the point. It is located five-sixths of the way from 0 to 1.

Use a fraction to name the point for each.

13.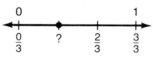

14.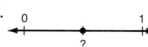

15.

★ 16.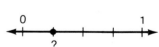

★ 17.

★ 18.

PROBLEM SOLVING • APPLICATIONS

Write a fraction to answer each question.

19. There are 7 apes. 4 of them are chimps. What part of the apes are chimps?

20. 15 animals in the park belong to the cat family. 2 of them are lions What part of the cats are lions?

★ 21. 12 workers care for the animals. 3 of them feed the animals. What part of the workers do not feed the animals?

★ 22. There are 9 reptiles. 2 of them are snakes. What part of the reptiles are not snakes?

Equivalent Fractions

Equivalent fractions name the same number. There are two ways to find equivalent fractions.

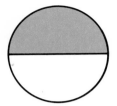 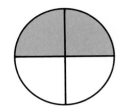 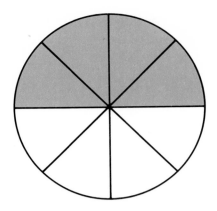

Multiply the numerator and the denominator by the same number.

$$\frac{1}{3}$$

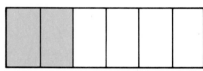

$$\frac{1}{3} = \frac{2 \times 1}{2 \times 3} = \frac{2}{6}$$

$\frac{1}{3}$ and $\frac{2}{6}$ are equivalent fractions. Make the fractions equivalent.

$$\frac{7}{8} = \frac{?}{16}$$

Think: What number times 8 is 16?

$$\frac{7}{8} = \frac{2 \times 7}{2 \times 8} = \frac{14}{16}$$

Divide the numerator and the denominator by the same number.

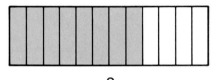

$$\frac{8}{12}$$

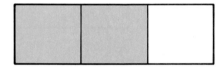

$$\frac{8}{12} = \frac{8 \div 4}{12 \div 4} = \frac{2}{3}$$

$\frac{8}{12}$ and $\frac{2}{3}$ are equivalent fractions. Make the fractions equivalent.

$$\frac{24}{32} = \frac{?}{4}$$

Think: 32 divided by what number is 4?

$$\frac{24}{32} = \frac{24 \div 8}{32 \div 8} = \frac{3}{4}$$

Practice • Complete.

1. $\frac{2}{3} = \frac{?}{6}$

2. $\frac{6}{15} = \frac{?}{5}$

3. $\frac{3}{7} = \frac{?}{28}$

4. $\frac{6}{24} = \frac{?}{4}$

5. $\frac{3}{4} = \frac{6}{?}$

6. $\frac{10}{16} = \frac{?}{8}$

7. $\frac{4}{7} = \frac{40}{?}$

8. $\frac{3}{36} = \frac{?}{12}$

Mixed Practice • Complete.

9. $\frac{3}{5} = \frac{?}{10}$ **10.** $\frac{5}{9} = \frac{?}{27}$ **11.** $\frac{8}{9} = \frac{64}{?}$ **12.** $\frac{1}{9} = \frac{?}{36}$

13. $\frac{4}{5} = \frac{?}{10}$ **14.** $\frac{3}{4} = \frac{?}{32}$ **15.** $\frac{4}{5} = \frac{?}{25}$ **16.** $\frac{9}{10} = \frac{?}{50}$

17. $\frac{14}{16} = \frac{7}{?}$ **18.** $\frac{10}{15} = \frac{?}{3}$ **19.** $\frac{8}{22} = \frac{16}{?}$ **20.** $\frac{21}{24} = \frac{?}{8}$

21. $\frac{4}{12} = \frac{?}{3}$ **22.** $\frac{6}{48} = \frac{?}{8}$ **23.** $\frac{18}{24} = \frac{?}{4}$ **24.** $\frac{18}{27} = \frac{?}{3}$

25. $\frac{2}{3} = \frac{4}{?}$ **26.** $\frac{12}{16} = \frac{?}{4}$ **27.** $\frac{2}{4} = \frac{6}{?}$ **28.** $\frac{?}{40} = \frac{3}{8}$

29. $\frac{?}{4} = \frac{10}{20}$ **30.** $\frac{?}{15} = \frac{2}{5}$ **31.** $\frac{?}{30} = \frac{4}{5}$ **32.** $\frac{12}{?} = \frac{3}{5}$

You can test fractions to find out if they are equivalent.
The cross products of equivalent fractions are equal.

Cross multiply.

$\frac{3}{4}$ $\frac{6}{8}$ $\frac{5}{6}$ ⬤ $\frac{3}{4}$

3×8 ⬤ 6×4 ⟵—————— cross product —————⟶ 5×4 ⬤ 3×6

$24 = 24$ $20 \ne 18$

                                                        ($\ne$ means "is not equal to.")

The fractions are equal.   The fractions are not equal.

Write = or ≠.

★ **33.** $\frac{4}{5}$ ⬤ $\frac{7}{8}$ ★ **34.** $\frac{3}{16}$ ⬤ $\frac{18}{96}$ ★ **35.** $\frac{3}{10}$ ⬤ $\frac{25}{100}$ ★ **36.** $\frac{1}{3}$ ⬤ $\frac{3}{8}$ ★ **37.** $\frac{5}{25}$ ⬤ $\frac{3}{15}$

PROBLEM SOLVING • APPLICATIONS

38. Peter and Mark walk to the park. The distance is 180 meters. They are $\frac{2}{3}$ of the way there. How many meters is this?

★ **39.** Peter and Mark are riding their unicycles to a friend's house. The distance is 3,200 meters. They are $\frac{3}{4}$ of the way there. How many meters is this? How many more meters do they have to ride?

Lowest Terms

$\frac{4}{8}$, $\frac{2}{4}$, and $\frac{1}{2}$ are equivalent fractions.

$\frac{4}{8}$ in lowest terms is $\frac{1}{2}$.

$\frac{2}{4}$ in lowest terms is $\frac{1}{2}$.

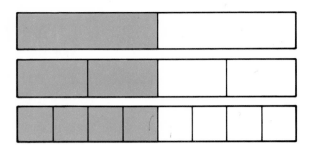

A fraction is in lowest terms when the numerator and the denominator have no common factor greater than 1.

Write $\frac{8}{12}$ in lowest terms.

Step 1 List the factors of 8 and 12 in order. Find the greatest common factor.

$$8 \longrightarrow 1, 2, 4, 8$$
$$12 \longrightarrow 1, 2, 3, 4, 6, 12$$

Step 2 Divide the numerator and the denominator by the greatest common factor, 4.

$$\frac{8}{12} = \frac{8 \div 4}{12 \div 4} = \frac{2}{3}$$

$\frac{8}{12}$ in lowest terms is $\frac{2}{3}$.

Practice • List the factors in order. Find the greatest common factor for each pair.

1. 12 and 16　　　　　2. 4 and 14　　　　　3. 8 and 10

4. 12 and 20　　　　　5. 8 and 32　　　　　6. 18 and 27

Write each fraction in lowest terms.

7. $\frac{12}{16}$　　8. $\frac{4}{14}$　　9. $\frac{8}{10}$　　10. $\frac{12}{20}$　　11. $\frac{8}{32}$　　12. $\frac{18}{27}$

Mixed Practice • List the factors in order. Find the greatest common factor for each pair.

13. 28 and 42　　　　　14. 30 and 32　　　　　15. 6 and 9

16. 10 and 15　　　　　17. 4 and 32　　　　　18. 50 and 60

Write each fraction in lowest terms.

19. $\dfrac{28}{42}$ **20.** $\dfrac{30}{32}$ **21.** $\dfrac{6}{9}$ **22.** $\dfrac{10}{15}$ **23.** $\dfrac{4}{32}$ **24.** $\dfrac{50}{60}$

25. $\dfrac{8}{16}$ **26.** $\dfrac{12}{18}$ **27.** $\dfrac{8}{20}$ **28.** $\dfrac{12}{36}$ **29.** $\dfrac{20}{25}$ **30.** $\dfrac{6}{10}$

31. $\dfrac{12}{15}$ **32.** $\dfrac{9}{24}$ **33.** $\dfrac{10}{40}$ **34.** $\dfrac{24}{36}$ **35.** $\dfrac{25}{30}$ **36.** $\dfrac{40}{56}$

37. $\dfrac{36}{48}$ **38.** $\dfrac{24}{60}$ **39.** $\dfrac{25}{75}$ **40.** $\dfrac{24}{100}$ **41.** $\dfrac{400}{600}$ **42.** $\dfrac{100}{300}$

We can use prime factors to write a fraction in lowest terms.

Write $\dfrac{18}{24}$ in lowest terms.

Step 1
Write the prime factors.

$$\frac{18}{24} = \frac{2 \times 3 \times 3}{2 \times 2 \times 2 \times 3} = ?$$

Step 2
Divide the numerator and the denominator by the common factors.

$$\frac{\overset{1}{\cancel{2}} \times \overset{1}{\cancel{3}} \times 3}{\underset{1}{\cancel{2}} \times 2 \times 2 \times \underset{1}{\cancel{3}}} = ?$$

Step 3
Multiply the remaining factors.

$$\frac{3}{2 \times 2} = \frac{3}{4}$$

Write each fraction in lowest terms. Use the prime factors.

★ **43.** $\dfrac{26}{36}$ ★ **44.** $\dfrac{12}{27}$ ★ **45.** $\dfrac{20}{44}$ ★ **46.** $\dfrac{27}{48}$ ★ **47.** $\dfrac{14}{35}$ ★ **48.** $\dfrac{39}{48}$

PROBLEM SOLVING • APPLICATIONS

Write each fraction in lowest terms.

49. Ramón orders 8 bags of fertilizer for Mrs. Brandon. He uses 6 bags on her front lawn. What fraction of the bags did Ramón use on the front lawn?

50. A garden center had 56 lawn mowers in stock. In March 40 lawn mowers were sold. What fraction of the lawn mowers was sold in March?

51. During the month of April, 35 lawn mowers were available for sale. 14 were sold. What fraction of the lawn mowers was not sold in April?

★ **52.** Mr. Warner had 88 lawn chairs in stock. He sold 26 wooden chairs and 40 metal ones. What fraction of lawn chairs was not sold?

Comparing Fractions

Compare $\frac{3}{5}$ and $\frac{4}{5}$.

To compare fractions when both have the same denominator, compare the numerators.

Think: 3 is less than 4,

and so $\frac{3}{5} < \frac{4}{5}$.

Compare $\frac{3}{4}$ and $\frac{2}{5}$.

You can use equivalent fractions with the same denominator to compare.

Use the **least common denominator** for $\frac{3}{4}$ and $\frac{2}{5}$.

Step 1 Find the least common multiple of the denominators. This multiple is the least common denominator.

$$4 \longrightarrow 4, 8, 12, 16, 20$$
$$5 \longrightarrow 5, 10, 15, 20$$

Step 2 Write equivalent fractions. Use 20 as the denominator.

$$\frac{3}{4} = \frac{5 \times 3}{5 \times 4} = \frac{15}{20} \qquad \frac{2}{5} = \frac{4 \times 2}{4 \times 5} = \frac{8}{20}$$

Since $\frac{15}{20} > \frac{8}{20}$, then $\frac{3}{4} > \frac{2}{5}$.

Practice • Find the least common multiple for each pair.

1. 4, 6   **2.** 7, 8   **3.** 6, 10   **4.** 6, 9

Find the least common denominator for each pair. Write equivalent fractions.

5. $\frac{3}{4}, \frac{5}{6}$ **6.** $\frac{4}{7}, \frac{3}{8}$ **7.** $\frac{1}{6}, \frac{3}{10}$ **8.** $\frac{5}{6}, \frac{5}{9}$

Write $>$, $<$, or $=$.

9. $\frac{1}{4}$ ⬤ $\frac{1}{5}$ **10.** $\frac{7}{8}$ ⬤ $\frac{5}{6}$ **11.** $\frac{6}{15}$ ⬤ $\frac{4}{10}$ **12.** $\frac{3}{4}$ ⬤ $\frac{7}{12}$

Mixed Practice • Find the least common multiple for each pair.

13. 8, 6   **14.** 9, 7   **15.** 3, 7   **16.** 8, 16

Find the least common denominator for each pair. Write equivalent fractions.

17. $\frac{3}{8}, \frac{5}{6}$ **18.** $\frac{1}{9}, \frac{1}{7}$ **19.** $\frac{2}{3}, \frac{3}{7}$ **20.** $\frac{5}{8}, \frac{9}{16}$

21. $\frac{2}{3}, \frac{1}{2}$ **22.** $\frac{1}{3}, \frac{2}{5}$ **23.** $\frac{1}{9}, \frac{5}{8}$ **24.** $\frac{3}{4}, \frac{5}{8}$

Write >, <, or =.

25. $\frac{4}{12}$ ⬤ $\frac{7}{12}$ **26.** $\frac{3}{4}$ ⬤ $\frac{7}{9}$ **27.** $\frac{5}{6}$ ⬤ $\frac{4}{5}$ **28.** $\frac{5}{8}$ ⬤ $\frac{11}{12}$

29. $\frac{5}{8}$ ⬤ $\frac{2}{3}$ **30.** $\frac{8}{14}$ ⬤ $\frac{12}{21}$ **31.** $\frac{3}{10}$ ⬤ $\frac{5}{16}$ **32.** $\frac{7}{12}$ ⬤ $\frac{2}{9}$

Write fractions in order from least to greatest.
Hint: Find an equivalent fraction for each.

33. $\frac{3}{4}, \frac{1}{2}, \frac{8}{9}$ **34.** $\frac{5}{8}, \frac{2}{3}, \frac{1}{2}$ **35.** $\frac{4}{5}, \frac{2}{5}, \frac{1}{2}$

★ **36.** $\frac{7}{8}, \frac{2}{3}, \frac{1}{4}, \frac{29}{36}$ ★ **37.** $\frac{3}{4}, \frac{4}{5}, \frac{1}{2}, \frac{3}{10}$ ★ **38.** $\frac{2}{3}, \frac{5}{6}, \frac{4}{5}, \frac{1}{2}$

PROBLEM SOLVING • APPLICATIONS

39. Anita and Lee each use a package of zinnia seeds for science projects. $\frac{3}{5}$ of Lee's seeds germinate. $\frac{2}{3}$ of Anita's seeds germinate. Who has more seeds that germinate?

★ **40.** Lee has 25 vegetable seedlings. Only 18 grow to be plants. Anita has 30 seedlings. 21 of them grow to be plants. Write a fraction to show the part of the seedlings that grow for each person. Who has the largest part of their seedlings grow to be plants?

Skills Maintenance

1. 29$\overline{)453}$ **2.** 65$\overline{)975}$ **3.** 82$\overline{)563}$ **4.** 15$\overline{)3,035}$ **5.** 46$\overline{)3,582}$ **6.** 57$\overline{)1,145}$

7. 23$\overline{)7,928}$ **8.** 73$\overline{)6,549}$ **9.** 38$\overline{)6,394}$ **10.** 42$\overline{)31,794}$ **11.** 35$\overline{)84,998}$ **12.** 24$\overline{)72,401}$

145

Whole Numbers, Mixed Numbers, and Fractions

A fraction names a whole number when the numerator is a multiple of the denominator.

$1 = \dfrac{3}{3}$

$4 = \dfrac{12}{3}$

You can change a whole number to a fraction by writing it over a denominator of 1 and finding an equivalent fraction.

$1 = \dfrac{1}{1} = \dfrac{3 \times 1}{3 \times 1} = \dfrac{3}{3}$

$4 = \dfrac{4}{1} = \dfrac{3 \times 4}{3 \times 1} = \dfrac{12}{3}$

$3\dfrac{1}{2}$ is a mixed number and means 3 and $\dfrac{1}{2}$.

$3\dfrac{1}{2}$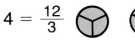

You can use addition to change a mixed number to a fraction.

$3\dfrac{1}{2} = 3 + \dfrac{1}{2}$

$\quad = \dfrac{3}{1} + \dfrac{1}{2}$

$\quad = \dfrac{6}{2} + \dfrac{1}{2}$

$\quad = \dfrac{7}{2}$

Here is another way to write $3\dfrac{1}{2}$ as a fraction. $3\dfrac{1}{2} = \dfrac{(2 \times 3) + 1}{2} = \dfrac{7}{2}$

Practice • Write the whole number or the mixed number for each.

1.  2. 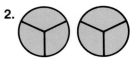 3.  4.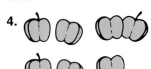

Complete.

5. $1 = \dfrac{?}{5}$ 6. $9 = \dfrac{?}{2}$ 7. $5 = \dfrac{?}{7}$ 8. $3 = \dfrac{?}{9}$

Write as fractions.

9. $6\dfrac{1}{2}$ 10. $3\dfrac{2}{3}$ 11. $2\dfrac{3}{8}$ 12. $1\dfrac{4}{9}$

146

Mixed Practice • Complete.

13. $6 = \frac{?}{4}$

14. $3 = \frac{?}{5}$

15. $4 = \frac{?}{8}$

16. $1 = \frac{?}{12}$

Write as fractions.

17. $3\frac{4}{7}$ **18.** $5\frac{1}{3}$ **19.** $9\frac{1}{5}$ **20.** $7\frac{3}{4}$ **21.** $6\frac{3}{5}$ **22.** $3\frac{1}{4}$

23. $7\frac{2}{4}$ **24.** $4\frac{3}{4}$ **25.** $10\frac{5}{12}$ **26.** $5\frac{5}{9}$ **27.** $4\frac{1}{3}$ **28.** $6\frac{1}{2}$

29. $6\frac{5}{8}$ **30.** $1\frac{2}{5}$ **31.** $7\frac{2}{9}$ **32.** $1\frac{1}{8}$ **33.** $5\frac{3}{4}$ **34.** $9\frac{3}{10}$

35. $4\frac{3}{8}$ **36.** $5\frac{3}{7}$ **37.** $8\frac{2}{3}$ **38.** $9\frac{4}{5}$ **39.** $6\frac{1}{5}$ **40.** $7\frac{8}{9}$

To compare mixed numbers, first compare the whole numbers and then compare the fractions.

$$6\frac{3}{8} \bigcirc 6\frac{5}{8}$$

$$6 = 6$$

$$\frac{3}{8} < \frac{5}{8}$$

$$\text{So } 6\frac{3}{8} < 6\frac{5}{8}.$$

If the fractions have different denominators, find equivalent fractions and then compare.

$$4\frac{2}{3} \bigcirc 4\frac{3}{5}$$

$$4 = 4$$

$$\frac{2}{3} = \frac{10}{15} \qquad \frac{3}{5} = \frac{9}{15}$$

$$\frac{10}{15} > \frac{9}{15}$$

$$\text{So } 4\frac{2}{3} > 4\frac{3}{5}.$$

Write >, <, or =.

★ **41.** $6\frac{7}{8} \bigcirc 6\frac{3}{8}$

★ **42.** $2\frac{4}{5} \bigcirc 5\frac{4}{5}$

★ **43.** $1\frac{2}{8} \bigcirc 1\frac{3}{12}$

★ **44.** $7\frac{2}{3} \bigcirc 7\frac{10}{15}$

★ **45.** $10\frac{5}{9} \bigcirc 10\frac{7}{12}$

★ **46.** $14\frac{5}{6} \bigcirc 14\frac{17}{24}$

PROBLEM SOLVING • APPLICATIONS

47. There are $5\frac{1}{4}$ cheese pies. How many fourths are there?

48. There are $6\frac{2}{3}$ pounds of beef. How many thirds of a pound are there?

★ **49.** There are $3\frac{1}{3}$ spinach pies. Are there enough thirds for each of 10 people to have one-third of a pie?

★ **50.** There are $2\frac{3}{8}$ pounds of spaghetti. Are there enough eighths for each of 18 people to have one-eighth pound of spaghetti?

Dividing to Find Mixed Numbers

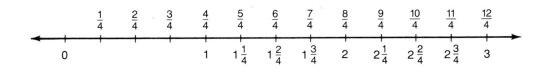

Find the mixed number for $\frac{11}{4}$.
You can use the number line.

Think: $\frac{11}{4} \longrightarrow \frac{8}{4} + \frac{3}{4} \longrightarrow 2 + \frac{3}{4} = 2\frac{3}{4}$

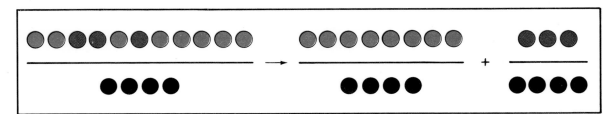

You can also divide to find the mixed number for $\frac{11}{4}$.

Step 1
Divide the numerator by the denominator.

$$4\overline{)11} \quad \begin{array}{r} 2 \\ \hline -8 \\ \hline 3 \end{array}$$

Step 2
Show the remainder as a fraction.
The remainder is the numerator.
The divisor is the denominator.

$$4\overline{)11} \quad \begin{array}{r} 2\frac{3}{4} \\ \hline -8 \\ \hline 3 \end{array}$$

A mixed number for $\frac{11}{4}$ is $2\frac{3}{4}$.

Practice • Divide. Show the remainders as fractions.

1. $4\overline{)9}$ 2. $20 \div 6$ 3. $5\overline{)17}$ 4. $6\overline{)41}$ 5. $52 \div 9$ 6. $8\overline{)75}$

Divide to find the mixed numbers.

7. $\frac{13}{4}$ 8. $\frac{29}{5}$ 9. $\frac{38}{7}$ 10. $\frac{22}{3}$ 11. $\frac{34}{7}$ 12. $\frac{19}{2}$

Mixed Practice • Divide. Show the remainders as fractions.

13. $7\overline{)17}$ 14. $23 \div 4$ 15. $33 \div 5$ 16. $7\overline{)48}$ 17. $9\overline{)65}$ 18. $3\overline{)29}$

148

Divide to find the mixed numbers. Write the answers in lowest terms.

19. $\frac{9}{2}$ **20.** $\frac{12}{5}$ **21.** $\frac{5}{4}$ **22.** $\frac{7}{4}$ **23.** $\frac{5}{2}$ **24.** $\frac{8}{6}$

25. $\frac{16}{3}$ **26.** $\frac{7}{6}$ **27.** $\frac{11}{2}$ **28.** $\frac{17}{4}$ **29.** $\frac{7}{2}$ **30.** $\frac{9}{5}$

31. $\frac{21}{4}$ **32.** $\frac{25}{2}$ **33.** $\frac{7}{3}$ **34.** $\frac{9}{7}$ **35.** $\frac{15}{4}$ **36.** $\frac{19}{4}$

37. $\frac{15}{2}$ **38.** $\frac{21}{10}$ **39.** $\frac{53}{6}$ **40.** $\frac{52}{8}$ **41.** $\frac{27}{5}$ **42.** $\frac{39}{8}$

43. $\frac{48}{5}$ **44.** $\frac{22}{7}$ **45.** $\frac{76}{9}$ **46.** $\frac{85}{10}$ **47.** $\frac{35}{4}$ **48.** $\frac{46}{6}$

Write the fraction and mixed number for each point on the number line.

★ **49.** $\frac{24}{4}$ A $\frac{28}{4}$ ★ **50.** $\frac{12}{6}$ B $\frac{19}{6}$

★ **51.**   ★ **52.**

$\frac{25}{5}$ C $\frac{30}{5}$ $\frac{8}{8}$ D $\frac{16}{8}$

PROBLEM SOLVING • APPLICATIONS

53. Each watermelon will be divided into 8 pieces. 57 pieces are needed. How many watermelons are needed?

54. 23 pieces of cantaloupe are needed. Each cantaloupe will be divided into fourths. How many cantaloupes are needed?

★ **55.** There are $3\frac{2}{3}$ dozen eggs. Are there enough eggs to make 14 omelettes if $\frac{1}{3}$ dozen eggs are used in each omelette?

★ **56.** Robin has $4\frac{3}{4}$ pounds of ground beef. Is there enough meat to make 20 hamburgers if $\frac{1}{4}$ pound of meat is used in each hamburger?

PROBLEM SOLVING • STRATEGIES

Using a Schedule

Schedules are used by airlines, bus companies, and train operators. A passenger must be able to read the schedule in order to choose which plane, bus, or train to take.

Lucia Brummel is a freelance artist. She travels by train from Dobbs Ferry to New York City several days each week. This is the train schedule she uses.

Dobbs Ferry to New York				New York to Dobbs Ferry			
Leave			Arrive	Leave	Arrive		
Dobbs Ferry	Hastings	Greystone	New York	New York	Greystone	Hastings	Dobbs Ferry
7:52 A.M.	7:55 A.M.	—	8:28 A.M.	10:20 A.M.	10:57 A.M.	11:00 A.M.	11:03 A.M.
9:31 A.M.	9:33 A.M.	9:36 A.M.	10:11 A.M.	12:20 P.M.	12:57 P.M.	1:00 P.M.	1:03 P.M.
11:51 A.M.	11:53 A.M.	11:56 A.M.	12:35 P.M.	3:50 P.M.	—	4:22 P.M.	4:25 P.M.
4:51 P.M.	4:53 P.M.	4:56 P.M.	5:30 P.M.	5:13 P.M.	5:48 P.M.	5:51 P.M.	5:54 P.M.
5:51 P.M.	5:53 P.M.	5:56 P.M.	6:30 P.M.	6:53 P.M.	7:30 P.M.	7:33 P.M.	7:36 P.M.
8:51 P.M.	8:53 P.M.	8:56 P.M.	9:33 P.M.	10:20 P.M.	10:57 P.M.	11:00 P.M.	11:03 P.M.

The train schedule has 2 sections. The section on the left shows the times Lucia can leave from three stations near her home. The section on the right shows the times Lucia can leave New York to return home.

The 7:52 A.M. train from Dobbs Ferry stops in Hastings at 7:55 A.M. This train does not stop at Greystone. It arrives in New York at 8:28 A.M., 36 minutes after it leaves Dobbs Ferry.

Use the train schedule to answer the questions.

1. At what times does the 4:51 P.M. train from Dobbs Ferry arrive in New York?

2. At what time does the 12:20 P.M. train from New York arrive in Hastings?

   Choose the correct schedule for the trip.

3. Lucia wants to stop in Greystone. Can she take the 3:50 P.M. train from New York?

4. An artist working with Lucia lives in Hastings. Can he take the 6:53 P.M. train home from New York?

150

5. Lucia must have some new sketches in New York by 1:00 P.M. Which trains can she take from Dobbs Ferry to be there on time?

Locate the cities and the times for leaving and arriving.

6. An editor wants to meet Lucia at the Greystone station at 12:15 P.M. Which trains can the editor take from Dobbs Ferry to be there on time?

7. Lucia has tickets for a New York play. It begins at 8:00 P.M. She is going with a friend from Greystone. Which train from Greystone can they take after 5:00 P.M.?

8. Lucia finishes work in New York at 4:30 P.M. She wants to arrive home before 7:00 P.M. Which train should she take?

9. How many minutes does it take for the second train leaving Dobbs Ferry to get to New York?

10. How many minutes does it take for the last train leaving New York to get to Hastings?

★ 11. Which train from Dobbs Ferry takes longer to get to New York, the 7:52 A.M. or the 9:31 A.M.? How much longer?

★ 12. Which train from Dobbs Ferry gets to New York in the least amount of time? Which train returns the fastest? If Lucia took these trains on the same day, how much time would she have to spend in New York?

6 CHAPTER — REVIEW

Write each number as a product of prime factors. (pages 130–131)

1. 18   **2.** 30   **3.** 45   **4.** 75

Find the greatest common factor for each. (pages 132–133)

5. 12, 16   **6.** 9, 27   **7.** 18, 45   **8.** 42, 35

Find the least common multiple for each. (pages 134–135)

9. 2, 7   **10.** 6, 9   **11.** 9, 12   **12.** 24, 36

Write the fraction that tells what part is blue for each. (pages 138–139)

13.   **14.**   **15.**

Complete. (pages 140–141)

16. $\frac{3}{7} = \frac{?}{21}$ **17.** $\frac{4}{5} = \frac{28}{?}$ **18.** $\frac{16}{24} = \frac{?}{3}$

Write each fraction in lowest terms. (pages 142–143)

19. $\frac{6}{8}$ **20.** $\frac{10}{12}$ **21.** $\frac{30}{45}$

Find the least common denominators. Write the equivalent fractions. (pages 144–145)

22. $\frac{2}{3}, \frac{3}{8}$ **23.** $\frac{5}{6}, \frac{3}{10}$ **24.** $\frac{4}{5}, \frac{1}{9}$

Write as fractions. (pages 146–147)

25. $3\frac{5}{6}$ **26.** $2\frac{3}{4}$ **27.** $5\frac{3}{10}$

Divide to find the mixed numbers. Write in lowest terms. (pages 148–149)

28. $\frac{9}{5}$ **29.** $\frac{13}{3}$ **30.** $\frac{30}{4}$

Solve.

31. Sandra drank $\frac{4}{5}$ of a glass of milk. Janice drank $\frac{7}{8}$ of a glass of milk. Who drank more milk? (p. 144)

32. Billy has $3\frac{1}{8}$ cheese pies. How many eighths are there? (p. 146)

Egyptian Numbers

One Egyptian number system was invented more than 5,000 years ago. The Egyptians used a system that was based on grouping by tens and is somewhat like our number system. Symbols were used to represent numbers.

Egyptian Code

1	10	100	1,000	10,000	100,000	1,000,000
│	∩	𝟿	🝪	𝄎	🐟	👤

Combinations of these symbols were used to write numbers. Egyptian numbers were written in either direction. When reading the numbers, the Egyptians always started with the symbol with the greatest value.

4,721 may be written as:

    [hieroglyphs]   or   [hieroglyphs]

Write the numbers.

1. [hieroglyphs]   **2.** [hieroglyphs]   **3.** [hieroglyphs]

Write the Egyptian numbers.

4. 19

5. 438

6. 1,250

7. 52,187

8. 2,351,746

153

CHAPTER 6

TEST

Write each number as a product of prime factors.

1. 20   **2.** 32   **3.** 56   **4.** 36

Find the greatest common factor for each.

5. 9, 15   **6.** 12, 40   **7.** 24, 60   **8.** 14, 48

Find the least common multiple for each.

9. 3, 8   **10.** 6, 10   **11.** 18, 24   **12.** 15, 20

Write the fraction that tells what part is blue for each.

13.   **14.**   **15.**

Complete.

16. $\frac{2}{5} = \frac{?}{15}$ **17.** $\frac{2}{9} = \frac{10}{?}$ **18.** $\frac{18}{30} = \frac{?}{5}$

Write each fraction in lowest terms.

19. $\frac{6}{10}$ **20.** $\frac{15}{30}$ **21.** $\frac{15}{18}$

Find the least common denominators. Write the equivalent fractions.

22. $\frac{3}{4}, \frac{3}{8}$ **23.** $\frac{5}{7}, \frac{1}{2}$ **24.** $\frac{5}{6}, \frac{4}{9}$

Write as fractions.

25. $2\frac{1}{4}$ **26.** $5\frac{3}{8}$ **27.** $13\frac{2}{5}$

Divide to find the mixed numbers. Write in lowest terms.

28. $\frac{8}{3}$ **29.** $\frac{17}{4}$ **30.** $\frac{20}{8}$

Solve.

31. Ellen solved 6 of her 9 math problems before dinner. What fraction of the problems has she completed? Write the fraction in lowest terms.

32. Mark sliced loaves of bread into 8 pieces each. He has $\frac{24}{8}$ loaves. How many loaves did he slice?

ENRICHMENT

Patterns

Choose the correct response.

⊤	⊢	⊣	⊥
a	b	c	d

A is to **V** as **T** is to ?

Think: **V** is the same as **A** except that it is upside down. Look for the upside-down letter **T**. It is **⊥**. Look for the box that shows this. It is box **d**. The correct choice is **d**.

Now try this one.

◯	▢	▫	◯
a	b	c	d

◯ is to ◯ as ▢ is to ?

Think: ◯ is the same as ◯ except that it is larger. Look for the same shape as ▢ but larger. It is ▢ The correct choice is **b**.

Try another one.

| °◯ ◯ | □ □ | □ | °◯ |
| a | b | c | d |

◦◦ ◦◦ is to °◦ as ▢▢ ▢▢ is to ?

Did you say **c**? That is the correct choice.

155

Choose the correct responses.

1. **P** is to **P** as **E** is to ___?___

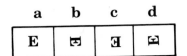

2. △ is to ▲ as ○ is to ___?___

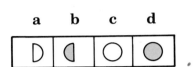

3. ○ is to ◖ as ⬤ is to ___?___

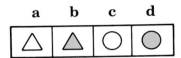

4. ▲ is to △ as ◼ is to ___?___

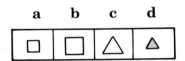

5. ◻ is to ⋀ as ⬤ is to ___?___

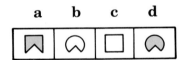

6. is to as is to ___?___

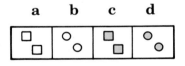

7. is to as is to ___?___

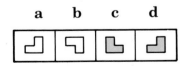

8. is to as is to ___?___

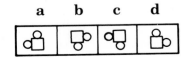

156

COMPUTER

Computer Dollars

Look at the numbers we must use to talk about computers.
Very large computers can cost over $1,000,000: one million dollars.
Scientific groups and companies have bought more than 5,000 of these computers.
5,000 of these computers have a total value of over $5,000,000,000.
Sometimes five billion dollars is written in the form $5 billion.

Large computers are called *data-processing equipment* or *mainframe computers*.
Smaller computers are called *personal computers* or *microcomputers*.
These cost under $10,000.
Middle-sized computers are called *minicomputers*.

$5,400,000,000 is an estimate of the value of personal computers produced in 1983.
More than a million computers were made in this one year.
One computer company may sell $40,000,000,000 worth of computers in a year.
$1,500,000,000 of that amount may be in personal computers.
That one company may sell 400,000 personal computers a year.

Choose the correct answers.

1. Large computers are called

   A. data-processing equipment.
   B. mainframe computers.
   C. both A and B.
   D. neither A nor B.

2. Smaller computers are called

   A. personal computers.
   B. minicomputers.
   C. both A and B.
   D. neither A nor B.

3. Middle-sized computers are called

   A. microcomputers.
   B. minicomputers.
   C. midicomputers.
   D. none of the above.

4. The number of computers made in 1983 was

   A. 10,000,000.
   B. 1,000,000,000.
   C. 1,000,000.
   D. none of the above.

5. An estimate of the value of personal computers produced in 1983 was

   A. four billion, five hundred million dollars.
   B. five million, four hundred thousand dollars.
   C. five trillion, five hundred billion dollars.
   D. none of the above.

Choose the correct answers.

1. Add.

$$\begin{array}{r} \$\ 60.93 \\ 25.61 \\ 397.18 \\ +\quad 4.57 \end{array}$$

A. $478.19
B. $488.29
C. $486.19
D. not here

2. Subtract.

$$\begin{array}{r} \$407.52 \\ -\ 219.75 \end{array}$$

A. $187.77
B. $188.77
C. $197.87
D. not here

3. Multiply.

$$\begin{array}{r} 4,708 \\ \times\quad 285 \end{array}$$

A. 1,330,680
B. 1,151,780
C. 1,341,780
D. not here

4. Divide.

$$136\overline{)45,087}$$

A. 330 r 71
B. 303 r 20
C. 338 r 119
D. not here

5. What is the average temperature in March?

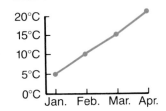

A. 5°C
B. 7°C
C. 15°C
D. not here

6. Which is a prime number?

14, 9, 53, 27

A. 14
B. 9
C. 53
D. not here

7. Choose the fraction that tells which part is red.

A. $\frac{1}{3}$
B. $\frac{1}{6}$
C. $\frac{2}{3}$
D. not here

8. Complete.

$$\frac{12}{32} = \frac{3}{?}$$

A. 6
B. 9
C. 8
D. not here

9. Compare.

$$\frac{7}{12} \bigcirc \frac{2}{9}$$

A. <
B. =
C. >
D. not here

10. Mrs. Mohzer orders 24 handbags for her shop. Each bag costs $12.95. What is the total cost of her order?

A. $310.80
B. $310.60
C. $307.60
D. not here

11. Mrs. Mohzer sells all 24 handbags for a total of $402.96. How much does each handbag sell for?

A. $16.29
B. $12.95
C. $15.95
D. not here

Fractions: Addition and Subtraction

Addition with Like and Unlike Denominators • More Addition with Mixed Numbers • Subtraction with Like and Unlike Denominators • Subtraction with Regrouping • Problem Solving: Missing Information Stock Market • Time Zones

Addition with Like Denominators

Juan eats $\frac{3}{8}$ of a meat pie.
Juanita eats $\frac{1}{8}$.
How much do they eat in all?

$$\frac{3}{8} + \frac{1}{8} = ?$$

Step 1
The denominators are the same.
Add the numerators.

$$\frac{3}{8} + \frac{1}{8} = \frac{4}{8}$$

Step 2
Write the answer in lowest terms.

$$\frac{3}{8} + \frac{1}{8} = \frac{4}{8} = \frac{1}{2}$$

They eat $\frac{1}{2}$ of the pie.

Add: $4\frac{1}{6} + 2\frac{2}{6}$.

Step 1
Add: $\frac{1}{6} + \frac{2}{6}$.

$$4\frac{1}{6}$$
$$+2\frac{2}{6}$$
$$\overline{\frac{3}{6}}$$

Step 2
Add: $4 + 2$.

$$4\frac{1}{6}$$
$$+2\frac{2}{6}$$
$$\overline{6\frac{3}{6}}$$

Step 3
Write the answer in lowest terms.

$$4\frac{1}{6}$$
$$+2\frac{2}{6}$$
$$\overline{6\frac{3}{6} = 6\frac{1}{2}}$$

Practice • Add. Write the answers in lowest terms.

1. $\frac{5}{8} + \frac{1}{8} = $ _____?_____

2. $\frac{3}{10} + \frac{4}{10} = $ _____?_____

3. $\frac{3}{7} + \frac{1}{7} = $ _____?_____

4. $3\frac{1}{5}$
 $+4\frac{3}{5}$

5. $2\frac{2}{7}$
 $+3\frac{3}{7}$

6. $1\frac{3}{8}$
 $+5\frac{3}{8}$

7. $4\frac{3}{10}$
 $+6\frac{5}{10}$

8. $10\frac{4}{12}$
 $+3\frac{6}{12}$

Mixed Practice • Add. Write the answers in lowest terms.

9. $\frac{4}{10} + \frac{2}{10} = $ _____?_____

10. $\frac{1}{9} + \frac{2}{9} = $ _____?_____

11. $\frac{3}{8} + \frac{2}{8} = $ _____?_____

12. $\frac{9}{12} + \frac{2}{12} = $ _____?_____

13. $\frac{5}{11} + \frac{4}{11} = $ _____?_____

14. $\frac{3}{15} + \frac{2}{15} = $ _____?_____

15. $3\frac{4}{10}$
 $+1\frac{1}{10}$

16. $6\frac{1}{4}$
 $+2\frac{2}{4}$

17. $3\frac{5}{13}$
 $+6\frac{5}{13}$

18. $4\frac{2}{8}$
 $+7\frac{2}{8}$

19. $12\frac{2}{6}$
 $+3\frac{2}{6}$

160

20. $3\frac{5}{12}$
$+4\frac{4}{12}$

21. $6\frac{6}{16}$
$+5\frac{6}{16}$

22. $8\frac{9}{21}$
$+3\frac{5}{21}$

23. $6\frac{5}{18}$
$+7\frac{3}{18}$

24. $15\frac{4}{24}$
$+\ 8\frac{6}{24}$

25. $\frac{4}{12}$
$\frac{2}{12}$
$+\frac{3}{12}$

26. $\frac{6}{15}$
$\frac{3}{15}$
$+\frac{4}{15}$

27. $1\frac{2}{9}$
$2\frac{1}{9}$
$+4\frac{4}{9}$

28. $3\frac{5}{20}$
$8\frac{6}{20}$
$+9\frac{3}{20}$

29. $14\frac{6}{35}$
$8\frac{3}{35}$
$+\ 5\frac{5}{35}$

Both denominators are the same for each. Write the missing denominators.

★ **30.** $\frac{1}{?} + \frac{3}{?} = \frac{1}{2}$

★ **31.** $\frac{3}{?} + \frac{5}{?} = \frac{4}{5}$

★ **32.** $\frac{1}{?} + \frac{2}{?} = \frac{1}{5}$

PROBLEM SOLVING • APPLICATIONS

Write the answers in lowest terms.

33. How much salad dressing can be made from $\frac{1}{8}$ cup of vinegar and $\frac{3}{8}$ cup of mayonnaise?

34. A recipe for baked apples calls for $1\frac{2}{8}$ teaspoons cinnamon, $1\frac{3}{8}$ teaspoons nutmeg, and $\frac{1}{8}$ teaspoon cloves. How many teaspoons of spices are needed?

★ **35.** A recipe for 1 batch of muffins requires $1\frac{1}{8}$ cups of whole wheat flour. How much flour is needed to make 4 batches of muffins?

★ **36.** Lenno has 3 cups of milk. He wants to make pancakes. Each batch of pancakes calls for $1\frac{1}{3}$ cups of milk. How many batches of pancakes can he make?

Addition with Unlike Denominators

Diana and Tracy are making clay sculptures for the Crafts Fair.

Diana uses $\frac{3}{4}$ of a block of clay.

Tracy uses $\frac{5}{8}$ of a block of clay.

How many blocks of clay do they use in all?

$$\frac{3}{4} + \frac{5}{8} = ?$$

The denominators are not the same. You can use equivalent fractions with the same denominator. Use the least common denominator.

Step 1
Find the least common denominator. Write equivalent fractions.

$$\frac{3}{4} = \frac{6}{8}$$
$$+\frac{5}{8} = \frac{5}{8}$$

Step 2
Add.

$$\frac{3}{4} = \frac{6}{8}$$
$$+\frac{5}{8} = \frac{5}{8}$$
$$\frac{11}{8}$$

Step 3
Write the answer using a mixed number.

$$\frac{3}{4} = \frac{6}{8}$$
$$+\frac{5}{8} = \frac{5}{8}$$
$$\frac{11}{8} = 1\frac{3}{8}$$

They use $1\frac{3}{8}$ blocks of clay.

Add: $3\frac{1}{4} + 2\frac{3}{5}$.

Step 1
Write equivalent fractions.

$$3\frac{1}{4} = 3\frac{5}{20}$$
$$+2\frac{3}{5} = 2\frac{12}{20}$$

Step 2
Add: $\frac{5}{20} + \frac{12}{20}$.

$$3\frac{1}{4} = 3\frac{5}{20}$$
$$+2\frac{3}{5} = 2\frac{12}{20}$$
$$\frac{17}{20}$$

Step 3
Add the whole numbers.

$$3\frac{1}{4} = 3\frac{5}{20}$$
$$+2\frac{3}{5} = 2\frac{12}{20}$$
$$5\frac{17}{20}$$

Practice • Add. Write the answers in lowest terms.

1. $\frac{1}{2}$
$+\frac{3}{8}$

2. $\frac{2}{3}$
$+\frac{1}{4}$

3. $\frac{2}{3}$
$+\frac{7}{12}$

4. $\frac{1}{8}$
$+\frac{3}{4}$

5. $\frac{3}{4}$
$+\frac{2}{3}$

6. $1\frac{2}{5}$
$+2\frac{3}{10}$

7. $2\frac{1}{6}$
$+1\frac{5}{12}$

8. $3\frac{1}{5}$
$+4\frac{2}{3}$

9. $4\frac{1}{6}$
$+2\frac{2}{9}$

10. $5\frac{3}{7}$
$+6\frac{1}{2}$

Mixed Practice • Add. Write the answers in lowest terms.

11. $\dfrac{5}{6}$
$+\dfrac{2}{3}$

12. $\dfrac{3}{4}$
$+\dfrac{1}{6}$

13. $\dfrac{3}{8}$
$+\dfrac{1}{6}$

14. $\dfrac{4}{12}$
$+\dfrac{5}{6}$

15. $\dfrac{2}{5}$
$+\dfrac{1}{10}$

16. $\dfrac{3}{8}$
$+\dfrac{2}{3}$

17. $\dfrac{5}{6}$
$+\dfrac{3}{4}$

18. $\dfrac{1}{2}$
$+\dfrac{2}{9}$

19. $\dfrac{3}{15}$
$+\dfrac{2}{5}$

20. $\dfrac{3}{8}$
$+\dfrac{1}{4}$

21. $4\dfrac{1}{4}$
$+5\dfrac{1}{4}$

22. $6\dfrac{2}{4}$
$+3\dfrac{2}{7}$

23. $4\dfrac{2}{6}$
$+5\dfrac{3}{5}$

24. $6\dfrac{4}{9}$
$+2\dfrac{2}{9}$

25. $7\dfrac{3}{10}$
$+4\dfrac{1}{2}$

★ 26. $\dfrac{1}{2} + \dfrac{1}{6} + \dfrac{1}{4} = $ _____?_____

★ 27. $\dfrac{2}{6} + \dfrac{1}{3} + \dfrac{1}{9} = $ _____?_____

★ 28. $5\dfrac{3}{7} + 5\dfrac{2}{35} + 6\dfrac{1}{5} = $ _____?_____

★ 29. $4\dfrac{2}{4} + 3\dfrac{2}{12} + 1\dfrac{1}{6} = $ _____?_____

PROBLEM SOLVING • APPLICATIONS

Write the answers in lowest terms.

30. Mandy entered a hat in the Crafts Fair contest. She used $2\dfrac{3}{4}$ rolls of pink ribbon and $1\dfrac{1}{8}$ rolls of green ribbon to make the hat. How much ribbon did she use in all?

31. Iye spent $1\dfrac{1}{4}$ hours sanding wood for his wall plaque entry. He spent $\dfrac{2}{3}$ hour varnishing it. How many hours did Iye spend on the project?

32. Theresa entered stuffed animals in the fair. She used $\dfrac{7}{8}$ bag of stuffing to make cats and $\dfrac{3}{5}$ bag to make dogs. How much stuffing did she use in all?

★ 33. Paul made macramé plant hangers for his entry. He used $3\dfrac{1}{6}$ balls of white cord, $1\dfrac{1}{3}$ balls of brown cord, and $2\dfrac{3}{8}$ balls of green cord for the hangers. How many balls of cord did he use in all?

Skills Maintenance

1. $2.56
$+ 3.89$

2. $4.49
$+ 2.67$

3. $3.89
$+ 5.15$

4. $2.88
$+ 7.05$

5. $2.29
$+ 5.92$

6. $59.00
$+ 18.75$

7. $24.95
$+ 35.16$

8. $57.13
$+ 14.69$

9. $33.75
$+ 42.27$

10. $17.65
$+ 25.89$

More Addition with Mixed Numbers

Doug Wilson works for the Ace Computer Company. He is in charge of logging the amount of time the computers are used.

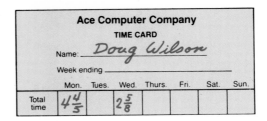

To find how many hours one computer was used in a day he adds.

$$4\frac{4}{5} + 2\frac{5}{8} = ?$$

Step 1
Write equivalent fractions.

Step 2
Add: $\frac{32}{40} + \frac{25}{40}$.

Step 3
Add: $4 + 2$.
$\frac{57}{40} > 1$. Regroup. Write the answer in lowest terms.
$6\frac{57}{40} = 6\frac{40}{40} + \frac{17}{40}$
Add: $6 + 1$.

$$4\frac{4}{5} = 4\frac{32}{40}$$
$$+2\frac{5}{8} = 2\frac{25}{40}$$

$$4\frac{4}{5} = 4\frac{32}{40}$$
$$+2\frac{5}{8} = 2\frac{25}{40}$$
$$\frac{57}{40}$$

$$4\frac{4}{5} = 4\frac{32}{40}$$
$$+2\frac{5}{8} = 2\frac{25}{40}$$
$$6\frac{57}{40} = 7\frac{17}{40}$$

More Examples

$$8\frac{7}{10} = 8\frac{21}{30}$$
$$+3\frac{5}{6} = 3\frac{25}{30}$$
$$11\frac{46}{30} = 12\frac{16}{30} = 12\frac{8}{15}$$

$$4\frac{7}{12}$$
$$+5\frac{5}{12}$$
$$9\frac{12}{12} = 10$$

Practice • Add. Write the answers in lowest terms.

1. $5\frac{2}{3}$
   $+1\frac{3}{6}$

2. $1\frac{1}{2}$
   $+2\frac{3}{5}$

3. $3\frac{3}{8}$
   $+5\frac{3}{4}$

4. $3\frac{2}{3}$
   $+4\frac{1}{2}$

5. $2\frac{3}{5}$
   $+4\frac{5}{8}$

6. $1\frac{3}{8}$
   $+1\frac{2}{3}$

7. $4\frac{5}{7}$
   $+3\frac{2}{3}$

8. $6\frac{4}{7}$
   $+8\frac{2}{4}$

9. $4\frac{3}{5}$
   $+4\frac{7}{10}$

10. $2\frac{4}{5}$
    $+4\frac{6}{15}$

Mixed Practice • Add. Write the answers in lowest terms.

11. $6\frac{2}{3}$
$+2\frac{3}{4}$

12. $5\frac{3}{4}$
$+2\frac{7}{10}$

13. $10\frac{9}{10}$
$+\ \ \frac{3}{5}$

14. $9\frac{5}{6}$
$+2\frac{7}{9}$

15. $5\frac{5}{8}$
$+5\frac{3}{4}$

16. $3\frac{4}{9}$
$+4\frac{5}{6}$

17. $8\frac{7}{10}$
$+4\frac{9}{15}$

18. $4\frac{3}{5}$
$+4\frac{5}{8}$

19. $5\frac{5}{6}$
$+2\frac{2}{4}$

20. $9\frac{3}{4}$
$+8\frac{3}{7}$

21. $\frac{7}{10}$
$+\frac{8}{15}$

22. $3\frac{3}{4}$
$+4\frac{5}{16}$

23. $5\frac{1}{8}$
$+3\frac{3}{4}$

24. $11\frac{7}{12}$
$+\ 5\frac{3}{4}$

25. $9\frac{2}{3}$
$+8\frac{4}{7}$

26. $2\frac{3}{4} + 6\frac{7}{8} = $ _____

27. $5\frac{2}{5} + 6\frac{7}{10} = $ _____

28. $3\frac{2}{3} + 9\frac{2}{4} = $ _____

29. $7\frac{4}{5} + 4\frac{2}{3} = $ _____

30. $5\frac{5}{12} + 6\frac{1}{12} = $ _____

31. $5\frac{9}{12} + 3\frac{2}{8} = $ _____

32. $\frac{3}{4} + \frac{5}{8} = $ _____

★ 33. $4\frac{2}{3} + 2\frac{5}{6} + 5\frac{2}{3} = $ _____

★ 34. $9\frac{4}{6} + 4\frac{3}{5} + 5\frac{8}{10} = $ _____

PROBLEM SOLVING • APPLICATIONS

Find the total number of hours worked.

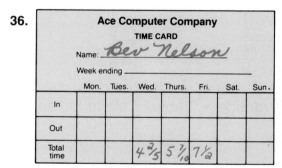

35.

Ace Computer Company TIME CARD							
Name: Mu Lan Chang							
Week ending _____							
	Mon.	Tues.	Wed.	Thurs.	Fri.	Sat.	Sun.
In							
Out							
Total time	$6\frac{1}{2}$	$7\frac{3}{4}$		6			

36.

Ace Computer Company TIME CARD							
Name: Bev Nelson							
Week ending _____							
	Mon.	Tues.	Wed.	Thurs.	Fri.	Sat.	Sun.
In							
Out							
Total time	$4\frac{2}{5}$	$5\frac{7}{10}$	$7\frac{1}{2}$				

37. Lettie used a computer $6\frac{2}{5}$ hours on Monday, $7\frac{1}{4}$ hours on Tuesday, and $5\frac{7}{10}$ hours on Wednesday. Did she use it more than 20 hours?

38. Carol used a computer $5\frac{1}{2}$ hours on Monday, $3\frac{3}{4}$ hours on Tuesday, and $7\frac{3}{10}$ hours on Wednesday. Did she use it more than 16 hours?

★ 39. Dale purchased $5\frac{2}{5}$ hours of computer time on Monday, $7\frac{1}{2}$ hours on Tuesday, and $6\frac{1}{10}$ hours on Wednesday. How much time did he purchase in all?

★ 40. Pearl programmed 7 hours on Monday, $4\frac{3}{4}$ hours on Tuesday, and $6\frac{1}{4}$ hours on Wednesday. How many hours in all did she program?

Subtraction with Like Denominators

$\frac{5}{8}$ of a farmer's produce is corn.

$\frac{3}{8}$ of his produce is potatoes.

How much more of his produce is corn than potatoes?

$\frac{5}{8} - \frac{3}{8} = ?$

Step 1
The denominators are the same. Subtract the numerators.

$\frac{5}{8} - \frac{3}{8} = \frac{2}{8}$

Step 2
Write the answer in lowest terms.

$\frac{5}{8} - \frac{3}{8} = \frac{2}{8} = \frac{1}{4}$

$\frac{1}{4}$ more of his produce is corn than potatoes.

Subtract: $5\frac{7}{9} - 2\frac{1}{9}$.

Step 1
Subtract:
$\frac{7}{9} - \frac{1}{9}$.

$\begin{array}{r} 5\frac{7}{9} \\ -2\frac{1}{9} \\ \hline \frac{6}{9} \end{array}$

Step 2
Subtract: $5 - 2$.

$\begin{array}{r} 5\frac{7}{9} \\ -2\frac{1}{9} \\ \hline 3\frac{6}{9} \end{array}$

Step 3
Write the answer in lowest terms.

$\begin{array}{r} 5\frac{7}{9} \\ -2\frac{1}{9} \\ \hline 3\frac{6}{9} = 3\frac{2}{3} \end{array}$

Practice • Subtract. Write the answers in lowest terms.

1. $\frac{5}{6} - \frac{1}{6} = $ _____

2. $\frac{7}{8} - \frac{2}{8} = $ _____

3. $\frac{5}{7} - \frac{2}{7} = $ _____

4. $\begin{array}{r} 8\frac{7}{8} \\ -2\frac{1}{8} \\ \hline \end{array}$

5. $\begin{array}{r} 7\frac{9}{10} \\ -1\frac{6}{10} \\ \hline \end{array}$

6. $\begin{array}{r} 3\frac{4}{5} \\ -1\frac{2}{5} \\ \hline \end{array}$

7. $\begin{array}{r} 8\frac{6}{7} \\ -5\frac{4}{7} \\ \hline \end{array}$

8. $\begin{array}{r} 15\frac{2}{9} \\ -3\frac{1}{9} \\ \hline \end{array}$

Mixed Practice • Subtract. Write the answers in lowest terms.

9. $\frac{7}{8} - \frac{5}{8} = $ _____

10. $\frac{5}{7} - \frac{3}{7} = $ _____

11. $\frac{7}{9} - \frac{6}{9} = $ _____

12. $\frac{7}{10} - \frac{3}{10} = $ _____

13. $\frac{13}{15} - \frac{7}{15} = $ _____

14. $\frac{5}{12} - \frac{1}{12} = $ _____

15. $3\frac{5}{8}$
$-2\frac{1}{8}$

16. $5\frac{2}{3}$
$-1\frac{1}{3}$

17. $7\frac{11}{20}$
$-3\frac{6}{20}$

18. $4\frac{6}{9}$
$-1\frac{1}{9}$

19. $10\frac{9}{11}$
$-4\frac{7}{11}$

20. $9\frac{19}{20}$
$-2\frac{7}{20}$

21. $16\frac{6}{7}$
$-3\frac{1}{7}$

22. $5\frac{7}{8}$
$-2\frac{3}{8}$

23. $8\frac{7}{12}$
$-3\frac{5}{12}$

24. $18\frac{9}{10}$
$-9\frac{3}{10}$

25. $9\frac{9}{12}$
$-3\frac{3}{12}$

26. $12\frac{7}{8}$
$-4\frac{3}{8}$

27. $13\frac{13}{16}$
$-2\frac{9}{16}$

★ 28. $768\frac{19}{20}$
$-321\frac{15}{20}$

★ 29. $419\frac{15}{36}$
$-212\frac{12}{36}$

PROBLEM SOLVING • APPLICATIONS

30. A Montana cattle rancher sets aside $58\frac{2}{3}$ acres for grazing. He sets aside $3\frac{1}{3}$ acres for raising poultry. How many more acres of land is set aside for grazing?

★ 31. Another rancher sets aside $\frac{3}{4}$ of her land to build on. She uses $\frac{1}{8}$ of this land to build a house and another $\frac{3}{8}$ of this land to build a barn. How much of her land for building is left over?

Midchapter Review

Add or subtract. Write the answers in lowest terms.

1. $\frac{3}{8}$
$+\frac{3}{8}$

2. $\frac{5}{8}$
$+\frac{1}{6}$

3. $\frac{2}{3}$
$+\frac{7}{9}$

4. $9\frac{1}{4}$
$+4\frac{2}{3}$

5. $3\frac{4}{9}$
$+5\frac{5}{6}$

6. $\frac{7}{8}$
$-\frac{3}{8}$

7. $\frac{11}{12}$
$-\frac{4}{12}$

8. $7\frac{9}{10}$
$-3\frac{3}{10}$

9. $8\frac{5}{6}$
$-2\frac{1}{6}$

10. $9\frac{5}{8}$
$-6\frac{3}{8}$

Subtraction with Unlike Denominators

Utina is going to visit her grandparents. She spends $\frac{1}{3}$ of an hour driving to the airport. Her flight takes $\frac{5}{6}$ of an hour. How much longer is the flight than the drive?

$$\frac{5}{6} - \frac{1}{3} = ?$$

Step 1
Find the least common denominator. Write equivalent fractions.

$$\begin{array}{r} \frac{5}{6} = \frac{5}{6} \\ -\frac{1}{3} = \frac{2}{6} \\ \hline \end{array}$$

Step 2
Subtract.

$$\begin{array}{r} \frac{5}{6} = \frac{5}{6} \\ -\frac{1}{3} = \frac{2}{6} \\ \hline \frac{3}{6} \end{array}$$

Step 3
Write the answer in lowest terms.

$$\begin{array}{r} \frac{5}{6} = \frac{5}{6} \\ -\frac{1}{3} = \frac{2}{6} \\ \hline \frac{3}{6} = \frac{1}{2} \end{array}$$

The flight is $\frac{1}{2}$ hour longer than the drive.

Subtract: $4\frac{2}{3} - 1\frac{1}{5}$.

Step 1
Write equivalent fractions.

$$\begin{array}{r} 4\frac{2}{3} = 4\frac{10}{15} \\ -1\frac{1}{5} = 1\frac{3}{15} \\ \hline \end{array}$$

Step 2
Subtract: $\frac{10}{15} - \frac{3}{15}$.

$$\begin{array}{r} 4\frac{2}{3} = 4\frac{10}{15} \\ -1\frac{1}{5} = 1\frac{3}{15} \\ \hline \frac{7}{15} \end{array}$$

Step 3
Subtract: $4 - 1$.

$$\begin{array}{r} 4\frac{2}{3} = 4\frac{10}{15} \\ -1\frac{1}{5} = 1\frac{3}{15} \\ \hline 3\frac{7}{15} \end{array}$$

Practice • Subtract. Write the answers in lowest terms.

1. $\begin{array}{r} \frac{7}{8} \\ -\frac{1}{2} \\ \hline \end{array}$

2. $\begin{array}{r} \frac{1}{2} \\ -\frac{3}{8} \\ \hline \end{array}$

3. $\begin{array}{r} \frac{1}{2} \\ -\frac{1}{3} \\ \hline \end{array}$

4. $\begin{array}{r} \frac{9}{10} \\ -\frac{3}{5} \\ \hline \end{array}$

5. $\begin{array}{r} \frac{4}{5} \\ -\frac{2}{3} \\ \hline \end{array}$

6. $\begin{array}{r} 8\frac{3}{4} \\ -3\frac{1}{6} \\ \hline \end{array}$

7. $\begin{array}{r} 2\frac{1}{2} \\ -1 \\ \hline \end{array}$

8. $\begin{array}{r} 7\frac{7}{12} \\ -5\frac{1}{3} \\ \hline \end{array}$

9. $\begin{array}{r} 9\frac{3}{8} \\ -7\frac{1}{4} \\ \hline \end{array}$

10. $\begin{array}{r} 8\frac{6}{7} \\ -5\frac{1}{2} \\ \hline \end{array}$

Mixed Practice • Subtract. Write the answers in lowest terms.

11. $\begin{array}{r} \frac{7}{9} \\ -\frac{1}{3} \\ \hline \end{array}$

12. $\begin{array}{r} \frac{5}{8} \\ -\frac{1}{4} \\ \hline \end{array}$

13. $\begin{array}{r} \frac{9}{10} \\ -\frac{3}{5} \\ \hline \end{array}$

14. $\begin{array}{r} \frac{6}{7} \\ -\frac{2}{3} \\ \hline \end{array}$

15. $\begin{array}{r} \frac{4}{6} \\ -\frac{2}{5} \\ \hline \end{array}$

16. $\dfrac{7}{12}$ $-\dfrac{1}{3}$

17. $\dfrac{8}{9}$ $-\dfrac{3}{4}$

18. $\dfrac{7}{8}$ $-\dfrac{3}{4}$

19. $\dfrac{8}{10}$ $-\dfrac{3}{4}$

20. $\dfrac{7}{8}$ $-\dfrac{5}{6}$

21. $9\dfrac{1}{4}$ $-8\dfrac{1}{7}$

22. $6\dfrac{3}{5}$ $-2\dfrac{3}{10}$

23. $4\dfrac{6}{9}$ $-1\dfrac{2}{5}$

24. $5\dfrac{5}{6}$ $-1\dfrac{1}{4}$

25. $8\dfrac{7}{12}$ $-3\dfrac{5}{12}$

26. $35\dfrac{1}{2}$ $-10\dfrac{3}{8}$

27. $14\dfrac{8}{16}$ $-\ 7\dfrac{4}{16}$

28. $9\dfrac{6}{7}$ $-3\dfrac{2}{4}$

29. $23\dfrac{3}{6}$ $-\ 8\dfrac{3}{8}$

30. $14\dfrac{4}{15}$ $-\ 6\dfrac{2}{15}$

31. $7\dfrac{2}{3} - 1\dfrac{5}{9} = $ _____?_____

32. $5\dfrac{3}{4} - 2\dfrac{1}{16} = $ _____?_____

33. $6\dfrac{1}{2} - 4\dfrac{3}{10} = $ _____?_____

34. $10\dfrac{5}{8} - 4\dfrac{1}{3} = $ _____?_____

35. $18\dfrac{9}{20} - 9\dfrac{3}{20} = $ _____?_____

36. $8\dfrac{6}{17} - 2\dfrac{4}{17} = $ _____?_____

Use $-$ and $+$ to make true sentences.

★ **37.** $\dfrac{3}{4}$ ⬤ $\dfrac{1}{6}$ ⬤ $\dfrac{2}{8} = \dfrac{5}{6}$

★ **38.** $\dfrac{2}{3}$ ⬤ $\dfrac{4}{5}$ ⬤ $\dfrac{1}{3} = 1\dfrac{2}{15}$

The time is 4:00.

$6\dfrac{1}{4}$ hours ago, the time was 9:45.

Look at each clock.

What time was it $6\dfrac{1}{4}$ hours ago?

4:00

★ **39.**  **3:30**

★ **40.**  **7:15**

★ **41.**  **2:45**

★ **42.**  **9:00**

PROBLEM SOLVING • APPLICATIONS

43. Utina spends $1\dfrac{1}{4}$ hours waiting at the airport for her plane. She changes planes at the next airport. This time she waits $3\dfrac{1}{2}$ hours for the plane. How much longer does she spend waiting for the second plane?

★ **44.** On the way home, Utina changes planes again. Her first flight takes $4\dfrac{5}{6}$ hours. Her second flight takes $1\dfrac{1}{4}$ hours. How much longer was the first flight than the second? She waits $2\dfrac{1}{3}$ hours between flights. How long did her return trip take in all?

169

Subtraction with Regrouping

Chef Herrera slices 8 pounds of turkey for a special luncheon. Only $5\frac{3}{4}$ pounds are served. How many pounds of sliced turkey are left?

$8 - 5\frac{3}{4} = ?$

Step 1
Write 8 as 7 + 1.
Then $7 + \frac{4}{4} = 7\frac{4}{4}$.

$$\begin{aligned} 8 &= 7\frac{4}{4} \\ -5\frac{3}{4} &= 5\frac{3}{4} \\ \hline \end{aligned}$$

Step 2
Subtract.

$$\begin{aligned} 8 &= 7\frac{4}{4} \\ -5\frac{3}{4} &= 5\frac{3}{4} \\ \hline & 2\frac{1}{4} \end{aligned}$$

$2\frac{1}{4}$ pounds of sliced turkey are left.

Subtract: $7\frac{1}{3} - 4\frac{2}{3}$.

Step 1
$\frac{2}{3} > \frac{1}{3}$. Regroup $7\frac{1}{3}$ as $6 + 1 + \frac{1}{3}$.
Then $6 + \frac{3}{3} + \frac{1}{3} = 6 + \frac{4}{3} = 6\frac{4}{3}$.

$$\begin{aligned} 7\frac{1}{3} &= 6\frac{4}{3} \\ -4\frac{2}{3} &= 4\frac{2}{3} \\ \hline \end{aligned}$$

Step 2
Subtract.

$$\begin{aligned} 7\frac{1}{3} &= 6\frac{4}{3} \\ -4\frac{2}{3} &= 4\frac{2}{3} \\ \hline & 2\frac{2}{3} \end{aligned}$$

Practice • Subtract. Write the answers in lowest terms.

1. $\begin{aligned} 2\frac{1}{6} \\ -1\frac{5}{6} \\ \hline \end{aligned}$

2. $\begin{aligned} 3\frac{3}{12} \\ -1\frac{9}{12} \\ \hline \end{aligned}$

3. $\begin{aligned} 2\frac{5}{16} \\ -1\frac{11}{16} \\ \hline \end{aligned}$

4. $\begin{aligned} 4 \\ -2\frac{4}{5} \\ \hline \end{aligned}$

5. $\begin{aligned} 8 \\ -6\frac{5}{8} \\ \hline \end{aligned}$

6. $\begin{aligned} 5 \\ -1\frac{2}{3} \\ \hline \end{aligned}$

7. $\begin{aligned} 6 \\ -4\frac{3}{5} \\ \hline \end{aligned}$

8. $\begin{aligned} 4\frac{1}{4} \\ -2\frac{3}{4} \\ \hline \end{aligned}$

9. $\begin{aligned} 6\frac{3}{10} \\ -3\frac{7}{10} \\ \hline \end{aligned}$

10. $\begin{aligned} 5\frac{1}{8} \\ -1\frac{7}{8} \\ \hline \end{aligned}$

Mixed Practice • Subtract. Write the answers in lowest terms.

11. $\begin{aligned} 4 \\ -1\frac{3}{7} \\ \hline \end{aligned}$

12. $\begin{aligned} 3 \\ -1\frac{1}{2} \\ \hline \end{aligned}$

13. $\begin{aligned} 5\frac{13}{20} \\ -2\frac{17}{20} \\ \hline \end{aligned}$

14. $\begin{aligned} 8 \\ -5\frac{4}{9} \\ \hline \end{aligned}$

15. $\begin{aligned} 10\frac{2}{6} \\ -8\frac{3}{6} \\ \hline \end{aligned}$

170

16. $4\frac{1}{18}$
   $-1\frac{7}{18}$

17. $9\frac{3}{9}$
   $-2\frac{7}{9}$

18. $8\frac{2}{10}$
   $-5\frac{8}{10}$

19. $7\frac{1}{3}$
   $-5\frac{2}{3}$

20. 9
   $-1\frac{4}{9}$

21. 19
   $-15\frac{2}{3}$

22. $32\frac{9}{10}$
   $-7\frac{7}{10}$

23. $11\frac{3}{11}$
   $-7\frac{6}{11}$

24. 8
   $-3\frac{5}{8}$

25. $12\frac{2}{7}$
   $-6\frac{6}{7}$

26. $4\frac{5}{12} - 3\frac{7}{12} = $ _____?_____

27. $9 - 4\frac{7}{8} = $ _____?_____

28. $7\frac{13}{16} - 2\frac{7}{16} = $ _____?_____

29. $8\frac{5}{11} - 2\frac{6}{11} = $ _____?_____

30. $6 - 2\frac{1}{3} = $ _____?_____

31. $9\frac{3}{8} - 1\frac{7}{8} = $ _____?_____

PROBLEM SOLVING • APPLICATIONS

Chef Herrera uses this chart to help him plan cooking times for the dinner meats he selects.

32. How much longer does it take to cook the pork loin than the rib eye roast?

33. How much longer does it take to cook the turkey than the ham?

34. How much longer does it take to cook the leg of lamb than the veal?

★ **35.** If the standing rib roast is to be ready by 5:00 P.M., what time should Chef Herrera put it in the oven?

★ **36.** If the ham is to be ready by 2:45 P.M., what time should Chef Herrera put it in the oven?

Kilograms	Dinner Meats	Roasting Time in Hours
10	Turkey	6
2	Veal	$2\frac{5}{6}$
1	Pork loin	$2\frac{1}{4}$
7	Ham	$4\frac{1}{3}$
2	Rib eye roast	$1\frac{3}{4}$
3	Standing rib roast	$2\frac{2}{3}$
2	Leg of lamb	$3\frac{1}{6}$

Skills Maintenance

1. $8.75
   $- 2.98$

2. $4.15
   $- 1.87$

3. $9.24
   $- 3.29$

4. $8.48
   $- 6.95$

5. $7.02
   $- 4.25$

6. $25.37
   $- 19.83$

7. $14.79
   $- 6.95$

8. $32.45
   $- 15.89$

9. $68.24
   $- 29.95$

10. $90.06
   $- 23.58$

More Subtraction with Regrouping

One week Theresa's dog, Barkus, ate $5\frac{2}{3}$ cans of dog food. The second week Barkus ate $8\frac{1}{2}$ cans of dog food. How many more cans of dog food did Barkus eat the second week?

$$8\frac{1}{2} - 5\frac{2}{3} = ?$$

Step 1
Write equivalent fractions.

$$8\frac{1}{2} = 8\frac{3}{6}$$
$$-5\frac{2}{3} = 5\frac{4}{6}$$

Step 2
Since $\frac{4}{6} > \frac{3}{6}$, regroup $8\frac{3}{6}$ as $7\frac{9}{6}$.

$$8\frac{1}{2} = 8\frac{3}{6} = 7\frac{9}{6}$$
$$-5\frac{2}{3} = 5\frac{4}{6} = 5\frac{4}{6}$$

Step 3
Subtract.

$$8\frac{1}{2} = 8\frac{3}{6} = 7\frac{9}{6}$$
$$-5\frac{2}{3} = 5\frac{4}{6} = 5\frac{4}{6}$$
$$2\frac{5}{6}$$

Barkus ate $2\frac{5}{6}$ more cans of dog food the second week.

Practice • Subtract. Write the answers in lowest terms.

1. $5\frac{1}{6}$
   $-2\frac{2}{3}$

2. $7\frac{1}{4}$
   $-3\frac{2}{5}$

3. $3\frac{1}{10}$
   $-1\frac{4}{5}$

4. $5\frac{1}{10}$
   $-2\frac{1}{2}$

5. $5\frac{1}{3}$
   $-\frac{3}{4}$

6. $7\frac{1}{2}$
   $-1\frac{3}{5}$

7. $8\frac{1}{4}$
   $-2\frac{2}{5}$

8. $4\frac{1}{4}$
   $-1\frac{7}{12}$

9. $4\frac{1}{8}$
   $-1\frac{2}{3}$

10. $9\frac{1}{6}$
    $-3\frac{5}{9}$

More Practice • Subtract. Write the answers in lowest terms.

11. $4\frac{1}{8}$
    $-2\frac{3}{4}$

12. $12\frac{1}{3}$
    $-8\frac{8}{15}$

13. $2\frac{3}{8}$
    $-1\frac{2}{3}$

14. $6\frac{2}{3}$
    $-\frac{3}{4}$

15. $2\frac{1}{5}$
    $-1\frac{1}{4}$

16. $8\frac{5}{6}$
    $-4\frac{8}{9}$

17. $5\frac{3}{4}$
    $-3\frac{11}{12}$

18. $6\frac{1}{3}$
    $-1\frac{5}{9}$

19. $2\frac{5}{8}$
    $-1\frac{5}{6}$

20. $4\frac{1}{6}$
    $-2\frac{3}{4}$

21. $11\frac{1}{6}$
$-10\frac{2}{3}$

22. $8\frac{3}{16}$
$-\ \ \frac{1}{4}$

23. $9\frac{1}{8}$
$-3\frac{7}{12}$

24. $5\frac{1}{6}$
$-2\frac{1}{3}$

25. $2\frac{3}{10}$
$-1\frac{7}{10}$

26. $18\frac{1}{6}$
$-\ 5\frac{3}{4}$

27. $20\frac{4}{5}$
$-17\frac{5}{6}$

28. $6\frac{1}{2}$
$-1\frac{3}{8}$

29. $2\frac{1}{2}$
$-1\frac{7}{8}$

30. $4\frac{1}{2}$
$-2\frac{7}{10}$

31. $5\frac{1}{6} - 3\frac{1}{2} = $ _____

32. $9\frac{3}{8} - 1\frac{3}{4} = $ _____

33. $8\frac{1}{2} - 2\frac{4}{5} = $ _____

34. $7\frac{2}{3} - \frac{7}{9} = $ _____

35. $6\frac{1}{4} - 2\frac{3}{4} = $ _____

★ **36.** $11\frac{1}{4} - 3\frac{7}{10} = $ _____

The time is 2:15.

$7\frac{3}{4}$ hours ago the time was 6:30.

Look at each clock.
What time was it $7\frac{3}{4}$ hours ago?

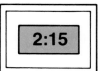

2:15

★ **37.** **6:20**

★ **38.** **7:35**

★ **39.** **4:10**

★ **40.** **8:40**

PROBLEM SOLVING • APPLICATIONS

Write the answers in lowest terms.

41. In March a pet store had $4\frac{3}{8}$ boxes of birdseed to feed the birds. By April only $2\frac{1}{2}$ boxes were left. How many boxes of birdseed did the birds at the pet store eat during one month?

★ **42.** Elliot worked for three days in the pet store for a total of $12\frac{1}{4}$ hours. On Monday he worked for $5\frac{1}{6}$ hours. On Tuesday he worked for $2\frac{1}{2}$ hours. How many hours did he work on the third day?

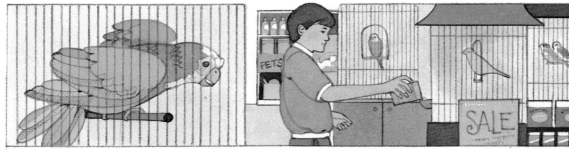

PROBLEM SOLVING • STRATEGIES

Missing Information

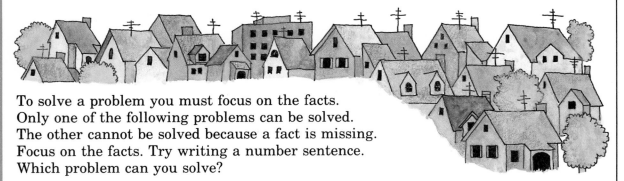

To solve a problem you must focus on the facts.
Only one of the following problems can be solved.
The other cannot be solved because a fact is missing.
Focus on the facts. Try writing a number sentence.
Which problem can you solve?

98 of 100 homes in the United States have at least one television set. What fraction of the homes do not have at least one television set?

Peg watched $2\frac{1}{2}$ hours of television on Saturday morning. Then she watched some more in the afternoon. How many hours of television did Peg watch in all?

Think:

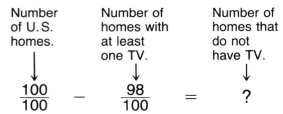

Number of U.S. homes.	Number of homes with at least one TV.	Number of homes that do not have TV.
$\frac{100}{100}$	$-$ $\frac{98}{100}$	$=$?

You have enough information. $\frac{2}{100}$ of the homes do not have television sets.

Think:

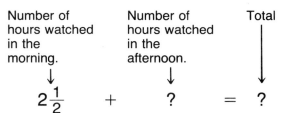

Number of hours watched in the morning.	Number of hours watched in the afternoon.	Total
$2\frac{1}{2}$	$+$?	$=$?

Information is missing. You need to know how many hours of television Peg watched in the afternoon.

Is there enough information to solve the problem? Write YES or NO.

1. The Ryan family watches $2\frac{1}{2}$ hours of television each day. The Walsch family watches 4 hours of television each day. How many more hours does the Walsch family watch television?

2. 48 of 100 of the homes in the United States have two or more television sets. What fraction of the homes have fewer than two television sets?

3. A variety show runs for $\frac{1}{2}$ hour. It is followed by a special show. How long will it take to view both shows?

Read the question. Think: Do I have all the information I need?

Solve if you have enough information. If not, tell what fact is missing.

4. One program is on television for $1\frac{1}{2}$ hours. Some of this time is used for commercials. What part of the program is not used for commercials?

5. A local television station shows a program for preschool children three times a week. The program is one hour long. How many hours is this program shown each week?

6. One-fourth of the people in the United States tuned in for a special sports show. One-third tuned in for a symphony. What fraction of the people in the United States tuned in for the sports show and the symphony?

Write a number sentence to help you decide if information is missing.

7. One television station in a city broadcasts 24 hours a day. Another station broadcasts for only part of each day. How much longer is the first station on the air each day?

8. $\frac{47}{100}$ of the homes with television receive 9 or more stations. What fraction of these homes receives only 9 stations?

9. John watches about $6\frac{1}{2}$ hours of educational television each week. Betty watches educational television for about $9\frac{3}{4}$ hours weekly. How many more hours of educational television does Betty watch?

10. A television magazine has television listings, advertisements, and articles. $\frac{2}{3}$ of the pages have television listings. What fraction of the pages is used for articles?

11. Adults watch $4\frac{1}{3}$ hours of television each day. Children between the ages of six and eleven watch less. How many more hours do adults watch television than 6-to-11-year olds.

12. A public television station broadcasts for 5 hours each weekday. How many hours less does it broadcast on weekends?

★ 13. Choose a number between 0 and $4\frac{1}{3}$. Use it to solve Exercise 11.

★ 14. Choose a number less than 5. Use it to solve Exercise 12.

REVIEW

Add. Write the answers in lowest terms. (pages 160–165)

1. $\dfrac{4}{6}$
$+\dfrac{1}{6}$

2. $\dfrac{1}{9}$
$+\dfrac{5}{9}$

3. $4\dfrac{1}{6}$
$+3\dfrac{1}{6}$

4. $\dfrac{1}{2}$
$+\dfrac{3}{8}$

5. $\dfrac{4}{5}$
$+\dfrac{1}{2}$

6. $1\dfrac{1}{4}$
$+2\dfrac{7}{12}$

7. $4\dfrac{7}{8}$
$+2\dfrac{2}{3}$

8. $3\dfrac{5}{6}$
$+1\dfrac{3}{4}$

Subtract. Write the answers in lowest terms. (pages 166–173)

9. $\dfrac{7}{10}$
$-\dfrac{2}{10}$

10. $\dfrac{3}{4}$
$-\dfrac{1}{4}$

11. $5\dfrac{6}{8}$
$-1\dfrac{4}{8}$

12. $4\dfrac{9}{10}$
$-2\dfrac{3}{10}$

13. $\dfrac{1}{2}$
$-\dfrac{2}{5}$

14. $\dfrac{9}{10}$
$-\dfrac{1}{4}$

15. $3\dfrac{2}{3}$
$-1\dfrac{1}{2}$

16. $6\dfrac{7}{12}$
$-2\dfrac{1}{3}$

17. 5
$-1\dfrac{1}{2}$

18. $3\dfrac{1}{4}$
$-\dfrac{3}{4}$

19. $7\dfrac{3}{8}$
$-2\dfrac{7}{8}$

20. $9\dfrac{7}{10}$
$-5\dfrac{9}{10}$

21. $2\dfrac{1}{3}$
$-1\dfrac{5}{6}$

22. $5\dfrac{1}{2}$
$-3\dfrac{5}{8}$

23. $8\dfrac{3}{4}$
$-2\dfrac{9}{10}$

24. $3\dfrac{1}{8}$
$-1\dfrac{1}{3}$

Solve.

25. Jacy hikes $\dfrac{1}{3}$ of the Pine Trail on Monday and $\dfrac{1}{2}$ of the trail on Tuesday. What part of the Pine Trail does he hike in those two days? (p. 162)

26. Lana picks $4\dfrac{1}{4}$ boxes of blueberries. Her family eats $1\dfrac{3}{4}$ boxes. How many boxes of blueberries are left? (pages 170–171)

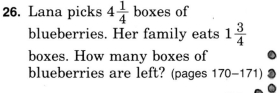

PROJECT

Stock Market

Here is how stock market prices are reported in newspapers. The dollar value of a share of stock is shown as a whole number or a mixed number.

The Change column shows the difference between yesterday's Last price and today's Last price.

A plus (+) in the Change column means the price went up. A minus (−) in the Change column means the price went down.

Stock	High	Low	Last	Change
AAK	45	44¼	44⅞	+ ⅛
ADQ	26⅜	25¼	25¼	+ 1⅝
BTG	51¼	49¼	50⅛	− 1⅛
Cing	34⅜	33⅞	34⅛	− ¼
ItF	45	45	45	.....
Mas	9½	9¼	9⅜	+ ¼
Sir	83¼	82¼	83¼	+ ¾
WIT	68	68	68	− 1

1. Today's High for one share of ADQ is $26\frac{3}{8}$. What is today's Low for one share of ADQ?

2. What is the difference between today's High price and today's Low price for one share of Cing?

Make a chart like the one below. Look up some stocks in a newspaper. You have $500 to spend. "Buy" only one share of any one stock. Use the Last price when you buy. "Sell" the stocks in one week. Use the Last price when you sell. Find your profit or loss.

Stock	Buy	Sell	Profit (Sell price higher)	Loss (Buy price higher)

TEST

Add. Write the answers in lowest terms.

1. $\frac{2}{8}$
$+\frac{4}{8}$

2. $\frac{1}{6}$
$+\frac{3}{6}$

3. $2\frac{6}{10}$
$+1\frac{2}{10}$

4. $\frac{1}{4}$
$+\frac{1}{2}$

5. $\frac{5}{8}$
$+\frac{1}{2}$

6. $2\frac{5}{12}$
$+1\frac{1}{3}$

7. $1\frac{3}{4}$
$+1\frac{5}{12}$

8. $3\frac{1}{8}$
$+5\frac{5}{6}$

Subtract. Write the answers in lowest terms.

9. $\frac{5}{6}$
$-\frac{2}{6}$

10. $\frac{3}{8}$
$-\frac{1}{8}$

11. $7\frac{7}{12}$
$-2\frac{2}{12}$

12. $3\frac{8}{10}$
$-1\frac{3}{10}$

13. $\frac{7}{9}$
$-\frac{2}{3}$

14. $\frac{3}{5}$
$-\frac{1}{2}$

15. $4\frac{2}{5}$
$-1\frac{1}{8}$

16. $5\frac{5}{6}$
$-4\frac{1}{3}$

17. 7
$-5\frac{1}{6}$

18. 6
$-3\frac{3}{10}$

19. $8\frac{1}{4}$
$-6\frac{3}{4}$

20. $5\frac{2}{5}$
$-1\frac{4}{5}$

21. $4\frac{3}{4}$
$-1\frac{7}{8}$

22. $6\frac{3}{5}$
$-2\frac{5}{6}$

23. $3\frac{1}{3}$
$-1\frac{1}{2}$

24. $5\frac{3}{10}$
$-2\frac{1}{3}$

Solve.

25. The grocer orders $7\frac{3}{4}$ cases of whole milk and $5\frac{1}{2}$ cases of lowfat milk. How many cases of milk does the grocer order in all?

26. There are 2 crates of apples at the store. $\frac{1}{4}$ of a crate is sold in the morning. How many crates of apples are left?

Time Zones

Mary's office is in Seattle. At 10:00 A.M. she calls John at the branch office in Chicago. He is at lunch.
What did Mary forget?

There are 24 time zones throughout the world.
Seattle is in the Pacific Time Zone.
Chicago is in the Central Time Zone.

The clocks show that when it is 10:00 A.M. in the Pacific Time Zone,
it is   11:00 A.M. in the Mountain Time Zone.
         12:00 Noon in the Central Time Zone.
         1:00 P.M. in the Eastern Time Zone.

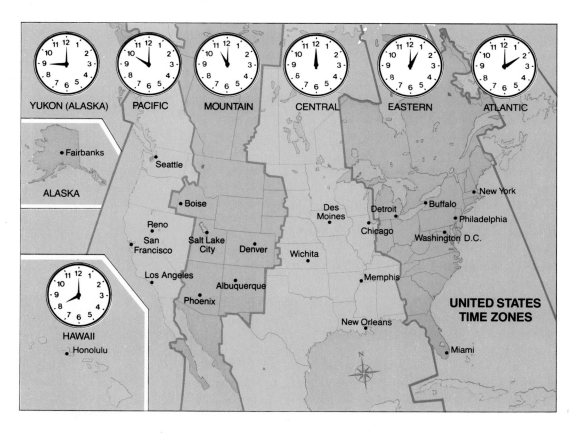

Mary forgot about the time difference.
When it is 10:00 A.M. in Seattle, it is 12:00 Noon in Chicago.

It is 8:45 A.M. in Memphis. What time is it in

1. Washington, D.C.?   **2.** Boise?   **3.** New Orleans?   **4.** Reno?

It is 12:00 midnight in Albuquerque. What time is it in

5. Des Moines? **6.** Honolulu? **7.** Los Angeles? **8.** Buffalo?

It is 9:15 P.M. in Washington, D.C. What time is it in

9. Wichita? **10.** Miami? **11.** Fairbanks? **12.** Salt Lake City?

13. A flight from Boston to San Francisco takes 6 hours. It leaves Boston at 8:00 P.M. What time will the flight arrive in San Francisco?

14. Bruce works at the Miami office. At 10:00 A.M. he decides to call Fred at the Phoenix branch. He knows the office opens at 9:00 A.M. How long must he wait to place the call?

15. Nigan leaves Salt Lake City at noon. He takes a $3\frac{1}{2}$ hour flight to Detroit. What time is it in Detroit when he arrives? Should he turn his watch forward or backward? By how many hours?

16. It is 1:30 A.M., May 8, in Wichita. What is the time and date in Fairbanks?

New York	London	Peking	Sydney
9:00 A.M.	2:00 P.M.	10:00 P.M.	12:00 Midnight

It is 5:00 A.M. in New York. What time is it in

17. London? **18.** Peking? **19.** Sydney?

20. It is 5:00 P.M., August 25, in London. What is the time and date in Sydney?

COMPUTER

Computer Cycle Time

Data-processing equipment is useful because it works very fast. Time is measured in a computer by means of an *internal clock.* The speed of a computer is usually measured in relation to cycle time. *Cycle time* is the amount of time for one tick of the computer's internal clock. At each internal clock tick, data move from one place to another inside the computer. In the time of one internal clock tick, a bit can turn from on to off. Today the fastest internal clock ticks eighty million times per second.

The smallest piece of a computer is a *switch* that turns a bit on or off. A switch is said to *change states* when it is turned on or off. Today an ordinary switch can change states eighty million times per second.

A *Josephson junction* is a special switch with an even faster switching time. It can change states 167,000,000,000 times in a second. That is an enormous number of times. To get an idea of that number of times, imagine that you started counting long ago. You started counting in ancient Egypt, in 3300 B.C. You counted once every second. You counted once every second through the 5,200 years before the turn of the twentieth century. You would still have to count, once every second, to the year 1995. (How old will you be?) By then you would count to 167,000,000,000. The Josephson junction changes states that many times in *one* second.

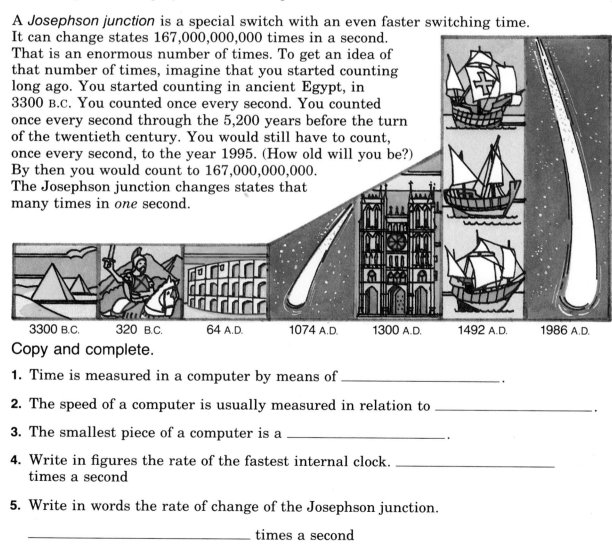

| 3300 B.C. | 320 B.C. | 64 A.D. | 1074 A.D. | 1300 A.D. | 1492 A.D. | 1986 A.D. |

Copy and complete.

1. Time is measured in a computer by means of _____ .

2. The speed of a computer is usually measured in relation to _____ .

3. The smallest piece of a computer is a _____ .

4. Write in figures the rate of the fastest internal clock. _____ times a second

5. Write in words the rate of change of the Josephson junction.

_____ times a second

SKILLS MAINTENANCE
Chapters 1 Through 7

Choose the correct answers.

1. Estimate. Round to the nearest thousand.

   7,398
   +2,503

   A. 9,500
   B. 10,000
   C. 9,000
   D. not here

2. Add.

   $397.49
   + 85.57

   A. $472.06
   B. $472.96
   C. $383.06
   D. not here

3. Subtract.

   $408.24
   − 39.95

   A. $368.29
   B. $378.39
   C. $368.39
   D. not here

4. Multiply.

   $27.95
   × 38

   A. $992.10
   B. $1,071.70
   C. $1,062.10
   D. not here

5. Divide.

   $16)\overline{\$63.52}$

   A. $3.67
   B. $3.97
   C. $3.90
   D. not here

6. Find the least common multiple.

   6, 8

   A. 2
   B. 48
   C. 24
   D. not here

7. Find an equivalent fraction.

   $\frac{5}{6} = \frac{?}{30}$

   A. 25
   B. 30
   C. 5
   D. not here

8. Add. Write the answer in lowest terms.

   $5\frac{2}{5} + 3\frac{1}{4} = \underline{\ ?\ }$

   A. $8\frac{3}{9}$
   B. $8\frac{7}{20}$
   C. $8\frac{13}{20}$
   D. not here

9. Subtract. Write the answer in lowest terms.

   $4\frac{5}{8} - 2\frac{1}{3} = \underline{\ ?\ }$

   A. $2\frac{4}{24}$
   B. $2\frac{4}{5}$
   C. $2\frac{7}{24}$
   D. not here

10. Sally works as a cashier two nights each week. On Tuesday she works $2\frac{3}{4}$ hours. On Wednesday she works $3\frac{1}{3}$ hours. What is the total number of hours Sally worked in one week?

    A. $5\frac{1}{12}$
    B. $6\frac{1}{12}$
    C. $5\frac{4}{12}$
    D. not here

11. Elia drives $12\frac{3}{5}$ miles to attend college. He drives $4\frac{1}{2}$ miles to the public library. How many miles farther did he drive to college than to the library?

    A. $8\frac{1}{10}$
    B. $8\frac{11}{20}$
    C. $17\frac{1}{10}$
    D. not here

Fractions: Multiplication and Division

CHAPTER

8

Multiplication • Multiplying Fractions and Whole Numbers • Multiplying Mixed Numbers • Reciprocals • Division • Dividing Fractions and Whole Numbers • Dividing Fractions and Mixed Numbers • Problem Solving: Too Much Information • Mail-Order Forms • Writing a Product in Lowest Terms

Multiplication

One-half of a garden is planted with flowers. One-fourth of the flower garden is planted with daisies. How much of the garden is planted with daisies?

What number is $\frac{1}{4}$ of $\frac{1}{2}$?

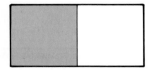

The garden is separated into 2 equal parts.

$$\frac{1}{2}$$

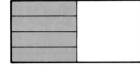

The flower garden is separated into 4 equal parts.

$$\frac{1}{4} \text{ of } \frac{1}{2}$$

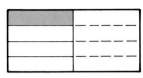

1 part is 1 of 8 equal parts.

$$\frac{1}{4} \text{ of } \frac{1}{2} \text{ is } \frac{1}{8}.$$

You can also multiply the fractions to find the answer.

$$\frac{1}{4} \times \frac{1}{2} = ?$$

Step 1
Multiply the numerators.

$$\frac{1}{4} \times \frac{1}{2} = \frac{1}{}$$

Step 2
Multiply the denominators.

$$\frac{1}{4} \times \frac{1}{2} = \frac{1}{8}$$

$\frac{1}{8}$ of the garden is planted with daisies.

Practice • Use the drawings to complete the sentences.

1.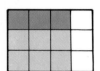

$\frac{1}{3}$ of $\frac{3}{4}$ is ___?___

2.

$\frac{1}{2}$ of $\frac{1}{5}$ is ___?___

3.

$\frac{3}{4}$ of $\frac{2}{3}$ is ___?___

Multiply. Write the answers in lowest terms.

4. $\frac{1}{5} \times \frac{1}{4} =$ ___?___

5. $\frac{1}{6} \times \frac{5}{8} =$ ___?___

6. $\frac{2}{5} \times \frac{1}{2} =$ ___?___

7. $\frac{3}{7} \times \frac{2}{5} =$ ___?___

8. $\frac{1}{4} \times \frac{8}{9} =$ ___?___

9. $\frac{3}{5} \times \frac{2}{9} =$ ___?___

Mixed Practice • Use the drawings to complete the sentences.

10.

$\frac{1}{3}$ of $\frac{1}{5}$ is ___?___

11.

$\frac{2}{3}$ of $\frac{1}{5}$ is ___?___

12.

$\frac{1}{4}$ of $\frac{3}{4}$ is ___?___

13.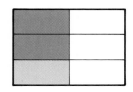

$\frac{2}{3}$ of $\frac{1}{2}$ is ___?___

14.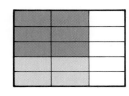

$\frac{3}{5}$ of $\frac{2}{3}$ is ___?___

15.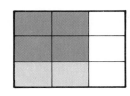

$\frac{2}{3}$ of $\frac{2}{3}$ is ___?___

Multiply. Write the answers in lowest terms.

16. $\frac{1}{2} \times \frac{6}{7} =$ ___?___

17. $\frac{1}{9} \times \frac{3}{10} =$ ___?___

18. $\frac{2}{3} \times \frac{4}{7} =$ ___?___

19. $\frac{8}{9} \times \frac{7}{11} =$ ___?___

20. $\frac{5}{6} \times \frac{8}{11} =$ ___?___

21. $\frac{1}{5} \times \frac{2}{5} =$ ___?___

22. $\frac{1}{3} \times \frac{3}{5} =$ ___?___

23. $\frac{2}{5} \times \frac{3}{5} =$ ___?___

24. $\frac{2}{3} \times \frac{1}{4} =$ ___?___

25. $\frac{2}{5} \times \frac{3}{4} =$ ___?___

26. $\frac{8}{9} \times \frac{2}{7} =$ ___?___

27. $\frac{1}{3} \times \frac{3}{4} =$ ___?___

★ **28.** $\frac{1}{2} \times \frac{2}{3} \times \frac{1}{4} =$ ___?___

★ **29.** $\frac{4}{5} \times \frac{2}{3} \times \frac{1}{8} =$ ___?___

★ **30.** $\frac{3}{4} \times \frac{5}{8} \times \frac{2}{5} =$ ___?___

PROBLEM SOLVING • APPLICATIONS

31. Asia makes up about $\frac{3}{10}$ of the land surface of the earth. The Soviet Union is about $\frac{1}{2}$ of Asia. What part of the land surface of the earth is the Soviet Union?

32. North America makes up about $\frac{1}{6}$ of the land surface of the earth. Canada is about $\frac{2}{5}$ of North America. What part of the land surface of the earth is Canada?

★ **33.** About $\frac{7}{10}$ of the earth's surface is covered by water. About $\frac{1}{4}$ of the water is the Atlantic Ocean. What part of the earth's water is not the Atlantic Ocean?

Skills Maintenance

1. $\frac{4}{16} = \frac{?}{4}$

2. $\frac{6}{30} = \frac{?}{5}$

3. $\frac{22}{40} = \frac{?}{20}$

4. $\frac{8}{14} = \frac{?}{7}$

5. $\frac{9}{?} = \frac{1}{4}$

6. $\frac{12}{36} = \frac{?}{9}$

7. $\frac{45}{63} = \frac{?}{21}$

8. $\frac{14}{?} = \frac{7}{12}$

9. $\frac{14}{44} = \frac{?}{22}$

10. $\frac{7}{10} = \frac{?}{50}$

Multiplying Fractions and Whole Numbers

Peter spends $\frac{3}{4}$ hour each day on his hobby. How many hours does he spend on his hobby in 5 days?

$$5 \times \frac{3}{4} = ?$$

Step 1
Write the whole number as a fraction. $\longrightarrow \frac{5}{1} \times \frac{3}{4} = ?$

Step 2
Multiply the numerators. $\longrightarrow \frac{5}{1} \times \frac{3}{4} = \frac{15}{}$

Step 3
Multiply the denominators. $\longrightarrow \frac{5}{1} \times \frac{3}{4} = \frac{15}{4}$

Step 4
Write a mixed number for the answer. $\longrightarrow \frac{5}{1} \times \frac{3}{4} = \frac{15}{4} = 3\frac{3}{4}$

He spends $3\frac{3}{4}$ hours on his hobby in 5 days.

More Examples

$$\frac{5}{12} \times 8 = \frac{5}{12} \times \frac{8}{1} = \frac{40}{12} = 3\frac{4}{12} = 3\frac{1}{3} \qquad 12 \times \frac{5}{6} = \frac{12}{1} \times \frac{5}{6} = \frac{60}{6} = 10$$

Practice • Multiply. Write the answers in lowest terms.

1. $7 \times \frac{1}{2} = $ _?_

2. $6 \times \frac{2}{5} = $ _?_

3. $\frac{2}{3} \times 9 = $ _?_

4. $\frac{5}{12} \times 5 = $ _?_

5. $4 \times \frac{1}{8} = $ _?_

6. $\frac{4}{5} \times 8 = $ _?_

Mixed Practice • Multiply. Write the answers in lowest terms.

7. $\frac{3}{4} \times 15 = $ _?_

8. $8 \times \frac{5}{8} = $ _?_

9. $\frac{2}{3} \times 18 = $ _?_

10. $9 \times \frac{1}{2} = $ _?_

11. $16 \times \frac{2}{3} = $ _?_

12. $\frac{5}{8} \times 9 = $ _?_

13. $\frac{3}{4} \times 32 =$ ___?___

14. $\frac{3}{8} \times 64 =$ ___?___

15. $\frac{5}{8} \times 13 =$ ___?___

16. $\frac{1}{20} \times 20 =$ ___?___

17. $27 \times \frac{2}{3} =$ ___?___

18. $\frac{5}{6} \times \frac{2}{3} =$ ___?___

19. $\frac{2}{3} \times 15 =$ ___?___

20. $\frac{7}{12} \times 9 =$ ___?___

21. $\frac{4}{5} \times 10 =$ ___?___

22. $\frac{6}{8} \times \frac{3}{4} =$ ___?___

23. $10 \times \frac{3}{5} =$ ___?___

24. $9 \times \frac{5}{6} =$ ___?___

25. $\frac{2}{7} \times 14 =$ ___?___

26. $\frac{2}{5} \times \frac{1}{2} =$ ___?___

27. $8 \times \frac{7}{10} =$ ___?___

★ 28. $20 \times \frac{2}{5} \times \frac{3}{10} =$ ___?___

★ 29. $\frac{1}{3} \times 9 \times \frac{2}{5} =$ ___?___

★ 30. $\frac{4}{9} \times 5 \times \frac{1}{6} =$ ___?___

Use this table to answer questions 31 through 38.

1 year (yr) = 12 months (mo)
2 years (yr) = 24 months (mo)
$\frac{1}{2}$ year (yr) = 6 months (mo)

Complete.

31. 5 yr = ___?___ mo

32. 10 yr = ___?___ mo

33. 100 yr = ___?___ mo

34. $\frac{1}{4}$ yr = ___?___ mo

35. $\frac{1}{3}$ yr = ___?___ mo

36. $\frac{1}{6}$ yr = ___?___ mo

37. $\frac{3}{4}$ yr = ___?___ mo

38. $\frac{2}{3}$ yr = ___?___ mo

PROBLEM SOLVING • APPLICATIONS

Peter spends $108 to build his racer. The circle graph shows how he spends his money.

39. How much money does Peter spend for wire?

40. What does he spend for tires?

41. How much money does he spend for tools?

★ 42. How much more money does Peter spend on wood than on tires?

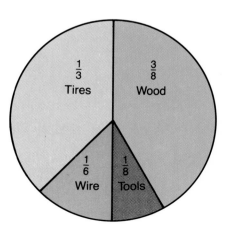

187

Multiplying Mixed Numbers

Marge works $5\frac{1}{3}$ hours every Saturday. She spends $\frac{3}{8}$ of this time making deliveries. How many hours does Marge spend making deliveries?

$$\frac{3}{8} \times 5\frac{1}{3} = ?$$

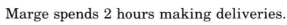

Step 1 Write the mixed number as a fraction.	$\frac{3}{8} \times \frac{16}{3} = ?$
Step 2 Multiply the numerators.	$\frac{3}{8} \times \frac{16}{3} = \frac{48}{}$
Step 3 Multiply the denominators.	$\frac{3}{8} \times \frac{16}{3} = \frac{48}{24}$
Step 4 Write the answer in lowest terms.	$\frac{3}{8} \times \frac{16}{3} = \frac{48}{24} = 2$

Marge spends 2 hours making deliveries.

More Examples

$4 \times 1\frac{2}{3} = ?$

$2\frac{1}{2} \times 1\frac{3}{4} = ?$

$3\frac{1}{4} \times 1\frac{1}{3} = ?$

$\frac{4}{1} \times \frac{5}{3} = ?$

$\frac{5}{2} \times \frac{7}{4} = ?$

$\frac{13}{4} \times \frac{4}{3} = ?$

$\frac{4}{1} \times \frac{5}{3} = \frac{20}{3} = 6\frac{2}{3}$

$\frac{5}{2} \times \frac{7}{4} = \frac{35}{8} = 4\frac{3}{8}$

$\frac{13}{4} \times \frac{4}{3} = \frac{52}{12} = 4\frac{4}{12} = 4\frac{1}{3}$

Practice • Multiply. Write the answers in lowest terms.

1. $\frac{1}{2} \times 3\frac{1}{2} = $ _____?_____

2. $5\frac{1}{3} \times 1\frac{1}{8} = $ _____?_____

3. $6\frac{2}{3} \times 3\frac{1}{4} = $ _____?_____

4. $2\frac{2}{5} \times \frac{7}{12} = $ _____?_____

5. $\frac{4}{5} \times 3\frac{1}{4} = $ _____?_____

6. $1\frac{3}{4} \times 2 = $ _____?_____

7. $4\frac{1}{3} \times \frac{3}{5} = $ _____?_____

8. $2\frac{5}{6} \times 8 = $ _____?_____

9. $1\frac{1}{3} \times 2\frac{1}{4} = $ _____?_____

More Practice • Multiply. Write the answers in lowest terms.

10. $3\frac{1}{4} \times 2\frac{2}{7} = $ _____?_____

11. $3 \times 2\frac{2}{3} = $ _____?_____

12. $\frac{2}{3} \times 3\frac{1}{2} = $ _____?_____

13. $\frac{1}{5} \times 2\frac{1}{2} = $ _____?_____

14. $4\frac{7}{8} \times 1\frac{1}{3} = $ _____?_____

15. $1\frac{3}{4} \times \frac{1}{2} = $ _____?_____

16. $3\frac{1}{2} \times 2\frac{1}{7} =$ ___?___

17. $\frac{2}{3} \times 4\frac{1}{2} =$ ___?___

18. $5 \times 1\frac{3}{4} =$ ___?___

19. $1\frac{1}{4} \times \frac{3}{5} =$ ___?___

20. $7\frac{4}{5} \times \frac{1}{3} =$ ___?___

21. $5\frac{1}{4} \times \frac{1}{7} =$ ___?___

22. $2\frac{1}{2} \times 2\frac{1}{2} =$ ___?___

23. $2\frac{1}{4} \times \frac{2}{3} =$ ___?___

24. $5\frac{3}{10} \times 1\frac{1}{4} =$ ___?___

25. $\frac{3}{4} \times 2 =$ ___?___

26. $1\frac{3}{8} \times 7 =$ ___?___

27. $\frac{1}{2} \times 1\frac{2}{5} =$ ___?___

28. $2\frac{1}{3} \times 6\frac{1}{2} =$ ___?___

29. $7\frac{1}{2} \times \frac{2}{5} =$ ___?___

30. $\frac{4}{5} \times \frac{1}{6} =$ ___?___

31. $\frac{4}{5} \times 10\frac{1}{2} =$ ___?___

32. $16 \times 8\frac{1}{2} =$ ___?___

33. $\frac{1}{3} \times 2\frac{1}{2} =$ ___?___

★ 34. $1\frac{1}{6} \times \frac{3}{7} \times 4\frac{2}{3} =$ ___?___

★ 35. $4 \times \frac{3}{5} \times 1\frac{3}{4} =$ ___?___

★ 36. $\frac{3}{4} \times 6\frac{1}{7} \times 2\frac{1}{3} =$ ___?___

PROBLEM SOLVING • APPLICATIONS

Write the answers in lowest terms.

37. There are $\frac{2}{3}$ dozen oranges in each bag. Marge delivers 4 bags of oranges. How many dozen oranges is that?

★ 38. It takes Raoul $1\frac{1}{4}$ hours to get to work. $\frac{1}{3}$ of this time is spent riding a train. How many minutes does he spend on the train?

★ 39. Raoul works at the store $3\frac{1}{2}$ hours on Friday and $5\frac{3}{4}$ hours on Saturday. $\frac{2}{5}$ of his time is spent stocking shelves. How many hours does he spend stocking shelves?

★ 40. Sharon works $4\frac{1}{4}$ hours on Friday, $5\frac{2}{3}$ hours on Saturday, and $1\frac{1}{2}$ hours on Sunday. $\frac{1}{3}$ of her time is spent taking inventory. How many hours does she spend taking inventory?

Midchapter Review

Multiply. Write the answers in lowest terms.

1. $\frac{2}{3} \times \frac{4}{5} =$ ___?___

2. $\frac{3}{4} \times \frac{2}{9} =$ ___?___

3. $6 \times \frac{2}{3} =$ ___?___

4. $\frac{5}{6} \times 11 =$ ___?___

5. $2\frac{1}{2} \times \frac{3}{4} =$ ___?___

6. $1\frac{1}{6} \times \frac{4}{7} =$ ___?___

7. $4\frac{2}{3} \times \frac{1}{2} =$ ___?___

8. $2\frac{3}{4} \times 1\frac{3}{5} =$ ___?___

9. $3 \times 2\frac{1}{3} =$ ___?___

Reciprocals

$$\frac{1}{3} \times \frac{3}{1} = \frac{3}{3} = 1 \qquad\qquad \frac{2}{5} \times \frac{5}{2} = \frac{10}{10} = 1$$

$$\frac{8}{3} \times \frac{3}{8} = \frac{24}{24} = 1 \qquad\qquad \frac{9}{1} \times \frac{1}{9} = \frac{9}{9} = 1$$

The product of each pair of factors is 1.
Two numbers are **reciprocals** when their product is 1.

Find the reciprocal of $\frac{3}{4}$, of $2\frac{4}{5}$, and of 6.

To find the reciprocal of $\longrightarrow$	$\frac{3}{4}$	$2\frac{4}{5}$	6
Step 1 Write the number as a fraction. $\longrightarrow$	$\frac{3}{4}$	$\frac{14}{5}$	$\frac{6}{1}$
Step 2 Exchange the numerator and the denominator. $\longrightarrow$	$\frac{4}{3}$	$\frac{5}{14}$	$\frac{1}{6}$

Practice • Find the reciprocals.

1. $\frac{3}{4}$
2. 2
3. $\frac{1}{7}$
4. $\frac{7}{2}$
5. $3\frac{3}{4}$
6. $10\frac{1}{3}$

7. $1\frac{1}{2}$
8. $\frac{2}{3}$
9. 8
10. $9\frac{2}{5}$
11. $\frac{6}{7}$
12. $\frac{15}{11}$

Mixed Practice • Find the reciprocals.

13. $\frac{2}{7}$
14. $1\frac{1}{3}$
15. $\frac{1}{8}$
16. 5
17. $\frac{5}{8}$
18. $\frac{7}{20}$

19. $12\frac{1}{2}$
20. $4\frac{1}{3}$
21. $\frac{8}{7}$
22. $\frac{1}{10}$
23. 9
24. $5\frac{2}{5}$

25. $\frac{25}{16}$
26. $\frac{5}{6}$
27. $3\frac{1}{16}$
28. $2\frac{1}{4}$
29. $\frac{3}{100}$
30. $3\frac{1}{7}$

31. $\frac{1}{2}$
32. $1\frac{3}{8}$
33. $\frac{9}{10}$
34. 4
35. $2\frac{4}{9}$
36. 7

Find the missing factors. If an answer is greater than 1, write it as a mixed number.

37. $\underline{\quad?\quad} \times \frac{4}{5} = 1$

38. $2\frac{1}{3} \times \underline{\quad?\quad} = 1$

39. $\underline{\quad?\quad} \times 3 = 1$

40. $1\frac{7}{10} \times \underline{\quad?\quad} = 1$

41. $\underline{\quad?\quad} \times \frac{3}{8} = 1$

42. $2\frac{5}{8} \times \underline{\quad?\quad} = 1$

43. $\underline{\quad?\quad} \times 6 = 1$

44. $3\frac{3}{4} \times \underline{\quad?\quad} = 1$

45. $\underline{\quad?\quad} \times \frac{5}{6} = 1$

46. $6\frac{2}{3} \times \underline{\quad?\quad} = 1$

47. $\underline{\quad?\quad} \times 9 = 1$

48. $8\frac{2}{9} \times \underline{\quad?\quad} = 1$

49. $\underline{\quad?\quad} \times \frac{9}{4} = 1$

50. $5\frac{1}{5} \times \underline{\quad?\quad} = 1$

51. $1\frac{3}{5} \times \underline{\quad?\quad} = 1$

★ **52.** $\frac{3}{8} \times \underline{\quad?\quad} = 4$

★ **53.** $\underline{\quad?\quad} \times 1\frac{1}{4} = 7$

★ **54.** $\underline{\quad?\quad} \times \frac{2}{7} = 3$

Use this table to answer questions 55 through 63.

1 day (d) = 24 hours (h)
2 days (d) = 48 hours (h)
$\frac{1}{2}$ day (d) = 12 hours (h)

Complete.

55. 7 d = $\underline{\quad?\quad}$ h

56. 30 d = $\underline{\quad?\quad}$ h

57. 365 d = $\underline{\quad?\quad}$ h

58. $\frac{1}{4}$ d = $\underline{\quad?\quad}$ h

59. $\frac{1}{3}$ d = $\underline{\quad?\quad}$ h

60. $\frac{1}{6}$ d = $\underline{\quad?\quad}$ h

61. $\frac{3}{4}$ d = $\underline{\quad?\quad}$ h

62. $\frac{2}{3}$ d = $\underline{\quad?\quad}$ h

63. $\frac{5}{6}$ d = $\underline{\quad?\quad}$ h

PROBLEM SOLVING • APPLICATIONS

64. Josh spent $\frac{1}{3}$ day raking leaves. How many hours did he rake leaves?

65. Julia was on a boat for $2\frac{1}{2}$ days. How many hours was that?

★ **66.** Mona practices playing the piano for 3 hours. Pat practices playing the guitar for $\frac{1}{6}$ of a day. Who practices longer?

★ **67.** José and Andy start working at 9:00 A.M. José works for 7 hours. Andy works for $\frac{1}{4}$ day. Who leaves work earlier?

Division

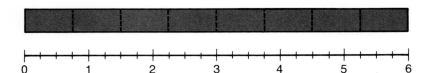

Brian is making bird feeders. He has a strip of wood that is 6 feet long. How many pieces $\frac{3}{4}$ foot long can he cut from the strip? (Count to find how many.)

$$6 \div \frac{3}{4} = 8 \qquad\qquad 6 \times \frac{4}{3} = 8$$

reciprocals

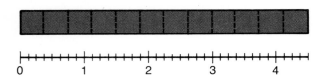

This strip of wood is $4\frac{1}{2}$ feet long. How many pieces $\frac{3}{8}$ foot long can Brian cut from the strip? (Count to find how many.)

$$\frac{9}{2} \div \frac{3}{8} = 12 \qquad\qquad \frac{9}{2} \times \frac{8}{3} = 12$$

reciprocals

To divide with fractions, multiply by the reciprocal of the divisor.

$$\frac{3}{5} \div \frac{4}{3} = \frac{3}{5} \times \frac{3}{4} = \frac{9}{20}$$

reciprocals

Practice • Copy and complete. Write the answers in lowest terms.

1. $\frac{1}{5} \div \frac{2}{3} = \frac{1}{5} \times \frac{3}{2} = \underline{\ ?\ }$

2. $\frac{3}{4} \div \frac{1}{2} = \frac{3}{4} \times \frac{2}{1} = \underline{\ ?\ }$

3. $\frac{8}{9} \div \frac{1}{3} = \frac{8}{9} \times \frac{3}{1} = \underline{\ ?\ }$

4. $\frac{4}{5} \div \frac{5}{6} = \frac{4}{5} \times \frac{?}{?} \quad \underline{\ ?\ }$

5. $\frac{5}{8} \div \frac{1}{4} = \frac{5}{8} \times \frac{?}{?} \quad \underline{\ ?\ }$

6. $\frac{7}{8} \div \frac{3}{4} = \frac{7}{8} \times \frac{?}{?} \quad \underline{\ ?\ }$

Divide. Write the answers in lowest terms.

7. $\frac{1}{8} \div \frac{4}{3} = \underline{\ ?\ }$

8. $\frac{6}{7} \div \frac{7}{6} = \underline{\ ?\ }$

9. $\frac{1}{2} \div \frac{2}{3} = \underline{\ ?\ }$

Mixed Practice • Divide. Write the answers in lowest terms.

10. $\frac{5}{6} \div \frac{2}{9} =$ ___?___

11. $\frac{7}{3} \div \frac{5}{6} =$ ___?___

12. $\frac{3}{2} \div \frac{4}{3} =$ ___?___

13. $\frac{3}{8} \div \frac{1}{4} =$ ___?___

14. $\frac{3}{4} \div \frac{1}{3} =$ ___?___

15. $\frac{5}{8} \div \frac{2}{3} =$ ___?___

16. $\frac{5}{4} \div \frac{3}{2} =$ ___?___

17. $\frac{2}{3} \div \frac{5}{6} =$ ___?___

18. $\frac{7}{2} \div \frac{3}{8} =$ ___?___

19. $\frac{4}{5} \div \frac{1}{3} =$ ___?___

20. $\frac{7}{2} \div \frac{3}{2} =$ ___?___

21. $\frac{11}{3} \div \frac{5}{6} =$ ___?___

22. $\frac{3}{4} \div \frac{1}{16} =$ ___?___

23. $\frac{10}{3} \div \frac{5}{6} =$ ___?___

24. $\frac{7}{8} \div \frac{1}{4} =$ ___?___

25. $\frac{10}{8} \div \frac{2}{9} =$ ___?___

26. $\frac{3}{4} \div \frac{1}{6} =$ ___?___

27. $\frac{1}{6} \div \frac{2}{9} =$ ___?___

★ 28. $\left(5 + \frac{1}{2}\right) \div \frac{3}{5} =$ ___?___

★ 29. $\left(2\frac{2}{3} + \frac{1}{2}\right) \div \frac{3}{8} =$ ___?___

★ 30. $\left(\frac{5}{8} \times \frac{3}{4}\right) \div \frac{3}{8} =$ ___?___

Use the table to answer questions 31 through 39.

1 hour (h) = 60 minutes (min)
2 hours (h) = 120 minutes (min)
$\frac{1}{2}$ hour (h) = 30 minutes (min)

Complete.

31. 8 h = ___?___ min

32. 12 h = ___?___ min

33. 24 h = ___?___ min

34. $\frac{1}{4}$ h = ___?___ min

35. $\frac{3}{4}$ h = ___?___ min

36. $\frac{1}{3}$ h = ___?___ min

37. $\frac{1}{20}$ h = ___?___ min

38. $1\frac{1}{2}$ h = ___?___ min

39. $2\frac{1}{2}$ h = ___?___ min

What are the next two numbers in the pattern?

★ 40.

$\frac{1}{3}$	$\frac{1}{6}$	$\frac{1}{12}$	?	?

★ 41.

$\frac{3}{4}$	1	$1\frac{1}{4}$	?	?

PROBLEM SOLVING • APPLICATIONS

Write the answers in lowest terms.

42. Brian has $\frac{7}{8}$ can of wood stain. It takes $\frac{1}{12}$ can to stain one bird feeder. How many bird feeders can Brian stain?

43. Now Brian is ready to fill his bird feeders. He has $4\frac{1}{2}$ bags of birdseed. Each feeder holds $\frac{3}{4}$ bag of birdseed. How many bird feeders can he fill?

Dividing Fractions and Whole Numbers

$\frac{3}{4}$ of a shipment of oil is pumped into 9 storage tanks. An equal amount of oil is pumped into each tank. What part of the shipment is in each tank?

$$\frac{3}{4} \div 9 = ?$$

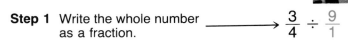

Step 1 Write the whole number as a fraction. $\longrightarrow \frac{3}{4} \div \frac{9}{1}$

Step 2 Rewrite as a multiplication problem. $\longrightarrow \frac{3}{4} \div \frac{9}{1} = \frac{3}{4} \times \frac{1}{9}$

Step 3 Multiply. $\longrightarrow \frac{3}{4} \div \frac{9}{1} = \frac{3}{4} \times \frac{1}{9} = \frac{3}{36}$

Step 4 Write the answer in lowest terms. $\longrightarrow \frac{3}{4} \div \frac{9}{1} = \frac{3}{4} \times \frac{1}{9} = \frac{3}{36} = \frac{1}{12}$

$\frac{1}{12}$ of the shipment is in each storage tank.

Divide: $6 \div \frac{2}{3}$.

Step 1 Write the whole number as a fraction. $\longrightarrow \frac{6}{1} \div \frac{2}{3}$

Step 2 Rewrite as a multiplication problem. $\longrightarrow \frac{6}{1} \div \frac{2}{3} = \frac{6}{1} \times \frac{3}{2}$

Step 3 Multiply. $\longrightarrow \frac{6}{1} \div \frac{2}{3} = \frac{6}{1} \times \frac{3}{2} = \frac{18}{2}$

Step 4 Write the answer in lowest terms. $\longrightarrow \frac{6}{1} \div \frac{2}{3} = \frac{6}{1} \times \frac{3}{2} = \frac{18}{2} = 9$

Practice • Divide. Write the answers in lowest terms.

1. $\frac{1}{10} \div 3 = \underline{\ ?\ }$

2. $\frac{8}{9} \div 8 = \underline{\ ?\ }$

3. $4 \div \frac{3}{5} = \underline{\ ?\ }$

4. $\frac{4}{5} \div 8 = \underline{\ ?\ }$

5. $9 \div \frac{3}{4} = \underline{\ ?\ }$

6. $\frac{1}{5} \div 7 = \underline{\ ?\ }$

More Practice • Divide. Write the answers in lowest terms.

7. $\frac{9}{10} \div 2 = $?

8. $\frac{5}{6} \div 5 = $?

9. $\frac{3}{8} \div 4 = $?

10. $10 \div \frac{10}{9} = $?

11. $2 \div \frac{9}{7} = $?

12. $7 \div \frac{2}{9} = $?

13. $\frac{3}{7} \div 8 = $?

14. $\frac{7}{2} \div 6 = $?

15. $\frac{4}{3} \div 2 = $?

16. $5 \div \frac{2}{3} = $?

17. $7 \div \frac{1}{2} = $?

18. $\frac{1}{2} \div \frac{3}{4} = $?

19. $\frac{2}{3} \div 4 = $?

20. $\frac{1}{10} \div \frac{5}{6} = $?

21. $\frac{1}{6} \div 2 = $?

22. $6 \div \frac{3}{4} = $?

23. $4 \div \frac{1}{3} = $?

24. $15 \div \frac{1}{5} = $?

25. $\frac{5}{9} \div 5 = $?

26. $\frac{2}{5} \div 2 = $?

27. $\frac{3}{8} \div \frac{2}{3} = $?

★ **28.** $\left(\frac{1}{2} + \frac{2}{3} \right) \div \frac{7}{8} = $?

★ **29.** $\left(5 \div \frac{3}{4} \right) \div \frac{2}{3} = $?

★ **30.** $9 \div \left(3 \div \frac{5}{3} \right) = $?

PROBLEM SOLVING • APPLICATIONS

Write the answers in lowest terms.

31. It takes a worker $\frac{5}{12}$ hour to check a section of pipeline for minor leaks. How many sections of pipeline can the worker check in 10 hours?

32. A pipe is leaking 1 liter of oil every $\frac{5}{6}$ hour. How many liters will it leak in 20 hours?

33. $\frac{1}{3}$ of each barrel of crude oil becomes fuel oil. How many barrels of crude oil are needed to make 60 barrels of fuel oil?

Skills Maintenance

1. $\begin{array}{r} \$3.64 \\ \times\ \ \ 8 \\ \hline \end{array}$

2. $\begin{array}{r} \$9.07 \\ \times\ \ \ 9 \\ \hline \end{array}$

3. $\begin{array}{r} \$8.59 \\ \times\ \ \ 4 \\ \hline \end{array}$

4. $\begin{array}{r} \$5.76 \\ \times\ \ \ 7 \\ \hline \end{array}$

5. $\begin{array}{r} \$9.87 \\ \times\ \ \ 3 \\ \hline \end{array}$

6. $\begin{array}{r} \$26.50 \\ \times\ \ \ 16 \\ \hline \end{array}$

7. $\begin{array}{r} \$18.55 \\ \times\ \ \ 23 \\ \hline \end{array}$

8. $\begin{array}{r} \$19.95 \\ \times\ \ \ 48 \\ \hline \end{array}$

9. $\begin{array}{r} \$37.08 \\ \times\ \ \ 29 \\ \hline \end{array}$

10. $\begin{array}{r} \$43.28 \\ \times\ \ \ 17 \\ \hline \end{array}$

195

Dividing Fractions and Mixed Numbers

Marian and her club help at a nursery school. Marian is making window ornaments out of plastic bottles. Each bottle holds $\frac{3}{4}$ pitcher of colored water. She has $3\frac{3}{4}$ pitchers of water. How many bottles can she fill?

$$3\frac{3}{4} \div \frac{3}{4} = ?$$

Step 1 Write the mixed number as a fraction. $\longrightarrow$ $\frac{15}{4} \div \frac{3}{4}$

Step 2 Rewrite as a multiplication problem. $\longrightarrow$ $\frac{15}{4} \div \frac{3}{4} = \frac{15}{4} \times \frac{4}{3}$

Step 3 Multiply. $\longrightarrow$ $\frac{15}{4} \div \frac{3}{4} = \frac{15}{4} \times \frac{4}{3} = \frac{60}{12}$

Step 4 Write the answer in lowest terms. $\longrightarrow$ $\frac{15}{4} \div \frac{3}{4} = \frac{15}{4} \times \frac{4}{3} = \frac{60}{12} = 5$

She can fill 5 bottles.

Divide: $2\frac{1}{2} \div 3\frac{1}{3}$.

Step 1 Write the mixed numbers as fractions. $\longrightarrow$ $\frac{5}{2} \div \frac{10}{3}$

Step 2 Rewrite as a multiplication problem. $\longrightarrow$ $\frac{5}{2} \div \frac{10}{3} = \frac{5}{2} \times \frac{3}{10}$

Step 3 Multiply. $\longrightarrow$ $\frac{5}{2} \div \frac{10}{3} = \frac{5}{2} \times \frac{3}{10} = \frac{15}{20}$

Step 4 Write the answer in lowest terms. $\longrightarrow$ $\frac{5}{2} \div \frac{10}{3} = \frac{5}{2} \times \frac{3}{10} = \frac{15}{20} = \frac{3}{4}$

Practice • Divide. Write the answers in lowest terms.

1. $2\frac{1}{3} \div \frac{3}{7} = \underline{\quad?\quad}$

2. $\frac{2}{3} \div 3\frac{1}{5} = \underline{\quad?\quad}$

3. $2\frac{1}{2} \div 1\frac{2}{3} = \underline{\quad?\quad}$

4. $3\frac{1}{5} \div \frac{2}{5} = \underline{\quad?\quad}$

5. $1\frac{1}{2} \div \frac{5}{6} = \underline{\quad?\quad}$

6. $\frac{1}{3} \div 4\frac{1}{2} = \underline{\quad?\quad}$

Mixed Practice • Divide. Write the answers in lowest terms.

7. $2\frac{1}{7} \div \frac{2}{7} = $ ___?___

8. $4\frac{1}{3} \div \frac{2}{5} = $ ___?___

9. $\frac{4}{5} \div 3\frac{1}{2} = $ ___?___

10. $1\frac{5}{6} \div \frac{4}{5} = $ ___?___

11. $5\frac{1}{4} \div \frac{3}{10} = $ ___?___

12. $1\frac{3}{4} \div \frac{2}{9} = $ ___?___

13. $3\frac{1}{5} \div 3\frac{2}{5} = $ ___?___

14. $21 \div 2\frac{1}{3} = $ ___?___

15. $2\frac{2}{3} \div \frac{5}{9} = $ ___?___

16. $1\frac{2}{7} \div 2\frac{1}{4} = $ ___?___

17. $\frac{9}{10} \div \frac{3}{5} = $ ___?___

18. $\frac{4}{9} \div 1\frac{2}{3} = $ ___?___

19. $1\frac{1}{2} \div 3 = $ ___?___

20. $18 \div 6\frac{3}{4} = $ ___?___

21. $2\frac{1}{10} \div 1\frac{1}{5} = $ ___?___

22. $\frac{1}{2} \div \frac{1}{3} = $ ___?___

23. $1\frac{1}{3} \div 2\frac{1}{3} = $ ___?___

24. $18 \div 5\frac{1}{4} = $ ___?___

★ 25. $1\frac{1}{4} \div $ ___?___ $ = \frac{1}{2}$

★ 26. $1\frac{1}{3} \div $ ___?___ $ = \frac{8}{15}$

★ 27. $2\frac{2}{5} \div $ ___?___ $ = \frac{3}{5}$

★ 28. $2\frac{1}{3} \div $ ___?___ $ = 4$

★ 29. $12 \div $ ___?___ $ = 21$

★ 30. $\frac{3}{7} \div $ ___?___ $ = \frac{8}{21}$

Use the table to answer questions 31 through 39.

1 minute (min) =	60 seconds (s)
2 minutes (min) =	120 seconds (s)
$\frac{1}{2}$ minute (min) =	30 seconds (s)

Complete.

31. 10 min = ___?___ s

32. 30 min = ___?___ s

33. 60 min = ___?___ s

34. $\frac{1}{4}$ min = ___?___ s

35. $\frac{3}{4}$ min = ___?___ s

36. $\frac{1}{3}$ min = ___?___ s

37. $1\frac{1}{2}$ min = ___?___ s

38. $1\frac{2}{3}$ min = ___?___ s

39. $2\frac{1}{2}$ min = ___?___ s

PROBLEM SOLVING • **APPLICATIONS**

Write the answers in lowest terms.

40. It takes each club member $1\frac{3}{4}$ hours to assemble an alphabet book. How many books can a member assemble in $10\frac{1}{2}$ hours?

41. Marian's group has 8 jars of dry beans to make bean bags for the children. It takes $1\frac{1}{3}$ jars to fill each bean bag. How many bean bags can they fill?

PROBLEM SOLVING • STRATEGIES

Too Much Information

To answer a question you must find the important facts.

Find the facts that you need to answer this question.

Question: How many cans of paint does Mr. Harrison use to paint the lawn chairs?

Facts: Mr. Harrison paints the back door.
Mr. Harrison uses $\frac{1}{4}$ can of paint on one lawn chair.
Mr. Harrison buys 4 cans of paint.
Mr. Harrison paints 5 lawn chairs.

These are the facts you need:

Mr. Harrison uses $\frac{1}{4}$ can of paint on one lawn chair.
Mr. Harrison paints 5 lawn chairs.

You multiply to find the answer.

$$5 \times \frac{1}{4} = \frac{5}{4} = 1\frac{1}{4}$$

Mr. Harrison uses $1\frac{1}{4}$ cans of paint.

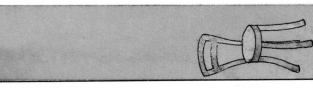

Which facts do you need to answer each question?

1. How many customers does Mr. Harrison have?

   He has 3 customers that live in Woodcliff. Mr. Harrison lives 3 blocks away from the paint store. He has 8 customers that live in Marshall. He has 4 customers that live in Riverside.

   _____

   Read all the facts carefully.

   _____

2. How many hours does Mr. Harrison work each week at his part-time job?

   Mr. Harrison works 3 days each week at his part-time job. It takes $2\frac{1}{2}$ hours for Mr. Harrison to prepare his garden for planting. Mr. Harrison works $4\frac{1}{2}$ hours each day at his part-time job. Mr. Harrison spends $1\frac{1}{4}$ hours buying groceries.

Answer the questions. Use only the facts you need.

3. How many hours does Mr. Harrison spend painting window frames at the Tuckers' house?

   It takes $\frac{3}{4}$ hour to paint one window frame. Mr. Harrison buys 5 cans of paint. Mr. Harrison spends 3 hours repairing the Tuckers' fence. Mr. Harrison paints 14 window frames at the Tuckers' house. Mr. Harrison paints 8 window frames at the Burkes' house.

Write a number sentence to help you solve the problem.

---

4. How much of the living room does Arlene paint?

   Mr. Harrison paints $\frac{1}{2}$ of the kitchen. Arlene paints $\frac{1}{4}$ of $\frac{1}{2}$ of the living room. Arlene paints the family room yellow. Mr. Harrison uses $\frac{1}{2}$ of his paint on the porch.

5. How many boards does Mr. Harrison use to repair the Shaws' deck?

   Mr. Harrison uses 4 boards to repair the east side of the Shaws' deck. There are 6 steps that need to be painted at the Shaw residence. Mr. Harrison uses 8 boards to repair the south side of the Shaws' deck. Mr. Harrison uses 12 boards to repair the Shaws' garage.

6. How many sections of fence can Mr. Harrison paint in 5 hours?

   The fence at the Burke house is 100 meters long. It takes $\frac{5}{6}$ hour to paint one section of fence. Mr. Harrison installs one new post in the fence. It takes $\frac{1}{2}$ hour to travel to this job.

7. How many tiles does Mr. Harrison use to repair the Beaumonts' roof?

   25 tiles are needed to repair the shed. There are 8 square meters of roof that need repair. Mr. Harrison worked for $10\frac{1}{2}$ hours to repair the roof. It takes 16 tiles to repair one square meter of roof.

8. How much material does Arlene use to make curtains for the windows?

   Arlene uses $2\frac{1}{3}$ meters of material for each curtain panel. It takes Arlene $1\frac{1}{4}$ hours to sew a curtain panel. There are 12 windows that need curtains. 20 panels are needed to make all the curtains.

★ 9. How many hours does Mr. Harrison spend clipping hedges at home?

   Mr. Harrison trims 6 sections of hedges across the front. He trims $2\frac{3}{4}$ sections of hedges along the side. It takes $\frac{3}{5}$ of an hour to trim one section of hedges. Mr. Harrison plants 3 small maple trees near his hedges.

★ 10. How much does Mr. Harrison charge Mr. Buchanan for repairing the backyard patio?

   It takes Mr. Harrison $7\frac{1}{2}$ hours to repair Mr. Buchanan's patio. Mr. Harrison repairs the front walk in $2\frac{3}{4}$ hours. Mr. Harrison earns $8.00 an hour. Mr. Harrison spends $7.50 on supplies for the patio repair.

199

Multiply. Write the answers in lowest terms. (pages 184–189)

1. $\frac{1}{3} \times \frac{5}{8} = \underline{\ ?\ }$

2. $\frac{2}{7} \times \frac{3}{4} = \underline{\ ?\ }$

3. $\frac{9}{10} \times \frac{1}{2} = \underline{\ ?\ }$

4. $\frac{3}{4} \times \frac{5}{6} = \underline{\ ?\ }$

5. $\frac{7}{8} \times \frac{4}{5} = \underline{\ ?\ }$

6. $\frac{2}{3} \times \frac{9}{16} = \underline{\ ?\ }$

7. $6 \times \frac{1}{4} = \underline{\ ?\ }$

8. $\frac{5}{6} \times 12 = \underline{\ ?\ }$

9. $9 \times \frac{2}{3} = \underline{\ ?\ }$

10. $\frac{2}{5} \times 3\frac{1}{2} = \underline{\ ?\ }$

11. $1\frac{1}{4} \times \frac{2}{3} = \underline{\ ?\ }$

12. $2\frac{3}{8} \times 4 = \underline{\ ?\ }$

13. $1\frac{1}{5} \times 2\frac{1}{3} = \underline{\ ?\ }$

14. $5\frac{5}{6} \times 1\frac{3}{5} = \underline{\ ?\ }$

15. $4\frac{1}{3} \times 3\frac{3}{8} = \underline{\ ?\ }$

Find the reciprocals. (pages 190–191)

16. $\frac{3}{4}$

17. $\frac{5}{2}$

18. 4

19. $2\frac{1}{3}$

20. $4\frac{4}{5}$

21. $\frac{21}{16}$

Divide. Write the answers in lowest terms. (pages 192–197)

22. $\frac{1}{7} \div \frac{2}{3} = \underline{\ ?\ }$

23. $\frac{3}{4} \div 1\frac{7}{8} = \underline{\ ?\ }$

24. $\frac{3}{8} \div \frac{1}{2} = \underline{\ ?\ }$

25. $\frac{3}{10} \div \frac{3}{5} = \underline{\ ?\ }$

26. $\frac{5}{6} \div \frac{2}{3} = \underline{\ ?\ }$

27. $\frac{7}{8} \div \frac{5}{6} = \underline{\ ?\ }$

28. $\frac{5}{6} \div 2 = \underline{\ ?\ }$

29. $10 \div \frac{5}{8} = \underline{\ ?\ }$

30. $12 \div \frac{2}{3} = \underline{\ ?\ }$

31. $1\frac{1}{3} \div \frac{1}{4} = \underline{\ ?\ }$

32. $3\frac{1}{2} \div \frac{7}{12} = \underline{\ ?\ }$

33. $\frac{7}{9} \div 2\frac{4}{5} = \underline{\ ?\ }$

34. $3\frac{1}{4} \div 6\frac{3}{8} = \underline{\ ?\ }$

35. $4\frac{2}{3} \div 4\frac{2}{3} = \underline{\ ?\ }$

36. $1\frac{5}{8} \div 1\frac{3}{10} = \underline{\ ?\ }$

Solve.

37. Toshi jogs $2\frac{1}{4}$ laps around the track. Ken jogs $\frac{1}{3}$ of this distance. How far does Ken jog? (p. 188)

38. Eric practices swimming 5 days a week. He swims the same amount each day. He swims a total of $8\frac{1}{4}$ hours each week. How much time does he swim each day? (p. 194)

PROJECT

Mail-Order Forms

You must fill out an order form to buy items from Mail-Order Gifts, Inc. Suppose you order these items.

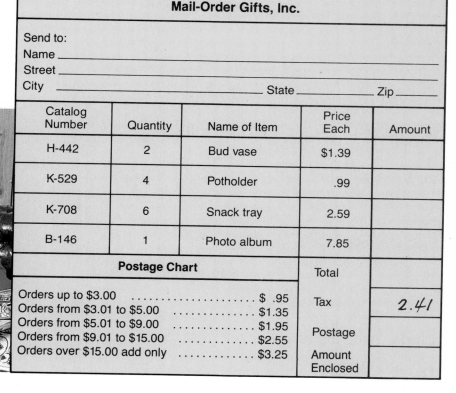

Mail-Order Gifts, Inc.

Send to:
Name _____
Street _____
City _____ State _____ Zip _____

Catalog Number	Quantity	Name of Item	Price Each	Amount
H-442	2	Bud vase	$1.39	
K-529	4	Potholder	.99	
K-708	6	Snack tray	2.59	
B-146	1	Photo album	7.85	

Postage Chart

Total	
Tax	2.41
Postage	
Amount Enclosed	

Orders up to $3.00 .... $ .95
Orders from $3.01 to $5.00 .... $1.35
Orders from $5.01 to $9.00 .... $1.95
Orders from $9.01 to $15.00 .... $2.55
Orders over $15.00 add only $3.25

Copy the order form. Then answer the questions.

1. Complete the top of the form. Use your name and address.

2. You order 2 bud vases. Each vase costs $1.39. Multiply to find how much 2 vases cost. Write the product in the Amount column. Complete the Amount column for the other items.

3. Add to find the total cost of the items. Write the sum in the Total box.

4. Use the Postage Chart. Write the correct amount in the Postage box.

5. Add to find the total amount that must be enclosed with this order. Write that amount in the Amount Enclosed box.

Find a mail-order catalog. Pretend you have $50.00 to spend. Fill out the order form. Then find the amount of money that must be enclosed with the order.

TEST

Multiply. Write the answers in lowest terms.

1. $\frac{4}{5} \times \frac{3}{8} =$ ___?___

2. $\frac{7}{10} \times \frac{5}{6} =$ ___?___

3. $\frac{5}{8} \times \frac{4}{5} =$ ___?___

4. $\frac{2}{5} \times \frac{5}{7} =$ ___?___

5. $\frac{2}{3} \times \frac{3}{4} =$ ___?___

6. $\frac{3}{8} \times \frac{4}{9} =$ ___?___

7. $9 \times \frac{1}{6} =$ ___?___

8. $\frac{2}{3} \times 15 =$ ___?___

9. $\frac{4}{5} \times 20 =$ ___?___

10. $\frac{1}{2} \times 5\frac{1}{4} =$ ___?___

11. $3\frac{3}{4} \times \frac{4}{5} =$ ___?___

12. $2\frac{2}{5} \times 5 =$ ___?___

13. $1\frac{3}{5} \times 2\frac{1}{8} =$ ___?___

14. $4\frac{2}{7} \times 2\frac{1}{10} =$ ___?___

15. $9\frac{1}{3} \times 1\frac{5}{7} =$ ___?___

Find the reciprocals.

16. $\frac{2}{3}$

17. $\frac{7}{3}$

18. 6

19. $3\frac{1}{4}$

20. $5\frac{6}{7}$

21. $\frac{35}{13}$

Divide. Write the answers in lowest terms.

22. $\frac{3}{10} \div \frac{1}{2} =$ ___?___

23. $\frac{11}{12} \div \frac{3}{4} =$ ___?___

24. $\frac{5}{8} \div \frac{7}{12} =$ ___?___

25. $\frac{7}{8} \div \frac{3}{4} =$ ___?___

26. $\frac{5}{6} \div \frac{3}{8} =$ ___?___

27. $\frac{3}{10} \div \frac{9}{5} =$ ___?___

28. $\frac{7}{9} \div 7 =$ ___?___

29. $\frac{2}{5} \div 6 =$ ___?___

30. $10 \div \frac{2}{5} =$ ___?___

31. $\frac{2}{3} \div 3\frac{1}{3} =$ ___?___

32. $1\frac{3}{4} \div \frac{5}{6} =$ ___?___

33. $2\frac{5}{8} \div \frac{3}{4} =$ ___?___

34. $4\frac{1}{2} \div 2\frac{2}{3} =$ ___?___

35. $3\frac{5}{8} \div 1\frac{1}{2} =$ ___?___

36. $6\frac{4}{5} \div 5\frac{2}{3} =$ ___?___

Solve.

37. A mechanic spends $2\frac{3}{4}$ hours tuning up each car. He has 3 cars to tune up. How long will it take him to finish the cars?

38. Mrs. Devon uses $4\frac{4}{5}$ cans of oil each time she changes the oil in her car. How many oil changes can she make with 24 cans of oil?

Writing a Product in Lowest Terms

This is a shortcut for finding the lowest term for a product.

$$\frac{4}{7} \times \frac{5}{6} = ?$$

Step 1

The numerator and the denominator have the common factor of 2. Divide each by 2.

$$\frac{\overset{2}{4}}{7} \times \frac{5}{\underset{3}{6}} = ?$$

$$\frac{4}{9} \times \frac{3}{8} = ?$$

Step 1

Look for common factors. Divide 4 and 8 by 4. Divide 9 and 3 by 3.

$$\frac{\overset{1}{4}}{\underset{3}{9}} \times \frac{\overset{1}{3}}{\underset{2}{8}} = ?$$

Step 2

Multiply: $\frac{2 \times 5}{7 \times 3} = \frac{10}{21}$.

$$\frac{\overset{2}{4}}{7} \times \frac{5}{\underset{3}{6}} = \frac{10}{21}$$

Step 2

Multiply: $\frac{1 \times 1}{3 \times 2} = \frac{1}{6}$.

$$\frac{\overset{1}{4}}{\underset{3}{9}} \times \frac{\overset{1}{3}}{\underset{2}{8}} = \frac{1}{6}$$

Multiply. Use the shortcut.

1. $\frac{4}{15} \times \frac{10}{28} = \underline{}$

2. $\frac{7}{12} \times \frac{8}{21} = \underline{}$

3. $\frac{9}{10} \times \frac{25}{21} = \underline{}$

4. $\frac{5}{12} \times \frac{3}{10} = \underline{}$

5. $\frac{3}{4} \times \frac{20}{27} = \underline{}$

6. $\frac{3}{8} \times \frac{8}{9} = \underline{}$

7. $\frac{5}{8} \times \frac{6}{15} = \underline{}$

8. $\frac{9}{15} \times \frac{7}{9} = \underline{}$

9. $\frac{7}{8} \times \frac{12}{14} = \underline{}$

10. $3\frac{3}{7} \times 2\frac{1}{6} = \underline{}$

11. $1\frac{3}{4} \times 4\frac{4}{5} = \underline{}$

12. $3\frac{1}{3} \times 6\frac{3}{7} = \underline{}$

COMPUTER

Computer Storage Density

A computer can process large amounts of data in the form of numbers or letters. *Storage density* measures the amount of data that can be stored in a small area. *Speed* is the most important feature of the computer. Storage density is the next most important feature. If every computer were the size of an entire building, not many people could afford to own one. A calculator displays eight or nine numbers in about one square inch of space. The storage density for a calculator display is nine digits per square inch. The storage density of this page is about 80 characters per square inch. The storage density of newspaper print is about 130 characters per square inch.

Microcomputers today have memories that store 400,000 bits per square inch. Remember that computers store one character in eight bits of storage. Researchers are studying a way to get 625,000,000,000 bits per square inch. The method, called *spectral memory*, involves laser technology using a spectrum of 1,000 colors. It will not be available for many years.

An encyclopedia may have 125 characters on each of 80 lines of print per page. Each page of an encyclopedia thus can contain about 10,000 characters. Large encyclopedias may have 30 volumes of 1,000 pages each, or 30,000 pages. So an encyclopedia holds about 300,000,000 characters, or 2,400,000,000 bits. Spectral memory will be able to hold 260 encyclopedias in one square inch. If you lined up 260 encyclopedias, they would stretch four football fields.

Copy and complete.

1. A computer processes large amounts of _____.

2. _____ is a measure of the amount of data stored in a space.

3. Computers store one character in _____ bits of storage.

4. A new laser method of high-density storage is called _____.

5. Spectral memory may store _____ bits per square inch.

6. Write the number, above, in words. _____

7. Write the number of bits in an encyclopedia in words. _____

_____

SKILLS MAINTENANCE
Chapters 1 Through 8

Choose the correct answers.

1. Complete.

5,968 ⬤ 6,986

- **A.** >
- **B.** <
- **C.** =
- **D.** not here

2. Add.

2,397
482
1,531
+   48

- **A.** 4,358
- **B.** 3,458
- **C.** 4,458
- **D.** not here

3. Subtract.

$42{,}813 - 6{,}928 = $ __?__

- **A.** 34,885
- **B.** 35,885
- **C.** 34,995
- **D.** not here

4. Multiply.

$341 \times 528 = $ __?__

- **A.** 17,480
- **B.** 178,048
- **C.** 179,048
- **D.** not here

5. Divide.

$138\overline{)52{,}195}$

- **A.** 397 r11
- **B.** 378 r31
- **C.** 313 r1
- **D.** not here

6. Write 36 as a product of prime factors.

- **A.** $3 \times 3 \times 4$
- **B.** $1 \times 3 \times 3 \times 2$
- **C.** $2 \times 2 \times 3 \times 3$
- **D.** not here

7. Find the greatest common factor of 12 and 18.

- **A.** 2
- **B.** 3
- **C.** 36
- **D.** not here

8. Write $\frac{38}{7}$ as a mixed number.

- **A.** $5\frac{3}{7}$
- **B.** $7\frac{3}{8}$
- **C.** $6\frac{2}{7}$
- **D.** not here

9. Add.

$7\frac{3}{5}$
$+4\frac{2}{8}$

- **A.** $12\frac{3}{20}$
- **B.** $11\frac{6}{13}$
- **C.** $11\frac{17}{20}$
- **D.** not here

10. Subtract.

$4\frac{3}{10}$
$-1\frac{3}{4}$

- **A.** $2\frac{1}{2}$
- **B.** $3\frac{7}{40}$
- **C.** $2\frac{11}{20}$
- **D.** not here

11. Multiply.

$\frac{2}{5} \times \frac{3}{4} = $ __?__

- **A.** $\frac{5}{9}$
- **B.** $\frac{3}{10}$
- **C.** $1\frac{3}{20}$
- **D.** not here

12. Divide.

$\frac{5}{8} \div \frac{1}{4} = $ __?__

- **A.** $\frac{5}{32}$
- **B.** $2\frac{1}{2}$
- **C.** $\frac{7}{8}$
- **D.** not here

Skills Maintenance continued

Choose the correct answers.

13. Johnny buys track shoes for $49.95, jeans for $35.29, and a denim jacket for $47.50. How much does he spend?

    A. $131.74   **B.** $132.64
    C. $121.74   **D.** not here

14. Ruby buys a purse for $17.85 and a dress for $34.29. How much change will she receive from a $100 bill?

    A. $47.86   **B.** $52.14
    C. $48.96   **D.** not here

15. Mr. O'Dwyer collects trading stamps. Each booklet can be filled with 85 stamps. How many stamps does he need to fill 35 booklets?

    A. 2,855   **B.** 2,955
    C. 2,975   **D.** not here

16. Becton Oil Company employs 76 clerical workers. A total of $13,224 was paid out in salary to the clerical workers in one week. What average weekly salary did each person earn?

    A. $168.22   **B.** $174.00
    C. $192.50   **D.** not here

17. Jenny attends classes for $2\frac{1}{3}$ hours on Tuesday, $3\frac{3}{4}$ hours on Wednesday, and $4\frac{1}{2}$ hours on Friday. What is the total number of hours she attends classes each week?

    A. $9\frac{7}{12}$ **B.** $10\frac{5}{12}$
    C. $10\frac{2}{3}$ **D.** not here

18. Sean jogs $5\frac{3}{10}$ miles. Jessie jogs $4\frac{4}{5}$ miles. How many more miles does Sean jog?

    A. $\frac{1}{2}$ **B.** $1\frac{1}{2}$
    C. $1\frac{1}{5}$ **D.** not here

19. A farmer sets aside $\frac{4}{5}$ of his land for growing crops. He plants corn on $\frac{1}{3}$ of this land. What part of the land has been set aside for corn?

    A. $\frac{7}{15}$ **B.** $1\frac{2}{15}$
    C. $\frac{4}{15}$ **D.** not here

20. John types one page of a report in $\frac{4}{10}$ hour. How many pages can he type in 5 hours?

    A. $\frac{4}{50}$ **B.** $12\frac{1}{2}$
    C. 2   **D.** not here

Decimals: Addition and Subtraction

Tenths and Hundredths • Thousandths • Place
Value • Comparing and Ordering Decimals
• Rounding Decimals • Adding Decimals • Problem
Solving: Take a Second Look • Subtracting
Decimals • Problem Solving: Writing Checks
• Balancing the Checkbook

Tenths and Hundredths

A square is divided into 10 parts of the same size.
Each part is one tenth of the square.

The shaded part may be named by a fraction or by a decimal.

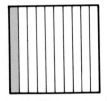 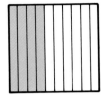

fraction   **decimal**
↓   ↓

$\frac{1}{10} = 0.1$ $\frac{4}{10} = 0.4$

one-tenth   four-tenths

You can use place value to show tenths.

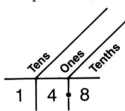

Read → fourteen and eight-tenths

Write → 14.8

Each tenth is divided into 10 parts of the same size.
Each part is one hundredth of the square.

The shaded part may be named by a fraction or by a decimal.

fraction   **decimal**
↓   ↓

$\frac{1}{100} = 0.01$ $\frac{27}{100} = 0.27$

one-hundredth   twenty-seven hundredths

You can use place value to show hundredths.

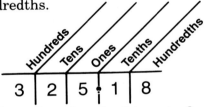

Read → three hundred twenty-five and eighteen-hundredths

Write → 325.18

Practice • Write the decimals that tell how much is blue.

1.   2.   3.   4.

Write the decimals.

5. $\frac{3}{10}$ 6. $14\frac{8}{10}$ 7. $\frac{15}{100}$ 8. $89\frac{67}{100}$ 9. $9\frac{6}{100}$ 10. $5\frac{4}{100}$

11. nine-tenths   12. fourteen-hundredths   13. six and one-tenth

Mixed Practice • Write the decimals.

14. $\frac{5}{10}$ 15. $\frac{8}{10}$ 16. $\frac{4}{100}$ 17. $17\frac{38}{100}$ 18. $4\frac{2}{10}$ 19. $6\frac{9}{100}$

20. $\frac{28}{100}$ 21. $\frac{9}{10}$ 22. $\frac{2}{10}$ 23. $\frac{16}{100}$ 24. $\frac{23}{100}$ 25. $7\frac{1}{10}$

26. $6\frac{5}{100}$ 27. $\frac{4}{10}$ 28. 87   29. $98\frac{1}{100}$ 30. $10\frac{49}{108}$ 31. $42\frac{7}{10}$

32. nine-hundredths

33. fifty-six and four-tenths

34. five thousand and fifty-four hundredths

35. three hundred seven and eighty-two hundredths

36. seven-tenths

37. eight hundred forty and twelve-hundredths

Write the decimals in words.

38. 146.1

39. 49.72

40. 7.03

41. 34.8

42. 14.01

43. 374.75

44. 9,010.6

45. 3,552.07

Tenths can be shown on the number line.

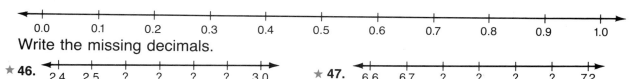

Write the missing decimals.

★ 46.   2.4 2.5 ? ? ? ? 3.0

★ 47.   6.6 6.7 ? ? ? ? 7.2

Complete the patterns.

48. 0.1 0.2 0.3 0.4 0.5 ___?___ ___?___ ___?___ ___?___ ___?___ ___?___

49. 0.91 0.92 0.93 ___?___ ___?___ ___?___ ___?___ ___?___ ___?___ ___?___ ___?___

★ 50. 1.0 1.3 1.6 1.9 2.2 ___?___ ___?___ ___?___ ___?___ ___?___ ___?___

★ 51. 10.7 10.3 9.9 9.5 9.1 ___?___ ___?___ ___?___ ___?___ ___?___ ___?___

★ 52. 14.98 14.83 14.68 ___?___ ___?___ ___?___ ___?___ ___?___ ___?___ ___?___ ___?___

PROBLEM SOLVING • APPLICATIONS

Write the decimals.

53. A sheet of paper is about twenty-nine thousandths of an inch thick.

54. The width of a chapter is one and three-hundredths of an inch.

Thousandths

There are 1,000 boxes in this grid.

Each box is $\frac{1}{1,000}$ of the grid.

$$\frac{1}{1,000} = 0.001$$

one-thousandth

235 of the boxes are green.

What part of the grid is green?

$$\frac{235}{1,000} = 0.235$$

two hundred thirty-five thousandths

Two hundred thirty-five thousandths of the grid is green.

You can use place value to show thousandths.

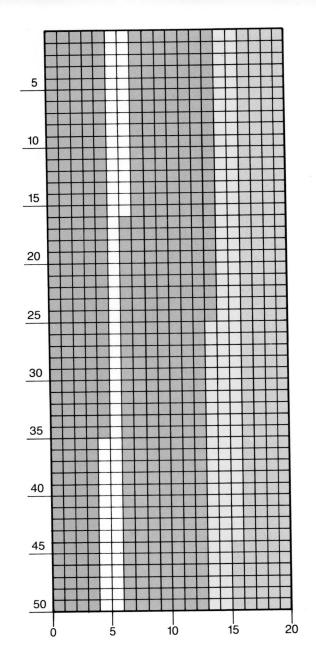

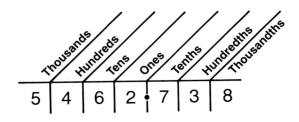

Read → five thousand, four hundred sixty-two and seven hundred thirty-eight thousandths

Write → 5,462.738

Practice • Write the decimals.

1. $\frac{895}{1,000}$ 2. $3\frac{48}{1,000}$ 3. $16\frac{7}{1,000}$ 4. $107\frac{136}{1,000}$ 5. $2,325\frac{95}{1,000}$ 6. $445\frac{20}{1,000}$

7. twenty-seven thousandths

8. twelve and nineteen-thousandths

9. nine-thousandths

10. five hundred and sixteen-thousandths

Mixed Practice • Write the decimals.

11. $\frac{328}{1,000}$ 12. $7\frac{17}{1,000}$ 13. $438\frac{4}{1,000}$ 14. $8,421\frac{39}{1,000}$ 15. $\frac{92}{1,000}$

16. $200\frac{7}{1,000}$ 17. $3\frac{26}{1,000}$ 18. $205\frac{60}{1,000}$ 19. $7,234\frac{14}{1,000}$ 20. $\frac{3}{1,000}$

21. $8\frac{98}{100}$ 22. $15\frac{20}{100}$ 23. $560\frac{1}{10}$ 24. $8,516\frac{23}{100}$ 25. $\frac{565}{1,000}$

26. $2\frac{9}{1,000}$ 27. $3,535\frac{432}{1,000}$ 28. $96\frac{40}{1,000}$

29. five-thousandths   30. forty-three thousandths

31. six thousand, thirty-eight and ten-thousandths

32. seven hundred ninety-six and fifty-two hundredths

33. twenty thousand, four hundred and three hundred seven-thousandths

Complete the patterns.

★ 34. 3.988 3.993 3.998 __?__ __?__ __?__ __?__ __?__

★ 35. 2.064 2.056 2.048 __?__ __?__ __?__ __?__ __?__

Use the three digits and a decimal point to write 18 different numbers.

★ 36. 6 4 8   ★ 37. 1 2 4   ★ 38. 7 3 5   ★ 39. 9 6 1

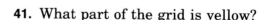

PROBLEM SOLVING • APPLICATIONS

Use the grid on page 210 to answer the questions.
Write the answer as a decimal.

40. What part of the grid is blue?   41. What part of the grid is yellow?

42. What part of the grid is red?   43. What part of the grid is white?

Skills Maintenance

Write >, <, or =.

1. $\frac{1}{3}$ ● $\frac{1}{9}$ 2. $\frac{3}{4}$ ● $\frac{2}{5}$ 3. $\frac{2}{3}$ ● $\frac{5}{9}$ 4. $\frac{7}{10}$ ● $\frac{5}{6}$ 5. $\frac{3}{4}$ ● $\frac{7}{9}$

6. $\frac{6}{10}$ ● $\frac{3}{5}$ 7. $\frac{3}{8}$ ● $\frac{5}{9}$ 8. $\frac{7}{8}$ ● $\frac{2}{3}$ 9. $\frac{7}{9}$ ● $\frac{5}{8}$ 10. $\frac{3}{4}$ ● $\frac{5}{6}$

Place Value

Each place in a decimal number has a value

    10 times the value of the place at its right,

    $\frac{1}{10}$ the value of the place at its left.

A digit in different places names different numbers.

The chart shows how 5 can name different numbers according to its place.

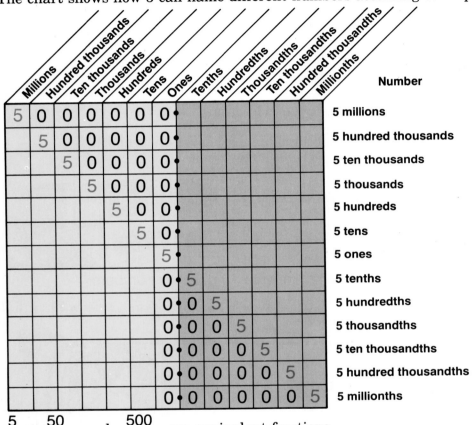

Millions	Hundred thousands	Ten thousands	Thousands	Hundreds	Tens	Ones	Tenths	Hundredths	Thousandths	Ten thousandths	Hundred thousandths	Millionths	Number
5	0	0	0	0	0	0							5 millions
	5	0	0	0	0	0							5 hundred thousands
		5	0	0	0	0							5 ten thousands
			5	0	0	0							5 thousands
				5	0	0							5 hundreds
					5	0							5 tens
						5							5 ones
						0	5						5 tenths
						0	0	5					5 hundredths
						0	0	0	5				5 thousandths
						0	0	0	0	5			5 ten thousandths
						0	0	0	0	0	5		5 hundred thousandths
						0	0	0	0	0	0	5	5 millionths

$\frac{5}{10}$, $\frac{50}{100}$, and $\frac{500}{1,000}$ are equivalent fractions.

Decimals that name the same number are **equivalent decimals**.

$$0.5 = 0.50 = 0.500$$
$$1.7 = 1.70 = 1.700$$

Practice • In what place is each blue digit?

1. 25.613   **2.** 37.946   **3.** 54.258   **4.** 246.088   **5.** 63.472

What number does each blue digit name?

6. 92.851   **7.** 30.789   **8.** 26.735   **9.** 343.004   **10.** 582.341

Mixed Practice • In which place is each blue digit?

11. 1.936   **12.** 21.483   **13.** 498.325   **14.** 6,432.363   **15.** 9.548

16. 5.042   **17.** 54.971   **18.** 135.006   **19.** 3,535.198   **20.** 3,384.212

What number does each blue digit name?

21. 2.672   **22.** 85.304   **23.** 548.652   **24.** 3,005.235   **25.** 54.208

26. 9.585   **27.** 27.216   **28.** 415.806   **29.** 7,723.008   **30.** 621.742

31. 4.684   **32.** 43.301   **33.** 540.016   **34.** 4,716.695   **35.** 6,584.271

In which number does the digit 5 have the greatest value?

36. 26.5   **37.** 16.526   **38.** 432.153   **39.** 8,451.77   **40.** 3,764.051
    265   15.626   432.5   8,541.77   3,764.005

Write decimals that name the same number.

41. $0.6 = 0.60 = \underline{\quad?\quad}$ **42.** $1.5 = 1.50 = \underline{\quad?\quad}$ **43.** $41.3 = 41.30 = \underline{\quad?\quad}$

44. $3.7 = \underline{\quad?\quad} = 3.700$ **45.** $\underline{\quad?\quad} = 2.80 = 2.800$ **46.** $\underline{\quad?\quad} = 95.20 = 95.200$

47. $9.1 = \underline{\quad?\quad} = \underline{\quad?\quad}$ **48.** $\underline{\quad?\quad} = \underline{\quad?\quad} = 5.100$ **49.** $67.5 = \underline{\quad?\quad} = \underline{\quad?\quad}$

★ **50.** $8.45 = \underline{\quad?\quad} = \underline{\quad?\quad}$ ★ **51.** $\underline{\quad?\quad} = 2.640 = \underline{\quad?\quad}$ ★ **52.** $95.29 = \underline{\quad?\quad} = \underline{\quad?\quad}$

★ **53.** $\underline{\quad?\quad} = 5.360 = \underline{\quad?\quad}$ ★ **54.** $3.76 = \underline{\quad?\quad} = \underline{\quad?\quad}$ ★ **55.** $\underline{\quad?\quad} = 32.890 = \underline{\quad?\quad}$

Use the digits 1 through 9. Use each digit only once.
Name the largest number possible for each.

★ **56.** ____ ____ . ____ ____   ★ **57.** ____ . ____ ____ ____   ★ **58.** ____ ____ ____ . ____

Name the smallest number possible for each.

★ **59.** ____ ____ . ____   ★ **60.** ____ ____ ____ ____   ★ **61.** ____ . ____ ____ ____

PROBLEM SOLVING • **APPLICATIONS**

★ **62.** Write the decimal that has 5 in the hundreds place, 4 in the hundredths place, 0 in the tens place, 6 in the tenths place, 6 in the ones place, and 2 in the thousandths place.

★ **63.** Write the decimal that has 9 in the ones place, 4 in the hundredths place, 3 in the hundreds place, 0 in the tenths place, 1 in the tens place, and 6 in the thousandths place.

Comparing and Ordering Decimals

A speed skater raced 500 meters
in 39.44 seconds. Another skater
raced 500 meters in 39.17 seconds.

Compare the decimals.
Use $>$, $<$, or $=$ to make a true sentence.

39.44 **39.17**

Think:
Same number of tens,
same number of ones.
Compare the tenths:
  $4 > 1$.

So, $39.44 > 39.17$.

Compare the decimals.

0.41 **0.415**

Think:
$0.41 = 0.410$
Compare 0.410 and 0.415.
Same number of tenths,
same number of hundredths.
Compare the thousandths:
  $0 < 5$.

So $0.410 < 0.415$.

Put these other speed-skating times
in order from least to greatest.

  43.4   40.2   43.1

Think: $40.2 < 43.1$
       $43.1 < 43.4$

So $40.2 < 43.1 < 43.4$.

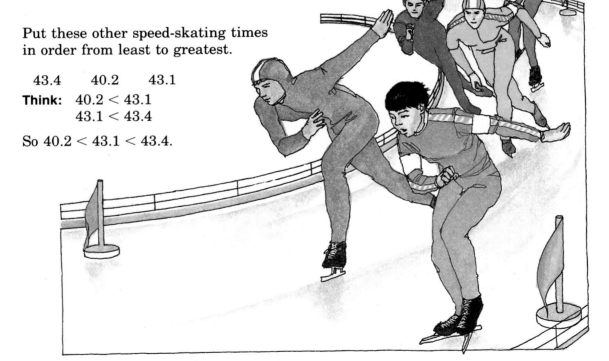

Practice • Write $>$, $<$, or $=$.

1. 0.22 0.37

2. 8.01 8.1

3. 92.6 92.56

4. 0.273 2.73

5. 6.75 6.7

6. 46.41 4.64

7. 0.964 0.97

8. 9.98 9.980

9. 72.03 72.3

Mixed Practice • Write >, <, or =.

10. 19.85 ● 18.9

11. 4.035 ● 4.3

12. 36.060 ● 36.06

13. 84.64 ● 86.46

14. 9.099 ● 9.99

15. 45.7 ● 45.57

16. 33.94 ● 34.0

17. 6.6 ● 6.066

18. 70.08 ● 70.7

19. 7.700 ● 7.70

20. 25.8 ● 25.9

21. 88.124 ● 88.421

22. 96.550 ● 96.55

23. 8.889 ● 8.888

24. 68.050 ● 68.05

Which is greater?

25. 6.4 m or 6.0 m

26. 2.2 km or 3.1 km

27. 9.0 cm or 9.1 cm

28. 37.5 cm or 38.0 cm

29. 18.4 km or 14.8 km

30. 16.4 cm or 14.6 cm

Write in order from least to greatest.

31. 7.06, 7.059, 7.013

32. 18.047, 1.8450, 18.046

★ 33. 26.073, 20.673, 25.898, 2.976, 2.959

★ 34. 8.063, 80.002, 8.603, 80.01, 80.009

PROBLEM SOLVING • APPLICATIONS

Compare the decimals. Use >, <, or = to write a true sentence.

35. George can swim the 100-meter backstroke in 68.2 seconds. Masaji can swim the same distance in 68.6 seconds.

36. Franz skis the 15-kilometer cross-country course. He receives 449.039 points. Johan skis the same course and receives 449.036 points.

Midchapter Review

Write the decimals.

1. $7\frac{5}{10}$

2. $\frac{4}{100}$

3. $\frac{37}{100}$

4. $2\frac{46}{1,000}$

In what place is each blue digit?

5. 563.79

6. 24.083

7. 6.174

8. 32.59

Write >, <, or =.

9. 2.46 ● 2.64

10. 15.04 ● 15.1

11. 8.12 ● 8.09

12. 12.65 ● 12.650

Rounding Decimals

The population density of the United States in 1920 was 35.605 people per square mile.

35.605 is between 35 and 36.
It is nearer to 36.
35.605 rounded to the nearest whole number is 36.

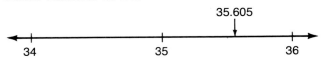

You can round numbers without using a number line.

Round 15.864 to the nearest hundredth.
　The digit in the hundredths place is 6.
　The digit to the right is less than 5.
　Keep the digit in the hundredths place the same.

15.864 rounded to the nearest hundredth is 15.86.

hundredths place
↓
15.864
↑

Round 15.864 to the nearest tenth.
　The digit in the tenths place is 8.
　The digit to the right is 5 or greater.
　Increase the digit in the tenths place by 1.

15.864 rounded to the nearest tenth is 15.9.

tenths place
↓
15.864
↑

Round 12.9163 to the nearest thousandth.
12.9163 rounded to the nearest thousandth is 12.916.

thousandths place
↓
12.9163
↑

Practice • Round to the nearest whole number.

1. 3.52   **2.** 6.20   **3.** 18.75   **4.** 326.14

Round to the nearest tenth.

5. 6.68   **6.** 9.24   **7.** 25.09   **8.** 459.83

Round to the nearest hundredth.

9. 8.065   **10.** 6.433   **11.** 72.011   **12.** 520.068

More Practice • Round to the nearest whole number.

13. 4.5   **14.** 9.06   **15.** 5.123   **16.** 6.4

17. 7.47   **18.** 8.674   **19.** 25.9   **20.** 35.12

Round to the nearest tenth.

21. 7.26   **22.** 2.60   **23.** 4.55   **24.** 6.41   **25.** 5.06

26. 56.35   **27.** 85.69   **28.** 592.55   ★ **29.** 355.96   **30.** 731.98

Round to the nearest hundredth.

31. 2.648   **32.** 6.002   **33.** 8.407   **34.** 3.502   **35.** 9.364

36. 84.111   **37.** 63.863   **38.** 143.105   **39.** 161.989   ★ **40.** 400.999

Round to the nearest thousandth.

41. 0.001429   **42.** 0.00973   **43.** 0.24654

44. 39.0983   **45.** 74.9216   **46.** 58.9332

Round to the nearest ten thousandth.

★ **47.** 9.130475   ★ **48.** 14.261132   ★ **49.** 58.1967349

PROBLEM SOLVING • APPLICATIONS

Complete the table.

	Year	People Per Square Mile	Round to the Nearest		
			Whole Number	Tenth	Hundredth
50.	1800	6.136	?	?	?
51.	1820	5.5106	?	?	?
52.	1840	9.759	?	?	?
53.	1860	10.59	?	?	?
54.	1880	16.8875	?	?	?
★ **55.**	1900	25.58754	?	?	?

Table title: **Population Density of the United States, 1800–1900**

Skills Maintenance

1. $\frac{5}{10}$ $+\frac{3}{10}$ **2.** $\frac{3}{8}$ $+\frac{1}{3}$ **3.** $3\frac{2}{5}$ $+9\frac{4}{7}$ **4.** $4\frac{3}{4}$ $+7\frac{5}{6}$ **5.** $15\frac{5}{8}$ $+7\frac{1}{6}$

6. $\frac{11}{15}$ $-\frac{7}{15}$ **7.** $\frac{7}{9}$ $-\frac{1}{6}$ **8.** $8\frac{2}{3}$ $-3\frac{5}{12}$ **9.** $5\frac{1}{2}$ $-2\frac{7}{8}$ **10.** $12\frac{2}{3}$ $-7\frac{5}{6}$

217

Adding Decimals

Sam enters a bicycle race. He rides 4.36 kilometers in the morning and 2.89 kilometers in the afternoon. How many kilometers does he ride in all?

4.36 + 2.89 = ?

Estimate first. **Think:** 4 kilometers plus 3 kilometers equals 7 kilometers. The answer is about 7.

Step 1
Line up the decimal points.
Add the hundredths.

```
  1
 4.3 6
+2.8 9
     5
```

Step 2
Add the tenths.

```
 1 1
 4.3 6
+2.8 9
   2 5
```

Step 3
Add the ones.
Write the decimal point
in the answer.

```
 1 1
 4.3 6
+2.8 9
 7.2 5
```

Sam rides 7.25 kilometers in all.

8.59 + 4.928 = ?

Step 1
Line up the decimal points.
Think: 8.59 = 8.590.
Add the thousandths.

```
 8.590
+4.928
     8
```

Step 2
Add the hundredths.

```
     1
 8.5 9 0
+4.9 2 8
     1 8
```

Step 3
Add the tenths.

```
   1 1
 8.5 9 0
+4.9 2 8
   5 1 8
```

Step 4
Add the ones.
Write the
decimal point.

```
   1 1
 8.5 9 0
+4.9 2 8
 1 3.5 1 8
```

Practice • Add.

1. 3.8
   +5.5

2. 16.11
   +25.92

3. 8.7
   +6.51

4. 23.1
   + 4.95

5. 98.07
   +57.385

Mixed Practice • Add.

6. 0.8
   +0.5

7. 21.7
   +67.9

8. 8.9
   +6.7

9. 9.6
   +8.0

10. 562.9
    + 49.3

11. 2.37
    +5.12

12. 8.31
    +7.70

13. 54.57
    +38.03

14. 816.018
    + 13.55

15. 319.08
    + 0.47

16.	17.	18.	19.	20.
6.682	8.756	3.049	1.357	8.995
2.316	6.297	5.106	2.876	4.760
+4.745	+2.214	+8.994	+7.245	+2.075

21.	22.	23.	24.	25.
12.95	15.6	43.67	0.1	198.1
17.3	7.8	812.55	21.976	45.06
8.246	10.365	8.1	98.02	713.948
+ 6.9	+ 0.84	+ 5.67	+ 0.338	+ 0.799

26. 9.57 + 3.4 = ___?___

27. 29.9 + 391.0 = ___?___

28. 8.9 + 0.76 + 3.075 = ___?___

29. 1.568 + 8.870 + 16.4 = ___?___

Write >, <, or =.

★ 30. 5.321 + 6.007 ⬤ 11.328

★ 31. 1.50 + 9.78 ⬤ 12.28

★ 32. 12.873 + 6.445 ⬤ 18.318

★ 33. 3.82 + 5.50 ⬤ 9.32

PROBLEM SOLVING • APPLICATIONS

34. Sam's bicycle weighs 18.6 kilograms. Sarita's bicycle weighs the same. What is the weight of the two bicycles?

★ 36. Evan, who placed third in a bike-a-thon, rode 16.45 kilometers. Rosa, who came in second place, rode 2.6 kilometers farther than Evan. Jody, the winner of the bike-a-thon, rode 11 kilometers farther than Rosa. How many kilometers did Jody ride?

35. Fran enters a bicycle race. She travels 16.20 kilometers in the morning, 11.56 kilometers in the afternoon, and 12.24 kilometers in the evening. How far does she travel that day?

★ 37. Use the map above. Four bike riders start at a crossroads. Each bike rider visits a different town and goes back to the crossroads. How many kilometers do they travel in all?

219

PROBLEM SOLVING • STRATEGIES

Take a Second Look

Sometimes it may seem that the answer to a problem is easy to find.

Sometimes, however, you may have to know something more. Take a second look at the problem.

Marcus and Naomi work part-time at the Ink Press. Marcus waits on customers, and Naomi proofreads. Marcus earns $4.00 an hour. Naomi earns $4.50 an hour. How much do Marcus and Naomi earn in one week?

$4.50 an hour

$4.00 an hour

What do you need to know before you can say how much each person earns in one week?

Think: How many hours does each person work in one week?

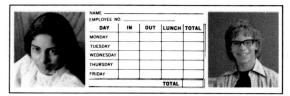

DAY	IN	OUT	LUNCH	TOTAL
MONDAY				
TUESDAY				
WEDNESDAY				
THURSDAY				
FRIDAY				
			TOTAL	

NAME _____
EMPLOYEE NO. _____

Read the problems. Then tell what you need to know before you can solve them.

1. Marcus lives 5.2 kilometers farther away from the Ink Press than Naomi. It takes Naomi 15 minutes to get to work. How many kilometers away from the Ink Press does Marcus live?

2. Henry delivers 15 packages of yellow paper and 20 packages of blue paper to the Ink Press. Does he deliver more yellow paper or more blue paper?

INK PRESS

BLUE   YELLOW

Identify the question carefully.
Locate the information you need.

Solve if there is enough information. If not, tell what fact is missing.

3. Cindi buys a package of paper that costs $9.60. Wayne buys a package of paper that costs $8.75. Who gets more paper?

4. Frederic unpacks one-half of a carton of packages of paper. Jerry unpacks one-half of a carton of packages of paper bags. Who unpacks more packages?

5. Mr. Diaz uses 3.5 more bottles of ink to print Madeline's order than Mr. Roese uses on the Fine Foods order. Mr. Roese uses 6 bottles of ink. How much ink does Mr. Diaz use?

6. Julius works for 2.5 hours at the linotype. Carmine works for 3 hours at the linotype. Who types more lines?

7. The owner of the Ink Press orders paper by the carton. A large carton costs $24.00 and a small carton costs $18.00. Which size carton is the better buy?

Do you have enough information to solve the problem?

---

8. String is used to wrap boxed orders. A new roll of string has 400 meters. One roll has 183.6 meters left on it. How much string was used from that roll?

9. Marcus carries a box of 100 envelopes to Mrs. Avery's car. Mr. Diaz carries a box of 50 envelopes to Mr. Dundee's car. Who carried the heavier box?

10. Naomi earns $6.00 for proofreading the order for Fine Foods. She earns $13.50 for filling the order. How much does Naomi earn in all for the job?

★ 11. Marcus earns $56.80 for his work one week. He earns $72.40 for his work another week. How many hours does Marcus work during the two weeks?

★ 12. Mr. Diaz uses 48 bottles of ink to print 15 orders. 36 bottles are blue ink. 12 bottles are red ink. How many bottles of ink does Mr. Diaz use for one order?

Subtracting Decimals

Dolly the dolphin can jump through a hoop 4.35 meters above the water. Dolores the dolphin can jump through the hoop 2.89 meters above the water. How much higher can Dolly jump?

4.35 − 2.89 = ?

Estimate first.
Think: 4 meters minus 3 meters equals 1 meter. The answer is about 1.

Step 1	**Step 2**	**Step 3**
Line up the decimal points. Subtract the hundredths.	Subtract the tenths.	Subtract the ones. Write the decimal point in the answer.

```
       2 15              12              12
                       3 2 15          3 2 15
   4.3 5               4.3 5           4.3 5
 − 2.8 9             − 2.8 9         − 2.8 9
 ───────             ───────         ───────
       6                 4 6           1.4 6
```

Dolly can jump 1.46 meters higher.

9.27 − 3.845 = ?

Step 1	**Step 2**	**Step 3**
Line up the decimal points. **Think:** 9.27 = 9.270. Subtract the thousandths.	Subtract the hundredths.	Subtract the tens and ones. Write the decimal point.

```
      6 10              6 10          8 126 10
   9.2 7 0            9.2 7 0         9.2 7 0
 − 3.8 4 5          − 3.8 4 5       − 3.8 4 5
 ─────────          ─────────       ─────────
         5                2 5         5.4 2 5
```

Practice • Subtract.

1.	2.	3.	4.	5.
8.7 −2.3	9.35 −4.73	19.15 − 6.50	7.1 −3.459	16 − 2.163

Mixed Practice • Subtract.

6.	7.	8.	9.	10.
146.7 − 82.8	371.2 − 45.6	387.6 −149.9	16.5 −11.6	100.4 − 97.9

11. 10.36
   − 5.38
	12. 5.89
	   −1.8
		13. 19.15
		   − 7.65
			14. 86.12
			   − 8.8
				15. 6.78
				   −5.07

16. 0.011
   −0.007
	17. 0.975
	   −0.460
		18. 0.49
		   −0.184
			19. 3.047
			   −1.829
				20. 15
				   − 3.644

21. 416.4
   − 11.468
	22. 58.164
	   − 2.09
		23. 14.42
		   − 5.247
			24. 18.87
			   − 4.5
				25. 32.9
				   −16.46

26. $9.8 - 2.4 =$ __?__

27. $3.1 - 1.7 =$ __?__

28. $91.43 - 77.68 =$ __?__

29. $45 - 36.99 =$ __?__

30. $567 - 36.982 =$ __?__

31. $645.362 - 289.86 =$ __?__

Use a plus sign, a minus sign, and a decimal point to solve.

Example: 1 3 7 9 4 6 = 87.4

$$13 + 79 - 4.6 = 87.4$$

★ **32.** 3 7 4 6 1 9 = 58.6

★ **33.** 7 8 6 5 2 7 = 45.8

★ **34.** 4 2 3 7 2 8 = 37.72

★ **35.** 5 6 4 9 3 7 = 58.07

PROBLEM SOLVING • APPLICATIONS

36. A common dolphin is 2.12 meters long. A bottle-nosed dolphin is 3.46 meters long. How much shorter is the common dolphin?

37. A bottle-nosed dolphin weighs 320.24 kilograms. A common dolphin weighs 59.78 kilograms. How much more does the bottle-nosed dolphin weigh?

38. Dolly dives to 211.65 meters beneath the surface of the water. She then rises 137.42 meters. How many meters beneath the surface is she now?

★ 39. Dolphins can swim as fast as 35.7 kilometers per hour, but their average speed is about 9.8 kilometers per hour. Dolly sometimes swims 15.3 kilometers per hour. How much slower than the fast speed is this? What is the difference between Dolly's speed and a dolphin's average speed?

PROBLEM SOLVING • STRATEGIES

Writing Checks

A customer buys an item in a store. It is paid for with this check.
The bank where the customer has a checking account will pay the
bank where the store has an account. The money is taken from the
customer's account.

James or Vera Marona
2100 Brooks Drive
Falls Church, Virginia 22041

No. *264*

March 5 19 *84*

Pay to the
order of *Audio Center, Inc.* $ *68.25*

Sixty-eight and 25/100 ————————— Dollars

Columbia Bank
West End Avenue
Falls Church, Virginia 22041

Memo *tape recorder*   *Vera Marona*

789 12345 123 0456

Use the check to answer questions 1 through 10.

1. What is the number of the check?

2. What is the date on this check?

3. To whom was the check written?

4. What is the amount of the check?

5. How many times is the amount of
   money filled in on the check?

6. What word takes the place of the decimal
   point where the amount is written?

7. Who signed this check?

8. Who else can sign this check?

9. Where does the customer live?

10. What did the customer purchase?

11. On April 11, 1984, Neil Baldwin bought stereo equipment at Bell
    and Company that cost $168.79. He paid with this check.
    Copy and complete the check.

Neil Baldwin
Greta Baldwin
2708 Orange Avenue
Scottsdale, Arizona 85253

No. *708*

———————— 19 ————

Pay to the
order of ————————————————————— $ ————

————————————————————————— Dollars

Mid-State Bank
Metropolitan Ave.
Mesan, Arizona 85201

Memo ——————   —————————————

0123 0456 789 12345

Neil makes a deposit to increase the amount of money in his account. He writes checks to pay his bills. Neil keeps a record of the amounts of money he deposits and withdraws from his account.

Check Number	Date	Item	Amount of Check		Amount of Deposit		Balance	
							$126	15
432	9/6	Central Bell Telephone	$35	56			93	59
433	9/7	Garden Restaurant	18	75			74	84
	9/10	deposit			483	92	?	
434	9/12	Island Trust Bank	516	25			?	

The balance column shows how much is in the account.
On September 6, the balance is $93.59.
On September 7, Neil writes a check for $18.75.
Subtract to find the new balance.

$93.59
$- \ 18.75$
93.59
$\overline{\$74.84}$

Use Neil's checkbook record to answer questions 12 through 17.

12. What is the amount of check number 433?

13. On what date did Neil make a deposit?

Read the checkbook record carefully to find needed information.

14. What is the balance before Neil's deposit?

15. What is the balance after the deposit?

16. What is the amount of the check paid to Island Trust Bank?

17. What is the balance after Neil writes check number 434?

Solve.

18. Lisa Rush has $212.75 in her checking account. She writes a check for $45.93. How much money does she have left?

19. Frank Tucker has $87.56 in his checking account. He makes a deposit of $2,083.72. What is the new balance?

★ **20.** George Sellers wants to write a check for $205.75. The balance in his checking account is $248.21. Does he need to make a deposit before writing the check, or does he have enough money in his account now?

★ **21.** Rosa Perez has $253.72 in her checking account. She writes a check for $72.85. Then she makes a deposit of $95.00. How much money is now in her account?

★ **22.** Lois Chang has $406.12 in her checking account. She writes two checks, one for $18.75 and the other for $264.95. How much money does she have left?

★ **23.** Barbara Miller has $375.42 in her checking account. She wants to buy a chair for $225.00 and a lamp for $148.95. Does she have enough money to write a check for both purchases? What will her balance be if she writes the check?

REVIEW

Write the decimals. (pages 208–211)

1. $\frac{7}{10}$

6. $\frac{483}{1,000}$

10. seven-tenths

2. $19\frac{1}{10}$

7. $\frac{62}{1,000}$

11. forty-one hundredths

12. five and two-hundredths

3. $\frac{9}{100}$

8. $9\frac{7}{1,000}$

13. two hundred nine thousandths

4. $2\frac{39}{100}$

9. $60\frac{840}{1,000}$

14. one and fifteen-thousandths

5. $51\frac{5}{100}$

15. fifty-two and seven-thousandths

In what place is the 9? (pages 212–213)

16. 1.297

17. 14.379

18. 495.862

Write >, <, or =. (pages 214–215)

19. 2.01 ● 2.010

20. 0.29 ● 0.287

21. 10.001 ● 10.756

22. 18.1 ● 18.089

23. 8.54 ● 8.24

24. 95.643 ● 95.8

Round to the nearest whole number. (pages 216–217)

25. 5.430

26. 19.71

27. 8.097

Round to the nearest tenth. (pages 216–217)

28. 2.69

29. 15.12

30. 26.08

Round to the nearest hundredth. (pages 216–217)

31. 1.075

32. 86.312

33. 0.9062

Round to the nearest thousandth. (pages 216–217)

34. 68.19752

35. 3.10849

36. 0.54972

Add. (pages 218–219)

37. $\begin{array}{r} 1.3 \\ +7.4 \\ \hline \end{array}$

38. $\begin{array}{r} 23.6 \\ +\ 8.8 \\ \hline \end{array}$

39. $\begin{array}{r} 12.598 \\ +28.261 \\ \hline \end{array}$

40. $\begin{array}{r} 78.676 \\ 5.9 \\ +\ 0.3 \\ \hline \end{array}$

Subtract. (pages 222–223)

41. $\begin{array}{r} 54.9 \\ -20.1 \\ \hline \end{array}$

42. $\begin{array}{r} 3.9 \\ -1.36 \\ \hline \end{array}$

43. $\begin{array}{r} 46.37 \\ -29.814 \\ \hline \end{array}$

44. $\begin{array}{r} 84 \\ -67.59 \\ \hline \end{array}$

Solve.

45. Brian has an odometer on his bike. This morning it read 23.8 kilometers. He rides 3.6 kilometers. What does it read now? (p. 218)

46. Brian is watching his odometer to see when it shows 100 kilometers. It shows 27.4 kilometers now. How much farther does he have to ride to reach 100 kilometers? (p. 222)

PROJECT

Magic Squares

In a magic square, the sum of the numbers in each row, column, and diagonal is the same. This sum is called the **magic sum.**

1. Find the sum of each row,
   column, and diagonal for
   this magic square.

   What is the magic sum?

4.85	4.91	5.3	5.24
5.06	5.27	4.88	5.09
5.21	5	5.15	4.94
5.18	5.12	4.97	5.03

For Exercises 2 and 3, use the magic square in Exercise 1 to make a new square.

2. Add 8.6 to each number.
   $4.85 + 8.6 = 13.45$

   Is this a magic square?
   If your answer is yes,
   what is the magic sum?

13.45	13.51	13.9	13.84
13.66	13.87	13.48	13.69
13.81	13.6	13.75	13.54
13.78	13.72	13.57	13.63

3. Subtract 1.08 from each number.
   $4.85 - 1.08 = 3.77$

   Is this a magic square?
   If your answer is yes,
   what is the magic sum?

3.77	3.83	4.22	4.16
3.98	4.19	3.8	4.01
4.13	3.92	4.07	3.86
4.1	4.04	3.89	3.95

TEST

Write the decimals.

1. $6\frac{9}{10}$

2. $15\frac{7}{10}$

3. $\frac{73}{100}$

4. $3\frac{4}{100}$

5. $78\frac{18}{100}$

6. $\frac{862}{1,000}$

7. $4\frac{39}{1,000}$

8. $70\frac{320}{1,000}$

9. $8\frac{2}{1,000}$

10. nine-tenths

11. fifty-six hundredths

12. six and three-hundredths

13. four hundred two thousandths

14. eight and twelve-thousandths

15. sixty-one and twenty-five thousandths

In what place is the 3?

16. 19.137

17. 325.85

18. 1.973

Write >, <, or =.

19. 0.065 ⬤ 0.65

20. 2.92 ⬤ 2.920

21. 0.813 ⬤ 0.810

22. 18.362 ⬤ 17.632

23. 5.2 ⬤ 5.098

24. 6.037 ⬤ 5.921

Round to the nearest whole number.

25. 6.7

26. 29.410

27. 15.55

Round to the nearest tenth.

28. 1.38

29. 0.75

30. 19.79

Round to the nearest hundredth.

31. 53.548

32. 3.081

33. 0.655

Round to the nearest thousandth.

34. 2.07169

35. 49.32804

36. 0.39175

Add or subtract.

37.
$$\begin{array}{r} 76.1 \\ +\ 1.7 \\ \hline \end{array}$$

38.
$$\begin{array}{r} 9.38 \\ +0.49 \\ \hline \end{array}$$

39.
$$\begin{array}{r} 0.83 \\ +0.565 \\ \hline \end{array}$$

40.
$$\begin{array}{r} 48.116 \\ 6.87 \\ +54.05 \\ \hline \end{array}$$

41.
$$\begin{array}{r} 3.2 \\ -0.8 \\ \hline \end{array}$$

42.
$$\begin{array}{r} 94.04 \\ -12.66 \\ \hline \end{array}$$

43.
$$\begin{array}{r} 8.67 \\ -0.412 \\ \hline \end{array}$$

44.
$$\begin{array}{r} 56 \\ -38.278 \\ \hline \end{array}$$

Solve.

45. The same gasoline pump fills two cars. One car takes 27.8 liters and the other car takes 36.3 liters. How much gasoline is taken from the pump for the two cars?

46. The gas tank in Miss Lee's car holds 45 liters. She stops at a gas station to fill the tank. It takes 38.7 liters. How much gasoline was in the tank already?

Balancing the Checkbook

Lou and Nancy have a checking account. They write checks to pay their bills. They make deposits when they want to increase the amount of money in their account.

Here are Lou and Nancy's checks and deposit tickets for one month.

Lou Peters or Nancy Peters	No. 603
June 4, 19 84	
Pay to the order of Lincoln Federal Bk. $ 547.54	
Five Hundred forty seven 54/100 Dollars	
United Bank	Lou Peters
Memo mortgage payment	

Lou Peters or Nancy Peters	No. 604
June 5, 19 84	
Pay to the order of Ohio Bell Telephone $ 28.76	
Twenty-eight and 76/100 — Dollars	
United Bank	Nancy Peters
Memo telephone bill	

Lou Peters or Nancy Peters	No. 605
June 6, 19 84	
Pay to the order of Dr. Fein $ 28.00	
Twenty-eight and 00/100 — Dollars	
United Bank	Nancy Peters
Memo eye exam	

Lou Peters or Nancy Peters	No. 606
June 8, 19 84	
Pay to the order of Grand Supermarket $ 87.92	
Eighty seven and 92/100 — Dollars	
United Bank	Lou Peters
Memo groceries	

Lou Peters or Nancy Peters	No. 607
June 12, 19 84	
Pay to the order of Union Gas Co. $ 95.15	
Ninety-five and 15/100 — Dollars	
United Bank	Nancy Peters
Memo gas bill	

Lou Peters or Nancy Peters	No. 608
June 15, 19 84	
Pay to the order of Mayer's Dept. Store $ 57.75	
Fifty seven and 75/100 — Dollars	
United Bank	Lou Peters
Memo coat	

Lou Peters or Nancy Peters	No. 609
June 23, 19 84	
Pay to the order of Bill's Pharmacy $ 8.12	
Eight and 12/100 — Dollars	
United Bank	Lou Peters
Memo drugs	

Lou Peters or Nancy Peters	No. 610
June 27, 19 84	
Pay to the order of Shelly's Bookshop $ 16.23	
Sixteen and 23/100 — Dollars	
United Bank	Nancy Peters
Memo books	

DEPOSIT TICKET

Lou Peters or Nancy Peters

Date June 7, 19 84

United Bank

CASH	150	00
CHECKS	32	50
TOTAL	182	50

DEPOSIT TICKET

Lou Peters or Nancy Peters

Date June 14, 19 84

United Bank

CASH		
CHECKS	675	00
TOTAL	675	00

These are other transactions the Peters made during the month of June.
They ordered new checks. On June 28, the bank charged
their account $6.87 to cover the cost of new checks.

On June 30, the bank credited the Peters' account with
a monthly dividend of $3.26.

On June 30, the bank charged their account a monthly
service fee of $5.00.

Shown here is a page from the Peters' checkbook record. Their
opening balance for the month is $635.42. Copy and complete the
checkbook page in order. Record all the checks written, deposits
made, and other transactions for June. Complete the balance column.

What is the Peters' balance at the end of the month?

Check Number	Date	Item	Amount of Check	Amount of Deposit	Balance	
			$	$		

COMPUTER

AND, OR, and NOT

A program is a step-by-step list of instructions to the computer. A program is software. One computer can contain many different programs. Although the software can change, the hardware stays the same. A program can be thought of as a set of rules for a computer. Software rules change from program to program. Hardware rules never change.

Hardware rules are called *rules of logic.* This logic is always the same. We said that switches were the smallest pieces of computer hardware. Bits were defined as 0 (off) or 1 (on). Switches turn bits on and off. Rules of logic define *how* switches turn bits on and off. Like computers, switches have input and output. One or two bits are input to a switch; one bit is output from a switch. Three rules of logic are called AND, OR, and NOT.

The *NOT rule of logic* is simplest. The NOT rule has one input bit and one output bit. The NOT rule says: Make the bit what it is NOT.

> If the input is 0, the output is 1.
> If the input is 1, the output is 0.

There is no other possibility. A bit can only be 0 (off) or 1 (on).

The AND and OR rules of logic are more complicated. The AND and OR rules have two input bits and one output bit. The *AND rule of logic* says: Turn on the output bit if BOTH input bits are 1.

> If the input is 0 and 0, or 1 and 0, or 0 and 1, the output is 0.
> If the input is 1 and 1, the output is 1.

The *OR rule of logic* says: Turn on the output bit if EITHER input bit is 1 or
if BOTH input bits are 1.

> If the input is 0 and 0, the output is 0.
> If the input is 0 and 1, or 1 and 0, or 1 and 1, the output is 1.

Copy and complete these tables of logic.

NOT rule		
Input	→	Output
1. 0	→	?
2. 1	→	?
3. 1	→	?
4. 0	→	?

AND rule		
Input	→	Output
5. 0 and 1	→	?
6. 1 and 0	→	?
7. 1 and 1	→	?
8. 0 and 0	→	?

OR rule		
Input	→	Output
9. 1 and 1	→	?
10. 0 and 0	→	?
11. 1 and 0	→	?
12. 0 and 1	→	?

Choose the correct answers.

1. Round 52,704 to the nearest thousand.

   A. 52,000
   B. 52,700
   C. 53,000
   D. not here

2. Add.

$$59,324$$
$$86,190$$
$$+\quad 452$$

   A. 145,966
   B. 155,966
   C. 146,866
   D. not here

3. Subtract.

$$86,040$$
$$-\quad 9,578$$

   A. 74,962
   B. 75,862
   C. 76,562
   D. not here

4. Multiply.

$$409$$
$$\times\ 76$$

   A. 31,844
   B. 31,084
   C. 30,625
   D. not here

5. Divide.

$$27\overline{)8,235}$$

   A. 305
   B. 35
   C. 3,500
   D. not here

6. Compare

$$\frac{5}{8}\ \bullet\ \frac{2}{3}.$$

   A. $<$
   B. $>$
   C. $=$
   D. not here

7. Subtract. Write the answer in lowest terms.

$$10\frac{3}{8} - 3\frac{1}{4} = \underline{\ ?\ }$$

   A. $7\frac{1}{8}$ **B.** 7
   C. $7\frac{3}{24}$ **D.** not here

8. Round 27.57 to the nearest tenth.

   A. 27
   B. 27.5
   C. 27.6
   D. not here

9. Subtract.

$$48.7$$
$$-\ 9.86$$

   A. 39.16
   B. 49.9
   C. 38.84
   D. not here

10. Oliver can run 100 meters in 18.2 seconds. Beth can run 100 meters in 15.7 seconds. How much faster is Beth than Oliver?

   A. 3.5 seconds
   B. 2.5 seconds
   C. 3.9 seconds
   D. not here

11. Allen runs 6.8 kilometers on Tuesday, 7 kilometers on Thursday, and 5.25 kilometers on Friday. How many kilometers does Allen run in all?

   A. 12.75
   B. 12.12
   C. 19.05
   D. not here

Decimals: Multiplication and Division

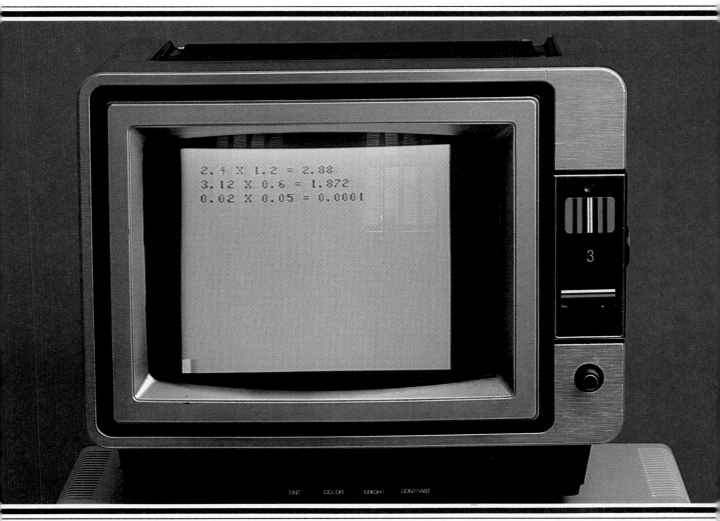

Estimating Products • Multiplying Decimals • Zeros in the Product • Problem Solving: Time Cards and Wages • Dividing by Whole Numbers • Zeros in Division • Multiplying or Dividing by 10, 100, or 1,000 • Dividing Decimals • Writing Decimals for Fractions • Problem Solving: Choose the Sensible Answer • Unit Pricing • Scientific Notation

Estimating Products

The length of this Spanish ship is 1.8 times the length of this Viking ship. What is the length of the Spanish ship?

The multiplication has been done for you. Estimate the product to know where to place the decimal point.

Think:
Round 24 to 20.
Round 1.8 to 2.
$2 \times 20 = 40$
The answer is about 40.
The answer must be 43.2.

```
    2 4
  ×1.8
  1 9 2
    2 4
  4 3 2
```

The Spanish ship is 43.2 meters long.

The length of this Egyptian cargo ship is 2.4 times the length of this riverboat. What is the length of the cargo ship?

The multiplication has been done for you. Estimate the product to know where to place the decimal point.

Think:
Round 16.7 to 20.
Round 2.4 to 2.
$2 \times 20 = 40$
The answer is about 40.
The answer must be 40.08.

```
   1 6.7
  ×  2.4
   6 6 8
   3 3 4
  4 0 0 8
```

The Egyptian cargo ship is 40.08 meters long.

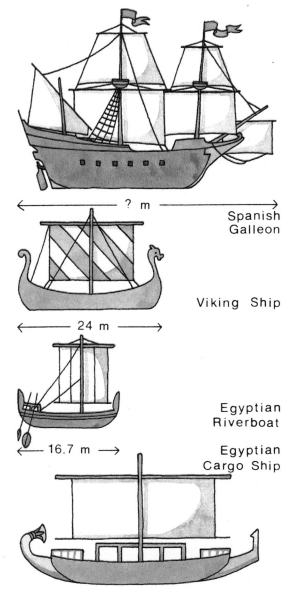

? m
Spanish Galleon

Viking Ship

24 m

Egyptian Riverboat

16.7 m

Egyptian Cargo Ship

? m

Practice • Estimate to place the decimal points in the answers.

1.	2.	3.	4.	5.
24	5.6	18.3	14.8	3.65
×1.7	×4.2	×2.76	× 3.9	× 2.3
408	2352	50508	5772	8395

Mixed Practice • Estimate to place the decimal point in the answers.

6.	7.	8.	9.	10.
83	74	126	403	19
×1.6	×9.5	× 3.2	× 1.9	×8.7
1328	7030	4032	7657	1653

234

11. 4.2	12. 5.5	13. 7.1	14. 10.2	15. 8.9
×6.3	×3.3	×1.4	× 9.8	×3.4
2646	1815	994	9996	3026

16. 19.7	17. 87.6	18. 54.6	19. 98.3	20. 46.3
×4.21	×3.19	×7.93	×1.45	×2.91
82937	279444	432978	142535	134733

21. 9.46	22. 7.98	23. 4.83	24. 6.42	25. 6.62
×8.12	×8.32	×2.96	×1.83	×2.47
768152	663936	142968	117486	163514

26. 5.31	27. 6.24	28. 8.99	29. 3.48	30. 5.62
× 4.5	× 8.7	× 3.2	× 6.5	× 9.1
23895	54288	28768	22620	51142

31. 3.7	32. 198	33. 9.5	34. 11.4	35. 9.37
×8.4	× 3.6	×8.7	×1.28	×8.14
3108	7128	8265	14592	762718

Estimate to place the decimal point in the underlined factors.

★ 36. $4.8 \times \underline{68} = 32.64$

★ 37. $\underline{134} \times 2.4 = 32.16$

★ 38. $8.76 \times \underline{345} = 30.222$

★ 39. $\underline{152} \times 3.8 = 57.76$

PROBLEM SOLVING • APPLICATIONS

Estimate to place the decimal point in the answers.

40. A modern steel sailing ship is 16 meters wide. The length is 8.25 times the width. How long is the ship?

$$\begin{array}{r} 16 \\ \times 8.25 \\ \hline 13200 \text{ meters} \end{array}$$

41. The length of the *United States* is 7.55 times the length of this Roman grain ship. How long is the *United States?*

$$\begin{array}{r} 40 \\ \times 7.55 \\ \hline 30200 \text{ meters} \end{array}$$

42. A Viking ship was 24 meters long. The *Queen Elizabeth 2* is 12.25 times as long. How long is the *Queen Elizabeth 2?*

$$\begin{array}{r} 24 \\ \times 12.25 \\ \hline 29400 \text{ meters} \end{array}$$

←——— 40 m ———→

★ 43. The width of a certain ship is 12 meters. It is 28.75 meters longer than 9.5 times the width. How long is the ship?

$(12 \times 9.5) + 28.75 = 14275$ meters

Multiplying Decimals

Angela Garret is designing the interior of a greeting card store. She multiplies the length of a room by the width to find out how many square meters of carpeting she needs for the store.

Find the number of square meters of carpeting needed.

$17.6 \times 3.2 = ?$

Step 1
Multiply as if you were multiplying whole numbers.

```
  1 7.6
×   3.2
  3 5 2
5 2 8 0
5 6 3 2
```

Step 2
Place the decimal point.
Think: Round each factor.
$3 \times 20 = 60$
The answer is about 60.

```
  1 7.6
×   3.2
  3 5 2
5 2 8 0
5 6.3 2
```

She needs 56.32 square meters of carpeting.

Each place to the right of the decimal point is a decimal place. Compare the number of decimal places in the product with the total number of decimal places in the factors.

```
  42.6 ←——— 1              3.75 ←——— 2              4.25 ←——— 2
×    8 ←——— 0            × 1.3 ←——— 1            ×0.75 ←——— 2
 340.8 ←——— 1            4.875 ←——— 3            3.1875 ←——— 4
```

The number of decimal places in the product equals the sum of the number of decimal places in the factors.

Practice • Multiply.

1. 37.8
    $\times\ \ \ 5$

2. 38
    $\times 0.9$

3. 0.16
    $\times\ 0.7$

4. 156.1
    $\times\ \ \ 8.7$

5. 2.25
    $\times 0.178$

Mixed Practice • Multiply.

6. 1.01
    $\times\ \ 99$

7. 4.2
    $\times\ \ 8$

8. 25
    $\times 1.1$

9. 3.6
    $\times 0.9$

10. 5.6
     $\times\ \ 9$

11. 4.2 ×3.7	12. 15.8 × 1.1	13. 79.6 ×0.54	14. 4.2 ×0.06	15. 2.76 × 1.3
16. 7.01 × 0.9	17. 10.06 ×0.302	18. 6.008 × 0.9	19. 10.12 × 0.22	20. 100.25 × 0.15
21. 7.03 ×21.4	22. 1.93 ×0.65	23. 200.8 × 3.45	24. 35.5 × 8.8	25. 0.84 ×0.303

26. $1.001 \times 246 =$ ___?___

27. $2.22 \times 200 =$ ___?___

28. $8.9 \times 1.5 =$ ___?___

29. $0.25 \times 0.83 =$ ___?___

30. $9.03 \times 5.78 =$ ___?___

31. $7.6 \times 0.9 =$ ___?___

32. $6.15 \times 0.23 =$ ___?___

33. $112 \times 0.387 =$ ___?___

34. $4.5 \times 8.3 =$ ___?___

Write the missing decimal point in each underlined factor to make the sentence true.

★ **35.** <u>209</u> $\times 5.32 = 11.1188$ ★ **36.** <u>134</u> $\times 0.03 = 0.402$ ★ **37.** <u>5614</u> $\times 3.8 = 21.3332$

PROBLEM SOLVING • APPLICATIONS

38. Angela uses 18.6 meters of wallpaper for the front room of the store. She needs 1.5 times as much wallpaper for the back room. How many meters does she need for the back room?

39. The width of the greeting card rack is 4.8 times the width of the display shelf. The width of the display shelf is 2.5 meters. How wide is the card rack?

★ **40.** For 9 days Angela works 2.5 hours each day planning the greeting card store. She also spends 3.25 hours every day in the store while the work is being done. What is the total number of hours she works on the card store during the 9 days?

★ **41.** Angela pays a carpenter $12.50 an hour. For each hour of overtime he works, she pays him $18.75. How much does she owe the carpenter for 37.5 hours of regular time and 15 hours of overtime?

Zeros in the Product

Each sheet of paper in Jan's science book is 0.0029 inch thick. The first chapter is 14 sheets long. How thick is that chapter?

$14 \times 0.0029 = ?$

Sometimes you need to place zeros in the product to locate the decimal point.

Step 1
Multiply.

$$
\begin{array}{r}
0.0029 \\
\times \quad 14 \\
\hline
116 \\
290 \\
\hline
406
\end{array}
$$

Step 2
Write one zero to show four decimal places in the answer. Place the decimal point.

$$
\begin{array}{r}
0.0029 \longleftarrow \boxed{4} \\
\times \quad 14 \longleftarrow \boxed{0} \\
\hline
116 \\
290 \\
\hline
0.0406 \longleftarrow \boxed{4}
\end{array}
$$

The first chapter is 0.0406 inch thick.

$0.036 \times 0.09 = ?$

$$
\begin{array}{r}
0.09 \longleftarrow \boxed{2} \\
\times 0.036 \longleftarrow \boxed{3} \\
\hline
54 \\
270 \\
\hline
0.00324 \longleftarrow \boxed{5} \quad \text{Write two zeros.}
\end{array}
$$

More Examples

$$
\begin{array}{r}
0.008 \longleftarrow \boxed{3} \\
\times \quad 3.2 \longleftarrow \boxed{1} \\
\hline
16 \\
24 \\
\hline
0.0256 \longleftarrow \boxed{4}
\end{array}
$$

$$
\begin{array}{r}
0.04 \longleftarrow \boxed{2} \\
\times 0.02 \longleftarrow \boxed{2} \\
\hline
0.0008 \longleftarrow \boxed{4}
\end{array}
$$

Practice • Multiply.

1.
$$
\begin{array}{r}
1.49 \\
\times 0.05
\end{array}
$$

2.
$$
\begin{array}{r}
0.37 \\
\times 0.04
\end{array}
$$

3.
$$
\begin{array}{r}
0.35 \\
\times 0.08
\end{array}
$$

4.
$$
\begin{array}{r}
16 \\
\times 0.006
\end{array}
$$

5.
$$
\begin{array}{r}
0.302 \\
\times \ 0.05
\end{array}
$$

6.
$$
\begin{array}{r}
0.012 \\
\times \ 0.82
\end{array}
$$

7.
$$
\begin{array}{r}
0.0037 \\
\times \quad 15
\end{array}
$$

8.
$$
\begin{array}{r}
0.43 \\
\times 0.02
\end{array}
$$

9.
$$
\begin{array}{r}
8.03 \\
\times 0.006
\end{array}
$$

10.
$$
\begin{array}{r}
0.62 \\
\times 0.104
\end{array}
$$

Mixed Practice • Multiply.

11. $\begin{array}{r} 24 \\ \times 0.004 \\ \hline \end{array}$	12. $\begin{array}{r} 0.085 \\ \times\ 0.07 \\ \hline \end{array}$	13. $\begin{array}{r} 0.95 \\ \times 0.08 \\ \hline \end{array}$	14. $\begin{array}{r} 0.076 \\ \times\ 1.3 \\ \hline \end{array}$	15. $\begin{array}{r} 0.454 \\ \times\ 0.2 \\ \hline \end{array}$
16. $\begin{array}{r} 0.506 \\ \times\ 0.12 \\ \hline \end{array}$	17. $\begin{array}{r} 0.253 \\ \times 0.006 \\ \hline \end{array}$	18. $\begin{array}{r} 0.25 \\ \times 0.15 \\ \hline \end{array}$	19. $\begin{array}{r} 2.31 \\ \times 0.03 \\ \hline \end{array}$	20. $\begin{array}{r} 0.027 \\ \times\ 1.5 \\ \hline \end{array}$
21. $\begin{array}{r} 0.106 \\ \times\ 0.17 \\ \hline \end{array}$	22. $\begin{array}{r} 0.793 \\ \times\ 0.5 \\ \hline \end{array}$	23. $\begin{array}{r} 0.94 \\ \times 0.03 \\ \hline \end{array}$	24. $\begin{array}{r} 0.008 \\ \times\ 4.5 \\ \hline \end{array}$	25. $\begin{array}{r} 13.4 \\ \times 0.003 \\ \hline \end{array}$
26. $\begin{array}{r} 8.6 \\ \times 0.004 \\ \hline \end{array}$	27. $\begin{array}{r} 0.038 \\ \times\ 0.04 \\ \hline \end{array}$	28. $\begin{array}{r} 1.89 \\ \times\ 0.3 \\ \hline \end{array}$	29. $\begin{array}{r} 0.007 \\ \times 0.009 \\ \hline \end{array}$	30. $\begin{array}{r} 0.005 \\ \times\ 3.57 \\ \hline \end{array}$

31. $0.07 \times 0.082 =$ ___?___

32. $8.45 \times 0.009 =$ ___?___

33. $1.5 \times 0.23 =$ ___?___

34. $0.002 \times 6.3 =$ ___?___

35. $0.004 \times 0.016 =$ ___?___

36. $0.02 \times 0.483 =$ ___?___

★ **37.** $0.075 \times 53 \times 0.009 =$ ___?___

★ **38.** $5.86 \times 0.14 \times 0.08 =$ ___?___

★ **39.** $0.125 \times 0.003 \times 0.045 =$ ___?___

★ **40.** $0.004 \times 0.07 \times 0.008 =$ ___?___

PROBLEM SOLVING • APPLICATIONS

41. Many workbooks are printed on paper that is 0.0093 inch thick. How thick is a 5-sheet stack of this paper?

★ **42.** A film company sells boxes of sheet film. There are 25 sheets in each box. Each sheet is 0.0036 inch thick. How thick is the stack of film in the box? How thick a stack would film from 2 boxes make?

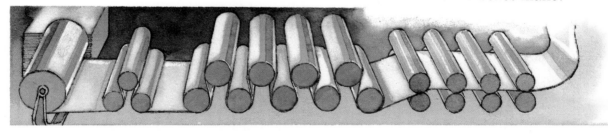

Skills Maintenance

Multiply. Write the answers in lowest terms.

1. $\frac{1}{2} \times \frac{2}{9} =$ ___?___

2. $\frac{3}{4} \times \frac{3}{8} =$ ___?___

3. $\frac{7}{8} \times \frac{6}{14} =$ ___?___

4. $\frac{2}{3} \times 3\frac{1}{5} =$ ___?___

5. $6 \times 3\frac{3}{4} =$ ___?___

6. $7 \times \frac{3}{5} =$ ___?___

7. $3\frac{1}{2} \times 4\frac{2}{5} =$ ___?___

8. $1\frac{3}{4} \times 4\frac{2}{7} =$ ___?___

9. $2\frac{4}{5} \times 2\frac{1}{7} =$ ___?___

PROBLEM SOLVING • STRATEGIES

Time Cards and Wages

A time card is a type of table. You can read it to find information.

Jessica Phillips works as a mechanic. Her time card shows the number of hours she works during one week.

This week's time card shows that on Monday Jessica came to work at 7:45 A.M. and worked until 3:15 P.M. She worked 7.5 hours on Monday. Jessica earns $6.50 an hour. How much did she earn on Monday?

Multiply Jessica's hourly wage by the number of hours she worked.

$$\begin{array}{r} \$6.50 \\ \times\ \ 7.5 \\ \hline \$48.75 \end{array}$$

Jessica earned $48.75 on Monday.

TIME CARD

Name _Jessica Phillips_

Week Ending _May 16_

	IN	OUT	TOTAL HOURS
Mon.	7:45 A.M.	3:15 P.M.	7.5
Tues.	9:00 A.M.	5:00 P.M.	8
Wed.	8:00 A.M.	4:30 P.M.	8.5
Thurs.	8:00 A.M.	5:30 P.M.	9.5
Fri.	8:15 A.M.	4:15 P.M.	8
Sat.	10:00 A.M.	12:45 P.M.	2.75
Sun			

Jessica worked 1 hour 30 minutes of overtime on Thursday and 2 hours 45 minutes of overtime on Saturday. How many hours of overtime is that in all?

Step 1
Add the minutes. Regroup 75 minutes as 1 hour 15 minutes.

$$\begin{array}{r} {\scriptstyle 1} \\ 1\,h\,30\,min \\ +\ 2\,h\,45\,min \\ \hline 15\,min \end{array}$$

Step 2
Add the hours.

$$\begin{array}{r} {\scriptstyle 1} \\ 1\,h\,30\,min \\ +\ 2\,h\,45\,min \\ \hline 4\,h\,15\,min \end{array}$$

Jessica worked 4 hours 15 minutes of overtime.

Use Jessica's time card to answer questions 1 through 5.

1. Jessica's regular hourly wage is $6.50. Her overtime wage is 1.5 times her regular wage. How much does she earn for each hour of overtime?

   Locate the day and read across to find the number of hours worked.

2. At the rate of $6.50 an hour, how much money does Jessica earn at her job on Friday alone?

3. Jessica did not work 8 hours on Monday. How much time did she need to make up? What day did she make up the time?

4. Jessica earns $10.00 an hour when she works on weekends. How much did she earn on Saturday?

Remember to place the dollar sign and decimal point in your answers when working with money.

---

5. How many hours did Jessica work during the week ending May 16?

Solve.

6. At Joe's Automotive Center, an oil change takes 45 minutes. A tune-up takes 1 hour 45 minutes. How long will it take a mechanic to give a car an oil change and a tune-up?

7. Jeff Faraday's time card at an automobile service shop shows that he worked 2.25 hours repairing the brakes of a car. The shop charges $22.00 an hour for repairs. What does the brake job cost the customer?

8. The time card for Jim Olden, a checker in a supermarket, shows that he worked a total of 38.5 hours. At $4.50 an hour, how much did Jim earn?

A time card is a record of hours worked.

---

9. On Wednesday Betty Wilder worked from 7:30 A.M. to 4:15 P.M. as a legal secretary. She usually works 8 hours a day. How much time more or less than 8 hours did she work on Wednesday?

10. Perry Marshall worked 144 hours this month. She earns $5.50 an hour as a tailor. How much did she earn this month?

★11. Steven Pole earned $8.25 an hour for 40 hours and $12.35 an hour for 6 hours of overtime. How much did he earn in all?

★12. Jane Carter, a welder on a construction job, earns $11.00 an hour for a 40-hour week. She is paid 1.5 times as much for each additional hour she works. How much does Jane earn for a week in which she works 45 hours?

Dividing by Whole Numbers

Bob watches Gerri fill piñatas with prizes. A total of 22.47 kilograms of toy rings, stickers, and pennies fill 7 piñatas. What is the average number of kilograms of prizes in each piñata?

You can estimate to place the decimal point in the quotient.

$$\begin{array}{r} 3\ 21 \\ 7\overline{)22.47} \end{array}$$

Think:
Round 22.47 to 22.
22 ÷ 7 is about 3. So the quotient is about 3.
The answer must be 3.21.

This is a way to divide a decimal by a whole number.

Step 1 Place the decimal point in the quotient directly above the decimal point in the dividend.

$$7\overline{)22.47}$$

Step 2 Divide as if you were dividing whole numbers.

$$\begin{array}{r} 3.21 \\ 7\overline{)22.47} \\ -21\downarrow \\ \hline 1\ 4 \\ -1\ 4\downarrow \\ \hline 07 \\ -\ 7 \\ \hline 0 \end{array}$$

There is an average of 3.21 kilograms of prizes in each piñata.

More Examples

$$\begin{array}{r} 0.028 \\ 6\overline{)0.168} \\ -\ 0 \\ \hline 16 \\ -12 \\ \hline 48 \\ -48 \\ \hline 0 \end{array} \qquad \begin{array}{r} 0.96 \\ 38\overline{)36.48} \\ -34\ 2 \\ \hline 2\ 28 \\ -2\ 28 \\ \hline 0 \end{array} \qquad \begin{array}{r} 4.633 \\ 16\overline{)74.128} \\ -64 \\ \hline 10\ 1 \\ -\ 9\ 6 \\ \hline 52 \\ -48 \\ \hline 48 \\ -48 \\ \hline 0 \end{array}$$

Practice • Write the quotients with the decimal points placed correctly.

1. $\begin{array}{r} 53 \\ 3\overline{)15.9} \end{array}$
2. $\begin{array}{r} 144 \\ 12\overline{)17.28} \end{array}$
3. $\begin{array}{r} 6 \\ 8\overline{)0.48} \end{array}$
4. $\begin{array}{r} 89 \\ 23\overline{)2.047} \end{array}$

Divide.

5. $6\overline{)3.54}$
6. $8\overline{)27.2}$
7. $6\overline{)404.4}$
8. $4\overline{)0.1516}$

Mixed Practice • Divide.

9. $5\overline{)21.5}$

10. $8\overline{)23.28}$

11. $2\overline{)74.4}$

12. $4\overline{)2.5528}$

13. $9\overline{)3.825}$

14. $3\overline{)27.3}$

15. $4\overline{)12.24}$

16. $7\overline{)66.7107}$

17. $6\overline{)24.36}$

18. $7\overline{)0.2667}$

19. $5\overline{)0.675}$

20. $9\overline{)0.0585}$

21. $4\overline{)6.48}$

22. $8\overline{)2.80}$

23. $9\overline{)77.67}$

24. $6\overline{)272.22}$

25. $23\overline{)20.47}$

26. $15\overline{)0.45}$

27. $27\overline{)5.481}$

28. $39\overline{)16.8402}$

29. $25\overline{)103.75}$

30. $63\overline{)2.646}$

31. $33\overline{)35.97}$

32. $74\overline{)8.0290}$

33. $54\overline{)127.98}$

34. $73\overline{)4.745}$

35. $49\overline{)287.63}$

36. $86\overline{)68.198}$

37. $341.6 \div 56 = \underline{\quad?\quad}$

38. $2.856 \div 34 = \underline{\quad?\quad}$

39. $1.508 \div 58 = \underline{\quad?\quad}$

40. $169.67 \div 47 = \underline{\quad?\quad}$

41. $15.25 \div 61 = \underline{\quad?\quad}$

42. $241.02 \div 39 = \underline{\quad?\quad}$

43. $263.63 \div 643 = \underline{\quad?\quad}$

44. $276.42 \div 542 = \underline{\quad?\quad}$

45. $1,000.5 \div 345 = \underline{\quad?\quad}$

What number does each letter stand for?

★ 46. $36\overline{)44.2B}$ with quotient $A.23$

★ 47. $25\overline{)10.05D}$ with quotient $0.4C2$

★ 48. $96\overline{)2.01F}$ with quotient $0.E21$

PROBLEM SOLVING • APPLICATIONS

49. Each package of napkins for the party weighs 43.2 grams. There are 16 napkins in each package. What does each napkin weigh?

★ 50. Bob has 170.8 grams of popcorn. He has 14 bowls that each hold 15 grams of popcorn. Does he have enough popcorn to fill all the bowls? If not, how much more does he need?

Midchapter Review

1. $\begin{array}{r} 13.9 \\ \times6 \\ \hline \end{array}$

2. $\begin{array}{r} 15 \\ \times1.3 \\ \hline \end{array}$

3. $\begin{array}{r} 1.965 \\ \times5.6 \\ \hline \end{array}$

4. $\begin{array}{r} 0.061 \\ \times0.04 \\ \hline \end{array}$

5. $\begin{array}{r} 19.4 \\ \times0.007 \\ \hline \end{array}$

6. $7\overline{)0.343}$

7. $6\overline{)46.8}$

8. $8\overline{)0.456}$

9. $12\overline{)7.608}$

10. $32\overline{)153.92}$

Zeros in Division

A chemist has 7.4 kilograms of powder to put into 4 containers. She puts the same amount into each container. How much does she put into each container?

$7.4 \div 4 = ?$

Sometimes you must write more zeros in the dividend in order to divide until there is a zero remainder.

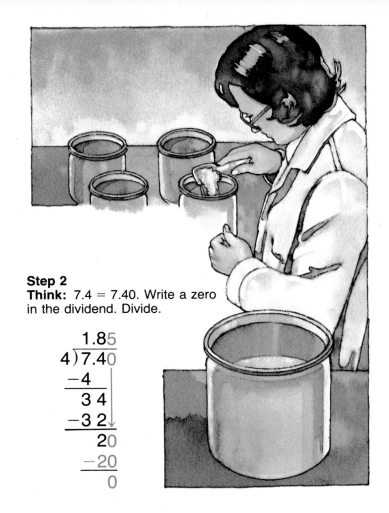

Step 1
Divide.
There is a remainder of 2.

```
      1.8
  4)7.4
   -4
    3 4
   -3 2
      2
```

Step 2
Think: 7.4 = 7.40. Write a zero in the dividend. Divide.

```
      1.85
  4)7.40
   -4
    3 4
   -3 2
      20
     -20
       0
```

She puts 1.85 kilograms into each container.

More Examples

```
        5.375
  4)21.500
   -20
     1 5
    -1 2
      30
     -28
      20
     -20
       0
```

```
          3.68
  55)202.40
    -165
      37 4
     -33 0
       4 40
      -4 40
         0
```

```
         0.675
  12)8.100
    -7 2
      90
     -84
      60
     -60
       0
```

Practice • Divide until the remainder is zero.

1. $6)\overline{8.7}$ **2.** $5)\overline{7.1}$ **3.** $6)\overline{0.57}$ **4.** $2)\overline{7.5}$ **5.** $4)\overline{8.2}$

6. $8)\overline{19.6}$ **7.** $4)\overline{12.6}$ **8.** $8)\overline{7.4}$ **9.** $15)\overline{34.8}$ **10.** $28)\overline{60.9}$

244

Mixed Practice • Divide until the remainder is zero.

11. $2\overline{)3.5}$ 12. $6\overline{)9.3}$ 13. $5\overline{)4.8}$ 14. $8\overline{)8.4}$ 15. $4\overline{)7.8}$

16. $8\overline{)17.2}$ 17. $4\overline{)30.7}$ 18. $4\overline{)0.46}$ 19. $6\overline{)57.3}$ 20. $2\overline{)38.7}$

21. $4\overline{)0.87}$ 22. $6\overline{)90.3}$ 23. $5\overline{)6.35}$ 24. $8\overline{)25.4}$ 25. $4\overline{)0.85}$

26. $18\overline{)4.5}$ 27. $24\overline{)29.4}$ 28. $16\overline{)43.6}$ 29. $52\overline{)98.8}$ 30. $65\overline{)0.104}$

31. $42\overline{)8.19}$ 32. $38\overline{)87.4}$ 33. $25\overline{)65.3}$ 34. $70\overline{)89.6}$ 35. $85\overline{)87.04}$

36. $0.27 \div 6 =$ ___?___

37. $13.9 \div 4 =$ ___?___

38. $5.1 \div 15 =$ ___?___

39. $26.6 \div 95 =$ ___?___

40. $140.4 \div 80 =$ ___?___

41. $0.56 \div 32 =$ ___?___

★ 42. $95.4 \div 48 =$ ___?___

★ 43. $47.1 \div 16 =$ ___?___

★ 44. $245.6 \div 125 =$ ___?___

★ 45. $25 \div$ ___?___ $= 2.5$

★ 46. $1.8 \div$ ___?___ $= 0.2$

★ 47. $15 \div$ ___?___ $= 0.75$

★ 48. $3.5 \div$ ___?___ $= 0.5$

★ 49. $0.42 \div$ ___?___ $= 0.07$

★ 50. $56 \div$ ___?___ $= 0.7$

PROBLEM SOLVING • APPLICATIONS

51. There are 4.5 liters of solution. The chemist stores the same amount of solution in 6 containers. How much does he put into each container?

52. A lab assistant does 5 experiments in 7.5 hours. What is the average amount of time spent on each experiment?

53. A lab assistant feeds a mouse a total of 28.56 milliliters of a new vitamin compound during a 7-day experiment. How much of the new compound is the mouse fed each day?

54. A chemist feeds 15 guinea pigs equal amounts of a solution. He uses a total of 5.4 milliliters. How much does each guinea pig get?

★ 55. A chemist mixes 1.6 liters of one solution and 1.8 liters of another solution. He pours an equal amount of the mixture into 8 beakers. How much does he put into each beaker?

★ 56. A chemist has 5 kilograms of a powder. She uses 0.7 kilograms for an experiment. She stores the rest of the powder equally in 4 containers. How much does she put into each container?

Multiplying or Dividing by 10, 100, or 1,000

Look for patterns. Watch the decimal points.

$10 \times 0.0572 = 0.572$
$10 \times 0.572 = 5.72$
$10 \times 5.72 = 57.2$

Multiplying by 10 moves the decimal point one place to the right.

$349.8 \div 10 = 34.98$
$34.98 \div 10 = 3.498$
$3.498 \div 10 = .3498$

Dividing by 10 moves the decimal point one place to the left.

$100 \times 0.6271 = 62.71$
$100 \times 62.71 = 6,271$

Multiplying by 100 moves the decimal point two places to the right.

$265.8 \div 100 = 2.658$
$2.658 \div 100 = 0.02658$

Dividing by 100 moves the decimal point two places to the left.

$1,000 \times 0.00654 = 6.54$
$1,000 \times 6.54 = 6,540$

Multiplying by 1,000 moves the decimal point three places to the right.

$597.2 \div 1,000 = 0.5972$
$0.5972 \div 1,000 = 0.0005972$

Dividing by 1,000 moves the decimal point three places to the left.

Practice • Multiply.

1. $10 \times 8.37 = $ __?__

2. $100 \times 9.365 = $ __?__

3. $1,000 \times 3.842 = $ __?__

Divide.

4. $69.3 \div 10 = $ __?__

5. $4.82 \div 100 = $ __?__

6. $71.04 \div 1,000 = $ __?__

More Practice • Multiply.

7. $10 \times 6.4 = \underline{\quad?\quad}$

8. $100 \times 9.04 = \underline{\quad?\quad}$

9. $1{,}000 \times 0.2354 = \underline{\quad?\quad}$

10. $100 \times 0.6 = \underline{\quad?\quad}$

11. $1{,}000 \times 4.86 = \underline{\quad?\quad}$

12. $100 \times 4.602 = \underline{\quad?\quad}$

13. $10 \times 5.132 = \underline{\quad?\quad}$

14. $100 \times 95.673 = \underline{\quad?\quad}$

15. $10 \times 0.007 = \underline{\quad?\quad}$

16. $1{,}000 \times 0.018 = \underline{\quad?\quad}$

17. $10 \times 29.46 = \underline{\quad?\quad}$

18. $100 \times 0.0143 = \underline{\quad?\quad}$

Divide.

19. $53.29 \div 10 = \underline{\quad?\quad}$

20. $1.666 \div 100 = \underline{\quad?\quad}$

21. $0.437 \div 1{,}000 = \underline{\quad?\quad}$

22. $7.924 \div 1{,}000 = \underline{\quad?\quad}$

23. $84.5 \div 10 = \underline{\quad?\quad}$

24. $372.4 \div 1{,}000 = \underline{\quad?\quad}$

25. $20.106 \div 1{,}000 = \underline{\quad?\quad}$

26. $54.8 \div 1{,}000 = \underline{\quad?\quad}$

27. $0.494 \div 10 = \underline{\quad?\quad}$

28. $750.2 \div 1{,}000 = \underline{\quad?\quad}$

29. $6.832 \div 100 = \underline{\quad?\quad}$

30. $117.6 \div 1{,}000 = \underline{\quad?\quad}$

Calculate.

★ **31.** $10{,}000 \times 0.6275 = \underline{\quad?\quad}$

★ **32.** $10{,}000 \times 6.275 = \underline{\quad?\quad}$

★ **33.** $10{,}000 \times 62.75 = \underline{\quad?\quad}$

★ **34.** $4{,}527.8 \div 10{,}000 = \underline{\quad?\quad}$

★ **35.** $452.78 \div 10{,}000 = \underline{\quad?\quad}$

★ **36.** $45.278 \div 10{,}000 = \underline{\quad?\quad}$

★ **37.** Write a rule for multiplying by 10,000.

★ **38.** Write a rule for dividing by 10,000.

★ **39.** Write a rule for multiplying by any power of ten.

★ **40.** Write a rule for dividing by any power of ten.

PROBLEM SOLVING • APPLICATIONS

41. A school orders 1,000 microscope slides. The slides cost $55.60. To the nearest cent, what is the cost of each slide?

42. An average cell is 0.0025 centimeters long. Under a microscope it looks 100 times longer. How long does the cell look?

43. An amoeba measures about 0.25 millimeters across. Theresa uses a microscope that magnifies 10 times. How wide does it look when magnified?

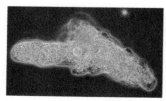

★ **44.** John looks at a cell that measures 0.003 centimeters under a microscope that magnifies 10 times. Then he looks at the same cell under a microscope that magnifies 100 times. How many centimeters longer does the cell look under the 100-power microscope than under the 10-power microscope?

247

Dividing Decimals

Multiply the dividend and the divisor by the same number.
The quotient does not change.

	Multiply both by 10.	Multiply both by 100.

$$\begin{array}{r} 7 \\ 6\overline{)42} \end{array} \qquad \begin{array}{r} 7 \\ 60\overline{)420} \end{array} \qquad \begin{array}{r} 7 \\ 600\overline{)4,200} \end{array}$$

When dividing with decimals, you need to divide by a whole number.
Sometimes, therefore, you must multiply the dividend and the
divisor by 10, 100, or 1,000.

6.12 ÷ 1.8. = ?

Step 1
There is one decimal place
in the divisor. Multiply the
dividend and the divisor by 10.
Move the decimal point
one place to the right.

$$1.8,\overline{)6.1.2}$$

Step 2
Place the decimal point
in the quotient directly above
the decimal point that you
wrote in the dividend.

$$1.8,\overline{)6.1.2}$$

Step 3
Divide as if you were
dividing whole numbers.

$$\begin{array}{r} 3.4 \\ 1.8,\overline{)6.1.2} \\ -5\ 4\downarrow \\ \hline 7\ 2 \\ -7\ 2 \\ \hline 0 \end{array}$$

More Examples

$$\begin{array}{r} 39.2 \\ 0.04.\overline{)1.56.8} \\ -1\ 2 \\ \hline 36 \\ -36 \\ \hline 8 \\ -8 \\ \hline 0 \end{array} \qquad \begin{array}{r} 2.7 \\ 0.65.\overline{)1.75.5} \\ -1\ 30 \\ \hline 45\ 5 \\ -45\ 5 \\ \hline 0 \end{array} \qquad \begin{array}{r} 347. \\ 0.006.\overline{)2.082.} \\ -1\ 8 \\ \hline 28 \\ -24 \\ \hline 42 \\ -42 \\ \hline 0 \end{array}$$

Practice • Write the quotients with the decimal points placed correctly.

1. $\begin{array}{r} 46 \\ 2.3\overline{)10.58} \end{array}$ 2. $\begin{array}{r} 19 \\ 0.4\overline{)0.76} \end{array}$ 3. $\begin{array}{r} 43 \\ 0.12\overline{)0.0516} \end{array}$ 4. $\begin{array}{r} 8 \\ 0.36\overline{)0.288} \end{array}$

Divide.

5. $0.4\overline{)0.212}$ 6. $0.7\overline{)2.59}$ 7. $0.65\overline{)0.780}$ 8. $0.003\overline{)0.0027}$

Mixed Practice • Write the quotients with the decimal points placed correctly.

9. $0.8\overline{)1.44}$ quotient 18

10. $0.9\overline{)0.099}$ quotient 11

11. $2.9\overline{)98.6}$ quotient 34

12. $9.5\overline{)45.505}$ quotient 479

Divide.

13. $1.2\overline{)49.2}$

14. $0.4\overline{)13.36}$

15. $4.1\overline{)0.3321}$

16. $1.6\overline{)64.32}$

17. $0.82\overline{)5.166}$

18. $0.23\overline{)10.35}$

19. $0.06\overline{)6.624}$

20. $0.36\overline{)339.48}$

21. $0.16\overline{)2.56}$

22. $5.8\overline{)3.48}$

23. $0.005\overline{)0.0185}$

24. $0.021\overline{)0.504}$

25. $0.83\overline{)42.33}$

26. $6.8\overline{)0.2312}$

27. $61.8\overline{)5.562}$

28. $0.551\overline{)23.142}$

29. $2.024 \div 0.08 =$ ___?___

30. $1.28 \div 3.2 =$ ___?___

31. $26.52 \div 0.39 =$ ___?___

32. $0.0522 \div 0.006 =$ ___?___

33. $1.8032 \div 0.046 =$ ___?___

34. $0.9204 \div 0.354 =$ ___?___

★ 35. Complete the table.

Dates	Kilometers Traveled	Liters of Gas Used	Kilometers per Liter
8/27–9/1	291.2	22.4	
9/2–9/7	516.6		14
9/8–9/15		16.6	12
9/15–9/20	544.7	41.9	

PROBLEM SOLVING • APPLICATIONS

36. Julie traveled a total of 291.5 kilometers. She used 26.5 liters of gasoline. How many kilometers per liter of gasoline did she average?

★ 37. On a business trip, Nick traveled 15.6 kilometers on Monday and 229.7 kilometers on Tuesday. His car averaged 11 kilometers per liter of gasoline. How many liters of gasoline did he use?

★ 38. Fill in the circles.

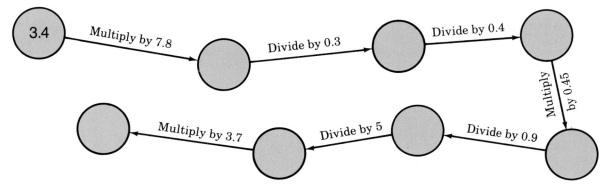

Zeros in the Dividend

The *Sea Star* returned to shore with a cargo of 18.2 kilograms of sea sponges. The average weight of each sponge was 0.07 kilograms. About how many sponges were on the *Sea Star*?

$18.2 \div 0.07 = ?$

Sometimes you must write more zeros in the dividend in order to locate the decimal point in the quotient.

Step 1
Multiply the divisor and dividend by 100. To move the decimal point two places to the right, you must write a zero in the dividend.

$$0.07\overline{)18.20.}$$

Step 2
Place the decimal point in the quotient.

$$0.07\overline{)18.20.}$$

Step 3
Divide.

$$
\begin{array}{r}
2\,60. \\
0.07\overline{)18.20.} \\
-14 \\
\hline
4\,2 \\
-4\,2 \\
\hline
00 \\
-\ 0 \\
\hline
0
\end{array}
$$

There were about 260 sponges on the *Sea Star*.

When you divide by decimals, you may need to write more zeros in the dividend in order to divide until there is a zero remainder.

Divide: $3.055 \div 2.5$.

Step 1
Multiply the divisor and dividend by 10. Place the decimal point in the quotient.

$$2.5\overline{)3.0.55}$$

Step 2
Divide. There is a remainder of 5.

$$
\begin{array}{r}
1.22 \\
2.5\overline{)3.0.55} \\
-2\,5 \\
\hline
5\,5 \\
-5\,0 \\
\hline
55 \\
-50 \\
\hline
5
\end{array}
$$

Step 3
Think: $3.055 = 3.0550$. Write a zero in the dividend. Divide.

$$
\begin{array}{r}
1.222 \\
2.5\overline{)3.0.550} \\
-2\,5 \\
\hline
5\,5 \\
-5\,0 \\
\hline
55 \\
-50 \\
\hline
50 \\
-50 \\
\hline
0
\end{array}
$$

Practice • Divide.

1. $0.7\overline{)42}$
2. $7.2\overline{)216}$
3. $0.22\overline{)31.9}$
4. $0.03\overline{)82.8}$

5. $0.4\overline{)2.9}$
6. $0.45\overline{)1.107}$
7. $0.06\overline{)1.41}$
8. $2.4\overline{)300}$

Mixed Practice • Divide.

9. $0.05\overline{)470}$
10. $0.29\overline{)153.7}$
11. $0.04\overline{)146.8}$
12. $2.5\overline{)60}$

13. $0.38\overline{)87.4}$
14. $0.2\overline{)16.7}$
15. $0.8\overline{)1.8}$
16. $4.4\overline{)37.4}$

17. $0.004\overline{)16}$
18. $1.6\overline{)0.84}$
19. $3.1\overline{)27.59}$
20. $0.5\overline{)7.5}$

21. $1.5\overline{)8.79}$
22. $0.006\overline{)0.504}$
23. $0.16\overline{)32}$
24. $0.08\overline{)0.576}$

25. $3.6\overline{)14.85}$
26. $0.48\overline{)40.8}$
27. $3.6\overline{)5.94}$
28. $8.4\overline{)31.5}$

29. $4.79 \div 0.5 = $ ___?___
30. $35.07 \div 4.2 = $ ___?___
31. $0.416 \div 0.08 = $ ___?___

32. $1.206 \div 0.268 = $ ___?___
33. $6.72 \div 0.064 = $ ___?___
34. $3.61 \div 0.8 = $ ___?___

★ 35. $0.01 \div 0.125 = $ ___?___
★ 36. $4.95 \div 0.004 = $ ___?___
★ 37. $3.98 \div 0.016 = $ ___?___

PROBLEM SOLVING • APPLICATIONS

38. Alex strings 1.54 kilograms of sponges. The average weight of each sponge is 0.055 kilogram. About how many sponges does he string?

39. John's string of sponges measures 3.4 meters long. The average length of each sponge is 0.025 meter. About how many sponges are on the string?

★ 40. The *Sea Star* often brings back shells. One kind of snail shell is so tiny that 30 of them in a row measure 2.34 centimeters long. What is the average length of each shell? How long would a row of 40 snail shells be?

★ 41. One bucket of shells weighs 4.13 kilograms. Another weighs 5.9 kilograms. The average weight of each shell is 0.295 kilogram. About how many shells are in both buckets?

Skills Maintenance

Divide. Write the answers in lowest terms.

1. $\frac{3}{5} \div \frac{2}{3} = $ ___?___
2. $\frac{7}{8} \div \frac{1}{2} = $ ___?___
3. $\frac{5}{6} \div \frac{3}{10} = $ ___?___

4. $6 \div \frac{1}{5} = $ ___?___
5. $\frac{2}{3} \div 6 = $ ___?___
6. $10 \div \frac{1}{4} = $ ___?___

7. $4\frac{3}{8} \div 1\frac{1}{4} = $ ___?___
8. $5\frac{1}{3} \div 4\frac{2}{3} = $ ___?___
9. $3\frac{1}{2} \div 2\frac{4}{5} = $ ___?___

251

Writing Decimals for Fractions

$\frac{3}{4}$ of the seats in the Astrodome are filled.
Find a decimal for $\frac{3}{4}$.

Divide the numerator by the denominator.
Divide until the remainder is 0.

$$3 \div 4 = ?$$

Step 1 Write a decimal point and a zero in the dividend. Place the decimal point in the quotient. Divide.

```
   0.7
4)3.0
 -2 8
 ────
    2
```

Step 2 Write another zero in the dividend. Divide.

```
   0.75
4)3.00
 -2 8↓
 ────
    20
   -20
   ───
     0
```

$\frac{3}{4} = 0.75$ Sometimes the remainder will never be 0.

Find a decimal for $\frac{2}{3}$. Find the answer to the nearest hundredth.
(Find the quotient to three decimal places.)

Step 1

```
   0.6
3)2 0
 -1 8
 ───
    2
```

Step 2

```
   0.66
3)2.00
 -1 8↓
 ────
    20
   -18
   ───
     2
```

Step 3

```
   0.666
3)2.000
 -1 8↓│
 ────  │
    20 │
   -18↓
   ───
    20
   -18
   ───
     2
```

0.666 is between 0.66 and 0.67. It is nearer to 0.67.
The decimal to the nearest hundredth for $\frac{2}{3}$ is 0.67.

Practice • Find the decimals. Divide until the remainder is 0.

1. $\frac{1}{4}$ 2. $\frac{3}{8}$ 3. $\frac{4}{5}$ 4. $\frac{3}{10}$ 5. $\frac{5}{8}$ 6. $\frac{1}{8}$

Find the decimals to the nearest hundredth.

7. $\frac{1}{3}$ 8. $\frac{2}{6}$ 9. $\frac{4}{9}$ 10. $\frac{9}{11}$ 11. $\frac{5}{7}$ 12. $\frac{3}{9}$

Mixed Practice • Find the decimals. Divide until the remainder is 0.

13. $\frac{3}{5}$ 14. $\frac{4}{25}$ 15. $\frac{2}{5}$ 16. $\frac{9}{10}$ 17. $\frac{7}{8}$ 18. $\frac{3}{50}$

19. $\frac{7}{20}$ 20. $\frac{21}{25}$ 21. $\frac{3}{16}$ 22. $\frac{5}{16}$ 23. $\frac{9}{4}$ 24. $\frac{15}{8}$

Find the decimals to the nearest hundredth.

25. $\frac{3}{11}$ 26. $\frac{7}{12}$ 27. $\frac{2}{7}$ 28. $\frac{7}{33}$ 29. $\frac{1}{9}$ 30. $\frac{5}{6}$

31. $\frac{2}{9}$ 32. $\frac{3}{22}$ 33. $\frac{5}{12}$ 34. $\frac{8}{6}$ 35. $\frac{26}{14}$ 36. $\frac{38}{17}$

You can find a baseball player's batting average.
Divide the number of hits by the number of times at bat.
Find the averages to the nearest thousandth.

	Batter	Number of Hits	Times at Bat	Batting Average
37.	Don	7	25	?
38.	Mary	8	26	?
39.	Paul	12	52	?
40.	Diane	14	58	?
41.	Ramon	16	62	?
42.	Bob	18	65	?
43.	Liz	23	81	?
★ 44.	Ellis	26	84	?

PROBLEM SOLVING • APPLICATIONS

Write the fractions as decimals. Then solve the problems.

45. $\frac{1}{5}$ of the 46,280 people at the stadium today have season passes. How many people at the stadium have season passes?

46. There are 56,216 fans at the game. $\frac{5}{8}$ of the fans are Yankee fans. How many are Yankee fans?

47. Tiger Stadium seats 53,676 people. $\frac{3}{4}$ of the seats in the stadium are filled. How many people are in the stadium?

★ 48. Candlestick Park seats 58,000 people. $\frac{3}{8}$ of the seats are taken by adults. $\frac{2}{5}$ of the seats are taken by children. How many seats are empty?

PROBLEM SOLVING • STRATEGIES

Choose the Sensible Answer

When solving a problem, you must think about whether or not your answer makes sense.

Read the problem.

Sara enjoyed woodworking classes in school. So she decided to become a carpenter. She worked as a carpenter's apprentice for 4 years. Now Sara is a carpenter and is in business for herself.

The Adams family wanted the roof of their house fixed and a new patio built. Sara charged $450.25 for her labor on the roof and $570.35 for her labor on the patio. Which of these answers is sensible for the total cost?

$102.06 or $1,020.60 or $10,206

Think: $450.25 is near $500.
$570.35 is near $600.
The answer is about $500 +
$600 or $1,100.

The sensible answer is $1,020.60.

Estimate to choose the sensible answers.

1. Sara bought a door for $79.50, a door frame for $34.45, a lock for $12.75, and hinges for $3.75. How much did she pay in all?

   $1,304.50 or $130.45 or $13.04

   Remember to round in order to estimate the answer.

2. Sara is building a stairway. The distance from the first floor to the landing is 338.7 centimeters. From the landing to the second floor is 696.8 centimeters. What is the height of the stairway?

   1,035.5 cm or 103.55 cm or 10,355.0 cm

254

Solve. Estimate to make sure that your answers are sensible.

3. A can of paint costs $15.39. Sara needs 12 cans. What will the total cost be?

4. Chair railing cost $0.24 a meter. Sara needs 35 meters. What is the total cost?

5. Sara charges $485.00 to build a sun deck. Materials cost her $302.78. How much does she earn?

6. Salvatore is Sara's apprentice. Together they work 76.25 hours on one job and 37.50 hours on another. How long do they work on both jobs?

7. A window screen takes about 0.75 hours to build. Salvatore builds 24 window screens. About how long does it take him?

8. Baseboard molding costs $0.32 per meter. Sara estimates she will need 16 meters to go around a new room. How much does she estimate the molding will cost?

9. Salvatore buys 18 meters of plastic pipe. The total cost is $58.50. What is the cost per meter?

10. Sara and Salvatore shingle a roof with 25 asphalt squares. The total cost is $287.50. What is the cost per square?

Reread the question. Does your solution make sense?

★ 11. Salvatore orders 6 boxes of nails at $6.95 each. Using a calculator, the clerk totals the bill to $59.70. Did the clerk make a mistake? If so, what was the mistake?

★ 12. Sara needs to buy 12 pieces of molding. Each piece must measure 2.8 meters long. The molding costs $2.25 per meter. What is the total cost of the molding?

Multiply. (pages 236–239)

1. 56.3
    × 7

2. 4.8
    ×0.9

3. 7.26
    × 5.3

4. 23.4
    ×0.62

5. 0.07
    ×0.08

6. 8
    ×0.004

7. 0.023
    × 0.05

8. 0.006
    × 3.4

Divide until the remainder is zero. (pages 242–245, 248–251)

9. $6\overline{)21.24}$

10. $9\overline{)4.932}$

11. $12\overline{)987.6}$

12. $41\overline{)133.414}$

13. $5\overline{)18.2}$

14. $6\overline{)35.1}$

15. $15\overline{)45.6}$

16. $8\overline{)2.7}$

17. $0.3\overline{)2.79}$

18. $0.08\overline{)0.448}$

19. $4.2\overline{)1.554}$

20. $0.007\overline{)2.5347}$

21. $0.8\overline{)2.74}$

22. $0.4\overline{)3}$

23. $0.06\overline{)4.2}$

24. $1.2\overline{)174}$

Find the decimals. Divide until the remainder is zero. (pages 252–253)

25. $\frac{6}{25}$

26. $\frac{7}{8}$

27. $\frac{12}{50}$

28. $\frac{3}{16}$

Find the decimals to the nearest hundredth. (pages 252–253)

29. $\frac{7}{9}$

30. $\frac{3}{7}$

31. $\frac{3}{11}$

32. $\frac{11}{12}$

Solve.

33. The S.S. *Atlantic* is 24.6 meters wide. Its length is 9.5 times its width. How long is the ship? (p. 236)

34. Each stateroom is 2.85 meters wide. Its length is 1.5 times its width. How long is the stateroom? (p. 236)

35. A school spends $25.00 for 100 pens. How much does each pen cost? (p. 246)

36. A case of pencils costs $150.00. There are 1,000 pencils in each case. How much does each pencil cost? (p. 246)

PROJECT

Unit Pricing

Louise is buying shampoo. She finds two different-sized bottles of the same brand. Which size bottle is the better buy?

She uses her calculator to find the **unit price.** The unit price for the shampoo is the price per ounce.

To find the unit price, Louise divides the cost by the number of ounces.

$$0.72 \div 18 = 0.04$$

The unit price is $0.04 per ounce for the 18-ounce bottle.

$$0.54 \div 12 = 0.045$$

The unit price is $0.045 per ounce for the 12-ounce bottle.
$$0.04 = 0.040$$

$$0.040 < 0.045$$

So the 18-ounce bottle is the better buy.

Which one is the better buy?

1. 12 ounces for $1.44
   or
   18 ounces for $2.25

2. 6 ounces for $.51
   or
   8 ounces for $.64

3. 5 pounds for $1.25
   or
   7 pounds for $1.68

4. 15 ounces for $1.14
   or
   18 ounces for $1.35

Cut out advertisements from the newspaper. Choose several of the same items advertised in two different stores. Divide to find the unit price for each item in each store. Then compare the unit prices to find the better buy.

TEST

Multiply.

1. 45.8
   × 9

2. 7.2
   ×0.6

3. 8.65
   × 4.9

4. 42.7
   ×0.85

5. 0.04
   ×0.09

6. 6
   ×0.007

7. 0.052
   × 0.08

8. 0.009
   × 5.1

Divide until the remainder is 0.

9. $4\overline{)140.8}$

10. $8\overline{)3.784}$

11. $12\overline{)507.72}$

12. $32\overline{)53.76}$

13. $4\overline{)52.2}$

14. $6\overline{)3.9}$

15. $5\overline{)2.63}$

16. $16\overline{)78.0}$

17. $0.6\overline{)7.26}$

18. $0.04\overline{)3.32}$

19. $0.012\overline{)0.5472}$

20. $0.005\overline{)0.1820}$

21. $0.4\overline{)9}$

22. $0.08\overline{)5.6}$

23. $0.003\overline{)5.4}$

24. $0.32\overline{)14.4}$

Find the decimals. Divide until the remainder is 0.

25. $\frac{9}{25}$

26. $\frac{17}{50}$

27. $\frac{7}{16}$

28. $\frac{3}{4}$

Find the decimals to the nearest hundredth.

29. $\frac{4}{11}$

30. $\frac{7}{12}$

31. $\frac{6}{7}$

32. $\frac{1}{9}$

Solve.

33. A turtle can travel 0.16 kilometer per hour. How far can the turtle travel in 2.5 hours?

34. A chemist has 2.4 liters of a solution. He stores the solution in 10 containers of equal size. How many liters does he put in each container?

35. A carpenter has 183.7 meters of molding. He cuts the molding into 100 pieces. How many meters is each piece?

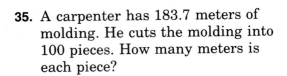

ENRICHMENT

Scientific Notation

The decimal numeration system is based on powers of ten.

Look for a pattern.

$10 = 10^1$ $100 = 10^2$ $1{,}000 = 10^3$ $10{,}000 = 10^4$

Compare the number of zeros in the number with the exponent in the exponent form.

Scientists often work with very large numbers. For example, the number 900,000 is a large number. They can rename this number by using **scientific notation.**

Step 1
Move the decimal point to the left to name a number less than 10 but not less than 1.

$$9.00000.$$

9×10^5 is scientific notation for 900,000.

Step 2
You have moved the decimal point 5 places to the left. You have divided by 10^5. So multiply by 10^5.

$$9 \times 10^5$$

Name 87,600 using scientific notation.

Step 1
Move the decimal point to the left to name a number less than 10 but not less than 1.

$$8.7600.$$

8.76×10^4 is scientific notation for 87,600.

Step 2
You have divided by 10^4. So multiply by 10^4.

$$8.76 \times 10^4$$

Write the exponent forms of the numbers.

1. 100

2. 10,000

3. 100,000

4. 1,000,000

5. 10,000,000

6. 100,000,000

7. 1,000,000,000

8. 10,000,000,000

9. 100,000,000,000

Enrichment continued

Write the numbers.

10. 6×10^5 **11.** 4×10^2 **12.** 7×10^7

13. 2×10^6 **14.** 6.25×10^3 **15.** 5.2×10^4

16. 9.3×10^3 **17.** 8×10^7 **18.** 4.32×10^5

19. 36.9×10^4 **20.** 7.34×10^6 **21.** 9.61×10^3

Complete the table.

	Planet	Distance from the Sun in km	Scientific Notation
22.	Mercury	22,500,000	?
23.	Venus	?	4.20×10^7
24.	Earth	58,100,000	?
25.	Mars	?	8.86×10^7
26.	Jupiter	302,000,000	?
27.	Saturn	556,000,000	?
28.	Uranus	?	1.11×10^9
29.	Neptune	1,750,000,000	?
30.	Pluto	2,300,000,000	?

Look for a pattern.

$0.1 = 10^{-1}$ $0.01 = 10^{-2}$ $0.001 = 10^{-3}$ $0.0001 = 10^{-4}$

Write the exponent forms of the numbers.

31. 0.000001   **32.** 0.00001   **33.** 0.000000001

Write the numbers.

34. 3×10^{-2} **35.** 8×10^{-4} **36.** 5×10^{-7}

CALCULATOR

Working with Decimals

The calculator takes care of decimal places for you.
But you must push the correct buttons.
You do not need to push the zero that comes before a decimal point for numbers less than one.
Always estimate your answer to make sure you pushed the correct buttons.

0.426	Estimate: 0.4 times 0.04 is about 0.016.
×0.036	

Push . 0 4 2 6 × . 0 3 6 = .

You should get 0.0015336. This number is not close to 0.016.
That means there must be too many zeros in one of the factors.

Push . 4 2 6 × . 0 3 6 = .

You should get 0.015336. That is close to 0.016, and so 0.015336 is the answer.

Multiply using the calculator. Add commas where needed in answers.

1. 42.04	2. 789.2	3. 13.089	4. 0.0662
× 4.35	× 36.8	× 0.004	× 4,287

Division with decimals works the same way as division without decimals.

Divide: 4.68 ÷ 36.

Estimate: 5.0 divided by 40 is about 0.1.

Push 4 . 6 8 ÷ 3 6 = . The answer is 0.13.

Divide using the calculator. Always estimate your answer first.
Write the dollar sign and the cents point where needed.

5. 96.2 ÷ 37 = ___?___

6. 36.57 ÷ 53 = ___?___

7. 2,184 ÷ 26 = ___?___

8. 18)$55.26

9. 79)0.474

10. 24)$23.76

11. 35)12.25

12. 85)88.40

13. 4)$83.28

14. 28)0.0028

15. 99)$99.99

16. $91.20 ÷ 95 = ___?___

17. $00.00 ÷ 35 = ___?___

18. 2,209 ÷ 47 = ___?___

261

SKILLS MAINTENANCE
Chapters 1 Through 10

Choose the correct answers.

1. Compare.

51,987 ⬤ 52,014

    A. >
    B. <
    C. =
    D. not here

2. Estimate. Round to the nearest thousand.

$$26,452$$
$$+\ 8,709$$

    A. 34,000
    B. 35,000
    C. 36,000
    D. not here

3. Subtract.

$$8,004$$
$$-2,756$$

    A. 6,252
    B. 5,358
    C. 5,248
    D. not here

4. Find the greatest common factor of 8 and 12.

    A. 2
    B. 4
    C. 8
    D. not here

5. How many runs did Jack score?

    A. 1   **B.** 3
    C. 2   **D.** not here

6. Round 412.058 to the nearest hundredth.

    A. 412.
    B. 412.05
    C. 412.06
    D. not here

7. Compare.

$\frac{5}{6}$ ⬤ $\frac{4}{5}$

    A. >
    B. <
    C. =
    D. not here

8. Subtract.

$$7\frac{3}{8}$$
$$-4\frac{3}{4}$$

    A. $3\frac{3}{4}$
    B. $2\frac{3}{8}$
    C. $3\frac{5}{8}$
    D. not here

9. Multiply.

$0.04 \times 7 =$ _____?_____

    A. 0.28
    B. 0.028
    C. 2.8
    D. not here

10. The length of Jeffrey's room is 1.6 times the width of the room. The width of the room is 2.5 meters. What is the length of the room?

    A. 4 meters   **B.** 40 meters
    C. 3.2 meters   **D.** not here

11. The school spends $16.20 for 36 pens. How much does each pen cost?

    A. $0.45   **B.** $4.50
    C. $0.36   **D.** not here

Measurement

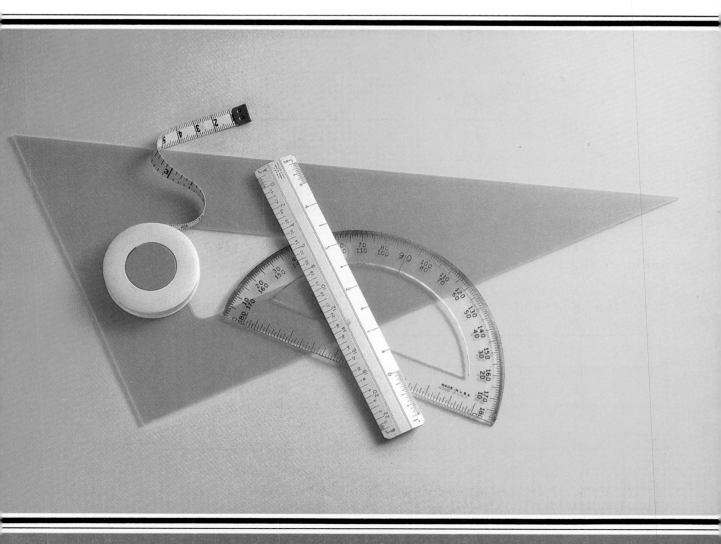

**Metric Units of Length • Changing Metric Units • Perimeter
and Circumference • Area of Rectangles, Parallelograms, and
Triangles • Surface Area • Volume and Rectangular Prisms
• Metric Units of Liquid Capacity and Mass
• Degrees Celsius • Time • Customary Units of Length
• Perimeter, Area, and Volume • Customary Units of Capacity
and Weight • Problem Solving: Operations with Measures
• Degrees Fahrenheit • Area of a Circle**

Metric Units of Length

The **kilometer, meter, decimeter, centimeter,** and **millimeter** are metric units of length.

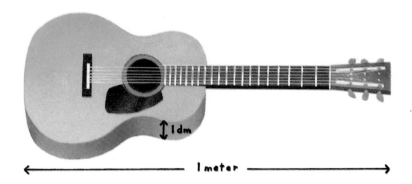

A guitar is about one **meter (m)** long.

A guitar is about one **decimeter (dm)** thick.

The distance between 2 guitar strings is about one **centimeter (cm)**.

The thickness of a guitar string is about one **millimeter (mm)**.

10 dm = 1 m
10 cm = 1 dm
100 cm = 1 m
10 mm = 1 cm
100 mm = 1 dm
1,000 mm = 1 m
1 km = 1,000 m

It takes Carmine about 12 minutes to walk at a steady pace to her guitar lesson. This is a distance of about 1 **kilometer (km)**.

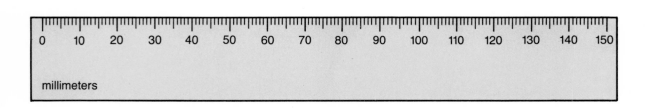

The length of this piece of guitar string is 88 millimeters to the **nearest millimeter**.

Practice • Estimate the lengths. Then measure each to the nearest unit.

1.
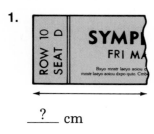

_____ cm

2.
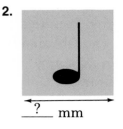

_____ mm

3.
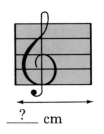

_____ cm

264

More Practice • Estimate the lengths. Then measure each to the nearest unit.

4.

___?___ mm

5.

___?___ cm

6.

___?___ cm

Use a ruler. Draw a picture of

7. a pencil that is 14 cm long.

8. a pen that is 122 mm long.

9. a piece of chalk that is 6 cm long.

10. a comb that is 180 mm long.

Which unit of measure would you use for each?
Write MILLIMETER, CENTIMETER, METER, or KILOMETER.

11. the thickness of a violin string

12. the distance from your house to the concert hall

13. the width of a stage

14. the length of a flute

Add the measures.

15.	23 cm	16.	48 cm	17.	123 mm	18.	295.5 m	19.	132.6 m
	36 cm		32 cm		146 mm		48.4 m		34.2 m
	+98 cm		+65 cm		+238 mm		+ 76.6 m		+396.9 m

PROBLEM SOLVING • APPLICATIONS

A group of musicians is on a concert tour. Give the distance they fly

20. from New York to Atlanta to Houston.

21. from Houston to Los Angeles to Chicago.

22. from New York to Chicago to San Francisco.

23. from New York to Chicago to Los Angeles.

★ 24. Which is the longer trip, from San Francisco to Chicago to New York to Atlanta or from San Francisco to Chicago to Los Angeles?

Changing Metric Units

Like the decimal system of numeration, the metric system is based on the number 10.

Each unit is 10 times the next smaller unit. Each unit is 0.1 times the next larger unit.

thousands	hundreds	tens	unit	tenths	hundredths	thousandths
kilometer km 1 km = 1,000 m 0.001 km = 1 m	hectometer hm 1 hm = 100 m 0.01 hm = 1 m	dekameter dam 1 dam = 10 m 0.1 dam = 1 m	meter m	decimeter dm 1 dm = 0.1 m 10 dm = 1 m	centimeter cm 1 cm = 0.01 m 100 cm = 1 m	millimeter mm 1 mm = 0.001 m 1,000 mm = 1 m

You can use the table to find the equivalent measures.

$$4 \text{ km} = ? \text{ m}$$

Kilometers are larger than meters, and so there will be more meters.

Think: 1 km = 1,000 m
4 km = 4 × 1,000 m
4 km = 4,000 m

You can also count the number of units you must move to the right. There are 3. Move the decimal point 3 places to the right.

$$4 \text{ km} = 4,000. \text{ m}$$

$$4.7 \text{ cm} = ? \text{ m}$$

Centimeters are smaller than meters, and so there will be fewer meters.

Think: 1 cm = 0.01 m
4.7 cm = 4.7 × 0.01 m
4.7 cm = 0.047 m

You can also count the number of units you must move to the left. There are 2. Move the decimal point 2 places to the left.

$$4.7 \text{ cm} = 0.047 \text{ m}$$

Practice • Complete.

1. 6 m = _?_ km

2. 3 km = _?_ m

3. 5 m = _?_ cm

4. 11 mm = _?_ m

5. _?_ mm = 14 m

6. _?_ mm = 9 m

7. _?_ m = 2.4 cm

8. 8.6 km = _?_ m

9. 0.63 km = _?_ m

Mixed Practice • Complete.

10. 1 m = _?_ km

11. 4 km = _?_ m

12. _?_ m = 800 cm

13. _?_ cm = 0.08 m

14. 16 m = _?_ cm

15. 9 km = _?_ m

16. 4 mm = _?_ m

17. _?_ m = 3,000 mm

18. 6 m = _?_ cm

19. 30.2 m = ___?___ km   **20.** ___?___ m = 190 cm   **21.** 0.06 m = ___?___ cm

22. 7.4 cm = ___?___ m   **23.** 0.027 m = ___?___ mm   **24.** ___?___ m = 7 mm

★ **25.** ___?___ cm = 5.28 dm   ★ **26.** 4.6 dm = ___?___ mm   ★ **27.** 52.4 km = ___?___ cm

★ **28.** 73.2 km = ___?___ dam   ★ **29.** ___?___ dam = 10.3 dm   ★ **30.** 48.5 hm = ___?___ cm

Complete.

	Kilometer	Hectometer	Dekameter	Meter	Decimeter	Centimeter	Millimeter
	0.006 km	0.06 hm	0.6 dam	6 m	60 dm	600 cm	6,000 mm
31.			3.7 dam				
32.		0.24 hm					
33.					40 dm		
34.						85 cm	
35.				9.8 m			
★ **36.**							8×10^9 mm

Use >, <, or = to make a true sentence.

342 cm ⬤ 3.36 m

You can change cm to m:	Or change m to cm:
342 cm = 3.42 m	3.36 m = 336 cm

Compare: 3.42 m ⟩ 3.36 m   Compare: 342 cm ⟩ 336 cm

Either way, you can see that 342 cm > 3.36 m.

Write >, <, or =.

★ **37.** 6.8 m ⬤ 69.2 cm   ★ **38.** 15.32 m ⬤ 1,500 cm   ★ **39.** 230 cm ⬤ 2.3 m

★ **40.** 2.18 m ⬤ 2,184 cm   ★ **41.** 30 cm ⬤ 0.003 m   ★ **42.** 61.4 cm ⬤ 0.6 m

PROBLEM SOLVING • APPLICATIONS

43. John runs 5,000 meters each day. How many kilometers is that?

44. Mary walks 6 kilometers each day. How many meters is that?

★ **45.** Paul swam 3 kilometers. Mark swam 2,500 meters. Who swam farther?

★ **46.** Tara hiked 9 kilometers. Jyu-li hiked 10,000 meters. Who hiked farther?

Perimeter

Tonya has a home near the beach. She plans to install a fence around her property. How many meters of fencing does she need?

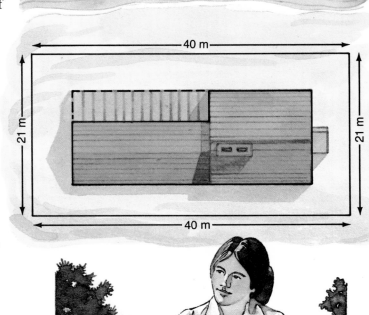

The distance around a figure is its **perimeter.**

The perimeter of a figure is the sum of the lengths of the sides.

Find the perimeter.

Step 1 Find the measure of each side.

Step 2 Find the sum of the measures.

$$40 + 21 + 40 + 21 = 122$$

Tonya needs 122 meters of fencing.

Practice • Find the perimeter of each figure.

1.

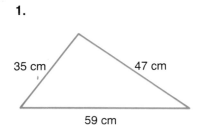

35 cm   47 cm   59 cm

2.

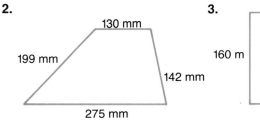

130 mm   199 mm   142 mm   275 mm

3.

88 m   160 m   160 m   88 m

4.

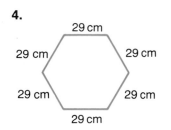

29 cm   29 cm   29 cm   29 cm   29 cm   29 cm

5.

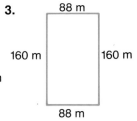

16 m   24 m   20 m   24 m

6.

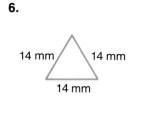

14 mm   14 mm   14 mm

268

More Practice • Find the perimeter of each figure.

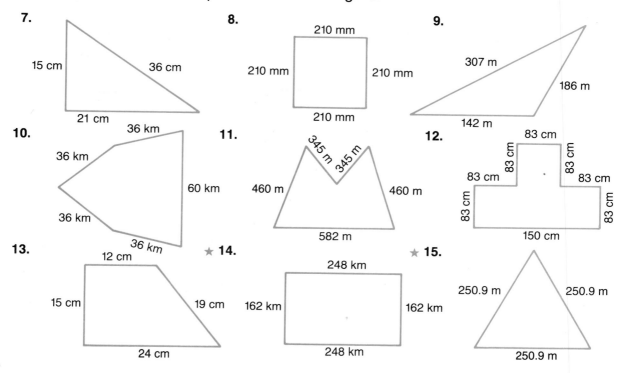

7. 15 cm, 36 cm, 21 cm

8. 210 mm, 210 mm, 210 mm, 210 mm

9. 307 m, 186 m, 142 m

10. 36 km, 36 km, 60 km, 36 km, 36 km

11. 345 m, 345 m, 460 m, 460 m, 582 m

12. 83 cm, 83 cm, 83 cm, 83 cm, 83 cm, 83 cm, 83 cm, 150 cm

13. 12 cm, 15 cm, 19 cm, 24 cm

★ **14.** 248 km, 162 km, 162 km, 248 km

★ **15.** 250.9 m, 250.9 m, 250.9 m

PROBLEM SOLVING • APPLICATIONS

16. What is the perimeter of Tonya's house?

17. What is the perimeter of Tonya's deck?

★**18.** Tonya uses yarn to frame her collection of shells. The shells are glued to a board. The sides of the board are 160 millimeters, 22 centimeters, 160 millimeters, and 22 centimeters. How many centimeters of yarn does she use?

★**19.** Place the end of a piece of string at START. Match the string to the outline of the shell. Mark the string where it meets START. Measure the string to find the perimeter to the nearest centimeter.

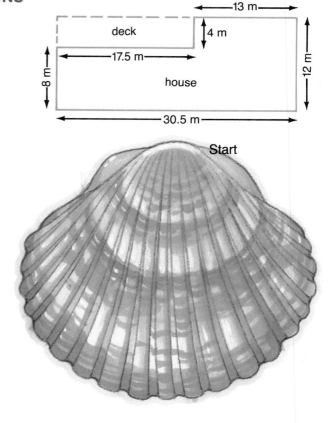

Tonya's house

deck — 13 m — 4 m — 17.5 m — 8 m — house — 12 m — 30.5 m

Start

Circumference of a Circle

The distance around a circle is its **circumference**.

Beth and David want to compare the circumference of a coin with the length of its diameter.

They place a piece of string around the coin. The length of the string is the circumference.

They mark off the diameter of the coin on the string. The string is a little longer than 3 diameters.

Beth and David try it with other coins. Each time the circumference is a little more than 3 diameters.

The circumference (C) divided by the length of a diameter (d) is always the same number. This number is named with the Greek letter π (**pi**). You pronounce the letter as "pie."

$$\frac{C}{d} = \pi$$

This is the formula for finding the circumference.

$$C = \pi \times d$$

Use 3.14 as an approximation for π.
The symbol $\approx$ means "is approximately equal to."

Find the circumference when the diameter is 8 centimeters.

$$C = \pi \times d$$
$$C \approx 3.14 \times 8$$
$$C \approx 25.12 \text{ cm}$$

The circumference is approximately equal to 25.12 centimeters.

Practice • Find the circumference of each.

1. 9 cm

2. 10 mm

3. 14 mm

4. 68 mm

5. $d = 40$ mm

6. $d = 21$ cm

7. $d = 35$ cm

8. $d = 5.3$ m

Mixed Practice • Find the circumference of each.

9.
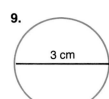
3 cm

10.

7 cm

11.

12 m

12.

46 km

13. $d = 4$ mm

14. $d = 11$ mm

15. $d = 18$ cm

16. $d = 27$ cm

17. $d = 62$ m

18. $d = 93$ m

19. $d = 325$ km

20. $d = 126$ km

21. $d = 8.6$ m

22. $d = 36.4$ m

23. $d = 17.9$ km

24. $d = 86.06$ km

Find the perimeter of each figure.

★ **25.**
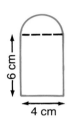
6 cm
4 cm

★ **26.**
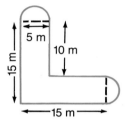
5 m
10 m
15 m
15 m

PROBLEM SOLVING • APPLICATIONS

27. Jenny is planning a flower garden in the shape of a circle. The diameter is 2.5 meters. What is the circumference?

28. Bob is watching his little brother Tim play in a wading pool. The pool is 1.6 meters in diameter. What is its circumference?

★ **29.** The Wilsons are putting a patio in their backyard. Jan needs to know the perimeter of the patio before she orders plants to go around the edge. Use the figure to find the perimeter.

★ **30.** If Jan can put a plant every 30 centimeters, how many plants will fit around the patio?

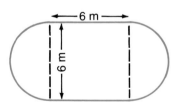
6 m
6 m

Skills Maintenance

1. 4.2
+6.5

2. 9.8
+7.4

3. 6.3
+5.72

4. 32.84
+15.5

5. $7.4 + 6.81 = $ ___?___

6. $3.28 + 0.7 = $ ___?___

7. $15.84 + 6.2 = $ ___?___

8. $5.983 + 3.25 = $ ___?___

9. $0.79 + 6.3 = $ ___?___

10. $8.374 + 5.8 = $ ___?___

Area of Rectangles

The number of square units that cover
a surface is the **area** of the surface.

A **square centimeter (cm²)** is a unit of area.

1 cm

1 cm

1 square centimeter (cm²)

You can count to find the area of the
rectangle. It is 15 square centimeters.

You can also multiply to find the area of a rectangle.

Multiply: length times width.

width, 3 cm

Area = length × width

A = l × w

$$A = 5 \times 3$$
$$A = 15$$
$$\text{Area} = 15 \text{ cm}^2$$

length, 5 cm

The area is 15 square centimeters.

Other metric units of area are the
square millimeter (**mm²**), square meter
(**m²**), and square kilometer (**km²**).

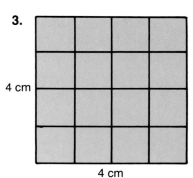

Practice • Count to find the area of each figure in square centimeters.

1.

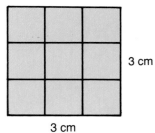

3 cm

3 cm

2.

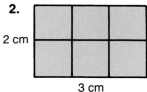

2 cm

3 cm

3.

4 cm

4 cm

The length and the width are given. Find the area of each.

4. $l = 6$ cm, $w = 5$ cm

5. $l = 12$ mm, $w = 7$ mm

Mixed Practice • Find the area of each figure.

6.

3 mm

6 mm

7.

4 cm

7 cm

8.

5 m

5 m

The length and the width are given. Find the area of each.

9. $l = 9$ mm, $w = 5$ mm

10. $l = 6$ mm, $w = 4$ mm

11. $l = 10$ cm, $w = 7$ cm

12. $l = 12$ cm, $w = 12$ cm

13. $l = 14$ cm, $w = 8$ cm

14. $l = 13$ cm, $w = 6$ cm

15. $l = 2.2$ km, $w = 7$ km

16. $l = 3.6$ km, $w = 10$ km

17. $l = 41.6$ m, $w = 15.2$ m

18. $l = 73.9$ m, $w = 73.9$ m

★ **19.** $l = 55$ mm, $w = 28$ cm

★ **20.** $l = 93$ m, $w = 0.8$ km

★ **21.** $l = 8.7$ m, $w = 129$ cm

★ **22.** $l = 134$ mm, $w = 185$ cm

PROBLEM SOLVING • APPLICATIONS

23. Mr. Miller plans to open a variety store in a shopping mall. There are two vacant stores that he can rent. Store A is 55 meters long and 20 meters wide. Store B is 40 meters long and 32 meters wide. Which store would give him more floor space? How much more?

24. In a box of blue facial tissues the tissues are 239 millimeters × 210 millimeters. A box of green tissues has tissues that are 24.1 centimeters × 20.3 centimeters. Which tissues are larger?

A **hectare** is a unit of area.
1 hectare = 10,000 square meters.

★ **25.** This map shows the layout of the shopping mall. What is the area of the mall in hectares?

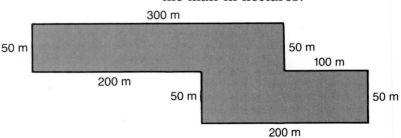

300 m

50 m

50 m

100 m

200 m

50 m

50 m

200 m

Area of Parallelograms

The **base** of the parallelogram is 6 centimeters long.

The **height** is 3 centimeters.

Use what you know about the area of a rectangle to find the area of a parallelogram.

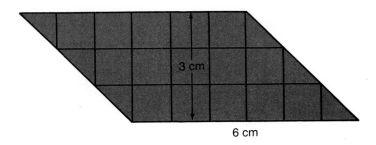

3 cm

6 cm

Step 1
Trace the parallelogram at the top of the page. Cut off one end of the parallelogram.

Step 2
Slide it around to the other end.

Step 3
You see a rectangle. The area of the parallelogram is equal to the area of the rectangle.

To find the area of a parallelogram, multiply: length of the base times height.

Area = base × height
A = b × h
$A = 6 \times 3$
$A = 18$
Area = 18 cm²

The area is 18 square centimeters.

Practice • Find the area of each figure.

1.

4 cm

6 cm

2.

3 cm

5 cm

3.

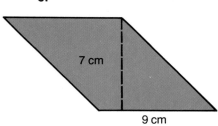

7 cm

9 cm

Mixed Practice • Find the area of each figure.

4.

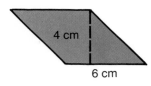

3 cm

7 cm

5.

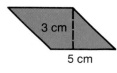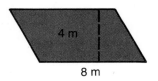

4 m

8 m

6.

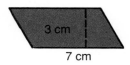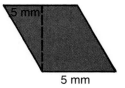

5 mm

5 mm

The base and the height are given. Find the area of each.

7. $b = 8$ mm, $h = 7$ mm

8. $b = 8$ m, $h = 3$ m

9. $b = 10$ dm, $h = 3$ dm

10. $b = 12$ cm, $h = 9$ cm

11. $b = 24$ cm, $h = 6$ cm

12. $b = 36$ mm, $h = 10$ mm

★ **13.** $b = 42$ cm, $h = 150$ mm

★ **14.** $b = 0.78$ km, $h = 28$ m

★ **15.** $b = 550$ mm, $h = 36$ cm

★ **16.** $b = 0.93$ m, $h = 4.4$ cm

How much paper is needed to make each shape?

★ **17.**

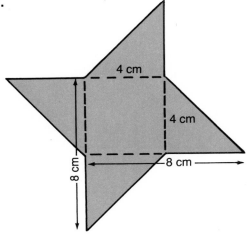

★ **18.**

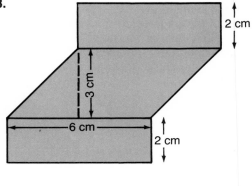

PROBLEM SOLVING • APPLICATIONS

Tell what you need to find, the AREA or the PERIMETER. Then solve.

19. A new clubhouse measures 10 meters by 7 meters. How much land does the clubhouse take up?

20. The club members cleared away the weeds from around a tree. They built a square fence guard to protect the tree. Each side of the square is 45 centimeters long. How much fencing did they use?

★ **21.** The members of the club put weather stripping around the windows in the clubhouse. The largest window measures 120 centimeters by 175 centimeters. How many meters of weather stripping did they use on this window?

★ **22.** Henry is using square tiles to form the shape of a parallelogram above the door of the clubhouse. Each tile is one square decimeter. The base of the parallelogram is 1.2 meters long. The height is 6 decimeters. How many tiles are needed?

275

Area of Triangles

The base of the triangle is 6 centimeters long.

The height is 3 centimeters.

Use what you know about the area of a parallelogram to find the area of a triangle.

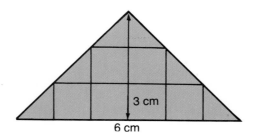

3 cm

6 cm

Step 1
Trace the triangle at the top of the page twice. Cut out each tracing. You now have two congruent triangles. They have the same area.

Step 2
Turn one around. Fit it against the other. You now have a parallelogram.

Step 3
The area of each triangle is $\frac{1}{2}$ the area of the parallelogram.

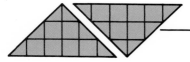  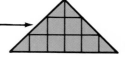 

To find the area of a triangle, multiply: $\frac{1}{2}$ times the base times the height.

$Area = \frac{1}{2} \times base \times height$

$A = \frac{1}{2} \times b \times h$

$$A = \frac{1}{2} \times 6 \times 3$$
$$A = 9$$
$$Area = 9 \text{ cm}^2$$

The area is 9 square centimeters.

Practice • Find the area of each figure.

1.

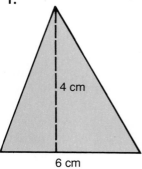

4 cm

6 cm

2.

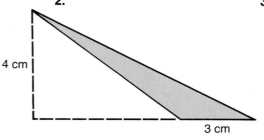

4 cm

3 cm

3.

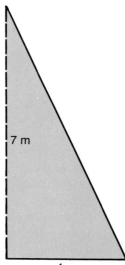

7 m

4 m

Mixed Practice • Find the area of each figure.

4.
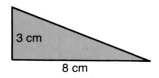
3 cm
8 cm

5.
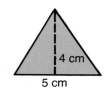
4 cm
5 cm

6.
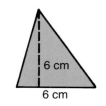
6 cm
6 cm

7.
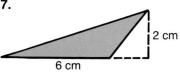
2 cm
6 cm

8.
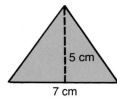
5 cm
7 cm

9.
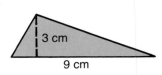
3 cm
9 cm

The base and the height are given. Find the area for each.

10. $b = 8$ cm, $h = 7$ cm

11. $b = 6$ cm, $h = 4$ cm

12. $b = 10$ m, $h = 3$ m

13. $b = 12$ cm, $h = 9$ cm

14. $b = 14$ cm, $h = 7$ cm

15. $b = 13$ m, $h = 8$ m

16. $b = 24$ m, $h = 6$ m

17. $b = 36$ cm, $h = 10$ cm

★ **18.** $b = 420$ mm, $h = 15$ cm

★ **19.** $b = 0.73$ m, $h = 28$ cm

★ **20.** $b = .5.5$ dm, $h = 0.36$ m

★ **21.** $b = 930$ mm, $h = 44$ cm

PROBLEM SOLVING • APPLICATIONS

22. An A-frame house has 2 walls shaped like triangles. The length of the base of each wall is 12 meters. The height of each wall is 9.6 meters. What is the area of the 2 walls in square meters?

23. John's tent has 3 sides shaped like triangles. The length of the base of each side is 4 meters. The height of each side is 2.8 meters. What is the area of the 3 sides of the tent?

★ **24.** Estimate the total area of the land shown on the map. Round each length to the nearest 10 meters.

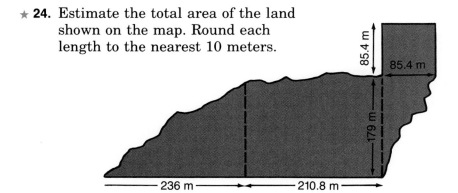

85.4 m
85.4 m
179 m
236 m
210.8 m

Surface Area

The dimensions of this box are
4 centimeters by 5 centimeters by 3 centimeters.

Look at the box opened up.
The six faces are rectangles.
This box is a rectangular
prism.

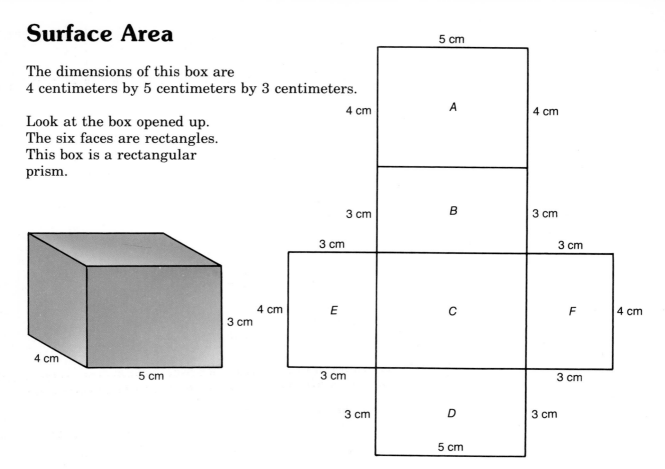

To find the **surface area** of a rectangular
prism, find the area of each face. Then add.

Area of face A $4 \times 5 = 20$ cm^2
Area of face B $3 \times 5 = 15$ cm^2
Area of face C $4 \times 5 = 20$ cm^2
Area of face D $3 \times 5 = 15$ cm^2
Area of face E $3 \times 4 = 12$ cm^2
Area of face F $3 \times 4 = \underline{12}$ cm^2
Surface area = 94 cm^2

Practice • Find the surface area of each figure.

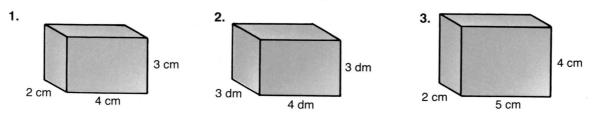

1.   3 cm   2 cm   4 cm

2.   3 dm   3 dm   4 dm

3.   4 cm   2 cm   5 cm

278

More Practice • Find the surface area of each figure.

4.

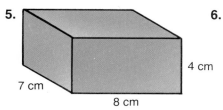

5 cm 6 cm 4 cm

5.

7 cm 8 cm 4 cm

6.

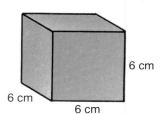

6 cm 6 cm 6 cm

7.

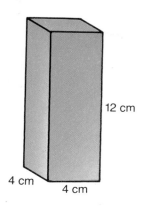

7 cm 5 cm 4 cm

8.

12 cm 4 cm 4 cm

★ **9.**

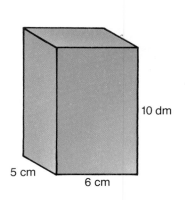

10 dm 5 cm 6 cm

PROBLEM SOLVING • APPLICATIONS

10. Carlos is ordering plastic to cover his greenhouse for the winter. He wants to cover 4 sides. How many square meters of plastic will he need if the plastic does not overlap?

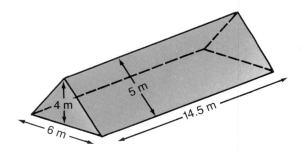

4 m 5 m 6 m 14.5 m

Carlos noticed that when a piece of pipe is cut and flattened, it is shaped like a rectangle.

The width of the rectangle is equal to the circumference of the circular opening.

To find the surface area of a piece of pipe, multiply the length of the pipe by the circumference of the pipe.

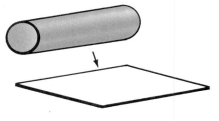

★ **11.** A water pipe in Carlos's greenhouse has a diameter of 45 millimeters. The pipe is 12 meters long. What is its surface area in square meters?

★ **12.** Carlos is going to install a sink in the greenhouse. He needs a pipe that is 3 meters long and has a diameter of 1.5 centimeters. What is the surface area of the pipe in square centimeters?

Volume and Rectangular Prisms

The **volume** of a box is the
number of cubic units that
will fit inside the box.

A **cubic centimeter (cm³)**
is a unit of volume.

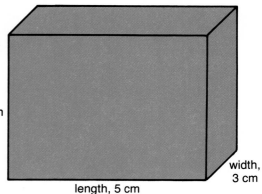

1 cm
1 cm
1 cm
cubic centimeter (cm³)

height, 4 cm

width, 3 cm

length, 5 cm

Find the volume of this box.

Step 1
Find how many cubic centimeters
will make one layer.

Step 2
Count the layers. Then find how many
cubic centimeters in all.

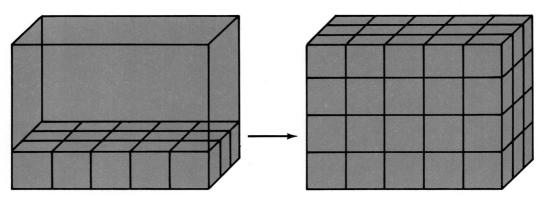

This box is a rectangular prism.
To find the volume of a rectangular prism,
multiply: length times width times height.

The volume of this box is 60 cubic centimeters.

Volume = length × width × height
$V = l \times w \times h$

$V = 5 \times 3 \times 4$
$V = 60$
Volume = 60 cm³

Other metric units of volume are the cubic millimeter (**mm³**)
and the cubic meter (**m³**).

Practice • Find the volume of each figure.

1.

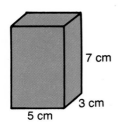

7 cm
3 cm
5 cm

2.

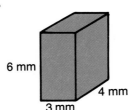

6 mm
4 mm
3 mm

3.

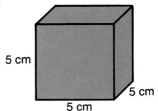

5 cm
5 cm
5 cm

280

Mixed Practice • Find the volume of each figure.

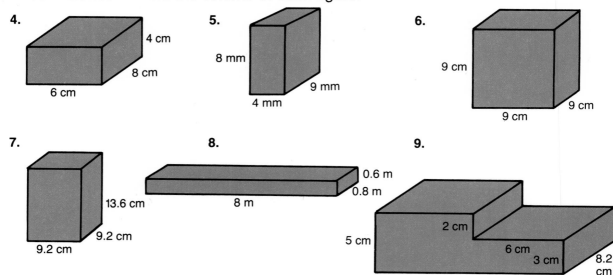

4.
4 cm
8 cm
6 cm

5.
8 mm
9 mm
4 mm

6.
9 cm
9 cm
9 cm

7.
13.6 cm
9.2 cm
9.2 cm

8.
0.6 m
0.8 m
8 m

9.
2 cm
5 cm
6 cm
3 cm
8.2 cm
12 cm

Complete.

	Length	Width	Height	Volume
10.	5 m	2 m	2 m	? m^3
11.	10 cm	12.5 cm	10 cm	? cm^3
12.	32 cm	20.6 cm	18 cm	? cm^3
★ 13.	8 m	5 m	? m	120 m^3
★ 14.	? m	9.8 m	4.3 m	505.68 m^3
★ 15.	70 cm	0.5 m	640 mm	? cm^3

PROBLEM SOLVING • APPLICATIONS

16. Dave knows that a cargo hold on a particular ship measures 9 meters by 11 meters by 3.5 meters. How much space is available for cargo?

17. The ship transports containers that measure 3 meters by 2 meters by 0.7 meters each. What is the volume of each container?

★ 18. Another cargo hold on the ship measures 8.5 meters by 12.2 meters by 3.9 meters. There is one container in the hold. The container measures 2.7 meters by 0.9 meters by 6.3 meters. How much space is still available for additional cargo?

★ 19. The cargo hold on one ship measures 8 meters by 10 meters by 4 meters. How many containers measuring 2 meters by 2 meters by 0.5 meters can fit into the hold?

281

Metric Units of Liquid Capacity

The **milliliter (mL), metric cup (c), liter (L),** and **kiloliter (kL)** are metric units used to measure liquid capacity.

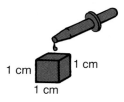

It takes 1 **milliliter** of water to fill 1 cubic centimeter.

The volume of a **metric cup** is 250 cubic centimeters. It takes 250 milliliters of water to fill a metric cup.

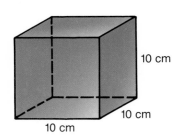

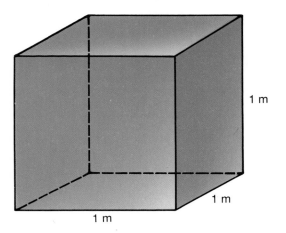

The volume of the cube is 1,000 cubic centimeters. It takes 4 metric cups of water to fill the cube. It takes 1,000 milliliters to fill the cube. The cube holds 1 **liter.**

1,000 mL = 1 L
1 mL = 0.001 L

The volume of the cube is 1 cubic meter. It takes 1,000 liters to fill the cube. The cube holds 1 **kiloliter.**

1,000 L = 1 kL
1 L = 0.001 kL

Practice • Choose the correct measure for each.

1.

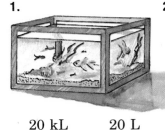

20 kL   20 L

2.

5 L   5 mL

3.

250 L   250 mL

4.

1 L   1 mL

Mixed Practice • Choose the correct measure for each.

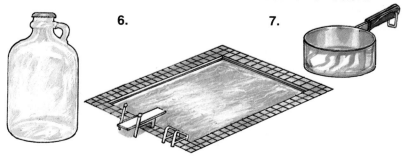

5.   6.   7.   8.

   4 L   4 mL   80 kL   80 L   2 L   2 mL   250 L   250 mL

Complete.

9. 34 L = __?__ mL   10. 0.5 kL = __?__ L   11. 3.2 L = __?__ mL

12. 2.86 L = __?__ mL   13. __?__ kL = 1,845 L   14. __?__ L = 482 mL

15. 9.41 L = __?__ mL   16. __?__ kL = 4,600 L   17. __?__ L = 5,000 mL

18. 0.25 kL = __?__ L   ★ 19. 9 kL = __?__ mL   ★ 20. 2.5 kL = __?__ mL

Add the measures.

21.	22.	23.	24.	25.
76 L	36 mL	562 kL	165.8 L	314.9 mL
76 L	19 mL	89 kL	209.6 L	85.2 mL
+98 L	+87 mL	+497 kL	+597.5 L	+268.7 mL

PROBLEM SOLVING • APPLICATIONS

26. A cube is 30 centimeters on each side. How many milliliters of water can it hold?

27. A pool is 15 meters long, 8 meters wide, and 2 meters deep. The pool is filled with water. How many kiloliters of water does it hold?

★ 28. A can of frozen concentrate makes 780 milliliters of juice. Is a 1.5 liter pitcher large enough to hold the juice made from 2 cans?

Metric Units of Mass

The **milligram (mg), gram (g),** and **kilogram (kg)** are metric units used to measure mass.

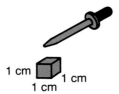

1 cm 1 cm
1 cm

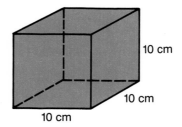

10 cm
10 cm
10 cm

The cube is 1 cubic centimeter. It holds 1 milliliter of water. 1 milliliter of water has a mass of 1 gram.

$$1,000 \text{ mg} = 1 \text{ g}$$
$$1 \text{ mg} = 0.001 \text{ g}$$

The cube is 1,000 cubic centimeters. It holds 1 liter of water. 1 liter of water has a mass of 1 kilogram.

$$1,000 \text{ g} = 1 \text{ kg}$$
$$1 \text{ g} = 0.001 \text{ kg}$$

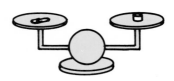

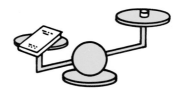

A paper clip has a mass of about 1 gram.

Your math book has a mass of about 1 kilogram.

Practice • Which unit of measure would you use? Write GRAM or KILOGRAM.

1.

2.

3.

4.

Mixed Practice • Choose the correct measure for each.

5.

5 g   5 kg

6.

500 mg   500 g

7.

3 g   3 kg

8.

6 g   6 kg

9.

7 g   7 kg

10.

315 g   315 kg

11.

1 g   1 kg

12.

150 g   150 kg

Complete.

13. 8 kg = __?__ g

14. 9 g = __?__ mg

15. __?__ g = 7 mg

16. 7.3 kg = __?__ g

17. __?__ kg = 88 g

18. __?__ g = 95 mg

19. __?__ kg = 348 g

20. 12.6 kg = __?__ g

21. 55.8 kg = __?__ g

22. __?__ kg = 500 g

★ **23.** 1.85 kg = __?__ mg

★ **24.** 53.9 kg = __?__ mg

Add the measures.

25. 96 mg
        14 mg
      +88 mg

26. 47 g
        58 g
      +33 g

27. 582 g
         46 g
       +353 g

28. 264.9 kg
        107.3 kg
      +497.8 kg

29. 517.2 kg
         85.1 kg
       +318.8 kg

PROBLEM SOLVING • APPLICATIONS

30. One egg has a mass of about 50 grams. What is the mass of 1 dozen eggs?

31. A piece of chalk has a mass of about 14.6 grams. What is the mass of 16 pieces of chalk?

★ **32.** Mrs. Chen orders 2.5 kilograms of apples, 800 grams of peaches, 350 grams of plums, and 1 kilogram of oranges. How many kilograms of fruit does Mrs. Chen order?

★ **33.** Peter has a pet gerbil that has a mass of 224 grams and a hamster that has a mass of 0.26 kilograms. Which pet has the greater mass? How much greater?

Degrees Celsius

Dr. Posen is a meteorologist. She reports the weather on the evening news. She uses a thermometer to read the temperature in **degrees Celsius**. To show 20 degrees Celsius she writes **20°C**.

Temperatures can fall below zero degrees Celsius. Ten degrees below zero is shown as **⁻10°C**.

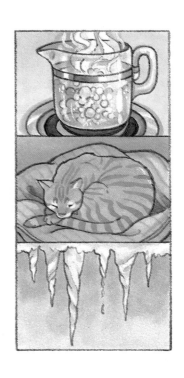

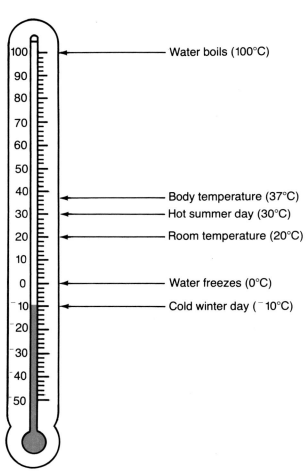

Water boils (100°C)

Body temperature (37°C)
Hot summer day (30°C)
Room temperature (20°C)

Water freezes (0°C)
Cold winter day (⁻10°C)

Practice • Choose the correct temperature for each.

1.

30°C   3°C

2.

80°C   ⁻8°C

3.

90°C   9°C

More Practice • Give the temperature in degrees Celsius for each.

4. 0 / ⁻10   **5.** 50 / 40   **6.** 100 / 90   **7.** ⁻20 / ⁻30   **8.** 10 / 0

PROBLEM SOLVING • APPLICATIONS

Dr. Posen keeps this record of the high and low temperatures for each day of the week. The **mean temperature** for a day is the average of the high and low temperatures for that day.

Find the mean temperature for each day.

	Day	High	Low	Mean
9.	Sunday	27°C	17°C	?
10.	Monday	25°C	19°C	?
11.	Tuesday	26°C	16°C	?
12.	Wednesday	23°C	19°C	?
13.	Thursday	23°C	15°C	?
14.	Friday	22°C	16°C	?
15.	Saturday	21°C	13°C	?

★ **16.** On Sunday the high temperature was 25°C. The mean was 20°C. What was the low temperature?

★ **17.** On Tuesday the low temperature was 18°C. The mean was 22°C. What was the high temperature?

Midchapter Review

1.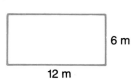
6 m
12 m

Perimeter __?__
Area __?__

2.
11 cm

Circumference __?__

3.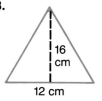
16 cm
12 cm

Area __?__

4.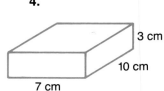
3 cm
10 cm
7 cm

Surface area __?__
Volume __?__

Complete.

5. 3 m = __?__ cm

6. 5 km = __?__ m

7. 652 mm = __?__ cm

8. 9,000 L = __?__ kL

9. 4 L = __?__ mL

10. 6.2 kg = __?__ g

Time

The table at the right shows some units that measure time.

60 seconds (s)	= 1 minute (min)
60 minutes (min)	= 1 hour (h)
24 hours (h)	= 1 day (d)
7 days (d)	= 1 week (wk)
12 months (mo)	= 1 year (yr)
52 weeks (wk)	= 1 year (yr)
100 years (yr)	= 1 century (cen)

Leroy spends $1\frac{1}{2}$ hours in dance class. How many minutes is this?

$$1\frac{1}{2} \text{ h} = ? \text{ min}$$

To change larger units into smaller units, multiply.

Think: 1 h = 60 min

$$1\frac{1}{2} \times 60 = ?$$

$$1\frac{1}{2} \times 60 = \frac{3}{\underset{1}{2}} \times \overset{30}{\cancel{60}}$$

$$1\frac{1}{2} \times 60 = 90$$

$1\frac{1}{2}$ hours is 90 minutes.

To change smaller units into larger units, divide.

$$540 \text{ min} = ?$$

Think: 60 min = 1 h

$$540 \div 60 = 9$$
$$540 \text{ min} = 9 \text{ h}$$

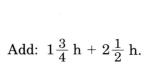

Add: $1\frac{3}{4}$ h + $2\frac{1}{2}$ h.

Find the least common denominator. Write equivalent fractions. Add. Then regroup. Write the answer in lowest terms.

$1\frac{3}{4}$ h + $2\frac{1}{2}$ h = $4\frac{1}{4}$ h

$$1\frac{3}{4} = 1\frac{3}{4}$$
$$+2\frac{1}{2} = 2\frac{2}{4}$$
$$\overline{\qquad\qquad 3\frac{5}{4} = 4\frac{1}{4}}$$

Subtract: 5 h 15 min − 3 h 30 min .

Regroup 60 minutes for 1 hour. Subtract.

5 h 15 min − 3 h 30 min = 1 hr 45 min

$$
\begin{array}{r}
\overset{4}{\cancel{5}} \text{ h} \quad \overset{7\ 5}{\cancel{15}} \text{ min} \\
-3 \text{ h} \quad 30 \text{ min} \\
\hline
1 \text{ h} \quad 45 \text{ min}
\end{array}
$$

Practice • Copy and complete.

1. $1\frac{3}{4}$ h = ____?____ min

2. 4 wk = ____?____ d

3. 7 yr = ____?____ mo

4. $2\frac{1}{2}$ d = ____?____ h

5. 240 s = ____?____ min

6. 72 h = ____?____ d

Add or subtract.

7. $2\frac{1}{2}$ h + $6\frac{2}{3}$ h = ____?____ h

8. $7\frac{3}{4}$ d − $5\frac{5}{6}$ d = ____?____ d

9. 11 h 46 min − 9 h 51 min = ____?____

10. 7 h 25 min + 3 h 54 min = ____?____

Mixed Practice • Copy and complete.

11. $1\frac{2}{5}$ h = ____?____ min

12. 360 s = ____?____ min

13. 96 h = ____?____ d

14. 7 wk = ____?____ d

15. 150 min = ____?____ h

16. 48 mo = ____?____ yr

Add or subtract.

17. $8\frac{3}{4}$ h − $6\frac{3}{8}$ h = ____?____ h

18. $10\frac{3}{4}$ d + $3\frac{1}{2}$ d = ____?____ d

19.   15 h 55 min
 − 7 h 58 min

20.   10 h 15 min
 − 3 h 38 min

21.   5 h 40 min
 −2 h 37 min

22.   5 h 17 min
 +11 h 29 min

23.   21 h 26 min
 + 1 h 32 min

24.   15 h 35 min
 + 8 h 28 min

★ 25.   2 d 15 h
 +3 d 12 h

★ 26.   5 d 20 h
 +1 d   6 h

★ 27.   5 d 18 h
 +   10 h

PROBLEM SOLVING • APPLICATIONS

28. On Tuesday, Nikki played soccer for 1 hour and 30 minutes. On Wednesday, she played for 1 hour and 45 minutes. How long did she play in all?

★ 30. Dwayne practiced the French horn for $1\frac{1}{4}$ hours on Tuesday, $1\frac{1}{2}$ hours on Thursday, and $1\frac{3}{4}$ hours on Saturday. How many minutes did he practice in all?

29. Last Saturday, Nikki's team played a game that lasted $1\frac{3}{4}$ hours. This Saturday the team played a game that lasted $1\frac{2}{3}$ hours. How much longer was last Saturday's game?

Customary Units of Length

The **inch (in.)** is a customary unit of length.
This ruler is marked in inches and in parts of an inch.

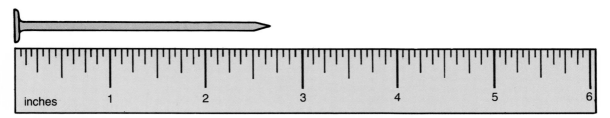

The length of the nail is 3 inches long to the nearest inch.

It is $2\frac{1}{2}$ inches long to the nearest $\frac{1}{2}$ inch.

It is $2\frac{3}{4}$ inches long to the nearest $\frac{1}{4}$ inch.

It is $2\frac{5}{8}$ inches long to the nearest $\frac{1}{8}$ inch.

It is $2\frac{11}{16}$ inches long to the nearest $\frac{1}{16}$ inch.

The **foot (ft)**, **yard (yd)**, and **mile (mi)** are other customary units used to measure length. The table shows how they are related.

12 inches (in.) = 1 foot (ft)
36 inches (in.) = 1 yard (yd)
3 feet (ft) = 1 yard (yd)
5,280 feet (ft) = 1 mile (mi)
1,760 yards (yd) = 1 mile (mi)

To change larger units to smaller units, multiply.

2 ft = ? in.

Think: 1 ft = 12 in.
$2 \times 12 = 24$
2 ft = 24 in.

To change smaller units to larger units, divide.

36 in. = ? ft

Think: 12 in. = 1 ft
$36 \div 12 = 3$
36 in. = 3 ft

Practice • Measure the nail to the nearest

1. inch.   **2.** $\frac{1}{2}$ inch.   **3.** $\frac{1}{4}$ inch.   **4.** $\frac{1}{8}$ inch.   **5.** $\frac{1}{16}$ inch.

Which unit of measure would you use for each? Write INCH, FOOT, YARD, or MILE.

6. the length of a clothespin   **7.** the length of a river

8. the height of a wall   **9.** the length of a fork

Mixed Practice • Which unit of measure would you use for each?
Write INCH, FOOT, YARD, or MILE.

10. the length of a football field

11. the width of this book

12. the distance from Dallas to Miami

13. the width of your classroom

Estimate the length to the nearest $\frac{1}{2}$ inch. Then measure to check your estimate.

14. 15.

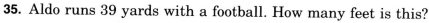

16.

Complete.

17. 3 ft = _?_ in.

18. 2 yd = _?_ in.

19. 3 mi = _?_ yd

20. 12 ft = _?_ in.

21. 27 ft = _?_ yd

22. 72 in. = _?_ yd

23. 132 in. = _?_ ft

24. 180 in. = _?_ yd

25. 3,520 yd = _?_ mi

26. 1 ft 4 in. = _?_ in.

27. 4 yd 2 ft = _?_ ft

28. 1,946 yd = _?_ mi _?_ yd

29. 145 in. = _?_ ft _?_ in.

30. 80 ft = _?_ yd _?_ ft

★ 31. 1 mi 92 yd = _?_ ft

★ 32. $4\frac{1}{3}$ yd = _?_ ft

★ 33. $1\frac{3}{8}$ mi = _?_ yd

★ 34. $\frac{3}{8}$ mi = _?_ in.

PROBLEM SOLVING • APPLICATIONS

35. Aldo runs 39 yards with a football. How many feet is this?

★ 36. Bill is $6\frac{1}{3}$ feet tall. How many inches is this?

★ 37. Mrs. Young buys $9\frac{1}{2}$ yards of fabric
to make uniforms for cheerleaders.
She uses $1\frac{1}{4}$ yards for each uniform.
She makes 7 uniforms. How many
inches of fabric does she have left over?

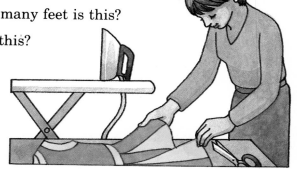

Skills Maintenance

1. 9.6
   −3.5

2. 7.8
   −5.9

3. 5.43
   −2.7

4. 45.6
   − 9.83

5. 5.29 − 2.85 = _?_

6. 16.08 − 4.7 = _?_

7. 32.3 − 1.52 = _?_

8. 15.2 − 4 = _?_

9. 27 − 3.84 = _?_

10. 64 − 0.79 = _?_

Perimeter, Area, and Volume

You can use customary units to find perimeter, area, and volume.

Find the perimeter in inches.

The perimeter of a figure is the sum of the length of the sides.

$$12 + 8 + 12 + 8 = 40$$

The perimeter is 40 inches.

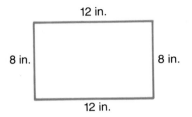

12 in.

8 in.　　　8 in.

12 in.

Find the area in square yards (yd²).

To find the area of a rectangle, multiply the length by the width.

$A = l \times w$
$A = 9 \times 6$
$A = 54$

The area is 54 square yards.

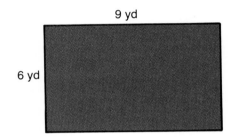

9 yd

6 yd

Find the volume in cubic feet (ft³).

To find the volume of a rectangular prism, multiply the length by the width by the height.

$V = l \times w \times h$
$V = 5 \times 3 \times 2$
$V = 30$

The volume is 30 cubic feet.

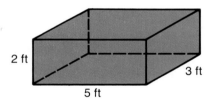

2 ft

5 ft

3 ft

Practice • Complete.

1.

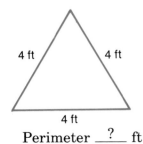

4 ft　　4 ft

4 ft

Perimeter ___?___ ft

2.

5 in.

5 in.　　5 in.

5 in.

Area ___?___ in.²

3.

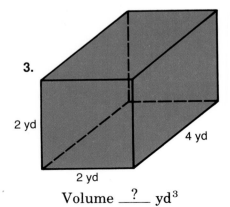

2 yd

2 yd

4 yd

Volume ___?___ yd³

292

Mixed Practice • Find the perimeter and the area of each figure.

4.

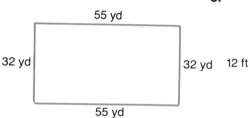
55 yd
32 yd
32 yd
55 yd

5.

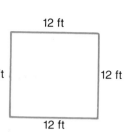
12 ft
12 ft
12 ft
12 ft

★ **6.**

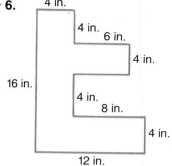
4 in.
4 in.
6 in.
4 in.
16 in.
4 in.
8 in.
4 in.
12 in.

Find the volume of each figure.

7.

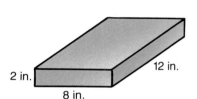
2 in.
12 in.
8 in.

8.

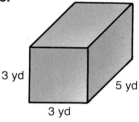
3 yd
5 yd
3 yd

★ **9.**

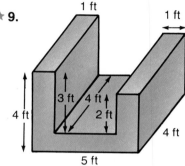
1 ft
1 ft
4 ft
3 ft
4 ft
2 ft
4 ft
5 ft

PROBLEM SOLVING • APPLICATIONS

10. How many square inches are in one square foot?

11. How many cubic inches are in one cubic foot?

12. How many square feet are in one square yard?

13. How many cubic feet are in one cubic yard?

★ **14.** The perimeter of a square patio is 64 feet. What is the area?

★ **15.** One cubic yard of gravel will cover an area of 160 square feet with a layer 2 inches deep. A patio is 20 feet by 20 feet. You want the layer of gravel to be 4 inches deep. How many cubic yards of gravel do you need?

An **acre** is used to measure large areas.
1 acre = 43,560 square feet
1 acre = 4,840 square yards

★ **16.** Ingrid buys 20 acres of land. The land is in the shape of a rectangle. The length of the land measures 400 yards. What is the width?

★ **17.** Paul buys a 15-acre farm that is shaped like a rectangle. The width of the farm is 600 feet. What is the length of the farm?

Customary Units of Capacity and Weight

These customary units are used to measure liquid capacity.

2 tablespoons
(1 fluid ounce)   **1 cup**   **1 pint**   **1 quart**   **1 half-gallon**   **1 gallon**

2 tablespoons (tbsp) = 1 fluid ounce (1 fl. oz)
8 fluid ounces (fl. oz) = 1 cup (c)
2 cups (c) = 1 pint (pt)
2 pints (pt) = 1 quart (qt)
2 quarts (qt) = 1 half-gallon $\left(\frac{1}{2} \text{ gal}\right)$
4 quarts (qt) = 1 gallon (gal)

These customary units are used to measure **weight.**

1 ounce   **1 pound**   **about 1 ton**

16 ounces (oz) = 1 pound (lb)
1 ton (T) = 2,000 pounds (lb)

Practice • Choose the correct measure for each.

1.

1 c   1 gal

2.

30 gal   30 fl. oz

3.

1 gal   1 pt

4.

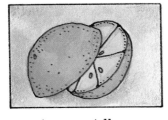

4 oz   4 lb

5.

2 lb   2 T

6.

6 lb   6 T

Mixed Practice • Complete.

7. 1 pt = __?__ fl. oz

8. 1 qt = __?__ c

9. 2 tbsp = __?__ fl. oz

10. 2 gal = __?__ qt

11. $\frac{1}{2}$ gal = __?__ qt

12. 2 pt = __?__ c

13. 3 gal 1 qt = __?__ qt

14. 14 pt = __?__ gal __?__ qt

15. 31 c = __?__ pt __?__ c

★ 16. $1\frac{3}{4}$ gal = __?__ c

★ 17. 4 gal = __?__ tbsp

★ 18. $4\frac{1}{2}$ qt = __?__ pt

Write >, <, or =.

19. 16 c ⬤ 1 gal

20. 2 qt ⬤ 8 c

21. 56 fl. oz ⬤ 7 c

22. $3\frac{1}{2}$ qt ⬤ 14 c

23. 32 tbsp ⬤ 2 pt

24. 2 qt ⬤ 5 pt

Complete.

25. 32 oz = __?__ lb

26. 80 oz = __?__ lb

27. 3 lb = __?__ oz

28. 4 lb = __?__ oz

29. 18 T = __?__ lb

30. $\frac{1}{2}$ T = __?__ lb

31. 46 oz = __?__ lb __?__ oz

32. 3 T 300 lb = __?__ lb

33. 4,800 lb = __?__ T __?__ lb

★ 34. 100 oz = __?__ lb

★ 35. $5\frac{3}{4}$ T = __?__ lb

★ 36. 8 oz = __?__ lb

Write >, <, or =.

37. 50 oz ⬤ 3 lb

38. 2 T ⬤ 6,000 lb

39. 9 lb ⬤ 144 oz

★ 40. 400 lb ⬤ $\frac{1}{2}$ T

★ 41. $2\frac{1}{2}$ T ⬤ 5,000 lb

★ 42. $\frac{1}{4}$ lb ⬤ 3 oz

PROBLEM SOLVING • APPLICATIONS

43. Mark is baking bread. He needs to mix 4 cups of white flour with 3 cups of whole wheat flour. Will the mixture fit into a 2-quart bowl?

44. Mark is making hamburgers. How many pounds of meat does he need to make 8 hamburgers if each hamburger weighs 4 ounces?

★ 45. Mary is making a fruit drink. She needs 24 fluid ounces of lemonade concentrate, 9 cups of water, and 3 quarts of cranberry juice. How many gallons of liquid is this?

★ 46. Mary buys 6 pounds of chicken for $8.16. She wants to serve 8 ounces to each person. How many people can she serve? How much does the chicken cost per serving?

PROBLEM SOLVING • STRATEGIES

Operations with Measures

We can use many of the rules we already know to work with units of measures.

Jay Osborne is a contractor. He keeps a record of the materials he uses on each job. On one job he used 3 feet 10 inches of wire for a kitchen light. He used 5 feet 8 inches of wire for a basement light.

12 in. = 1 ft
3 ft = 1 yd
16 oz = 1 lb
4 qt = 1 gal
60 min = 1 hour

Jay adds to find how much wire he used in all.

```
  3 ft 10 in.
+ 5 ft  8 in.
```

Step 1 Add.

```
  3 ft 10 in.
+ 5 ft  8 in.
  8 ft 18 in.
```

Step 2 18 in. > 1 ft
Regroup.

18 in. = 1 ft 6 in.
8 ft 18 in. = 9 ft 6 in.

Jay used 9 feet 6 inches of wire.

How much more wire did Jay use for the basement light than the kitchen light?

```
  5 ft  8 in.
− 3 ft 10 in.
```

Step 1 10 in. > 8 in.
Regroup.

1 ft = 12 in.
5 ft 8 in. = 4 ft 20 in.

Step 2 Subtract.

```
    4    20
    5̸ ft  8̸ in.
  − 3 ft 10 in.
    1 ft 10 in.
```

Jay used 1 foot 10 inches more wire for the basement light.

Solve.

1. On Tuesday a worker delivered 7 gallons of paint. The painters used 4 gallons 3 quarts. How much paint was left over?

2. It takes Ms. Hicks 8 hours to paint the outside of a house. She has been painting for 6 hours 15 minutes. How much longer must she work to finish the job?

Solve.

3. Sally Hicks is painting shutters. She uses $\frac{1}{2}$ pint of paint for each shutter. The house has 24 shutters. The paint is sold only in half-gallon cans. How many cans of paint does she need to buy?

Read the questions carefully. What operations should you use?

4. Jay Osborne has 100 yards of weather stripping. He uses 35 yards 2 feet on one house. He uses 42 yards 1 foot on another house. How much weather stripping does he have left?

5. A living room needs new wallpaper. Each roll of wallpaper covers 30 square feet. There are 420 square feet of wall to cover. How many rolls of wallpaper does the paperhanger need?

6. The paperhanger must mix the wallpaper paste with water. 5 quarts of water are needed for each pound of wallpaper paste. He is mixing 2 pounds of paste. How many gallons of water will he use?

7. Julia has $150.00 to spend on carpeting. The carpet she chooses costs $8.99 a square yard. She bought 14 square yards of carpeting. How much money does Julia have left over?

8. The plumber needs 6 feet 7 inches of pipe for the bathroom and 8 feet 9 inches of pipe for the kitchen. How much pipe does he need in all?

9. The carpenter uses 12 pounds 8 ounces of nails for one job and 10 pounds 12 ounces of nails on another job. How much do the nails he uses weigh in all?

★ 10. Cherry paneling will be used in a basement room. The walls and panels are 8 feet high. The room is 16 feet long and 12 feet wide. Each panel is 4 feet wide. How many panels will the carpenter need for this room?

Remember to use the correct unit of measure in your answer.

★ 11. Julia is buying new vinyl flooring for two hallways. The length of one hall is 6.5 yards. The width of that hall is 2 yards. Another hallway is 4.2 yards long and 3 yards wide. How many square yards of vinyl flooring does she need in all?

★ 12. Jay Osborne hires a gardener to plant pine trees along three sides of the perimeter of a backyard. The length of the yard is 80 feet and the width is 50 feet. If the pine trees are placed 9 feet apart, how many trees can be planted? If they are planted 6 feet apart, how many more trees can be planted?

Complete. (pages 268–281)

1.
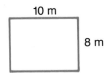
Perimeter = ___?___

2.

Circumference = ___?___

3.

Area = ___?___

4.
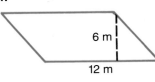
Area = ___?___

5.
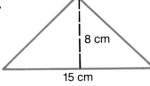
Area = ___?___

6.
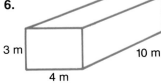
Surface area = ___?___
Volume = ___?___

Complete. (pages 266–267, 282–285, 288–295)

7. 7 cm = ___?___ m

8. 9,000 m = ___?___ km

9. 6 cm = ___?___ mm

10. 4,000 mL = ___?___ L

11. 9.2 kg = ___?___ g

12. 0.9 kL = ___?___ L

13. 4 d = ___?___ h

14. 360 sec = ___?___ min

15. 3 wk 5 d = ___?___ d

16. 4 ft = ___?___ in.

17. 6 yd = ___?___ ft

18. 2 mi = ___?___ ft

19. 3 gal = ___?___ qt

20. 18 c = ___?___ pt

21. 8 fl. oz = ___?___ tbsp

22. 5 lb = ___?___ oz

23. 8,000 lb = ___?___ T

24. 2 lb 6 oz = ___?___ oz

25.

Perimeter = ___?___

26.

Area = ___?___

27.
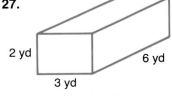
Volume = ___?___

Solve.

28. On Wednesday the high temperature was 26°C. The low temperature was 20°C. What was the mean temperature for the day? (p. 286)

29. Jay bought 25 feet of weather stripping to place around his front door. He used 20 feet 8 inches. How much weather stripping was left over? (p. 296)

PROJECT

Degrees Fahrenheit

This thermometer measures temperature in **degrees Fahrenheit**.
Each mark stands for 2 degrees Fahrenheit. The temperatures can fall
below zero degrees Fahrenheit. Ten degrees below zero is shown as ⁻**10°F**.

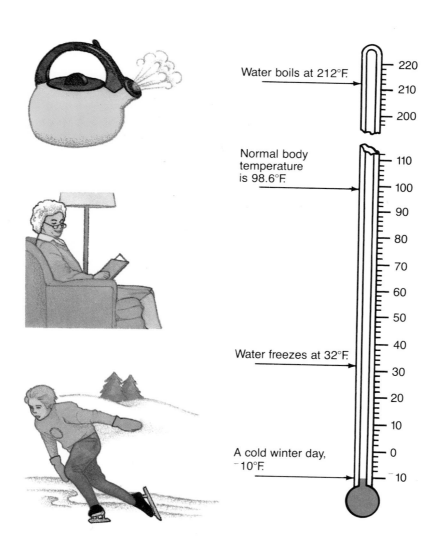

Water boils at 212°F.

Normal body temperature is 98.6°F.

Water freezes at 32°F.

A cold winter day, ⁻10°F.

Use a Fahrenheit thermometer.

Read the outdoor temperature at noon each day for five days.

Record your findings.

After you collect the data, show the temperatures on a line graph.

TEST

Complete.

1.

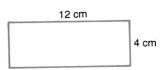
12 cm
4 cm

Perimeter = ___?___

2.

8 mm

Circumference = ___?___

3.

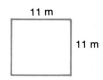
11 m
11 m

Area = ___?___

4.

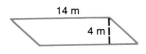
14 m
4 m

Area = ___?___

5.

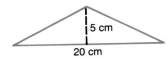
5 cm
20 cm

Area = ___?___

6.

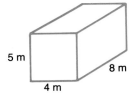
5 m
8 m
4 m

Surface area = ___?___
Volume = ___?___

Complete.

7. 12 cm = ___?___ m

8. 17,000 m = ___?___ km

9. 30 cm = ___?___ mm

10. 18,000 mL = ___?___ L

11. 0.8 kg = ___?___ g

12. 0.6 kL = ___?___ L

13. 5 d = ___?___ h

14. 420 sec = ___?___ min

15. 2 wk 4 d = ___?___ d

16. 6 ft = ___?___ in.

17. 9 yd = ___?___ ft

18. 3 mi = ___?___ ft

19. 6 gal = ___?___ qt

20. 20 c = ___?___ pt

21. 6 fl. oz = ___?___ tbsp

22. 3 lb = ___?___ oz

23. 12,000 lb = ___?___ T

24. 4 lb 2 oz = ___?___ oz

25.

13 ft
13 ft

Perimeter = ___?___

26.

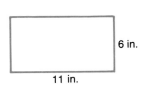
6 in.
11 in.

Area = ___?___

27.

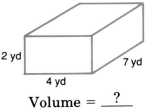
2 yd
7 yd
4 yd

Volume = ___?___

Solve.

28. On Saturday the high temperature was 20°C. The low temperature was 14°C. What was the mean temperature for the day?

29. Ellen has 3 gallons of paint. She uses 1 gallon 3 quarts to paint her room. How much paint is left?

ENRICHMENT

Area of a Circle

This circle has a radius of 3 centimeters. The area of each small blue square is 3×3, or 3^2. The area of the large square is 4 times 3^2.

The area of the circle is more than 3 but less than 4 times 3^2.

Ancient mathematicians found that π times the radius squared could be used to find the area of a circle. π is a decimal number between 3 and 4. We use 3.14 for π.

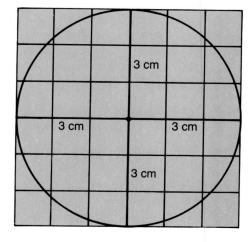

This is the formula for finding the area of a circle.

$$\text{Area} = \pi \times \text{radius}^2$$
$$A = \pi \times r^2$$

Find the area of a circle when the radius is 4 cm. Use 3.14 for π.

$$A = \pi \times r^2$$
$$A \approx 3.14 \times 4 \times 4$$
$$A \approx 50.24$$

The area of the circle is 50.24 square centimeters.

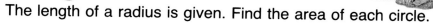

The length of a radius is given. Find the area of each circle.

1. 6 cm   **2.** 2 cm   **3.** 8 cm   **4.** 10 m

5. 7 m   **6.** 3 m   **7.** 5 m   **8.** 9 m

9. 12 m   **10.** 15 m   **11.** 8.1 cm   **12.** 3.3 cm

COMPUTER

Computer Switches

There are about ten types of computer switches.

Switches are made of materials that carry electric current. If the current is on, the bit is on, or 1. If the current is off, the bit is off, or 0. The first switch is called the *NOT switch*. It makes a bit what it is NOT. This is the simplest switch. It has one input (A) and one output (NOT A).

NOT rule: If the input is 0, the output is 1.
If the input is 1, the output is 0.

There is absolutely no other possibility of operation for the NOT switch.

This is the symbol for a NOT switch:

Practice using the NOT switch.

1. 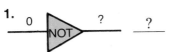 ? ?
　　　　　　　　　　　　　　　　　　　　———

2.  ? ?
　　　　　　　　　　　　　　　　　　　　———

3. Any other possibilities? _____

This is the symbol for an *AND switch:*

AND rule: If the input is 0 and 0, or 1 and 0, or 0 and 1, the output is 0.
If the input is 1 and 1, the output is 1.

Practice using the AND switch.

4. ? _____

5. ? _____

6. 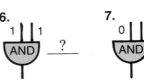 ? _____

7. ? _____

8. If the output of an AND switch is 1, what was the input?

This is the symbol for an *OR switch:*

OR rule: If the input is 0 and 0, the output is 0.
If the input is 0 and 1, or 1 and 0, or 1 and 1, the output is 1.

Practice using the OR switch.

9. ? _____

10. ? _____

11. ? _____

12. ? _____

13. If the output of an OR switch is 0, what was the input?

SKILLS MAINTENANCE
Chapters 1 Through 11

Choose the correct answers.

1. Multiply.

$$876 \times 57$$

A. 48,324
B. 49,062
C. 49,932
D. not here

2. Divide.

$$8\overline{)7,256}$$

A. 97
B. 907
C. 917
D. not here

3. Divide.

$$46\overline{)16,284}$$

A. 354
B. 402
C. 396 r4
D. not here

4. Compare.

19.36  19.089

A. >
B. <
C. =
D. not here

5. What digit is in the thousandths place in 4,386.0259?

A. 4
B. 2
C. 5
D. not here

6. Add.

$$8.63 + 92.1 + 34 = \underline{\ ?\ }$$

A. 21.24
B. 18.18
C. 181.8
D. not here

7. Multiply.

$$0.06 \times 0.3$$

A. 0.018
B. 0.18
C. 1.8
D. not here

8. Subtract.

$$12\frac{1}{4} - 6\frac{5}{8}$$

A. $5\frac{5}{8}$
B. $6\frac{5}{8}$
C. $5\frac{3}{8}$
D. not here

9. Divide.

$$14 \div 2\frac{4}{5} = \underline{\ ?\ }$$

A. 5
B. $39\frac{1}{5}$
C. 7
D. not here

10. 8 cm = __?__ mm

A. 0.8
B. 80
C. 800
D. not here

11. 7 L = __?__ mL

A. 0.007
B. 70
C. 7,000
D. not here

12. 8 yd = __?__ ft

A. 3
B. 18
C. 24
D. not here

Choose the correct answers.

13. Joan must drive 276 kilometers from her house to her grandparents' house. She has already driven $\frac{2}{3}$ of the way. How far does she still have to travel?

    A. 184 km
    B. 414 km
    C. 215 km
    D. not here

14. During a 40-hour work week, Marcy worked $\frac{4}{5}$ of the time. How many hours did she work?

    A. 18
    B. 50
    C. 32
    D. not here

15. From a board that was 3 meters long, Jeff cut a piece that was 1.67 meters long. How long was the piece that was left?

    A. 1.37 m
    B. 1.33 m
    C. 2.67 m
    D. not here

16. Cary drives 1,247.5 kilometers in 5 days. What is the average number of kilometers he drives each day?

    A. 232
    B. 249.5
    C. 187.7
    D. not here

17. Alberto earns $4.80 an hour. He worked 6.5 hours on Monday. How much did he earn?

    A. $31.20
    B. $28.80
    C. $312.00
    D. not here

18. Carol has $3\frac{1}{4}$ yards of fabric. She uses $1\frac{2}{3}$ yards to make a shirt. How much fabric is left?

    A. $1\frac{5}{12}$ yd
    B. 2 yd
    C. $1\frac{7}{12}$ yd
    D. not here

19. Ellen cut a shelf that measured 3 feet 7 inches from a board that measured 5 feet 6 inches. How much of the board was left?

    A. 2 ft 1 in.
    B. 1 ft 11 in.
    C. 9 ft 1 in.
    D. not here

20. Daniel uses 4.6 kilograms of apples, 3.5 kilograms of melon, and 3 kilograms of bananas for a fruit salad. How many kilograms of fruit are in the salad?

    A. 11.1
    B. 8.4
    C. 10.1
    D. not here

CHAPTER 12

Geometry

Vocabulary of Geometry • Angles • Using a Protractor • Parallel, Intersecting, and Perpendicular Lines • Polygons • Congruent Polygons • Circles • Symmetry and Reflections • Solid Figures • Problem Solving: Make a Drawing • Angles of a Triangle • Translations

The Vocabulary of Geometry

A line **segment** is straight. It has two **endpoints**. A segment is named by its endpoints.

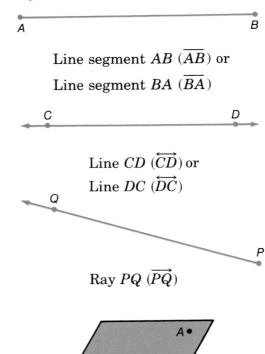

Line segment AB ($\overline{AB}$) or

Line segment BA ($\overline{BA}$)

A **line** has no endpoints. It goes on forever in both directions. A line is named by two of its points.

Line CD ($\overleftrightarrow{CD}$) or

Line DC ($\overleftrightarrow{DC}$)

A **ray** has one endpoint. It goes on forever in one direction only. Name the endpoint first.

Ray PQ ($\overrightarrow{PQ}$)

A **plane** is a flat surface that goes on forever in all directions. Points A, B, and C all lie in the same plane.

Plane ABC

Practice • Name the figures.

1.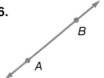

2.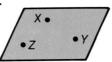

3.

4.

Mixed Practice • Name the figures.

5.

6.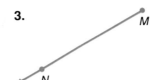

7.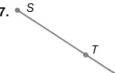

8.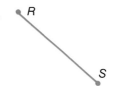

9. Draw a line segment. Call it $\overline{XY}$.

10. Draw a line. Call it $\overleftrightarrow{RS}$.

11. Draw a ray. Call it $\overrightarrow{PB}$.

12. Draw a ray. Call it $\overrightarrow{BP}$.

13. Draw a line segment. Call it $\overline{PE}$.

14. Draw a line. Call it $\overleftrightarrow{AR}$.

Congruent line segments are the same length.
You can use a compass and a straightedge to construct a line segment
congruent to $\overline{AB}$.

Step 1
Draw $\overleftrightarrow{CD}$ to be
longer than $\overline{AB}$.

Step 2
Open the compass
to length AB.

Step 3
Put the compass point on C.
Draw a mark where the
compass meets line $\overleftrightarrow{CD}$.
Label it X.

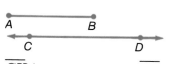

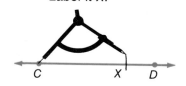

$\overline{CX}$ is congruent to $\overline{AB}$.

Use a compass and a straightedge to construct a line segment
congruent to each.

15.
E   F

16.
Q   R

17.
Y   Z

18.
L   M

PROBLEM SOLVING • APPLICATIONS

Draw points X, Y, and Z not on the same line. Then answer the questions.

19. How many line segments can you draw using points X, Y, and
Z as endpoints?

20. How many lines can you draw using points X, Y, and Z?

21. How many lines can you draw through point Z?

Use the diagram to answer the questions.

★**22.** Name 1 plane.

★ **23.** Name 3 lines.

★ **24.** Name 4 line segments.

★ **25.** Name 1 ray.

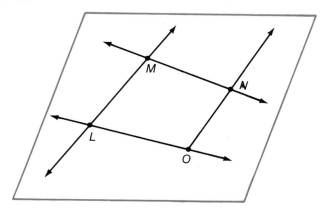

Angles

Two rays that have the same endpoint form an **angle**.

The endpoint is the **vertex**.

The rays are the sides of the angle.

Angle PAT ($\angle PAT$)
or
Angle TAP ($\angle TAP$)

The unit of measure for an angle is a **degree** (1°).

One degree

The measure of a **right angle** is 90°.

The measure of an **acute angle** is greater than 0° and less than 90°.

The measure of an **obtuse angle** is greater than 90° and less than 180°.

Practice • Name the angles. Then write RIGHT, ACUTE, or OBTUSE.

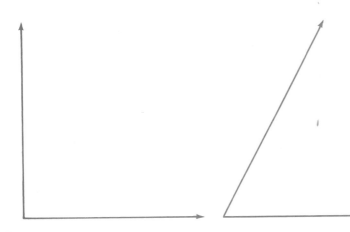

1.

2.

3.

4.

Mixed Practice • Name the angles. Then write RIGHT, ACUTE, or OBTUSE.

5.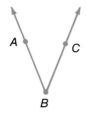

6.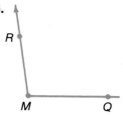

7.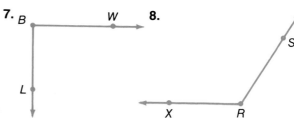

8.

9. Name the vertex of the angle.

10. Name the sides of the angle.

11. Name the angle.

12. Is the angle right, acute, or obtuse?

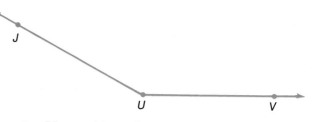

13. ∠*ABC* is an angle of the triangle.
Name the other angles of the
triangle.

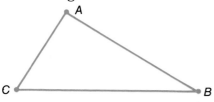

★ **14.** Name 10 angles.

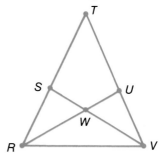

PROBLEM SOLVING • APPLICATIONS

15. Draw $\overrightarrow{AB}$.
Draw $\overrightarrow{AC}$.
Did you draw an
angle?

16. Draw $\overrightarrow{PQ}$.
Draw $\overrightarrow{XY}$.
Did you draw an
angle?

17. Draw $\overleftrightarrow{MJ}$.
Draw $\overrightarrow{JN}$.
Did you draw an
angle?

18. Draw $\overleftrightarrow{RS}$.
Draw $\overrightarrow{RT}$.
Name the angle you
drew.

19. Draw $\overline{GH}$.
Draw $\overline{HZ}$.
Name the angle you
drew.

★ **20.** Draw $\overleftrightarrow{EF}$, $\overleftrightarrow{EL}$,
and $\overrightarrow{FQ}$.
Name 2 different
angles.

Skills Maintenance

1. 0.9
× 8

2. 5.6
×3.2

3. 931.4
× 0.8

4. 0.16
×0.04

5.   5.2
×0.003

6. 86.1
×0.73

7. 2.35
× 5.4

8. 0.08
× 0.6

9. 586.5
× 0.3

10. 0.14
× 15

Using a Protractor

You can use a **protractor** to measure angles.

Place the protractor so that the center mark is on the vertex of the angle and the edge is on one side of the angle. Read the scale where the other side crosses the protractor.

There are two numbers where the other side crosses the protractor. The numbers are 130 and 50. Since ∠ABC is obtuse, the measure of ∠ABC is 130°.

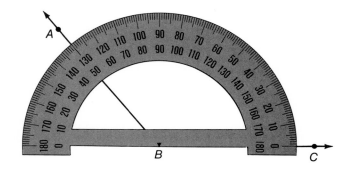

For ∠DEF, the two numbers on the scale are 110 and 70. Since ∠DEF is acute, the measure of ∠DEF is 70°.

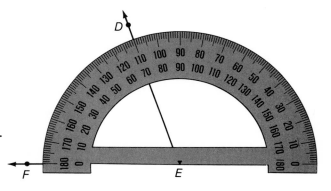

You can use a protractor to draw angles.

Follow the directions.

Draw ∠ZXY with a measure of 45°.

1. Draw $\overrightarrow{XY}$.

2. Place the protractor so that the center mark is at point X.

3. Line up the 0° mark with $\overrightarrow{XY}$.

4. Locate point Z at the 45° mark.

5. Draw $\overrightarrow{XZ}$.

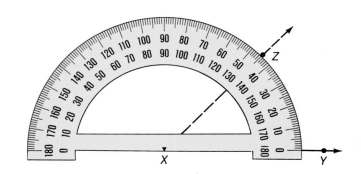

Practice • Measure the angles.

1.

2.

3.

Mixed Practice • Measure the angles.

4.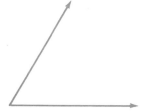

5.

6.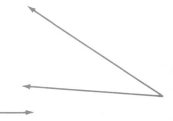

Use a protractor to draw the angles.

7. $\angle DEF$: 30°   **8.** $\angle JKL$: 150°   **9.** $\angle MNO$: 75°   **10.** $\angle PQR$: 100°

PROBLEM SOLVING • APPLICATIONS

Congruent angles have the same measure.
The measure of $\angle PQR$ is 45°.
The measure of $\angle STU$ is 45°.

$\angle PQR$ is congruent to $\angle STU$.

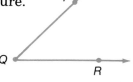
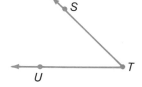

Measure each angle. Then use your protractor to draw a congruent angle for each.

11.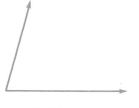

12.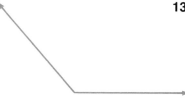

13.

★ **14.** Draw $\overleftrightarrow{MN}$. Mark point Q between M and N.

★ **15.** Draw $\angle NQR$ with a measure of 55°.

★ **16.** Find the measure of $\angle RQM$.

★ **17.** Find the sum of the measures of $\angle NQR$ and $\angle RQM$.

Parallel, Intersecting, and Perpendicular Lines

Lines *AB* and *CD* will never meet.
They are **parallel lines**.
Line *AB* is parallel to line *CD*.

$$\overleftrightarrow{AB} \parallel \overleftrightarrow{CD}$$

Lines *PQ* and *RS* meet at point *X*.
They are **intersecting lines**.

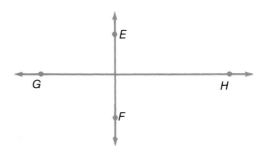

Lines *EF* and *GH* intersect. They
form right angles. They are
perpendicular lines. Line *EF*
is perpendicular to line *GH*.

$$\overleftrightarrow{EF} \perp \overleftrightarrow{GH}$$

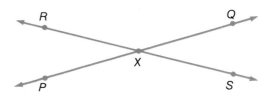

Practice • Write PARALLEL, INTERSECTING, or PERPENDICULAR.

1.

2.

3.

4.

5.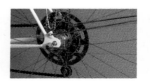
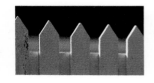

6.

7.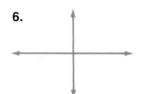

8.

312

Mixed Practice • Study the figure.

9. Name a pair of parallel lines.

10. Name 3 pairs of intersecting lines.

11. Name a pair of perpendicular lines.

12. Name 4 right angles.

13. Name 3 acute angles.

14. Name 3 obtuse angles.

15. Will $\overleftrightarrow{QP}$ intersect $\overleftrightarrow{GJ}$?

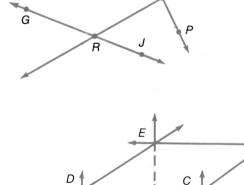

Lines that are not parallel and do not intersect are called **skew lines**.

Are they skew lines? Write YES or NO.

★ 16. $\overleftrightarrow{AB}$ and $\overleftrightarrow{FG}$ ★ 17. $\overleftrightarrow{DC}$ and $\overleftrightarrow{CB}$

★ 18. $\overleftrightarrow{DA}$ and $\overleftrightarrow{BG}$ ★ 19. $\overleftrightarrow{DE}$ and $\overleftrightarrow{CF}$

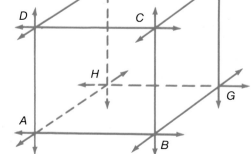

PROBLEM SOLVING • APPLICATIONS

Write PARALLEL, INTERSECTING, or PERPENDICULAR to describe the lines.

20. two lanes of a highway

21. the top and the legs of a table

22. Draw a pair of lines that intersect at point Q. Call them $\overleftrightarrow{RS}$ and $\overleftrightarrow{LM}$.

★ 23. Use a protractor to draw a pair of lines that are perpendicular. Call them $\overleftrightarrow{RS}$ and $\overleftrightarrow{LM}$.

Midchapter Review

Name the figures.

1.

2.

Name the angles. Then write RIGHT, ACUTE, or OBTUSE.

3.

4.

Draw the angles.

5. $\angle KLM$: $120°$ 6. $\angle BCD$: $45°$ 7. $\angle RST$: $60°$ 8. $\angle MNO$: $90°$

Polygons

The sides of a **polygon** are line segments.
The sides meet to form angles.

Names are given to polygons according to the number of sides and the number of angles they have.

Triangles are polygons that have three sides.
Some triangles have special names.

Equilateral

There are three congruent sides.

Isosceles

There are at least two congruent sides.

Scalene

There are no congruent sides.

Quadrilaterals are polygons that have four sides.
Some quadrilaterals have special names.

Parallelogram

a quadrilateral whose opposite sides are parallel and congruent

Rhombus

a parallelogram with four congruent sides

Rectangle

a parallelogram with four right angles

Square

a rectangle with four congruent sides

Trapezoid

a quadrilateral with two and only two sides parallel

These polygons are also named according to the number of sides and angles.

Pentagon
5 sides
5 angles

Hexagon
6 sides
6 angles

Octagon
8 sides
8 angles

Decagon
10 sides
10 angles

Practice • Name the polygons.

1.    2.   3.    4.

314

Mixed Practice • Name the polygons.

5.  6.  7.   8.

Which polygons below are

9. quadrilaterals?   10. rectangles?   11. squares?

12. rhombuses?   13. parallelograms?   14. trapezoids?

a.    b.   c.   d.   e.   f.

A **diagonal** is a line segment that joins vertices of a polygon but is not a side.

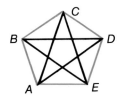

$\overline{AC}$ is a diagonal.

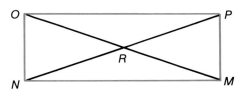

$\overline{NP}$ is a diagonal.

15. Name the triangles formed by the diagonals in each figure.

16. Trace pentagon *ABCDE*. Draw the other diagonals. Name them.

★ 17. How many triangles are formed by the diagonals of the pentagon?

★ 18. Trace a hexagon and an octagon. Draw all the diagonals. How many does each polygon have?

PROBLEM SOLVING • APPLICATIONS

Name the polygons.

19. a rectangle with four congruent sides

20. a rhombus with four right angles

★ 21. The length of each side of a hexagon is 2 centimeters. What is the perimeter of the hexagon?

★ 22. The length of one side of an equilateral triangle is 4 centimeters. What is the perimeter of the triangle?

315

Congruent Polygons

Congruent polygons are the same size and shape.

Trace triangle *STU*.
Place the tracing over triangle *MNO*.
The tracing fits exactly.
Triangle *STU* **is congruent to**
triangle *MNO*.

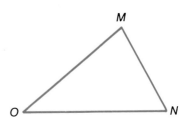

The parts that fit together are
called **corresponding parts**.
If the polygons are congruent,
then their corresponding parts
are also congruent. The symbol
↔ means "corresponds to."

Corresponding sides	Corresponding angles
$\overline{ST} \leftrightarrow \overline{MN}$	$\angle S \leftrightarrow \angle M$
$\overline{TU} \leftrightarrow \overline{NO}$	$\angle T \leftrightarrow \angle N$
$\overline{US} \leftrightarrow \overline{OM}$	$\angle U \leftrightarrow \angle O$

Practice • Are they congruent? Write YES or NO. Use a tracing to help you.

1.

2.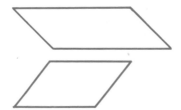

3.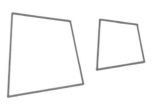

Triangles *EFG* and *QRS* are congruent. Name the corresponding parts.

4. $\overline{EF} \leftrightarrow$ ___?___

5. $\angle E \leftrightarrow$ ___?___

6. $\overline{FG} \leftrightarrow$ ___?___

7. $\angle F \leftrightarrow$ ___?___

8. $\overline{GE} \leftrightarrow$ ___?___

9. $\angle G \leftrightarrow$ ___?___

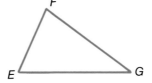
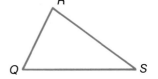

Mixed Practice • Are they congruent? Write YES or NO.
Use a tracing to help you.

10.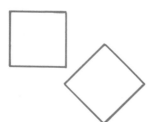

11.

12.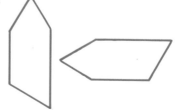

Quadrilaterals *JKLM* and *WXYZ* are congruent. Name the corresponding parts.

13. $\overline{JK}$ ↔ ___?___   14. $\angle J$ ↔ ___?___

15. $\overline{KL}$ ↔ ___?___   16. $\angle K$ ↔ ___?___

17. $\overline{LM}$ ↔ ___?___   18. $\angle L$ ↔ ___?___

19. $\overline{MJ}$ ↔ ___?___   20. $\angle M$ ↔ ___?___

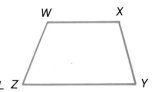

21. Find two pairs of congruent polygons. Use a tracing to help you. Then name the corresponding parts of the congruent polygons.

a. 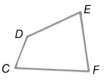   b.   c. 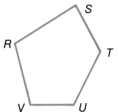   d.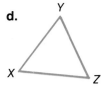

e. 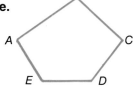   f. 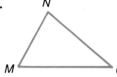   g. 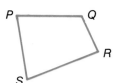   h.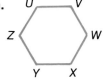

You must use three letters to name an angle when two angles have the same vertex.

$\angle EDH$ $\angle EDF$

★ 22. Name two pairs of congruent triangles.

★ 23. List their corresponding sides and angles.

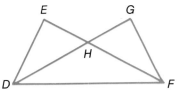

PROBLEM SOLVING • APPLICATIONS

24. A page of Jessica's notebook measures 26 centimeters by 20 centimeters. A page of Jonathan's notebook measures 30 centimeters by 20 centimeters. Are the two pages congruent?

25. Takara draws a triangle whose sides measure 15 centimeters, 18 centimeters, and 24 centimeters. Kevin draws a triangle that is congruent to Takara's triangle. What are the lengths of the sides of Kevin's triangle?

26. A page of Mandy's book measures 18 centimeters by 15 centimeters. A page of Michael's book measures 0.18 meters by 0.15 meters. Are the two pages congruent?

★ 27. Sara draws isosceles triangle *ABC*. $\overline{AB}$ and $\overline{AC}$ measure 12 centimeters. $\overline{BC}$ measures 8 centimeters. Daniel draws isosceles triangle *PQR* congruent to triangle *ABC*. Angle *P* corresponds to angle *A*. How long is side $\overline{QR}$?

Circles

You can use a **compass** to construct a circle.

Point P is the **center** of the circle. This circle is called circle P.

A **radius** of the circle is a segment that joins the center and a point on the circle. All radii of the same circle have the same length.

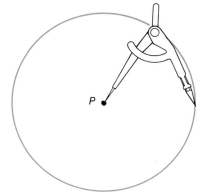

$\overline{PB}$ and $\overline{PA}$ are radii of circle P. The length of $\overline{PB}$ is 3 centimeters.

A **chord** is a segment that joins two points on the circle.

$\overline{DE}$ is a chord.

A **diameter** is a chord that passes through the center of the circle. It is twice as long as the length of a radius.

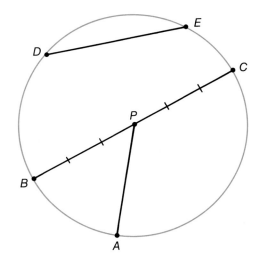

$\overline{BC}$ is a diameter. The length of $\overline{BC}$ is 6 centimeters.

Practice • Study the figure.

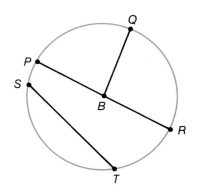

1. What is the name of this circle?

2. Name two chords of this circle.

3. How long is radius $\overline{BR}$?

4. How long is radius $\overline{BQ}$?

5. If you drew another radius for this circle, how long would it be?

6. How long is diameter $\overline{PR}$?

7. How is the length of diameter $\overline{PR}$ related to the length of radius $\overline{PB}$?

Mixed Practice • Study the figure.

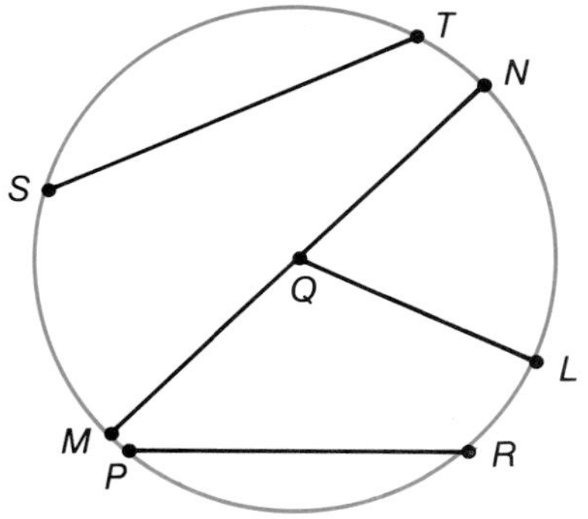

8. Name the circle.
9. Name three radii.
10. Name three chords.
11. Name a diameter.
12. Name an obtuse angle.
13. Name an acute angle.

In each circle point M is the center.
Name the segments that are radii.

14.

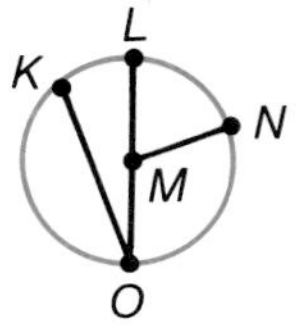

15.

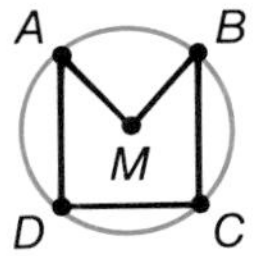

16.

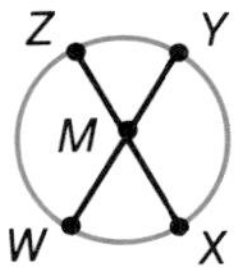

17.

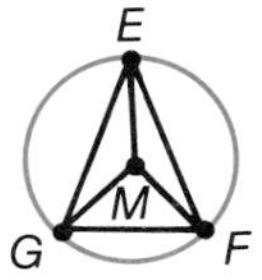

In each circle point L is the center.
Name the segments that are diameters.

18.

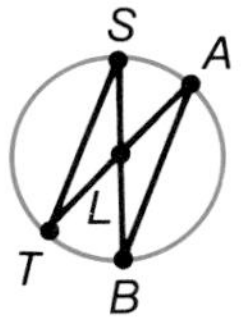

19.

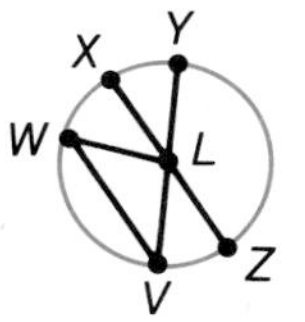

20.

21.

Complete.

	22.	23.	24.	25.	26.	27.	★ 28.	★ 29.
Radius	8 cm	?	13 km	?	9.8 m	?	?	?
Diameter	?	124 mm	?	264 m	?	32.4 cm	5.52 m	1.06 m

Draw segments with the lengths given.
Use each as a radius to construct a circle.

30. 4 cm **31.** 6 cm **32.** 2.5 cm **33.** 6.5 cm **34.** 30 mm

PROBLEM SOLVING • APPLICATIONS

35. Circle P is congruent to circle R. The radius of circle P is 19 centimeters. What is the diameter of circle R?

36. Circle O is congruent to circle Q. The diameter of circle O is 24 meters. What is the radius of circle Q?

37. Circle S has a radius of 15 centimeters. Circle P has a diameter of 15 centimeters. Are the circles congruent?

★ **38.** Circle R has a radius of 45 millimeters. Circle N has a diameter of 0.90 centimeters. Are the two circles congruent?

Symmetry and Reflections

Trace the figure and the dotted line. Cut it out. Fold along the dotted line. Do the halves match?

The figure is **symmetric**.

The dotted line is a **line of symmetry**.

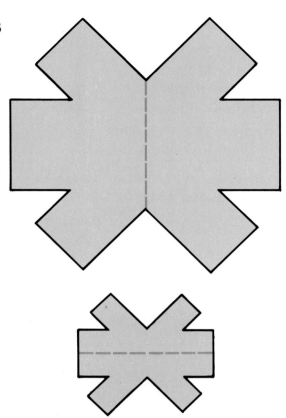

Unfold the figure. Now fold it along the line shown in the small picture.

How many lines of symmetry have you found for this figure?

Are there other lines of symmetry for this figure?

There are only two lines of symmetry.

Trace the parallelogram and cut it out.

How many lines of symmetry does this figure have?
The figure has no lines of symmetry.

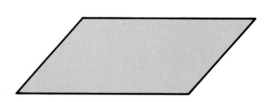

You can **flip** a figure along a line of symmetry to see a **mirror image** (or **reflection image**) of the figure.

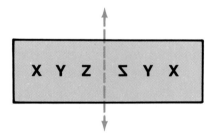

Practice • Is the dotted line a line of symmetry for the figure? Write YES or NO.

1.   2.   3.

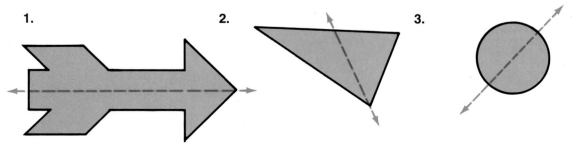

320

Mixed Practice • Trace the figures. Draw the lines of symmetry.

4.

5.

6.
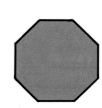

Do the pictures show mirror images? Write YES or NO.

7.
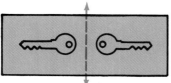

8.

9.

Trace the drawings. Then complete them to make figures that are symmetric.

10.
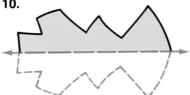

11.
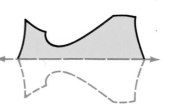

12.
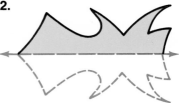

★ **13.** Make your own snowflake.

Draw a circle. Cut it out.   Fold it in half.   Fold again into thirds.   Cut out a pattern. Unfold a snowflake.

PROBLEM SOLVING • APPLICATIONS

Use a mirror to answer the questions.

14. Trace around one of your hands. Stand a mirror perpendicular along the drawing of your middle finger. Does it make a symmetric picture? Is a handprint symmetric?

★ **15.** Draw a picture of a drinking mug. Stand a mirror perpendicular from top to bottom along the middle. Move the picture to look at each side in the mirror. Which way resembles a glass? a sugar bowl? Which of the three images are symmetric?

Skills Maintenance

1. $7\overline{)135.1}$ **2.** $8\overline{)42.56}$ **3.** $0.5\overline{)39.2}$

4. $0.6\overline{)5.586}$ **5.** $1.2\overline{)67.452}$ **6.** $1.5\overline{)0.654}$

7. $0.09\overline{)0.477}$ **8.** $0.002\overline{)1.97}$ **9.** $0.034\overline{)0.2312}$

Solid Figures

This solid figure is a **cube**. Each flat surface of a cube is a **face**. A cube has six faces.

The shape of each face is a square. Two faces meet at an **edge**. Edges meet at a **vertex**. The cube rests on its **base**.

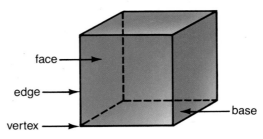

The cube and the solid figures below are **prisms**. The shape of the base is used to name the prism. What is the shape of each of the other faces?

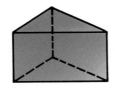

Triangular Prism   Rectangular Prism   Hexagonal Prism

The shape of the other faces is a rectangle. The top face of each prism is the same shape as the base.

These solid figures are **pyramids**. The shape of the base is used to name the pyramid. What is the shape of each of the other faces?

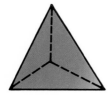 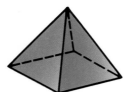  

Triangular Pyramid   Square Pyramid   Rectangular Pyramid   Hexagonal Pyramid

The shape of each of the other faces is a triangle.

These are some other special solid figures.   Cylinder   Cone   Sphere

Practice • Name the shapes.

1.

2.

3.

4.

Mixed Practice • Name the shapes.

5.

6.

7.

8.

Complete.

	Figure	Number of Faces	Number of Edges	Number of Vertices
9.	Cube	6	?	?
10.	Triangular pyramid	?	?	?
11.	Hexagonal pyramid	?	?	?
12.	Rectangular prism	?	?	?
13.	Triangular prism	?	?	?
14.	Hexagonal prism	?	?	?
15.	Square pyramid	?	?	?

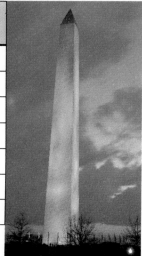

PROBLEM SOLVING • APPLICATIONS

Name the solid figure that does not belong.

16.

17.

Each of these patterns can be folded to make a solid figure.
Name the figures.

★ 18.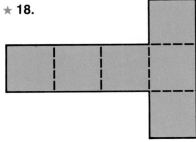

★ 19.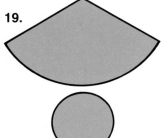

★ 20.

PROBLEM SOLVING · STRATEGIES

Make a Drawing

A quilt is decorated with 5 rows of flowers. There are either 3 or 4 flowers in each row. The top row has 3 flowers. The next row has 4 flowers. This pattern is repeated. How many flowers are there in all?

You can make a drawing to help you solve the problem.

Draw 3 flowers for the first row.
Draw 4 flowers for the second row.
Draw 3 flowers for the third row.
Draw 4 flowers for the fourth row.
Draw 3 flowers for the fifth row.

Count the flowers.
There are 17 flowers on the quilt.

Make a drawing to help you solve the problems.

1. A banner is decorated with 6 rows of stars. There are either 8 or 10 stars in each row. The top row has 10 stars. The next row has 8 stars. This pattern is repeated. How many stars are there in all?

2. A rug has 9 stripes. The first stripe is brown. The second stripe is white. This pattern is repeated across the rug. What color is the seventh stripe?

3. Rami put 8 knitted strips together to make an afghan. The first strip is yellow. The second strip is white. The third strip is green. This pattern is repeated. What color is the last strip?

4. A wall hanging is decorated with 7 rows of flowers. There are either 4 or 5 flowers on each row. The top row has 4 flowers. The next row has 5 flowers. This pattern is repeated. How many flowers in all?

5. Jun makes a quilt with 25 squares. There are 5 squares in each row. The center and the corner squares are red. How many red squares are there in all?

Read the problem carefully to decide how you will use the information.

6. A placemat is made out of 15 squares. There are 5 squares in each row. There are 3 rows. The center square is white. Each square around the center is brown. How many brown squares are there?

7. Sherle is designing a quilt that has 24 squares. There are 4 squares in each row. There are 6 rows. She wants to embroider tigers on all of the squares that make up the border of the quilt. She wants to embroider elephants on all of the other squares. How many tigers does she need to embroider? How many elephants does she need to embroider?

8. A quilt is 8 squares wide and 8 squares long. The first square in the first row is green. The second square in the first row is printed. The first square in the second row is striped. The second square in the second row is yellow. This pattern of 4 squares is repeated. How many yellow squares are there in all?

9. A bedspread has 67 stripes. The first stripe is navy blue. The second stripe is white. The third stripe is light blue. This pattern is repeated. How many times does the pattern appear?

10. Mary makes a quilt with 16 squares. There are 4 squares in each row. She wants to embroider flowers on all of the squares that make up the border. How many squares do not need to be embroidered?

★ **11.** Rami is making a potholder on a loom. He puts 20 loops on the loom. The first 3 loops are gold. The next 2 loops are white. This pattern is repeated. Then he weaves through 20 more loops in the same pattern to complete the potholder. How many gold loops does he need? How many white loops does he need?

★ **12.** A wall hanging is made out of 35 squares. There are 7 squares in each row. There are 5 rows. The corner squares and the center square are red. Each square around a red square is blue. The other squares are white. How many blue squares are there in all?

Name the figures. (page 306)

1.

2.

3.

Measure the angles. Write RIGHT, ACUTE, or OBTUSE. (pages 308–311)

4.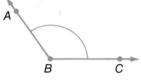

5.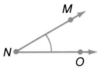

6.

Write PARALLEL, INTERSECTING, or PERPENDICULAR. (pages 312–313)

7.

8.

9.

Name the types of polygons. Then name the sides and the angles. (pages 314–315)

10.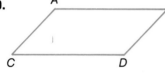

11.

12.

13. Triangles *XYZ* and *RST* are congruent. Name the corresponding parts. (p. 316)

14. Name the circle and four radii. (p. 318)

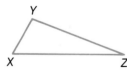

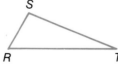

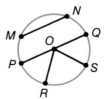

Name the shapes and tell how many. (pages 322–323)

15.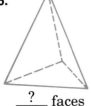

_?_ faces

16.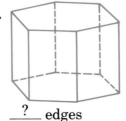

_?_ edges

17.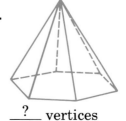

_?_ vertices

PROJECT

Angles of a Triangle

Try an experiment.

Step 1
Draw any triangle.
Label the angles.
Cut out the triangle.

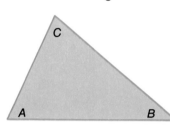

Step 2
Cut the triangle apart
as shown.

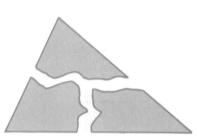

Step 3
Fit the angles together
along a line. Measure
them with your protractor.

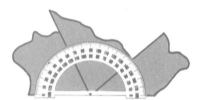

Try this with other triangles.

What is the sum of the measures of the angles of each triangle?

Find the sum of the measures.

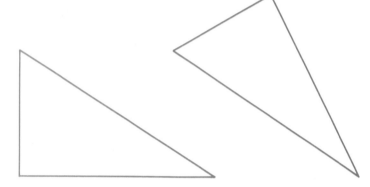

The sum of the measures of the angles of a triangle is 180°.

Find the missing measures.

1.
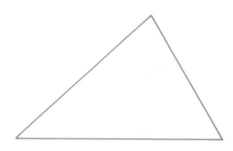

$90° + 40° + \underline{} = 180°$

2.

$\underline{} + 45° + 110° = 180°$

3.
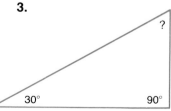

$30° + 90° + \underline{} = 180°$

327

TEST

Name the figures.

1.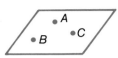

2.

3.

Measure the angles. Write RIGHT, ACUTE, or OBTUSE.

4.

5.

6.

Write PARALLEL, INTERSECTING, or PERPENDICULAR.

7.

8.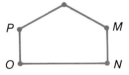

9.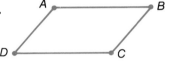

Name the types of polygons. Then name the sides and the angles.

10.

11.

12.

13. Triangles *PQR* and *STU* are congruent. Name the corresponding parts.

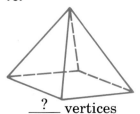

14. Name the circle and four radii.

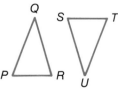

Name the shapes and tell how many.

15.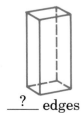

_____ edges

16.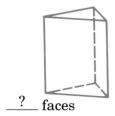

_____ vertices

17.

_____ faces

Translations

As you learned in Chapter 5, you can use an ordered pair of numbers to locate points on a grid.

Study parallelogram $ABCD$. Point A is located at (8, 5). Name the locations of points B, C, and D.

Suppose you wanted to slide parallelogram $ABCD$ to a new position—4 units to the right and 5 units up. Follow these steps:

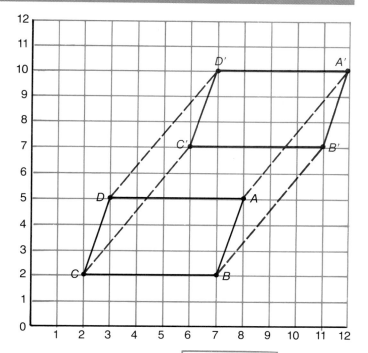

Step 1 Mark point A' at (12, 10), the point that is 4 units to the right and 5 units up from point A.

> Read A' as "A prime."

Step 2 Mark point B' at (11, 7), the point that is 4 units to the right and 5 units up from point B.

Step 3 Mark point C' at (6, 7), the point that is 4 units to the right and 5 units up from point C.

Step 4 Mark point D' at (7, 10), the point that is 4 units to the right and 5 units up from point D.

Step 5 Connect points A', B', C', and D' in order.

The new parallelogram, $A'B'C'D'$, is called a **slide image** or **translation image** of parallelogram $ABCD$. Are parallelograms $ABCD$ and $A'B'C'D'$ congruent? How can you prove your answer?

On a piece of graph paper, make three copies of the grid and parallelogram $ABCD$. Then make three translation images, sliding the parallelogram to these new positions.

1. 7 units up   **2.** 2 units to the right and 3 units up
3. 1 unit to the left and 2 units down

Addition with a Carry

Recall the binary addition facts:

$$\begin{array}{cccc} 0 & 0 & 1 & 1 \\ +0 & +1 & +0 & +1 \\ \hline 0 & 1 & 1 & 10 \end{array}$$

Note that the binary sum of 1 and 1 produces a *carry bit* of 1.

Add with binary addition. Count how many carries each problem has.

1. 101
$+101$, ___?___ carries

2. 1111
$+1111$, ___?___ carries

3. 1010
$+\ \ 101$, ___?___ carries

In general a binary number can receive a carry from the next lower place and pass a carry to the next higher place. This is the same as in decimal addition: The tens place can receive a ten regrouped from the ones place and can pass a regrouped hundred to the hundreds place.

Switches can be combined into *circuits*.
Little circles are used to show *inputs* and *outputs*.
These are the rules for this circuit:

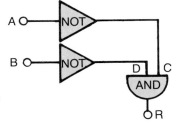

The A bit goes through a NOT switch.
    The output bit, C, is then input to an AND switch.

The B bit goes through a NOT switch.
    The output bit, D, is then input to the same AND switch.

The result bit, R, is the output from the AND switch.

Practice with this circuit.

4. A = 1,   B = 0,   C = ___?___,   D = ___?___,   R = ___?___.

5. A = 1,   B = 1,   C = ___?___,   D = ___?___,   R = ___?___.

6. A = 0,   B = 0,   C = ___?___,   D = ___?___,   R = ___?___.

7. A = 0,   B = 1,   C = ___?___,   D = ___?___,   R = ___?___.

Note, again, that this is every possible input combination. There is no other possible combination of bits being on and off. Circuits can get very complicated. A computer is, in fact, one very complicated electrical circuit.

COMPUTER

The Binary Adder

A *binary adder* is formed with one NOT switch, four AND switches, and four OR switches. The circuit shown is for a binary adder for one binary digit. Dots, ○ ○ ○ ○ ○ , show where circuit lines are connected. The same current goes in two directions. Current flows only from top to bottom in AND and OR switches. Current flows only from left to right in NOT switches. Where current lines cross without dots, ──┼── , currents continue in straight lines. Current lines are not connected at these points.

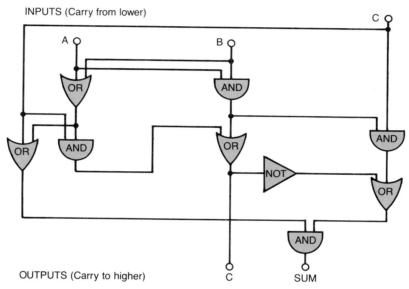

This last exercise shows how a computer "adds." Switches turn bits on or off, but no numbers are ever really added in any computer. This is only one of many surprising facts that people do not know about computers: Computers cannot add!

Follow the circuits in the binary adder to find the sum bit and the carry bit.

8. A = 1, B = 0, C = 1
   SUM = __?__ , CARRY = __?__

9. A = 0, B = 1, C = 1
   SUM = __?__ , CARRY = __?__

10. A = 1, B = 1, C = 1
   SUM = __?__ , CARRY = __?__

11. A = 0, B = 0, C = 1
   SUM = __?__ , CARRY = __?__

12. A = 1, B = 1, C = 0
   SUM = __?__ , CARRY = __?__

13. A = 0, B = 1, C = 0
   SUM = __?__ , CARRY = __?__

14. A = 1, B = 0, C = 0
   SUM = __?__ , CARRY = __?__

Choose the correct answers.

1. Write the expanded form of 864.

   A. $800 + 64$
   B. $800 + 60 + 4$
   C. $8,000 + 60 + 4$
   D. not here

2. Round 38.09 to the nearest whole number.

   A. 37
   B. 38
   C. 38.1
   D. not here

3. Compare.

   9.3 ● 9.07

   A. $>$
   B. $<$
   C. $=$
   D. not here

4. Subtract.

   $$6\frac{1}{3}$$
   $$-1\frac{5}{6}$$

   A. $5\frac{1}{2}$ C. $5\frac{5}{6}$
   B. $4\frac{1}{2}$ D. not here

5. Divide.

   $$4\frac{2}{5} \div 3\frac{2}{3} = \underline{\ ?\ }$$

   A. $1\frac{1}{5}$ C. $1\frac{2}{3}$
   B. $\frac{2}{15}$ D. not here

6. Subtract.

   $$42 - 0.36 = \underline{\ ?\ }$$

   A. 6.00   C. 41.64
   B. 38.4   D. not here

7. Name the figure.

   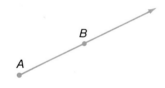

   A. line AB
   B. segment AB
   C. ray AB
   D. not here

8. Name a radius of the circle.

   A. $\overline{DC}$
   B. $\overline{AD}$
   C. $\overline{QD}$
   D. not here

9. What kind of angle is PQR?

   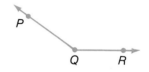

   A. acute
   B. obtuse
   C. right
   D. not here

10. Michi buys a gift for $12.58. How much change does she get from $20.00?

    A. $7.42
    B. $7.52
    C. $8.52
    D. not here

11. Danny buys a pair of sneakers that costs $28.50. The sales tax is $1.71. What is the total cost of the sneakers?

    A. $2.28
    B. $30.21
    C. $51.30
    D. not here

Ratio and Percent

Ratio

Ratio is one way of comparing numbers.

How many baseball bats do you see?
How many baseball mitts do you see?
The ratio of bats to mitts is 4 to 3.

Here are three ways to show the ratio.

$$4 \text{ to } 3 \qquad 4{:}3 \qquad \frac{4}{3}$$

You can show other ratios.

The ratio of mitts to bats is 3 to 4.
The fraction $\frac{3}{4}$ names this ratio.

4 of the 7 pieces of baseball gear are bats.
The fraction $\frac{4}{7}$ names this ratio.

3 of the 7 pieces of baseball gear are mitts.
Which fraction names this ratio, $\frac{3}{7}$ or $\frac{7}{3}$?

The fraction $\frac{3}{7}$ names this ratio.

Practice • Write a fraction for each ratio.

1. roller skates to ice
skates

2. ice skates to roller
skates

3. roller skates to all the
skates

4. 3 to 8

5. 7 to 4

6. 10 to 1

7. 2 to 9

8. 14:3

9. 25:100

10. 45:23

11. 26:50

334

Mixed Practice • Write a fraction for each ratio.

12. baseballs to mitts

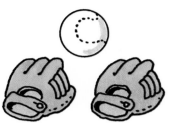

13. hats to whistles

14. hockey sticks to golf clubs

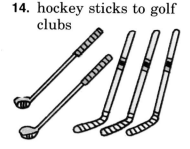

15. golf balls to tees

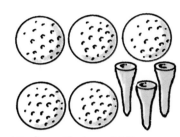

16. tennis rackets to bats and rackets

17. skis to boots

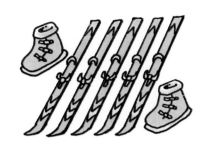

18. length to width

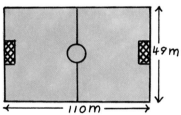

19. length of the base to height

★20. length of a side to perimeter

21. 2 to 5	**22.** 7 to 13	**23.** 9 to 4	**24.** 17 to 32
25. 6 to 1	**26.** 4 to 7	**27.** 8 to 21	**28.** 5 to 92
29. 225:48	**30.** 15:19	**31.** 72:10	**32.** 47:100

PROBLEM SOLVING • APPLICATIONS

33. Mavis is putting away 3 helmets and 4 hats. What is the ratio of hats to helmets?

34. In the basement Sally found 1 baseball in a mitt. What is the ratio of baseballs to mitts?

★35. Jane and Shasha have 2 pairs of yellow shoelaces, 3 pairs of orange shoelaces, and 2 pairs of skates. What is the ratio of pairs of shoelaces to pairs of skates?

★36. There are 2 wooden hockey sticks, 3 wooden baseball bats, and 4 metal tennis rackets in the garage. What is the ratio of wooden objects to metal objects?

Equal Ratios

MIX 1 CAN OF FROZEN JUICE WITH 3 CANS OF WATER.

Cans of juice mix	1	2	3	4
Cans of water	3	6	9	12
Ratio of juice to water	$\frac{1}{3}$	$\frac{2}{6}$	$\frac{3}{9}$	$\frac{4}{12}$

The ratio of juice to water remains the same.
$\frac{1}{3}, \frac{2}{6}, \frac{3}{9}$, and $\frac{4}{12}$ are **equal ratios.**

A recipe calls for 2 cups of milk for each 3 cups of flour.
Suppose you use 8 cups of milk. How much flour should you use?

cups of milk ⟶ $\quad \dfrac{2}{3} = \dfrac{8}{?}$

cups of flour ⟶

Think: $4 \times 2 = 8$,
and so $4 \times 3 = 12$.

Use 12 cups of flour.

A recipe for 12 servings of salad calls for 8 apples. Suppose you use
2 apples. How many servings can you make?

servings ⟶ $\quad \dfrac{12}{8} = \dfrac{?}{2}$

apples ⟶

Think: $8 \div 4 = 2$,
and so $12 \div 4 = 3$.

You can make 3 servings.

Practice • Complete.

1. $\frac{2}{3} = \frac{6}{?}$ **2.** $\frac{3}{8} = \frac{9}{?}$ **3.** $\frac{10}{15} = \frac{2}{?}$ **4.** $\frac{4}{7} = \frac{?}{14}$

5. $\frac{5}{6} = \frac{?}{36}$ **6.** $\frac{12}{32} = \frac{?}{8}$ **7.** $\frac{12}{21} = \frac{4}{?}$ **8.** $\frac{35}{42} = \frac{?}{6}$

Mixed Practice • Complete.

9. $\frac{7}{8} = \frac{14}{?}$ **10.** $\frac{21}{35} = \frac{?}{5}$ **11.** $\frac{4}{9} = \frac{12}{?}$ **12.** $\frac{15}{24} = \frac{?}{8}$

13. $\frac{2}{7} = \frac{?}{21}$ **14.** $\frac{4}{11} = \frac{?}{33}$ **15.** $\frac{14}{18} = \frac{7}{?}$ **16.** $\frac{15}{20} = \frac{3}{?}$

17. $\frac{3}{10} = \frac{12}{?}$ **18.** $\frac{30}{65} = \frac{?}{13}$ **19.** $\frac{25}{35} = \frac{?}{7}$ **20.** $\frac{9}{10} = \frac{27}{?}$

336

21. $\frac{12}{14} = \frac{?}{7}$ **22.** $\frac{12}{45} = \frac{4}{?}$ **23.** $\frac{5}{9} = \frac{?}{36}$ **24.** $\frac{10}{11} = \frac{?}{22}$

25. $\frac{?}{4} = \frac{3}{12}$ **26.** $\frac{2}{?} = \frac{4}{10}$ ★ **27.** $\frac{?}{10} = \frac{0.3}{6}$ ★ **28.** $\frac{?}{16} = \frac{0.7}{56}$

Complete the table of equal ratios.

29.

5	?	15	?	25	?	35
6	12	?	24	?	36	?

★ **30.**

7	?	28	?	42	?	56
4	12	?	20	?	28	?

PROBLEM SOLVING • APPLICATIONS

31. Jessup is making lemonade. The ratio of lemons to liters of water is 3 to 2. Jessup has 15 lemons. How many liters of water does he use?

32. Barbara is making tomato soup. For each package of soup mix she needs 4 cups of water. She uses 4 packages of soup mix. How many cups of water does she use?

33. Thelma uses 6 cups of flour to make 36 biscuits. How much flour does she use to make 1 dozen biscuits?

34. Tisa uses 90 milliliters of vinegar and 135 milliliters of mayonnaise to make salad dressing. How many milliliters of vinegar are used for every 3 milliliters of mayonnaise?

35. There are 32 bouillon cubes in 4 layers of a box. How many bouillon cubes are in 3 of the layers?

★ **36.** Juanita is making fruit punch. She uses 4 liters of orange concentrate and 6 liters of grapefruit concentrate. The ratio of liters of fruit concentrate to liters of water is 5 to 8. How many liters of water does she need?

The smaller gear makes 4 turns for every 3 turns of the larger gear.

★ **37.** How many turns will the larger gear make if the smaller gear makes 20 turns?

★ **38.** How many turns will the smaller gear make if the larger gear makes 27 turns?

Ratio and Proportion

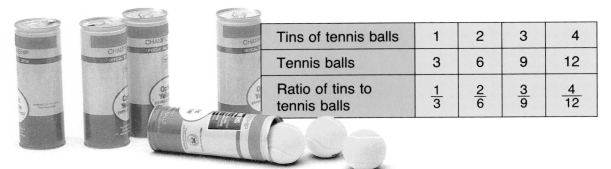

Tins of tennis balls	1	2	3	4
Tennis balls	3	6	9	12
Ratio of tins to tennis balls	$\frac{1}{3}$	$\frac{2}{6}$	$\frac{3}{9}$	$\frac{4}{12}$

Each tin contains 3 tennis balls. The ratio is 1 to 3.
No matter how many tins you buy, the ratio will remain the same.

A **proportion** is a statement that two ratios are equal.

number of tins $\longrightarrow$ $\dfrac{2}{6}$ $=$ $\dfrac{3}{9}$ $\longleftarrow$ number of tins
number of tennis balls $\longrightarrow$ $\phantom{\dfrac{2}{6}}$ $\phantom{\dfrac{3}{9}}$ $\longleftarrow$ number of tennis balls

You can use **cross products** to test a proportion.
If the cross products are equal, then the proportion is true.
The ratios are equal.

Is the proportion $\frac{2}{6} = \frac{7}{21}$ true?

$$\frac{2}{6} \overset{?}{=} \frac{7}{21}$$

$2 \times 21 \ \bullet \ 7 \times 6 \longleftarrow$ cross products

$42 = 42$

Yes, the proportion is true.
The ratios are equal.

Is the proportion $\frac{11}{31} = \frac{3}{9}$ true?

$$\frac{11}{31} \overset{?}{=} \frac{3}{9}$$

$\longrightarrow 11 \times 9 \ \bullet \ 3 \times 31$

$99 \neq 93$

No, the proportion is not true.
The ratios are not equal.

Practice • Is the proportion true? Compare the cross products.
Then write YES or NO.

1. $\dfrac{4}{5} = \dfrac{16}{20}$

2. $\dfrac{2}{3} = \dfrac{20}{40}$

3. $\dfrac{3}{4} = \dfrac{18}{24}$

4. $\dfrac{1}{2} = \dfrac{4}{6}$

Write = or ≠.

5. $\dfrac{1}{8} \ \bullet \ \dfrac{3}{24}$

6. $\dfrac{4}{7} \ \bullet \ \dfrac{2}{3}$

7. $\dfrac{5}{9} \ \bullet \ \dfrac{4}{7}$

8. $\dfrac{6}{20} \ \bullet \ \dfrac{3}{10}$

Mixed Practice • Is the proportion true? Compare the cross products. Then write YES or NO.

9. $\frac{2}{5} = \frac{10}{25}$

10. $\frac{2}{9} = \frac{14}{64}$

11. $\frac{3}{8} = \frac{9}{24}$

12. $\frac{7}{10} = \frac{18}{25}$

13. $\frac{4}{15} = \frac{6}{22}$

14. $\frac{7}{8} = \frac{28}{32}$

15. $\frac{9}{3} = \frac{3}{1}$

16. $\frac{5}{6} = \frac{3}{4}$

17. $\frac{9}{2} = \frac{18}{4}$

18. $\frac{27}{18} = \frac{3}{2}$

19. $\frac{5}{9} = \frac{8}{14}$

20. $\frac{17}{2} = \frac{35}{4}$

21. $\frac{15}{18} = \frac{2}{3}$

22. $\frac{7}{8} = \frac{21}{24}$

23. $\frac{10}{45} = \frac{8}{30}$

24. $\frac{4}{8} = \frac{5}{10}$

Write = or ≠.

25. $\frac{5}{8}$ ⬤ $\frac{15}{24}$

26. $\frac{1}{4}$ ⬤ $\frac{1}{3}$

27. $\frac{2}{7}$ ⬤ $\frac{5}{28}$

28. $\frac{10}{4}$ ⬤ $\frac{5}{2}$

29. $\frac{3}{14}$ ⬤ $\frac{5}{12}$

30. $\frac{35}{40}$ ⬤ $\frac{7}{8}$

31. $\frac{4}{9}$ ⬤ $\frac{12}{27}$

32. $\frac{3}{5}$ ⬤ $\frac{4}{6}$

33. $\frac{8}{3}$ ⬤ $\frac{32}{12}$

34. $\frac{5}{1}$ ⬤ $\frac{30}{4}$

35. $\frac{16}{3}$ ⬤ $\frac{10}{2}$

36. $\frac{5}{8}$ ⬤ $\frac{25}{49}$

★ 37. $\frac{0.3}{12}$ ⬤ $\frac{0.5}{20}$

★ 38. $\frac{0.9}{12}$ ⬤ $\frac{1}{15}$

★ 39. $\frac{10}{2.5}$ ⬤ $\frac{9}{1.5}$

★ 40. $\frac{0.6}{15}$ ⬤ $\frac{0.9}{22.5}$

PROBLEM SOLVING • APPLICATIONS

41. The ratio of packages to golf balls is 1 to 6. Will 9 packages contain 54 golf balls?

42. The ratio of table tennis balls to packages is 6 to 1. Will there be 40 balls in 7 packages?

★ 43. One croquet set contains 4 mallets and 2 balls. Will a dozen sets have 36 mallets and 24 balls?

★ 44. A tennis set contains 3 balls and 2 rackets. Can 24 balls and 18 rackets be made into complete sets with no pieces left over?

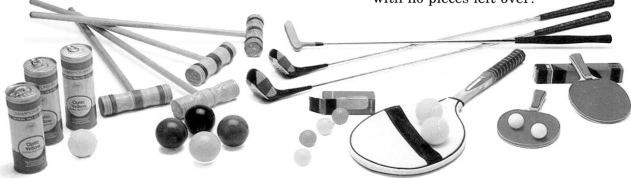

Solving Proportions

You can use cross products to help you solve proportions.

It takes Joan 3 hours to ride 72 kilometers on her bicycle. If she continues to travel at the same rate, how long does it take her to ride 120 kilometers?

hours ⟶ $\dfrac{3}{72} = \dfrac{?}{120}$
kilometers ⟶

$72 \times ? = 3 \times 120$
$72 \times ? = 360$
$? = 360 \div 72$
$? = 5$

It takes Joan 5 hours.

One class sells 30 student tickets and 48 adult tickets for the school play. For every 5 student tickets, how many adult tickets are sold?

student tickets ⟶ $\dfrac{30}{48} = \dfrac{5}{?}$
adult tickets ⟶

$30 \times ? = 48 \times 5$
$30 \times ? = 240$
$? = 240 \div 30$
$? = 8$

For every 5 student tickets, 8 adult tickets are sold.

Practice • Solve the proportions.

1. $\dfrac{8}{12} = \dfrac{6}{?}$
2. $\dfrac{3}{9} = \dfrac{?}{12}$
3. $\dfrac{5}{1} = \dfrac{?}{6}$
4. $\dfrac{6}{4} = \dfrac{36}{?}$

5. $\dfrac{6}{7} = \dfrac{?}{56}$
6. $\dfrac{2}{8} = \dfrac{?}{12}$
7. $\dfrac{10}{45} = \dfrac{8}{?}$
8. $\dfrac{4}{10} = \dfrac{?}{35}$

More Practice • Solve the proportions.

9. $\dfrac{6}{8} = \dfrac{9}{?}$
10. $\dfrac{9}{15} = \dfrac{6}{?}$
11. $\dfrac{3}{9} = \dfrac{?}{21}$
12. $\dfrac{12}{9} = \dfrac{?}{12}$

13. $\dfrac{15}{20} = \dfrac{?}{16}$
14. $\dfrac{14}{4} = \dfrac{42}{?}$
15. $\dfrac{12}{8} = \dfrac{?}{18}$
16. $\dfrac{12}{30} = \dfrac{6}{?}$

★ 17. $\dfrac{0.9}{1.8} = \dfrac{?}{2.4}$
★ 18. $\dfrac{1.6}{2.8} = \dfrac{4}{?}$
★ 19. $\dfrac{2.5}{4} = \dfrac{?}{6}$
★ 20. $\dfrac{0.99}{5} = \dfrac{5.94}{?}$

PROBLEM SOLVING • APPLICATIONS

Write the proportion. Then solve the problem.

21. The students painting scenery use 6 cans of white paint and 8 cans of green paint. For every 3 cans of white paint, how many cans of green paint do they use?

22. Monty buys some masking tape for the props department. 3 rolls cost $4.47. He spends $22.35. How many rolls of masking tape does he buy?

23. A student typed the program for the play at an average rate of 32 words per minute. One page of the program has 480 words on it. About how many minutes did it take the student to type this page?

24. Sasha is making costumes for the dancers. She uses 3 meters of material to make 2 costumes. How much material does she use to make 18 costumes?

★ **25.** One of the dancers exercises by riding his bicycle. He rides at an average rate of 18 kilometers per hour. How many minutes does it take him to ride 27 kilometers?

★ **26.** Ralph has quarters and dimes in his pocket. The ratio of quarters to dimes is 4 to 5. He has $4.50. How many dimes does Ralph have?

Skills Maintenance

1. 50 mm = __?__ cm

2. 5 m = __?__ km

3. 2.81 cm = __?__ mm

4. 235 mm = __?__ m

5. 6.2 L = __?__ mL

6. 72 mL = __?__ L

7. 5,200 g = __?__ kg

8. 15 mg = __?__ g

9. 28 g = __?__ mg

341

Scale Drawing

Scale: 1 cm = 8 m

Mammals	Reptiles and Amphibians	Late Dinosaurs
Trees / Biology of Invertebrates	Special Exhibits	
Biology of Humans	Space Room	Minerals and Gems / Fossils
Biology of Birds / Biology of Fish	Entrance Hall	Early Dinosaurs

This is a scale drawing of a museum.

Each centimeter in the scale drawing represents 8 meters in the museum.
The scale can be written as a ratio.

centimeters $\longrightarrow \dfrac{1}{8}$
meters $\longrightarrow$

In the drawing the length of the entrance hall is 4 centimeters.
Use cross products to find the actual length of the entrance hall.

$\dfrac{1}{8} = \dfrac{4}{?}$ $\longrightarrow$ length in drawing
$\phantom{\dfrac{1}{8} = \dfrac{4}{?}}$ $\longrightarrow$ actual length

$1 \times ? = 4 \times 8$
$1 \times ? = 32$
$? = 32 \div 1$
$? = 32$

The actual length of the entrance hall is 32 meters.

Find the actual width of the entrance hall.

$\dfrac{1}{8} = \dfrac{2}{?}$ ⟶ width in drawing
⟶ actual width

$1 \times ? = 2 \times 8$
$1 \times ? = 16$
$? = 16 \div 1$
$? = 16$

The actual width of the entrance hall is 16 meters.
The dimensions of the entrance hall are 32 meters by 16 meters.

Practice • Measure the drawing. Find the dimensions of the rooms.

1. Trees

2. Biology of Fish

3. Space Room

More Practice • Measure the drawing. Find the dimensions of the rooms.

4. Special Exhibits

5. Biology of Humans

6. Late Dinosaurs

7. Biology of Birds

★ 8. Minerals and Gems

★ 9. Fossils

★ 10. Find the actual dimensions of the entire museum.

PROBLEM SOLVING • APPLICATIONS

11. An excavation site is in the shape of a square. In a scale drawing, one side of the excavation is 26 centimeters. On the drawing each centimeter represents 3 meters. What is the perimeter of the site?

12. The museum is going to add a new wing. On a scale drawing, the new wing measures 13 centimeters by 6 centimeters. On the drawing each centimeter represents 6 meters. What are the actual dimensions of the new wing?

★ 13. Suppose you are making a scale drawing of an exhibit area. Use 1 centimeter to represent 4.5 meters. The actual dimensions of the area are 18 meters by 9 meters. What will be the length and the width of the exhibit area in the drawing?

★ 14. Make a scale drawing of your room or of your home. Be sure to mark the scale you use on the drawing. You may wish to include furniture.

The museum is building a model of the Great Pyramid. In the model 1 centimeter represents 3 meters.

★ 15. The pyramid was 147 meters high when it was first built. What will the height be in the model?

★ 16. The grand gallery of the pyramid was 47 meters long and 8.5 meters high. What will these dimensions be in the model? (Round to the nearest hundredth.)

Ratio and Similar Polygons

Rosemary has pictures that she took while on vacation. She had one of them enlarged. The original picture and the enlargement have the same shape. They are **similar** polygons.

Side *AB* corresponds to side *EF*.
Side *BC* corresponds to side *FG*.
Side *CD* corresponds to side *GH*.
Side *DA* corresponds to side *HE*.

The ratios of the lengths of the **corresponding sides** are equal.

You can write a proportion to show how these lengths are related.

Compare the cross products to show that the proportion is true.

$$\text{side } AB \longrightarrow \frac{8}{20} = \frac{12}{30} \longleftarrow \text{side } BC$$
$$\text{side } EF \longrightarrow \qquad \qquad \longleftarrow \text{side } FG$$
$$8 \times 30 = 12 \times 20$$
$$240 = 240$$

These triangles are similar.

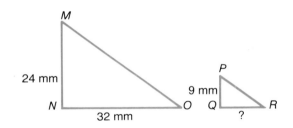

Side *MN* corresponds to side *PQ*.
Side *NO* corresponds to side *QR*.
Side *OM* corresponds to side *RP*.

Use cross products to find the length of side *QR*.

$$\text{side } MN \longrightarrow \frac{24}{9} = \frac{32}{?} \longleftarrow \text{side } NO$$
$$\text{side } PQ \longrightarrow \qquad \qquad \longleftarrow \text{side } QR$$
$$24 \times ? = 32 \times 9$$
$$24 \times ? = 288$$
$$? = 288 \div 24$$
$$? = 12$$

The length of $\overline{QR}$ is 12 millimeters.

Practice • Rectangles *JKLM* and *WXYZ* are similar.
Name the side that corresponds to

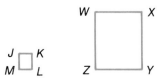

1. side *JK*.

2. side *KL*.

3. side *WZ*.

4. side *ZY*.

Find the missing measures.

5. $\overline{JK}$ = 4 cm
$\overline{KL}$ = 5 cm
$\overline{WX}$ = 16 cm
$\overline{XY}$ = ____?____

6. $\overline{JK}$ = 6 mm
$\overline{KL}$ = 14 mm
$\overline{WX}$ = 24 mm
$\overline{XY}$ = ____?____

Mixed Practice • Triangles *EFG* and *RST* are similar. Name the side that corresponds to

7. side *EF*.
8. side *FG*.
9. side *GE*.

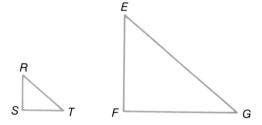

Find the missing measures.

10. $\overline{EF}$ = 3 cm
$\overline{FG}$ = 4 cm
$\overline{RS}$ = 9 cm
$\overline{ST}$ = ____?____

11. $\overline{EF}$ = 5 mm
$\overline{FG}$ = 8 mm
$\overline{RS}$ = 40 mm
$\overline{ST}$ = ____?____

Rectangles *RSTU* and *BCDE* are similar. Name the side that corresponds to

12. side *RS*.

13. side *RU*.

14. side *DC*.

15. side *ED*.

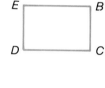

Find the missing measures.

16. $\overline{RS}$ = 8 cm
$\overline{RU}$ = 32 cm
$\overline{BC}$ = 12 cm
$\overline{BE}$ = ____?____

17. $\overline{RS}$ = 10 mm
$\overline{RU}$ = 15 mm
$\overline{BC}$ = 28 mm
$\overline{BE}$ = ____?____

★ **18.** $\overline{RS}$ = 2.1 cm
$\overline{RU}$ = 2.8 cm
$\overline{BC}$ = 1.8 cm
$\overline{BE}$ = ____?____

PROBLEM SOLVING • APPLICATIONS

19. Rosemary is making wooden frames for some of her pictures. Side *LM* of her larger frame is 50 centimeters. Side *MN* is 35 centimeters. The two frames are similar. For the smaller picture frame, side *EF* is 30 centimeters. What is the length of side *FG*?

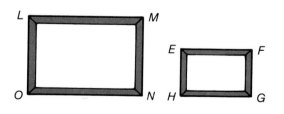

20. Rosemary is mailing pictures to her friends. She uses similar envelopes. One envelope is 20 centimeters long and 8 centimeters wide. The other envelope is 30 centimeters long. How wide is it?

★ **21.** Rosemary has three pictures. Picture A is 60 centimeters long and 44 centimeters wide. Picture B is 51 centimeters long and 35 centimeters wide. Picture C is 45 centimeters long and 33 centimeters wide. Which two pictures are similar?

Ratio and Probability

The spinner can stop on 1 of 4 symbols. Suppose you want a star. You can expect to get 1 star in 4 spins. The **probability** of getting a star is $\frac{1}{4}$. How many stars can you expect in 8 spins? Write a proportion to solve.

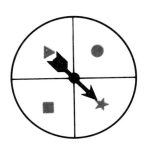

number of stars $\longrightarrow \dfrac{1}{4} = \dfrac{?}{8}$
number of spins $\longrightarrow$

You can use cross products.

$$1 \times 8 = ? \times 4$$
$$8 = ? \times 4$$
$$8 \div 4 = ?$$
$$2 = ?$$

You can expect to get 2 stars in 8 spins.

On which shape is this spinner most likely to stop? There are 3 spaces with stars. The spinner is most likely to stop on a star.

The probability of getting a star is $\frac{3}{6}$. You can expect to get 3 stars in 6 spins. How many stars can you expect in 24 spins? Write a proportion to solve.

number of stars $\longrightarrow \dfrac{3}{6} = \dfrac{?}{24}$
number of spins $\longrightarrow$

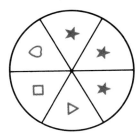

$$3 \times 24 = ? \times 6$$
$$72 = ? \times 6$$
$$72 \div 6 = ?$$
$$12 = ?$$

You can expect to get 12 stars in 24 spins.

Practice • How many stars can you expect to get

1. in 6 spins?

2. in 10 spins?

3. in 10 spins?

4. in 18 spins?

More Practice • How many stars can you expect to get

5. in 6 spins?

6. in 12 spins?

7. in 18 spins?

8. in 24 spins?

9. in 4 spins?   **10.** in 8 spins?   **11.** in 12 spins?   **12.** in 16 spins?

PROBLEM SOLVING • APPLICATIONS

There are 7 red, 5 green, and 3 blue marbles in a jar. You pick a marble without looking. What is the probability of picking a marble that is

13. red?   **14.** green?   **15.** blue?

Suppose you pick a marble from the jar 30 times. Each time you return the marble to the jar. How many times can you expect to get a

16. red marble?   **17.** green marble?   **18.** blue marble?

A number cube has faces numbered 2, 4, 6, 8, 10, and 12. The probability of tossing an even number is $\frac{6}{6}$, or 1. If the event will **always** occur, we say the probability is 1.

The probability of tossing an odd number is $\frac{0}{6}$, or 0. If the event will **never** occur, we say the probability is 0.

★ **19.** What is the probability of tossing a number less than 13?

★ **20.** What is the probability of tossing an odd number greater than 5?

Midchapter Review

Write the fractions for the ratios.   **1.** 8 to 5   **2.** 7 to 9   **3.** 6:3

Write = or ≠.   **4.** $\frac{7}{9}$ ◯ $\frac{5}{8}$ **5.** $\frac{6}{5}$ ◯ $\frac{4}{10}$ **6.** $\frac{12}{9}$ ◯ $\frac{4}{3}$

Solve the proportions.   **7.** $\frac{11}{12} = \frac{?}{36}$ **8.** $\frac{3}{12} = \frac{20}{?}$ **9.** $\frac{8}{20} = \frac{6}{?}$

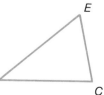 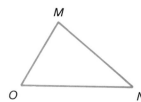

Triangles *CDE* and *MNO* are similar. Name the side that corresponds to

10. side *CD*.   **11.** side *CE*.   **12.** side *NO*.

Percent

Another way to show a ratio is to use **percent**. Percent means per hundred. The symbol for percent is %. Use a percent to show the ratio of blue blocks to all 100 blocks.

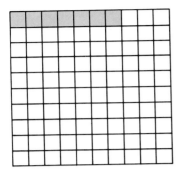 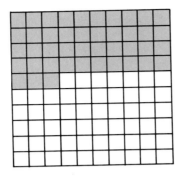 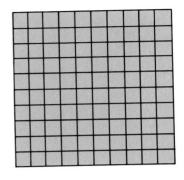

	7 out of 100	43 out of 100	100 out of 100
Ratio	$\frac{7}{100}$	$\frac{43}{100}$	$\frac{100}{100}$
Decimal	0.07	0.43	1.00
Percent	7%	43%	100%

Practice • Write the percent that tells what part is shaded.

1.   2.   3.   4.

Write the percents for the ratios.

5. 9 out of 100   6. 58 out of 100   7. 77 out of 100

8. $\frac{6}{100}$ 9. $\frac{17}{100}$ 10. $\frac{42}{100}$ 11. $\frac{1}{100}$ 12. $\frac{25}{100}$ 13. $\frac{13}{100}$

Write the percents for the decimals.

14. 0.87   15. 0.65   16. 0.45   17. 0.15   18. 0.99   19. 0.37

Mixed Practice • Write the percent that tells what part is shaded.

20.

21.

22.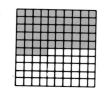

23.

Write the percents for the ratios.

24. 3 out of 100
25. 8 out of 100
26. 36 out of 100

27. 50 out of 100
28. 66 out of 100
29. 89 out of 100

30. 5 per 100
31. 49 per 100
32. 93 per 100

33. $\frac{4}{100}$
34. $\frac{39}{100}$
35. $\frac{19}{100}$
36. $\frac{23}{100}$
37. $\frac{11}{100}$
38. $\frac{31}{100}$

39. $\frac{27}{100}$
40. $\frac{90}{100}$
41. $\frac{63}{100}$
42. $\frac{29}{100}$
43. $\frac{52}{100}$
44. $\frac{74}{100}$

Write the percents for the decimals.

45. 0.34
46. 0.22
47. 0.02
48. 0.88
49. 1.00
50. 0.67

51. 0.75
52. 0.28
53. 0.97
54. 0.61
55. 0.56
56. 0.35

57. 0.01
58. 0.72
★ 59. 0.8
★ 60. 0.6
★ 61. 0.1
★ 62. 0.9

PROBLEM SOLVING • APPLICATIONS

63. In a collector's catalog, 70 out of 100 pages show coins. What percent of the pages show coins?

64. 54 out of 100 coins are in an album. What percent of the coins are in an album?

65. Flip 100 pennies. 48 land on heads. What percent of the pennies land on heads?

66. There are 100 coins. 23 are copper. What percent are copper?

★ 67. There are 100 coins. 74 are silver. What percent of the coins are not silver?

★ 68. There are 100 coins. 56 are nickels. What percent of the coins are not nickels?

Decimals and Fractions for Percents

41 out of the 100 bicycles are red.
This is 41% of the bicycles.
Write the decimal for 41%.

Think: 41% is 41 hundredths.

41% = 0.41

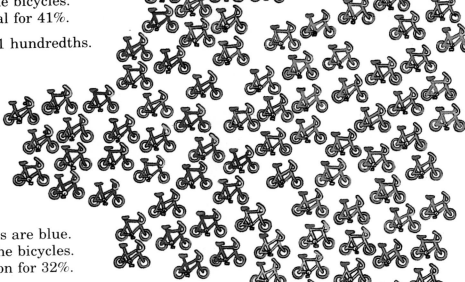

32 of the bicycles are blue.
This is 32% of the bicycles.
Write the fraction for 32%.

Think: 32% is 32 hundredths.

Step 1 32% means 32 hundredths. ⟶ $\dfrac{32}{100}$

Step 2 Write the fraction in lowest terms. ⟶ $\dfrac{8}{25}$

$32\% = \dfrac{8}{25}$

Practice • Write the decimals for the percents.

1. 33%   2. 48%   3. 6%   4. 80%   5. 30%   6. 12%

Write the fractions for the percents. Write the answers in lowest terms.

7. 25%   8. 50%   9. 20%   10. 30%   11. 28%   12. 55%

Mixed Practice • Write the decimals for the percents.

13. 11%   14. 8%   15. 54%   16. 35%   17. 75%   18. 70%

19. 29%   20. 42%   21. 38%   22. 96%   23. 99%   24. 86%

25. 7%   26. 16%   27. 65%   28. 13%   29. 83%   30. 77%

31. 93%   32. 23%   33. 58%   34. 25%   35. 67%   36. 59%

Write the fractions for the percents. Write the answers in lowest terms.

37. 37%   **38.** 44%   **39.** 13%   **40.** 40%   **41.** 21%   **42.** 16%

43. 81%   **44.** 66%   **45.** 98%   **46.** 85%   **47.** 71%   **48.** 90%

49. 4%   **50.** 75%   **51.** 56%   **52.** 64%   **53.** 15%   **54.** 48%

55. 70%   **56.** 45%   **57.** 68%   **58.** 83%   **59.** 95%   **60.** 72%

The manager at Pohanka Cycle sets a sales goal of 100 bikes per year for each salesperson.

Last year Clare sold 136 bikes.
The ratio of bikes sold to the sales goal is $\frac{136}{100}$.

bikes sold $\longrightarrow$ $\frac{136}{100} = 136\%$
sales goal $\longrightarrow$

Clare sold 136% of the goal.

Write the percents for the ratios.

★ **61.** 125 to 100   ★ **62.** 360 to 100   ★ **63.** 500 to 100   ★ **64.** 256 to 100

PROBLEM SOLVING • APPLICATIONS

65. Sal orders 100 new bikes for his shop. 65 of them are dirt bikes. What fraction of the bikes are dirt bikes?

66. 36% of the bikes Sal orders are imported. Write the decimal to show the percent of imported bikes that Sal orders.

★ **67.** A shipment of 100 bikes arrives. 72% of them are ten-speed. How many bikes in the shipment are not ten-speed?

★ **68.** Sal sends in an order for 50 bikes. 16% of them are five-speed. The rest are three-speed. How many three-speed bikes does he order?

Percents for Fractions

The ratio of trucks to cars is
2 to 5.
What percent names this ratio?

Find an equal ratio with 100
as the denominator.

$$\frac{2}{5} = \frac{?}{100}$$

Use cross products to solve.

$2 \times 100 = ? \times 5$

$\qquad 200 = ? \times 5$

$200 \div 5 = ?$

$\qquad\quad 40 = ?$

$$\frac{2}{5} = \frac{40}{100}$$

40% names the same ratio as $\frac{2}{5}$.

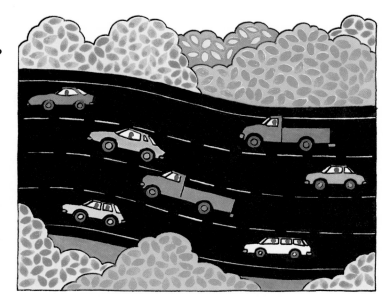

You can also divide to find the percent for $\frac{2}{5}$. Carry out the division to the hundredths place.

Step 1 Divide.

$$\begin{array}{r} 0.40 \\ 5\overline{)2.00} \\ -2\,0\!\downarrow \\ \hline 00 \\ -\;0 \\ \hline 0 \end{array}$$

Step 2 Write the quotient as a percent.

$0.40 = 40\%$

Divide to find the percent for $\frac{4}{7}$.

Step 1 Divide.

$$\begin{array}{r} 0.57\tfrac{1}{7} \\ 7\overline{)4.00} \\ -3\,5\!\downarrow \\ \hline 50 \\ -49 \\ \hline 1 \end{array}$$

Step 2 Write the quotient as a percent.

$0.57\frac{1}{7} = 57\frac{1}{7}\%$

Practice • Write the percents for the fractions.

1. $\frac{1}{2}$ 2. $\frac{1}{4}$ 3. $\frac{3}{4}$ 4. $\frac{7}{10}$ 5. $\frac{1}{10}$ 6. $\frac{5}{10}$

7. $\frac{3}{8}$ 8. $\frac{2}{3}$ 9. $\frac{5}{6}$ 10. $\frac{4}{9}$ 11. $\frac{5}{8}$ 12. $\frac{3}{7}$

Mixed Practice • Write the percents for the fractions.

13. $\frac{3}{20}$ 14. $\frac{1}{5}$ 15. $\frac{8}{10}$ 16. $\frac{6}{25}$ 17. $\frac{17}{20}$ 18. $\frac{9}{50}$

19. $\frac{4}{5}$ 20. $\frac{9}{20}$ 21. $\frac{23}{25}$ 22. $\frac{13}{50}$ 23. $\frac{27}{50}$ 24. $\frac{3}{10}$

25. $\frac{1}{3}$ 26. $\frac{7}{9}$ 27. $\frac{5}{12}$ 28. $\frac{2}{7}$ 29. $\frac{7}{8}$ 30. $\frac{1}{6}$

31. $\frac{4}{15}$ 32. $\frac{6}{13}$ 33. $\frac{13}{15}$ 34. $\frac{11}{24}$ 35. $\frac{5}{13}$ 36. $\frac{7}{11}$

37. $\frac{7}{15}$ 38. $\frac{8}{11}$ 39. $\frac{17}{24}$ ★ 40. $\frac{50}{39}$ ★ 41. $\frac{35}{6}$ ★ 42. $\frac{46}{15}$

Complete.

	Fraction	Decimal	Percent
43.	$\frac{1}{4}$	?	?
44.	?	0.8	?
45.	?	?	75%
46.	$\frac{4}{25}$	?	?
47.	?	0.29	?

PROBLEM SOLVING • APPLICATIONS

48. There are 25 antique automobiles. 6 are Model T's. What percent are Model T's?

49. There are 40 trailers. 15 are blue. What percent are blue?

★ 50. $\frac{2}{9}$ of the trucks are more than ten years old. What percent of the trucks are not more than ten years old?

★ 51. There are 60 cars. 45 are sports cars. What percent of the cars are not sports cars?

Skills Maintenance

1. 2 yd = __?__ in.

2. 30 ft = __?__ yd

3. 4 mi = __?__ ft

4. 8 c = __?__ qt

5. 8 qt = __?__ pt

6. 1 gal 1 qt = __?__ pt

7. 1 yd 2 ft = __?__ in.

8. 36 oz = __?__ lb __?__ oz

9. 7 T = __?__ lb

Percent of a Number

Eva drives a taxi. Yesterday she made 20 trips. 15% of them were to the airport. How many trips did she make to the airport?

15% of 20 = ?

Here are two ways to find the answer.

Step 1
Use a fraction to name the percent. Then multiply.

$$15\% = \frac{15}{100} \text{ or } \frac{3}{20}$$

$$\frac{3}{20} \times \frac{20}{1} = \frac{60}{20} = 3$$

Step 2
Use a decimal to name the percent. Then multiply.

$$15\% = 0.15$$

$$\begin{array}{r} 20 \\ \times 0.15 \\ \hline 1\,00 \\ 2\,00 \\ \hline 3.00 \end{array}$$

Eva made 3 trips to the airport.

Practice • Use fractions to find the answers.

1. 50% of 42 = __?__

2. 25% of 24 = __?__

3. 75% of 12 = __?__

Use decimals to find the answers.

4. 32% of 74 = __?__

5. 16% of 28 = __?__

6. 55% of 72 = __?__

Mixed Practice • Find the answers.

7. 20% of 55 = __?__

8. 45% of 500 = __?__

9. 94% of 46 = __?__

10. 15% of 400 = __?__

11. 16% of 48 = __?__

12. 25% of 140 = __?__

13. 2% of 350 = __?__

14. 50% of 94 = __?__

15. 5% of 860 = __?__

16. 30% of 40 = __?__

17. 45% of 330 = __?__

18. 78% of 120 = __?__

What percent of 20 is 3?

? % of 20 = 3

What percent of 90 is 45?

? % of 90 = 45

Think: $\dfrac{3}{20} = \dfrac{?}{100}$

$3 \times 100 = ? \times 20$

$300 = ? \times 20$

$300 \div 20 = ?$

$15 = ?$

15% of 20 is 3.

Think: $\dfrac{45}{90} = \dfrac{?}{100}$

$45 \times 100 = ? \times 90$

$4500 = ? \times 90$

$4500 \div 90 = ?$

$50 = ?$

50% of 90 is 45.

Find the answers.

★ **19.** __?__ % of 30 = 6

★ **20.** __?__ % of 8 = 4

★ **21.** __?__ % of 25 = 15

★ **22.** __?__ % of 50 = 33

★ **23.** __?__ % of 10 = 1

★ **24.** __?__ % of 80 = 60

PROBLEM SOLVING • APPLICATIONS

25. Joan drives a bookmobile. Her route has 20 stops. 35% of her stops are at schools. How many of her stops are at schools?

26. Zuri flies a traffic-control helicopter. She flies for 4 hours in the morning. 75% of this time she flies over expressways. How many hours does she fly over expressways in the morning?

★ **27.** Jennifer lands her small plane on a runway that is 3 kilometers long. She uses 28% of the runway to land. How many meters does she use to land?

★ **28.** Elvin drives a trailer truck. The truck's fuel tank holds 400 liters of gasoline. He starts a trip with a full tank. At his first stop the tank is 75% full. How much fuel did he use?

Circle Graphs

Jim has a part-time job at a service station. Because he wants to use his money wisely, he makes a **budget**. A budget is a plan for using money.

Jim earns more some weeks than others. By using percents he can tell how to use the money he earns each week. Jim shows his budget on a **circle graph.**

The circle graph tells him that 10% of his earnings should be saved. If he earns $25.00 one week, how much should be saved?

10% of $25.00 = ?

$$\begin{array}{r} \$25.00 \\ \times\ \ \ 0.10 \\ \hline \$\ \ 2.50 \end{array}$$

Jim should save $2.50 of the $25.00.

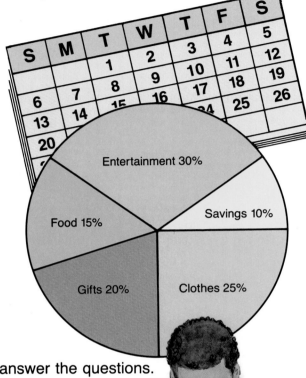

Practice • Use Jim's circle graph to answer the questions.

1. What is the sum of the percents shown on the graph?

2. On which item does Jim spend the most money?

3. For which item does he budget the least money?

What percent of Jim's earnings is used for

4. entertainment?   5. food?   6. gifts?   7. clothes?

If Jim earns $40.00, how much is budgeted for

8. entertainment?   9. food?   10. gifts?   11. clothes?

12. Suppose Jim earns $32.80 one week. How much would Jim budget for each item that week?

356

Mixed Practice • Use Eric's circle graph to answer the questions.

13. What is the sum of the percents shown on the graph?

Eric's yearly income is $18,000. How much money does he spend on

14. housing? **15.** food?

16. taxes? **17.** clothing?

18. How much more does he spend on medical care than on transportation?

★ **19.** For which item does Eric budget $1,620?

★ **20.** For which item does Eric budget $1,080?

★ **21.** Suppose Eric's yearly income is $26,500. List how it is budgeted according to the graph.

ERIC STANTON'S ANNUAL EXPENSES

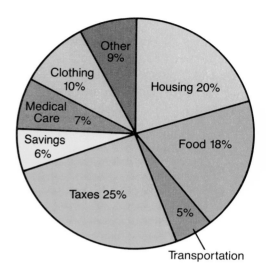

PROBLEM SOLVING • APPLICATIONS

Gary works at Fred's sport shop. He gets a 15% employee discount. A **discount** is an amount that is subtracted from the original cost. Use the percent to find how much the discount will be.

Gary buys a tennis racket that sells for $65.00. How much is his discount?

15% of $65.00 = ?
$$\begin{array}{r} \$65.00 \\ \times\ \ 0.15 \\ \hline \$\ 9.75 \end{array}$$

Gary gets a discount of $9.75.

How much does the tennis racket cost Gary?
Original cost − discount = new cost
$$\begin{array}{r} \$65.00 \\ -\ \ 9.75 \\ \hline \$55.25 \end{array}$$
The racket costs Gary $55.25.

Find the discount.

22. original cost: $18.75
discount: 40%

23. original cost: $172.60
discount: 10%

24. original cost: $14.76
discount: 25%

What is the discount and the new cost of each item?

25. 20% discount on a football jersey that sells for $15.95

26. 18% discount on golf clubs that sell for $175.00

Sales Tax

States and cities need money for the services that they provide.
One way to raise this money is to charge a **sales tax.**
This is an amount added to the price of something you buy.

Doris wants to buy a jewel fish
for her aquarium. It costs $7.99.
A sales tax of 6% must be added
to the cost. How much money does
Doris need to buy the fish?

Find the total cost of the fish.

Step 1
Find the amount of tax.
Round the tax to the
nearest whole cent.
$.4794 rounds to $.48.

$7.99
× 0.06
$.4794

Step 2
Add the tax to the price.

$7.99
+ .48
$8.47

The total cost is $8.47.

Practice • Find the amount of tax.

1. price: $2.50
   sales tax: 8%

2. price: $5.90
   sales tax: 6%

3. price: $450.00
   sales tax: 4%

Find the total cost.

4. price: $35.00
   sales tax: 3%

5. price: $86.49
   sales tax: 7%

6. price: $110.00
   sales tax: 5%

Mixed Practice • Find the amount of tax.

7. price: $12.95
   sales tax: 3%

8. price: $45.00
   sales tax: 8%

9. price: $38.75
   sales tax: 6%

10. price: $3.99
    sales tax: 7%

11. price: $74.50
    sales tax: 4%

12. price: $343.00
    sales tax: 5%

Find the total cost.

13. price: $7.35
sales tax: 7%

14. price: $99.98
sales tax: 3%

15. price: $162.00
sales tax: 5%

16. price: $5.25
sales tax: 4%

17. price: $37.80
sales tax: 7%

18. price: $958.50
sales tax: 6%

Find the total cost of each item if the sales tax is 7%.

★ **19.**

The Fishbowl	
Plastic plants	$4.00
3 packages gravel	1.76
Subtotal	?
Tax	?
Total	?

★ **20.**

The Fishbowl	
4 silver angelfish	$5.16
1 quill plant	1.49
Subtotal	?
Tax	?
Total	?

★ **21.**

The Fishbowl	
#17 fish tank	$23.99
hood with light	34.99
Subtotal	?
Tax	?
Total	?

PROBLEM SOLVING • APPLICATIONS

22. A glass fishbowl costs $5.79. There is a sales tax of 5%. What is the amount of sales tax? What is the total cost of the fishbowl?

23. Eli buys a can of tropical fish food for $4.99. He also buys a net for $3.19. There is a sales tax of 6%. What is the total cost of Eli's purchase?

★ **24.** Faith buys a large fish tank for $78.99. She also buys a pump for $62.00 and 3 bags of gravel at $4.15 each. The sales tax is 6%. What is the total cost of Faith's purchase?

★ **25.** Kit is finding the total cost of a customer's order. The customer buys 6 shells at $.85 each, a sword plant for $6.99, and 2 bronze catfish at $1.79 each. The sales tax is 4%. How much change would the customer receive from a $20.00 bill?

PROBLEM SOLVING · STRATEGIES

Reading Maps

A map is a special kind of scale drawing. We use maps to find places and distances.

This section of a highway map shows the city of Syracuse and some of the surrounding area.

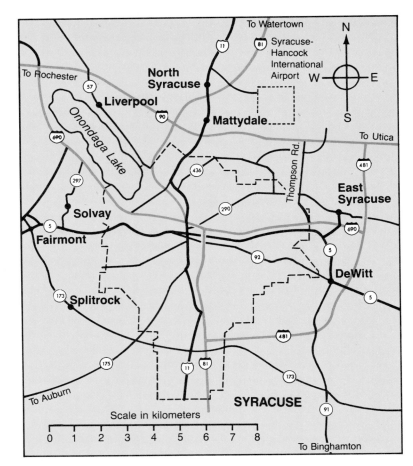

City boundary

Interstate highway

U.S. highway

State highway

About how far is it from (57) to (81) along (90) ?

A scale for this map is shown in kilometers. Measure the approximate distance on the map.

1. Copy the scale on the edge of an index card.

2. Now use the card like a ruler.

3. Place the card along the highway to be measured.

4. Read the distance to the nearest kilometer.

It is about 4 kilometers from (57) to (81) along (90).

Use the map scale to find distances.
Use the arrows for direction.

Use the map to answer the questions.

About how far is it from

1. (81) to (91) along (481) ?

2. (690) to (481) along (81) ?

3.  81 to 481 along 690?

4. 690 to 57 along 90?

5. 290 to 90 along Thompson Road?

6. 57 to 11 along 90?

Be sure you understand all the symbols on the map.

7. In which direction would you go to travel from North Syracuse to Mattydale?

8. In which direction would you go to travel from Syracuse to Utica?

9. In which direction would you go to travel from East Syracuse to Fairmont?

10. Suppose you want to drive to Binghamton from Syracuse. What interstate highway should you take?

11. Suppose you want to drive to Watertown from Syracuse. What U.S. highway should you take?

★ 12. You want to drive from Mattydale to Liverpool. You want to take the shortest route. Name the highways you would take.

★ 13. You want to drive from Split Rock to Solvay. Name the highways you would take. Then name the direction in which you would be traveling on each highway.

Write the fractions for the ratios. (pages 334–335)

1. $2:3$ **2.** 8 to 15   **3.** 7 to 1   **4.** $85:100$

Complete. (pages 336–337)

5. $\frac{2}{3} = \frac{6}{?}$ **6.** $\frac{10}{12} = \frac{?}{6}$ **7.** $\frac{5}{8} = \frac{?}{40}$ **8.** $\frac{15}{25} = \frac{3}{?}$

Write = or ≠. (pages 338–339)

9. $\frac{4}{5} \bullet \frac{12}{20}$ **10.** $\frac{3}{8} \bullet \frac{27}{72}$ **11.** $\frac{4}{9} \bullet \frac{20}{45}$ **12.** $\frac{5}{8} \bullet \frac{15}{18}$

Solve the proportions. (pages 340–341)

13. $\frac{2}{3} = \frac{?}{27}$ **14.** $\frac{3}{8} = \frac{6}{?}$ **15.** $\frac{6}{10} = \frac{?}{25}$ **16.** $\frac{6}{8} = \frac{?}{12}$

Write as a percent. (pages 348–349)

17. 8 out of 100   **18.** $\frac{16}{100}$ **19.** 0.36   **20.** 0.09

Write the fractions and the decimals. (pages 350–351)

21. 23%   **22.** 40%   **23.** 5%   **24.** 75%

Write the percents for the fractions. (pages 352–353)

25. $\frac{1}{2}$ **26.** $\frac{3}{5}$ **27.** $\frac{7}{20}$ **28.** $\frac{5}{11}$

Find the answers. (pages 354–355)

29. 65% of 200 = __?__   **30.** 80% of 360 = __?__   **31.** 24% of 72 = __?__

Solve.

32. Bian made a scale drawing of her room. In the drawing the length is 3 centimeters and the width is 2 centimeters. Each centimeter represents 2 meters. What are the actual dimensions of Bian's room? (p. 342)

33. Lauren's monthly allowance is $10.00. She budgets 25% for food. How much money does she budget for food? (p. 356)

PROJECT

Probability

Toss a coin.

The probability that it will land heads is 1 out of 2, or $\frac{1}{2}$.

About how many times can you expect it to land heads if you toss it 2 times? 4 times? 6 times?

Complete the prediction table.

Now toss a coin and complete the results table.

Compare the results with your prediction.

Prediction

Tosses	2	4	6	8	10
Heads	1	?	?	?	?

Results

Tosses	2	4	6	8	10
Heads	?	?	?	?	?

A number cube has faces numbered 1, 2, 3, 4, 5, and 6.

Toss the number cube. The probability of tossing a 4 or a 5 is 2 out of 6, or $\frac{2}{6}$.

Make a prediction table.

Now toss the number cube and complete the results table.

Compare the results with your prediction.

Prediction

Tosses	6	12	18	24	30	36
4 or 5	2	?	?	?	?	?

Results

Tosses	6	12	18	24	30	36
4 or 5	?	?	?	?	?	?

Look at a book.

The probability that the letter *e* will appear in 1,000 letters is about 1 out of 13, or $\frac{1}{13}$.

Complete the prediction table.

Look at your book. Use it to complete the results chart.

Compare the results with your prediction.

Prediction

Letters	13	26	39	52	65
e	1	?	?	?	?

Results

Letters	13	26	39	52	65
e	?	?	?	?	?

TEST

Write the fractions for the ratios.

1. $5:3$ **2.** 9 to 16   **3.** 12 to 1   **4.** $15:100$

Complete.

5. $\dfrac{3}{4} = \dfrac{?}{24}$ **6.** $\dfrac{16}{18} = \dfrac{8}{?}$ **7.** $\dfrac{11}{12} = \dfrac{?}{144}$ **8.** $\dfrac{65}{100} = \dfrac{13}{?}$

Write $=$ or $\neq$.

9. $\dfrac{5}{6} \bullet \dfrac{25}{30}$ **10.** $\dfrac{7}{15} \bullet \dfrac{56}{150}$ **11.** $\dfrac{5}{9} \bullet \dfrac{22}{55}$ **12.** $\dfrac{7}{20} \bullet \dfrac{35}{100}$

Solve the proportions.

13. $\dfrac{4}{5} = \dfrac{?}{40}$ **14.** $\dfrac{12}{7} = \dfrac{48}{?}$ **15.** $\dfrac{8}{10} = \dfrac{?}{55}$ **16.** $\dfrac{2}{4} = \dfrac{?}{10}$

Write as a percent.

17. 79 out of 100   **18.** $\dfrac{6}{100}$ **19.** 0.91   **20.** 0.06

Write the fractions and the decimals.

21. 27%   **22.** 1%   **23.** 20%   **24.** 65%

Write the percents for the fractions.

25. $\dfrac{19}{50}$ **26.** $\dfrac{4}{25}$ **27.** $\dfrac{3}{8}$ **28.** $\dfrac{7}{10}$

Find the answers.

29. 75% of 400 = __?__   **30.** 15% of 76 = __?__   **31.** 40% of 45 = __?__

Solve.

32. Sona made a scale drawing of her school. In the drawing the length is 25 centimeters and the width is 19 centimeters. In the drawing each centimeter represents 6 meters. What are the actual dimensions of the school?

33. Manchu buys a record album for $8.95. He gets a 20% discount on the album. How much does Manchu pay for the album?

ENRICHMENT

Interest

Savings banks pay **interest** to customers on money deposited in savings accounts. Suppose the First Savings Bank is paying interest at the rate of 5% per year. Tana has $200 in a savings account at this bank. How much interest will the bank pay on the $200 at the end of one year?

5% of $200 = ?   Amount of savings ⟶ $200
                  Rate of interest ⟶ ×0.05
                  Amount of interest ⟶ $10.00

The First Savings Bank will pay $10.00 in interest on $200 at the end of one year.

Find the amount of interest paid after one year.

	1.	2.	3.	4.	5.	6.
Amount of savings	$400	$250	$875	$4,000	$7,000	$10,000
Rate of interest	6%	7%	5%	12%	9%	11%
Interest	?	?	?	?	?	?

Banks also charge interest on money borrowed by their customers.

Jonathan borrows $100 for one year.   Amount of loan ⟶ $100
The bank charges 18% interest per year.   Rate of interest ⟶ ×0.18
How much interest will Jonathan have to pay? Amount of interest ⟶ $18.00

18% of $100 = ?

Jonathan will pay $18.00 in interest.

Solve. Round to the nearest cent.

7. Jennifer borrows $650 from a bank for one year. The bank charges 15% interest yearly. How much interest will Jennifer have to pay?

8. Kazuo has $852.25 in the bank. The bank pays 6% interest per year. How much does Kazuo have in the bank at the end of the year?

9. Jeff opens a savings account. He deposits $1,875. The bank pays 6% interest per year. How much will Jeff have in his savings account at the end of the year?

10. Bernice borrows $700 to improve her home. The bank charges 19% interest per year. How much interest will Bernice have to pay if the loan is for one year?

Enrichment continued

11. Nina borrows $8,600 to set up a new business. The bank charges 18% interest per year. How much interest will Nina have to pay if the loan is for one year?

12. Rachel takes out a new-car loan for $6,200.00. The bank charges 14% interest per year. How much interest will Rachel have to pay for a one-year loan?

13. Antoan borrows $400 for one year to buy a new display case for his store. The bank is charging 14% interest on a one-year loan. How much interest will Antoan have to pay?

14. Taro needs $950 to repair his car. He borrows the money from a bank that charges a yearly interest rate of 12%. How much interest will he have to pay on a one-year loan?

★ **15.** David opens a bank account with $100. The bank pays 5% interest each year. David leaves the money in the bank for 2 years. How much money does he have at the end of 2 years?

★ **16.** Sue deposits $2,500 in the bank. The bank pays 5% interest each year. Sue makes no deposits or withdrawals. How much money does she have in the bank at the end of 2 years?

Complete the savings account bankbooks.

17.

Name _Sara Johnson_

Account No. _L 2553011_

Interest rate _6% per year_

Date	Memo	Deposit		Withdrawal		Interest		Balance	
Jan. 1		250	00					250	00
Dec. 31	Interest paid					?		?	

18.

Name _Gregg Strong_

Account No. _G 0028316-1_

Interest rate _6% per year_

Date	Memo	Deposit		Withdrawal		Interest		Balance	
Jan. 1		1,575	00					1,575	00
Dec. 31	Interest paid					?		?	

CALCULATOR

Calculator Percents

Some calculators have a percent (%) button.

If your calculator has a percent button, you can calculate sales tax using it.
Find 7% of $4.95.   Estimate: $\frac{7}{100}$ of $5 is about $.35.
Push 4 . 9 5 × 7 % .

Pushing the percent button usually displays the product.
On some calculators, you may need to push = .
The displayed answer is 0.3465.
With sales tax, always round the tax up to the next whole cent.
The tax is $0.35.

If your calculator has no percent button, change 7% to a decimal: 7% = 0.07.

Push 4 . 9 5 × . 0 7 = . The answer is the same: 0.3465.

Find the amount of tax to the next whole cent. Use your calculator.

1. Price: $93.62
Sales tax: 5%

2. Price: $4.25
Sales tax: 6%

3. Price: $10.10
Sales tax: 7%

4. Price: $87.14
Sales tax: 1%

5. Price: $38.63
Sales tax: 6%

6. Price: $27.99
Sales tax: 0%

You can find the total cost using the calculator.

Price: $580.37
Sales tax: 6%

Estimate: $\frac{6}{100}$ of $600 is about $36.00.

Push 5 8 0 . 3 7 × 6 %
(or × . 0 6) = .

The displayed answer is 34.8222. Round to the next whole cent.
Add the dollar sign and write the tax as $34.83.
Then add the price and the tax to find the total cost.

Push 5 8 0 . 3 7 + 3 4 . 8 3 = .

Write the total cost as $615.20.

Find the total cost using the calculator.

7. Price: $238.44
Sales tax: 2%

8. Price: $48.22
Sales tax: 5%

9. Price: $103.59
Sales tax: 0%

10. Price: $64.99
Sales tax: 3%

11. Price: $43.21
Sales tax: 10%

12. Price: $462.87
Sales tax: 4%

Choose the correct answers.

1. Write the exponent form.

$10 \times 10 \times 10 \times 10$

- **A.** 10^{10}
- **B.** 10^2
- **C.** 1,000
- **D.** not here

2. Multiply.

$$7,209$$
$$\times \quad 86$$

- **A.** 619,974
- **B.** 619,284
- **C.** 624,374
- **D.** not here

3. Round 86.083 to the nearest tenth.

- **A.** 86
- **B.** 90
- **C.** 86.1
- **D.** not here

4. Add.

$$17\frac{5}{8}$$
$$+ \ 6\frac{3}{10}$$

- **A.** $23\frac{37}{40}$
- **B.** $23\frac{8}{40}$
- **C.** $23\frac{8}{18}$
- **D.** not here

5. Multiply.

$$3\frac{1}{8} \times 2\frac{4}{5} = \underline{\quad ? \quad}$$

- **A.** $6\frac{4}{40}$
- **B.** $8\frac{3}{4}$
- **C.** $8\frac{2}{3}$
- **D.** not here

6. Divide.

$$0.6\overline{)19.5}$$

- **A.** 32.5
- **B.** 3.25
- **C.** 325
- **D.** not here

7. Which lines are perpendicular?

A.   **B.**

C. **D.** not here

8. Triangles *LMN* and *PQR* are congruent. Which side corresponds to $\overline{MN}$?

- **A.** $\overline{RP}$
- **B.** $\overline{PQ}$
- **C.** $\overline{RQ}$
- **D.** not here

9. What is the percent for $\frac{3}{20}$?

- **A.** 20%
- **B.** 15%
- **C.** 3%
- **D.** not here

10. Hoy drives a gasoline truck. The tank holds 8,000 liters of gasoline. At his first stop he delivers 45% of the gasoline. How many liters of gasoline does he deliver?

- **A.** 360
- **B.** 36,000
- **C.** 3,600
- **D.** not here

11. The cost for a liter of gasoline at the gas station is $.43. The sales tax on each liter is 9%. What is the total cost of a liter of gasoline to the nearest cent?

- **A.** $.81
- **B.** $.47
- **C.** $4.30
- **C.** not here

Integers

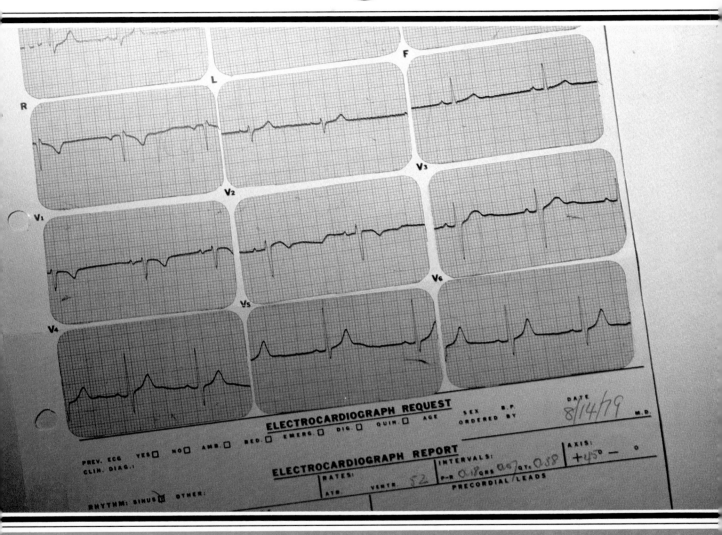

**Opposites • Integers • Adding With Like and Unlike
Signs • Subtracting With Like and Unlike Signs
• Graphing Ordered Pairs of Integers • Problem Solving:
Write Your Own Questions • Number Cubes • Square Root**

Opposites

The diving board is 2 meters *above* the surface of the water. The drain for the pool is 3 meters *below* the surface of the water.

Above is the **opposite** of *below*.

Right is the opposite of *left*.

What is the opposite of *east*?
West is the opposite of *east*.

You can use **positive numbers** and **negative numbers** to show opposites.

The surface of the water is 0.

$$2 \text{ meters above} \longrightarrow {}^+2$$
$$\text{Read } {}^+2 \longrightarrow \text{positive two}$$
$$3 \text{ meters below} \longrightarrow {}^-3$$
$$\text{Read } {}^-3 \longrightarrow \text{negative three}$$

${}^+5$ is a positive number that can describe 5 blocks to the right. What negative number can describe 5 blocks to the left?

${}^-5$ is a negative number that can describe 5 blocks to the left.

Practice • What is the opposite?

1. North   2. Down   3. West   4. Stop

Name the opposite numbers.

5. ${}^+7$ 6. ${}^-5$ 7. ${}^-16$ 8. ${}^+24$ 9. ${}^+54$ 10. ${}^-73$

11. ${}^-127$ 12. ${}^+450$ 13. ${}^+777$ 14. ${}^-813$ 15. ${}^+690$ 16. ${}^-907$

More Practice • Name the opposite numbers.

17. ${}^+3$ 18. ${}^-3$ 19. ${}^+5$ 20. ${}^-4$ 21. ${}^-8$ 22. ${}^+7$

23. ${}^+16$ 24. ${}^+18$ 25. ${}^-12$ 26. ${}^-17$ 27. ${}^+15$ 28. ${}^-11$

29. ${}^+42$ 30. ${}^-36$ 31. ${}^+50$ 32. ${}^-28$ 33. ${}^-92$ 34. ${}^+76$

35. $^-35$	**36.** $^+72$	**37.** $^+96$	**38.** $^-45$	**39.** $^-67$	**40.** $^-83$
41. $^+126$	**42.** $^-328$	**43.** $^-240$	**44.** $^+163$	**45.** $^+238$	**46.** $^-333$
47. $^-216$	**48.** $^+512$	**49.** $^+380$	**50.** $^-741$	**51.** $^-652$	**52.** $^+491$
53. $^+632$	**54.** $^-809$	**55.** $^+555$	**56.** $^-199$	**57.** $^+817$	**58.** $^-902$

Name the opposites.

★ **59.** 55 meters above sea level

★ **60.** 20 kilometers southeast

★ **61.** 18 revolutions faster

★ **62.** 2 hours before

★ **63.** earn 14 dollars

★ **64.** 145 kilograms heavier

PROBLEM SOLVING • APPLICATIONS

65. Tim's football team gains 10 yards. This is shown by $^+10$. What number would show a loss of 10 yards?

66. You get on an elevator and go up 23 floors. This is shown by $^+23$. What number would show going down 23 floors?

67. Death Valley, California, is 85 meters below sea level. This is shown by $^-85$. What number would show 85 meters above sea level?

68. Ingrid spends 12 dollars. This is shown by $^-12$. What number would show earning 12 dollars?

69. The countdown for a rocket blastoff is at minus 8 seconds. This is shown by $^-8$. What number would show 8 seconds after blastoff?

70. It is 2 hours before the airplane departure. This is shown by $^-2$. What number would show 2 hours after departure?

★ **71.** The high temperature is 4° above zero. This is shown by $^+4$. What number would show 4° below zero? How many degrees difference is there between the two temperatures?

★ **72.** Harold was riding his bike to Jim's house 7 blocks away. Harold was daydreaming and rode 12 blocks. Use a negative number to show the number of blocks that Harold rode that he should not have ridden.

Skills Maintenance

Name the figures.　**1.**　　　　　**2.**　　　　　**3.**　　　　　**4.**

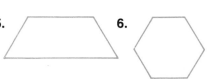

Name the polygons.　**5.**　　　**6.**　　　**7.**　　　**8.**

371

Integers

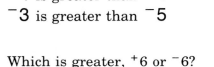

Integers can be shown on the number line.
Those to the right of 0 are **positive integers**.
Those to the left of 0 are **negative integers**.
0 is an integer, but it is neither positive nor negative.

$^+5$ and $^-5$ are the same distance from 0.
$^+5$ and $^-5$ are opposite integers.

Move your finger along the number line from left to right.
Notice that the numbers become greater.

$^+6$ is greater than $^+5$ $^+6 > ^+5$
$^+4$ is greater than $^-4$ $^+4 > ^-4$
$^-3$ is greater than $^-5$ $^-3 > ^-5$

Which is greater, $^+6$ or $^-6$?
$^+6$ is greater than $^-6$. $^+6 > ^-6$

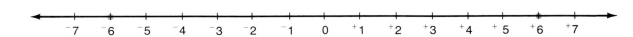

Which is greater, $^-7$ or $^-5$?
$^-5$ is greater than $^-7$. $^-5 > ^-7$

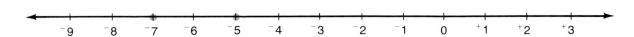

Practice • Name the opposite integers.

1. $^+6$ 2. $^-4$ 3. $^+9$ 4. $^-10$ 5. $^+2$ 6. $^+3$

7. $^-12$ 8. $^+7$ 9. $^+38$ 10. $^-17$ 11. $^+52$ 12. $^+93$

Which is greater?

13. $^+8, ^+9$ 14. $^-6, ^-5$ 15. $^+2, ^-2$ 16. $^+1, ^-8$ 17. $^-7, ^+3$

18. $^+6, ^-4$ 19. $^-12, ^+12$ 20. $^-8, ^+6$ 21. $^+4, ^-9$ 22. $^-11, ^-16$

372

Mixed Practice • Name the opposite integers.

23. $^+10$ **24.** $^-9$ **25.** $^+1$ **26.** $^-7$ **27.** $^-16$ **28.** $^+20$

29. $^-26$ **30.** $^+42$ **31.** $^+25$ **32.** $^-64$ **33.** $^+22$ **34.** $^-5$

Which is greater?

35. $^+1, ^+4$ **36.** $^-1, ^-4$ **37.** $0, ^-6$ **38.** $^+2, ^+20$ **39.** $^-2, ^-20$

40. $^+5, ^-5$ **41.** $^+10, ^-3$ **42.** $^-10, ^+3$ **43.** $^-9, ^+4$ **44.** $^+9, ^-4$

Write > or <.

45. $^+8$ ⬤ $^+3$ **46.** $^+2$ ⬤ $^+7$ **47.** $^-2$ ⬤ $^+7$

48. $^-9$ ⬤ $^-4$ **49.** $^-3$ ⬤ $^-6$ **50.** $^-6$ ⬤ $^+2$

51. $^+12$ ⬤ $^-15$ **52.** $^-12$ ⬤ $^+15$ **53.** $^-26$ ⬤ $^+13$

Write in order from least to greatest.

★ **54.** $^+3, ^-4, 0, ^-6, ^+6$ ★ **55.** $^-8, ^-3, ^-1, ^+7, ^-7$

★ **56.** $^+6, ^+4, 0, ^-5, ^-7$ ★ **57.** $^-19, ^+78, ^-45, ^+23, ^-89$

The temperature at A is $^+20$ degrees Celsius ($^+20°$C).
The temperature at B is $^-10°$C.

Give the temperature for each of the
other points.

58. C   **59.** D   **60.** H

61. E   **62.** G   **63.** F

Which temperature is warmer?

64. $0°$C, $^+6°$C   **65.** $^-22°$C, $^-12°$C   **66.** $^+10°$C, $^-10°$C

PROBLEM SOLVING • APPLICATIONS

67. The temperature in Chicago is
$^-9°$C. The temperature in Montreal
is $^+2°$C. Which city has the higher
temperature?

68. The morning temperature was
$^-1°$C. The evening temperature
was $^-4°$C. Did the temperature go
up or down?

★ **69.** The temperature was $^+8°$C. It rose
$3°$. What was the new temperature?

★ **70.** The temperature was $0°$C. It
dropped $9°$. What was the new
temperature?

Adding with Like Signs

Warnerville's football team gains 3 yards. Then the team gains 7 yards. How many yards does the team gain in all?

Think: Gain of 3 yards ⟶ $^+3$

Gain of 7 yards ⟶ $^+7$

$^+3$ and $^+7 = ?$

You can use a number line to help you add integers.

Start at 0.
A positive sign means a move to the right. Move 3 spaces to the right.
Move 7 more spaces to the right. You stop at $^+10$.

$^+3 + {}^+7 = {}^+10$

The team gains 10 yards.

Add: $^-3 + {}^-7$.

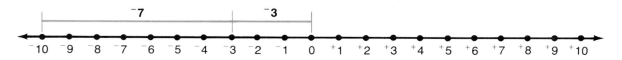

Start at 0.
A negative sign means a move to the left. Move 3 spaces to the left.
Move 7 more spaces to the left. You stop at $^-10$.

$^-3 + {}^-7 = {}^-10$

Practice • Add.

1. $^+2 + {}^+5 = $ ___?___

2. $^-2 + {}^-5 = $ ___?___

3. $^+3 + {}^+5 = $ ___?___

4. $^-3 + {}^-5 = $ ___?___

5. $0 + {}^-3 = $ ___?___

6. $^+5 + 0 = $ ___?___

Mixed Practice • Add.

7. $^+5 + {}^+2 = $ ___?___

8. $^-5 + {}^-2 = $ ___?___

9. $^+3 + {}^+4 = $ ___?___

10. $^-3 + {}^-4 = $ ___?___

11. $^+4 + {}^+3 = $ ___?___

12. $^-4 + {}^-3 = $ ___?___

374

13. $^+6 + 0 = $ ___?___

14. $^-6 + 0 = $ ___?___

15. $^-1 + {}^-3 = $ ___?___

16. $^+1 + {}^+3 = $ ___?___

17. $^+9 + {}^+8 = $ ___?___

18. $^-9 + {}^-8 = $ ___?___

19. $^+5 + {}^+7 = $ ___?___

20. $^-7 + {}^-5 = $ ___?___

21. $0 + {}^+8 = $ ___?___

22. $^-8 + 0 = $ ___?___

23. $^-2 + {}^-3 = $ ___?___

24. $^-5 + {}^-1 = $ ___?___

25. $^+7 + {}^+2 = $ ___?___

26. $^-4 + {}^-6 = $ ___?___

27. $^+7 + {}^+1 = $ ___?___

★ **28.** $0 + $ ___?___ $ = {}^-4$

★ **29.** $^-8 + $ ___?___ $ = {}^-10$

★ **30.** ___?___ $ + {}^+5 = 10$

★ **31.** $^+8 + $ ___?___ $ = {}^+15$

★ **32.** ___?___ $ + {}^-6 = {}^-6$

★ **33.** $^-9 + $ ___?___ $ = {}^-12$

A record of temperature is kept during each football game played at the Warnersville Stadium.

Complete the table.

	Games	Start of Game	Change	End of Game
34.	Game 1	$^+8°C$	$^+4°$	?
35.	Game 2	$^+10°C$	$^+7°$	?
36.	Game 3	$^-2°C$	$^-6°$	?
37.	Game 4	$^-14°C$	$^-4°$	?
38.	Game 5	$0°C$	$^+6°$	?
39.	Game 6	$0°C$	$^-6°$	?

PROBLEM SOLVING • APPLICATIONS

Use integers to write the number sentences. Then solve.

40. The Tigers lost 2 yards. Then they lost 4 yards. How many yards did they lose in all?

41. The Bears gained 3 yards. Then they gained 14 yards. How many yards did they gain in all?

42. Tina was saving money to go to a football game. She saved 9 dollars one week. The next week she saved 8 dollars. How many dollars did she save in all?

43. Frank spent 3 dollars on a banner and 2 dollars on refreshments at the football game. How many dollars did he spend in all?

★ **44.** The championship game began at 1:00 P.M. The temperature was 9°C. The temperature rose 3°C between 1:00 P.M. and 2:00 P.M. The temperature rose 2°C between 2:00 P.M. and 3:00 P.M. What was the temperature at 3:00 P.M.?

★ **45.** The Lions have the football on their 10-yard line. On the first play, they gain 5 yards. On the second play, they gain 3 yards. On what yard line is the ball placed at the end of the two plays?

Adding with Unlike Signs

A share of stock gains 6 points
before noon. After noon it loses
4 points. What is the total gain
or loss of this stock in one day?

Think: Gain of 6 points $\longrightarrow$ $^+6$

Loss of 4 points $\longrightarrow$ $^-4$

$^+6$ and $^-4 = ?$

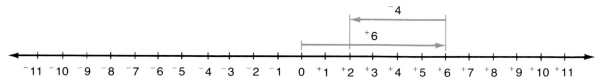

You can use a number line to help you add integers.

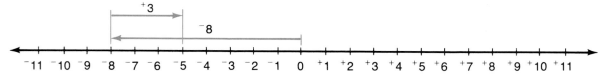

Start at 0.
Move 6 spaces to the right to show $^+6$.
Move 4 spaces to the left to show $^-4$.
You stop at $^+2$.

$^+6 + {}^-4 = {}^+2$

This stock gains 2 points in one day.

Add: $^-8 + {}^+3$.

Start at 0.
Move 8 spaces to the left to show $^-8$.
Move 3 spaces to the right to show $^+3$.
You stop at $^-5$.

$^-8 + {}^+3 = {}^-5$

Practice • Add.

1. $^+5 + {}^-2 =$ ___?___

2. $^-5 + {}^+2 =$ ___?___

3. $^+5 + {}^-5 =$ ___?___

4. $^+4 + {}^-5 =$ ___?___

5. $^-4 + {}^+5 =$ ___?___

6. $^-5 + {}^+4 =$ ___?___

376

Mixed Practice • Add.

7. $^+3 + ^-5 = $ ____?____

8. $^-3 + ^+5 = $ ____?____

9. $^-4 + ^-4 = $ ____?____

10. $^-4 + ^+4 = $ ____?____

11. $^+8 + ^-3 = $ ____?____

12. $^-8 + ^+3 = $ ____?____

13. $^-3 + ^+4 = $ ____?____

14. $^+4 + ^-3 = $ ____?____

15. $^+3 + ^-4 = $ ____?____

16. $^-4 + ^+3 = $ ____?____

17. $^+11 + ^-3 = $ ____?____

18. $^+3 + ^-11 = $ ____?____

19. $^-9 + ^+2 = $ ____?____

20. $^+2 + ^-9 = $ ____?____

21. $^-3 + ^+3 = $ ____?____

22. $^+6 + ^-7 = $ ____?____

23. $^+12 + ^-5 = $ ____?____

24. $^-14 + ^+8 = $ ____?____

25. $^+3 + ^+6 = $ ____?____

26. $^-4 + ^-2 = $ ____?____

27. $^-6 + ^-4 = $ ____?____

★ **28.** $^+7 + ^+3 + ^+10 = $ ____?____

★ **29.** $^-7 + ^-5 + ^-6 = $ ____?____

★ **30.** $^+9 + ^-2 + ^+4 = $ ____?____

★ **31.** $^-2 + ^+8 + ^-7 = $ ____?____

Each day Hiromi keeps a record of the price of his stocks. A plus sign (+) in the change column means the price went up. A minus sign (−) means the price went down.

Complete the table.

	Stock	Today's Opening Price	Change	Today's Closing Price
32.	Arnen	40	$^-5$	?
33.	Botel	6	$^+6$	?
34.	Clavid	35	$^-8$	?
35.	Dabel	106	$^-9$	?
36.	Evark	62	$^+3$	?
37.	Frifton	14	$^-1$	?

PROBLEM SOLVING • APPLICATIONS

Use integers to write the number sentences. Then solve.

38. A share of Glison dropped 3 points on Tuesday. On Wednesday it gained 5 points. What was the total gain or loss for both days?

★ **39.** During three days a share of Howle gained 4 points, lost 6 points, and then gained 3 points. What was the total gain or loss for the three days?

Midchapter Review

Name the opposite integer.

Write > or <.

1. $^+11$

2. $^-15$

3. $^-10$ ⬤ $^-4$

4. 0 ⬤ $^-7$

Add.

5. $^+8 + ^+2 = $ ____?____

6. $^+7 + 0 = $ ____?____

7. $^-4 + ^-9 = $ ____?____

8. $^-3 + ^-5 = $ ____?____

9. $^+6 + ^-1 = $ ____?____

10. $^+2 + ^-13 = $ ____?____

Subtracting with Like Signs

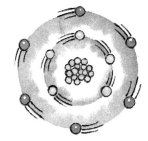

An atom has an electrical charge of $^-11$.
4 of the negative charges are taken
away. What is the charge on the atom now?

$$^-11 - {^-4} = ?$$

Addition and subtraction are related. You can think of subtraction
as finding a missing addend.

Change the subtraction sentence to an addition sentence.

$$^-11 - {^-4} = ? \longrightarrow {^-4} + ? = {^-11}$$

Start at 0.
Move 4 spaces to the left.
You want to reach $^-11$. You must now move 7 spaces to the left.
The answer is $^-7$.
The new charge on the atom is $^-7$.

Subtract: $^+6 - {^+8}$.

Change the subtraction sentence to an addition sentence.

$$^+6 - {^+8} = ? \longrightarrow {^+8} + ? = {^+6}$$

Start at 0.
Move 8 spaces to the right.
You want to reach $^+6$. You must move 2 spaces to the left.
The answer is $^-2$.

$$^+6 - {^+8} = {^-2}$$

Practice • Find the missing addends.

1. $^+3 + \underline{\quad?\quad} = {^+7}$
2. $^-4 + \underline{\quad?\quad} = {^-6}$
3. $^-5 + \underline{\quad?\quad} = {^-2}$

Subtract.

4. $^+8 - {^+4} = \underline{\quad?\quad}$
5. $^-6 - {^-2} = \underline{\quad?\quad}$
6. $^-2 - {^-7} = \underline{\quad?\quad}$

Mixed Practice • Subtract.

7. $^-4 - {^-1} = \underline{\quad?\quad}$
8. $^+4 - {^+1} = \underline{\quad?\quad}$
9. $^+5 - {^+2} = \underline{\quad?\quad}$

10. $^-5 - {^-2} = \underline{\quad?\quad}$
11. $^+3 - {^+4} = \underline{\quad?\quad}$
12. $^-3 - {^-4} = \underline{\quad?\quad}$

13. $^-9 - {}^-2 = \underline{?}$

14. $^+9 - {}^+2 = \underline{?}$

15. $^-3 - {}^-8 = \underline{?}$

16. $^+11 - {}^+7 = \underline{?}$

17. $^+3 - {}^+10 = \underline{?}$

18. $^-3 - {}^-10 = \underline{?}$

19. $^+6 - {}^+5 = \underline{?}$

20. $^-6 - {}^-5 = \underline{?}$

21. $^-6 - {}^-7 = \underline{?}$

22. $^+6 - {}^+7 = \underline{?}$

23. $^+4 - {}^+6 = \underline{?}$

24. $^-4 - {}^-6 = \underline{?}$

25. $^+13 - {}^+3 = \underline{?}$

26. $^-13 - {}^-3 = \underline{?}$

27. $^+2 - {}^+8 = \underline{?}$

28. $^-2 - {}^-8 = \underline{?}$

29. $^+10 - {}^+7 = \underline{?}$

30. $^-10 - {}^-7 = \underline{?}$

31. $^+8 - {}^+9 = \underline{?}$

32. $^-8 - {}^-9 = \underline{?}$

33. $^-3 - {}^-3 = \underline{?}$

★ **34.** $^+3 - \underline{?} = 0$

★ **35.** $\underline{?} - {}^-6 = {}^+6$

★ **36.** $^+3 - \underline{?} = {}^-3$

The temperature is $^+10°C$.
It was $^+7°C$ an hour ago.
The temperature changed
$^+3°$. It went up 3°C.

Complete the table.

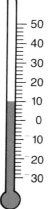

	Now	Before	Change
37.	$^+10°C$	$^+7°C$	$^+3°C$
38.	$^+6°C$	$^+2°C$	?
39.	$^-10°C$	$^-7°C$	?
40.	$^-6°C$	$^-2°C$	?
41.	$^+8°C$	$^+12°C$	?
42.	$^-4°C$	$^-6°C$	?

PROBLEM SOLVING • APPLICATIONS

Use integers to write the number sentences. Then solve.

43. An atom has an electrical charge of $^-9$. 6 of the negative charges are removed. What is the charge on the atom now?

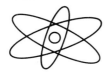

★ **44.** At the beginning of an experiment, the electrical charge on an atom was $^-2$. 3 more negative charges were added. Then 4 negative charges were removed. What was the charge on the atom at the end of the experiment?

Skills Maintenance

Complete the ratios.

1. $\frac{5}{8} = \frac{?}{24}$

2. $\frac{18}{45} = \frac{2}{?}$

3. $\frac{7}{10} = \frac{?}{40}$

4. $\frac{36}{42} = \frac{6}{?}$

Write the percents.

5. $\frac{8}{100}$

6. 0.55

7. $\frac{19}{50}$

8. $\frac{3}{5}$

Find the answers.

9. 65% of 80 = $\underline{?}$

10. 40% of 135 = $\underline{?}$

11. 15% of 90 = $\underline{?}$

Subtracting with Unlike Signs

At 8:00 A.M. today the temperature was
$^+8°C$. Yesterday at 8:00 A.M. the temperature
was $^-3°C$. What was the temperature change
for this twenty-four-hour period?

$^+8 - ^-3 = ?$

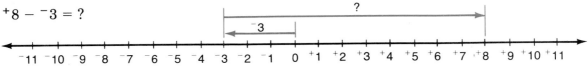

Change the subtraction sentence to an addition sentence.

$$^+8 - ^-3 = ? \longrightarrow {}^-3 + ? = {}^+8$$

Start at 0.
Move 3 spaces to the left.
You want to reach $^+8$.
You must move 11 spaces to the right.
The answer is $^+11$.

$^+8 - ^-3 = ^+11$ The temperature change was $^+11°C$.

Subtract: $^-7 - ^+5$.

Change the subtraction sentence to an addition sentence.

$$^-7 - ^+5 = ? \longrightarrow {}^+5 + ? = {}^-7$$

Start at 0.
Move 5 spaces to the right.
You want to reach $^-7$.
You must move 12 spaces to the left.
The answer is $^-12$.

$^-7 - ^+5 = ^-12$

Practice • Find the missing addends.

1. $^-4 + \underline{\ \ ?\ \ } = {}^+3$

2. $^+5 + \underline{\ \ ?\ \ } = {}^-2$

3. $^-6 + \underline{\ \ ?\ \ } = {}^+10$

Subtract.

4. $^+7 - ^-3 = \underline{\ \ ?\ \ }$

5. $^-4 - ^+1 = \underline{\ \ ?\ \ }$

6. $^-6 - ^+2 = \underline{\ \ ?\ \ }$

Mixed Practice • Subtract.

7. $^+8 - ^-3 = \underline{\ \ ?\ \ }$

8. $^-8 - ^+3 = \underline{\ \ ?\ \ }$

9. $^-9 - ^+6 = \underline{\ \ ?\ \ }$

10. $^+9 - ^-6 = \underline{\ \ ?\ \ }$

11. $^-11 - ^+4 = \underline{\ \ ?\ \ }$

12. $^+11 - ^-4 = \underline{\ \ ?\ \ }$

13. $^+10 - ^-3 = \underline{\ \ ?\ \ }$

14. $^-10 - ^+3 = \underline{\ \ ?\ \ }$

15. $^+6 - ^-5 = \underline{\ \ ?\ \ }$

16. $^-6 - ^+5 = \underline{\ \ ?\ \ }$

17. $^-5 - ^+5 = \underline{\ \ ?\ \ }$

18. $^+5 - ^-5 = \underline{\ \ ?\ \ }$

19. $^+4 - {}^-6 =$ ___?___   **20.** $^-4 - {}^+6 =$ ___?___   **21.** $^-7 - {}^+10 =$ ___?___

22. $^+7 - {}^-10 =$ ___?___   **23.** $^+2 - {}^-8 =$ ___?___   **24.** $^-2 - {}^+8 =$ ___?___

25. $^-8 - {}^+6 =$ ___?___   **26.** $^-8 - {}^-6 =$ ___?___   **27.** $^+6 - {}^+13 =$ ___?___

28. $^+6 - {}^-13 =$ ___?___   **29.** $^+2 - {}^-10 =$ ___?___   **30.** $^-2 - {}^+10 =$ ___?___

31. $^+15 - {}^+6 =$ ___?___   **32.** $^-15 - {}^+6 =$ ___?___   **33.** $^-9 - {}^-15 =$ ___?___

Write + and − to make a true sentence.

★ **34.** $^+6 \bigcirc {}^-3 \bigcirc {}^+4 = {}^-1$ ★ **35.** $^+5 \bigcirc {}^-2 \bigcirc {}^+8 = {}^+15$ ★ **36.** $^+2 \bigcirc {}^+7 \bigcirc -5 = {}^+14$

The temperature is $^+4°C$.
It was $^-2°C$ an hour ago.
The temperature changed
$^+6°$.

Complete the table.

	Now	Before	Change
37.	$^+4°C$	$^-2°C$	$^+6°$
38.	$^+8°C$	$^-3°C$	?
39.	$^-4°C$	$^+2°C$	?
40.	$^-8°C$	$^+3°C$	?
41.	$^-6°C$	$^+6°C$	?
42.	$^+3°C$	$^-5°C$	?

PROBLEM SOLVING • APPLICATIONS

Use integers to write the number sentences. Then solve.

43. A share of Robox Corporation is now selling for 19 dollars. Yesterday the stock sold for 24 dollars. What is the change in the price of the stock?

44. A share of Bitel now sells for 12 dollars. The price has gone down 4 dollars since noon. How much was the stock selling for at noon?

★ **45.** Follow the directions. Complete the path through the maze.

Enter the maze at $^-3$. Choose an adjacent box. Subtract the second number from the first.

For example: $^-3 - {}^-6 = {}^+3$.

Look for the difference in an adjacent box. It does not appear. Start at $^-3$ again. Choose another adjacent box. Subtract. $^-3 - {}^+4 = {}^-7$.

Enter

-3 ⇣	$^-6$	$^+7$	$^-2$	$^+5$
$^+4$	$^-1$	$^-6$	$^+9$	$^+2$
$^-7$ ↓	$^-8$	$^+1$	$^-3$	$^+7$
$^+6$	$^-3$	$^-10$	$^+2$	$^+5$
$^-4$	$^-11$	$^+12$	$^+14$	$^-2$

Exit

Look for the difference. Move to the box where $^-7$ appears. Mark the path you have taken.

Now use $^-7$ as the first number. Choose an adjacent box. Subtract. Look for the difference. Continue to move horizontally or vertically, not diagonally. Make a continuous path to the exit.

381

Graphing Ordered Pairs of Integers

You can use an ordered pair of numbers to locate a point on a grid.

The ordered pair ($^-4$, $^+3$) means
start at 0,
move 4 spaces to the left,
and then move 3 spaces up.

The ordered pair ($^-4$, $^+3$) locates point D.

The ordered pair ($^-2$, $^-2$) locates point E. Point E is 2 spaces to the left and 2 spaces down.

The ordered pair ($^+2$, $^-4$) locates point F. Point F is 2 spaces to the right and 4 spaces down.

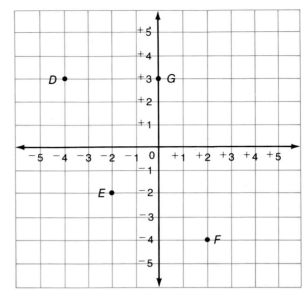

Point G is 0 spaces to the left or right and 3 spaces up.

The ordered pair that locates point G is (0, $^+3$).

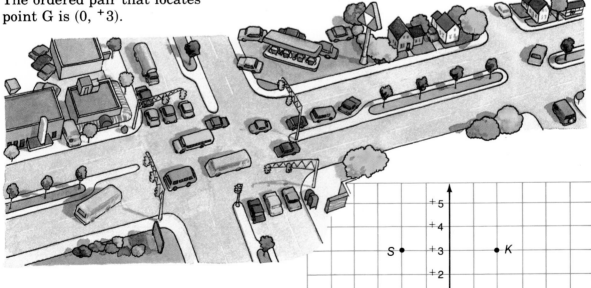

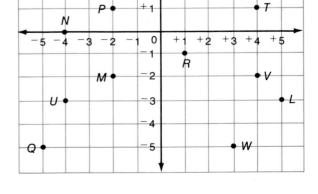

Practice • What letter is at the point?

1. ($^+5$, $^-3$)   2. ($^-2$, $^-2$)   3. ($^+3$, $^-5$)

4. ($^+1$, $^-1$)   5. ($^+4$, $^+1$)   6. ($^+4$, $^-2$)

Give the ordered pair for the point.

7. K   8. N   9. P

10. Q   11. S   12. U

382

Mixed Practice • What letter is at the point?

13. $(^+3, ^-3)$ **14.** $(^-6, ^-2)$

15. $(^-5, 0)$ **16.** $(^-1, ^+5)$

17. $(^+1, ^-2)$ **18.** $(^-3, ^-2)$

Give the ordered pair for the point.

19. A **20.** D

21. F **22.** H

23. J **24.** L

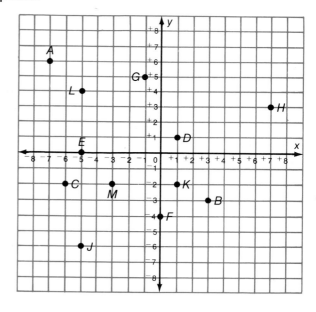

PROBLEM SOLVING • APPLICATIONS

Use a sheet of graph paper.
Locate the ordered pairs.
Draw a dot at each point.
Label the dot with the letter.
Connect the dots to form a picture.

25.

Point	Ordered Pair
S	$(^+2, ^+5)$
T	$(^+2, ^-3)$
U	$(^-3, ^-5)$
V	$(^-3, ^+3)$
S	$(^+2, ^+5)$

26.

Point	Ordered Pair
A	$(^+4, ^-4)$
B	$(^+4, ^-1)$
C	$(^+3, ^-2)$
D	$(0, ^+3)$
E	$(^-2, ^+1)$
F	$(^+2, ^-3)$
G	$(^+1, ^-4)$
A	$(^+4, ^-4)$

Follow the rule. Complete the table. Use the ordered pairs (INPUT, OUTPUT) to locate the points on a grid.

Draw a line through the points.

★ **27. Subtract** $^-4$.

INPUT	OUTPUT
$^-3$	$^+1$
$^-2$	?
$^-1$	?
0	?
$^+1$	?
$^+2$	?
$^+3$	?

★ **28. Add** $^-2$.

INPUT	OUTPUT
$^-3$	$^-5$
$^-2$	?
$^-1$	?
0	?
$^+1$	?
$^+2$	?
$^+3$	?

PROBLEM SOLVING • STRATEGIES

Write Your Own Questions

This is one page from Richard's savings account bankbook.

All of the transactions for Richard's account are shown in this book.

Interest is paid by the bank for the use of Richard's money.

	DATE	WITHDRAWAL	DEPOSIT	INTEREST	BALANCE
	IN ACCOUNT WITH				41612373
	** Richard Cado **				DAY OF DEPOSIT TO DAY OF WITHDRAWAL
1 N SEP 2 82			$125.00		$470.15
2 N̄ SEP 11 82		$75.00			$395.15
3 N̄ SEP 15 82		$100.00			$295.15
4					
5	SEP 30 82			$6.08	$301.23
6	DEC 31 82			$4.26	$305.49
7	MAR 31 83			$4.28	$309.77
8	JUN 30 83			$4.34	$314.11
9	AUG 11 83		$10.00		$324.11
10					
11	SEP 30 83			$4.53	$328.64
12	DEC 31 83			$4.65	$333.29
13	JAN 2 84		$5.00		$338.29
14	FEB 14 84		$70.00		$408.29
15	MAR 9 84	$167.58			$240.71

Royal Savings Bank

On September 2, 1982, the balance in Richard's account was $470.15.

On September 11, 1982, the balance was $395.15.

Which of the following questions could you ask, using the information given?

Is this Richard Cado's only bank account?
How much was deposited in the account on April 30, 1984?
How much money was withdrawn from Richard's account?
Where is the Royal Savings Bank located?

The only question you could ask is: How much money was withdrawn from Richard's account?

Make up one question that can be answered using the information given.

1. The balance in Richard's account on February 14, 1984, was $408.29. Then $167.58 was withdrawn from the account.

2. On August 11, 1983, the balance in Richard's savings account was $324.11. On September 30, 1983, the balance was $328.64.

Royal Savings Bank
Withdrawal Ticket
Date _____

Use the title at the top of each column in the bankbook to help you find the correct information.

Solve.

3. Richard received $4.53 interest on September 30, 1983. His balance had been $324.11.

4. Richard had $395.15 in his account on September 11, 1982. He withdrew $100.00 on September 15, 1982.

Read the information carefully to decide what question you will ask.

---

5. The balance in Richard's account on September 2, 1982, was $470.15. Then he withdrew $75.00.

6. Richard received $4.53 interest on September 30, 1983. His new balance was $328.64.

7. Richard made four deposits between September 2, 1982, and March 9, 1984. The deposits were $125.00, $10.00, $5.00, and $70.00.

8. The balance in Richard's account on September 30, 1982, was $301.23. Then Richard received $4.26 interest.

9. On March 31, 1983, the balance in Richard's account was $309.77. He received $4.34 interest. Then Richard deposited $10.00.

10. On December 31, 1982, the balance in Richard's account was $305.49. He made no deposits or withdrawals. Then he received $4.28 and $4.34 interest.

Write one question.
Then find the answer.

★11. Between December 31, 1983, and February 14, 1984, $79.65 was added to Richard's account. The amount of money added was the sum of the deposits and the interest earned. The interest earned was $4.65.

★12. From October 1, 1982, to September 30, 1983, Richard had interest added to his account four times. The amounts were $4.26, $4.28, $4.34, and $4.53.

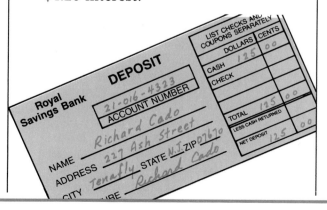

REVIEW

Name the opposite integers. (pages 370–371)

1. $^-11$ **2.** $^+2$ **3.** $^+9$ **4.** $^-67$

Write $>$ or $<$. (pages 372–373)

5. $^+3$ ⬤ $^-1$ **6.** $^-5$ ⬤ $^-1$ **7.** $^+11$ ⬤ $^+14$

8. $^-7$ ⬤ $^-9$ **9.** $^-2$ ⬤ $^+1$ **10.** $^+6$ ⬤ $^+4$

Add. (pages 374–377)

11. $^+5 + {^+4} = \underline{\quad?\quad}$ **12.** $^-3 + {^-3} = \underline{\quad?\quad}$

13. $^+2 + {^-4} = \underline{\quad?\quad}$ **14.** $^-6 + {^+8} = \underline{\quad?\quad}$

15. $^-12 + {^+8} = \underline{\quad?\quad}$ **16.** $^-10 + {^+5} = \underline{\quad?\quad}$

Subtract. (pages 378–381)

17. $^+7 - {^+3} = \underline{\quad?\quad}$ **18.** $^-5 - {^-6} = \underline{\quad?\quad}$

19. $^+6 - {^-3} = \underline{\quad?\quad}$ **20.** $^-9 - {^+9} = \underline{\quad?\quad}$

21. $^+14 - {^-10} = \underline{\quad?\quad}$ **22.** $^-13 - {^+12} = \underline{\quad?\quad}$

What letter is at the point? (pages 382–383)

23. $(^-2, {^-4})$ **24.** $(^-4, {^+3})$

25. $(^+5, {^+2})$ **26.** $(^+6, {^-5})$

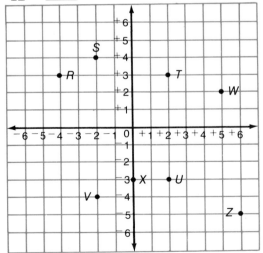

Give the ordered pair for the point.
(pages 382–383)

27. T   **28.** S

29. U   **30.** X

Solve.

31. On Saturday morning the outside temperature was $^+14°C$. By the afternoon the temperature had dropped 18°C. What was the afternoon temperature? (p. 370)

32. On Monday shares of Frifton stock and Botel stocks were each selling for 12 dollars. By Friday Frifton was selling for 7 dollars a share and Botel had dropped 4 dollars. Which share of stock was worth more on Friday? How much more? (p. 376)

PROJECT

Number Cubes

Trace this pattern twice. Mark the six faces of one pattern with 0, $^+1$, $^+2$, $^+3$, $^+4$, and $^+5$. Mark the six faces of the other pattern with 0, $^-1$, $^-2$, $^-3$, $^-4$, and $^-5$.

Cut out the pattern along the solid lines. Fold along the broken lines. Tape or glue the figure together with the tabs inside.

Toss the two number cubes and add the numbers on the faces.

Copy the table. Enter the sums. Continue to toss the cubes, and complete the table to show the sums.

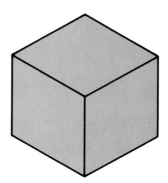

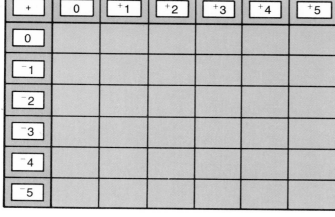

+	0	$^+1$	$^+2$	$^+3$	$^+4$	$^+5$
0						
$^-1$						
$^-2$						
$^-3$						
$^-4$						
$^-5$						

In how many ways can the sum of the two number cubes be:

$^+5$	$^+4$	$^+3$	$^+2$
$^+1$	0	$^-1$	$^-2$
$^-3$	$^-4$	$^-5$	

Which sum occurs most often?

Name the opposite integers.

1. $^+5$ **2.** $^-12$ **3.** $^+39$ **4.** $^-75$

Write > or <.

5. $^+2$ ⬤ $^+9$ **6.** $^-6$ ⬤ $^+1$ **7.** $^+5$ ⬤ $^+3$

8. $^-5$ ⬤ $^-7$ **9.** $^+12$ ⬤ $^-14$ **10.** $^-3$ ⬤ $^-1$

Add.

11. $^+7 + {}^+6 = $ _?_   **12.** $^-2 + {}^-2 = $ _?_

13. $^+3 + {}^-6 = $ _?_   **14.** $^-6 + 0 = $ _?_

15. $^-10 + {}^+9 = $ _?_   **16.** $^-8 + {}^+8 = $ _?_

Subtract.

17. $^+8 - {}^+7 + $ _?_   **18.** $^-10 - {}^-6 = $ _?_

19. $^+5 - {}^-1 = $ _?_   **20.** $^-2 - {}^+1 = $ _?_

21. $^+4 - {}^-7 = $ _?_   **22.** $^-1 - {}^+6 = $ _?_

What letter is at the point?

23. $(^+3, {}^-2)$ **24.** $(^+4, {}^+5)$

25. $(^-4, {}^-3)$ **26.** $(^+2, 0)$

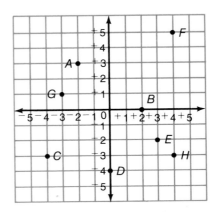

Give the ordered pair for the point.

27. G   **28.** A

29. H   **30.** D

Solve.

31. When the ice show began the temperature was $^-3°C$. When it ended the temperature had risen 4°C. What was the temperature at the end of the show?

★ **32.** On Tuesday the opening price of one share of Dabel was 104 dollars. The price went up 6 dollars on Tuesday and down 3 dollars on Wednesday. What was the closing price on Wednesday?

Square Root

To find the number of tiles that are needed to cover this square, multiply the number of rows by the number in each row.

$4 \times 4 = 16$

When the two factors are the same, the product is the **square** of the factor. The factor is the **square root** of the product. The symbol for square root is $\sqrt{}$ and is read "the square root of."

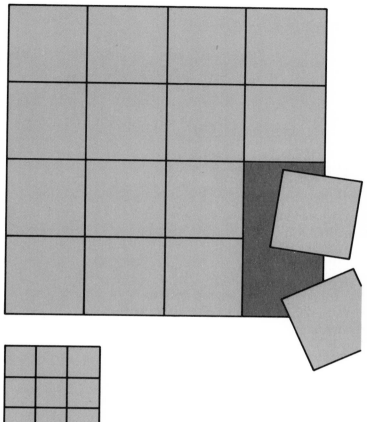

Since $4 \times 4 = 16$, then $\sqrt{16} = 4$.
The square of 4 is 16.
The square root of 16 is 4.

Since $3 \times 3 = 9$, then $\sqrt{9} = 3$.
The square of 3 is 9.
The square root of 9 is 3.

Copy and complete the table.

Number	1	2	3	4	5	6	7	8	9	10
Square	1	4	9	16	?	?	?	?	?	?

Use the table to find the square roots.

1. $\sqrt{16}$ **2.** $\sqrt{9}$ **3.** $\sqrt{49}$ **4.** $\sqrt{4}$ **5.** $\sqrt{81}$

6. $\sqrt{1}$ **7.** $\sqrt{25}$ **8.** $\sqrt{100}$ **9.** $\sqrt{36}$ **10.** $\sqrt{64}$

CALCULATOR

Estimating Multiplication

If you forget to enter a digit in a greater number, your answer will be wrong.
Always estimate a calculator answer first.
It is easier to make a mistake when pushing buttons than it is
when multiplying or dividing by hand.

$$\begin{array}{r} 4{,}725 \\ \times\ \ 832 \end{array}$$

Estimate: 5,000 times 800 is about 40 followed by five zeros.
The answer is about 4,000,000.

First do the example correctly.

Push 4 7 2 5 × 8 3 2 .

Write your answer with commas. You should get 3,931,200.
That looks like the correct answer.

Now suppose you had pushed 4 7 5 × 8 3 2 = .
Write your answer with a comma. You should get 395,200.
But 395,200 is not close to 4,000,000.
Your answer is much lower than your estimate.
You left out the 2 in the second factor.

Now suppose you had pushed 4 7 2 2 5 × 8 3 2 = .
Write your answer with commas.
You should get 39,291,200.
But 39,291,200 is not close to 4,000,000.
Your answer is much higher than your estimate.
You pushed the 2 once too often.
Leaving out or adding a digit is a very common mistake when using calculators.

Estimate the product before multiplying. Write your answers with commas.

1. $\begin{array}{r} 8{,}302 \\ \times\ \ 753 \end{array}$

2. $\begin{array}{r} 9{,}126 \\ \times\ \ 904 \end{array}$

3. $\begin{array}{r} 428 \\ \times 824 \end{array}$

4. $\begin{array}{r} 6{,}547 \\ \times\ \ 391 \end{array}$

5. $\begin{array}{r} 7{,}293 \\ \times\ \ 841 \end{array}$

6. $\begin{array}{r} 0 \\ \times 863 \end{array}$

7. $\begin{array}{r} 3{,}105 \\ \times\ \ 137 \end{array}$

8. $\begin{array}{r} 4{,}999 \\ \times\ \ \ \ \ 6 \end{array}$

9. $2{,}483 \times 710 =$ _____?_____

10. $8{,}562 \times 439 =$ _____?_____

Choose the correct answers.

1. Divide.

$$12\overline{)96,072}$$

A. 86
B. 806
C. 8,006
D. not here

2. Compare.

$$\frac{2}{3} \quad \bullet \quad \frac{7}{8}$$

A. <
B. >
C. =
D. not here

3. Subtract.

$$7\frac{5}{6}$$
$$-2\frac{7}{8}$$

A. $4\frac{23}{24}$
B. $5\frac{23}{24}$
C. $5\frac{1}{24}$
D. not here

4. What digit is in the thousandths place in 26,148.035?

A. 2
B. 6
C. 3
D. not here

5. Add.

$$8.6 + 94 + 0.52 = \underline{\quad?\quad}$$

A. 103.12
B. 232
C. 23.2
D. not here

6. Multiply.

$$7.2$$
$$\times 0.06$$

A. 0.432
B. 4.32
C. 43.2
D. not here

7. Divide.

$$0.8\overline{)2.592}$$

A. 324
B. 32.4
C. 0.324
D. not here

8. Write 0.76 as a percent.

A. 24%
B. 7.6%
C. 76%
D. not here

9. Solve the proportion.

$$\frac{4}{5} = \frac{?}{30}$$

A. 1
B. 4
C. 24
D. not here

10. 75% of 600 = $\underline{\quad?\quad}$

A. 450
B. 100
C. 75
D. not here

11. Add.

$$^+8 + {}^-10 = \underline{\quad?\quad}$$

A. $^-18$
B. $^+18$
C. $^-2$
D. not here

12. Subtract.

$$^-6 - {}^-4 = \underline{\quad?\quad}$$

A. $^-2$
B. $^+2$
C. $^-10$
D. not here

Choose the correct answers.

13. Lien buys a record album for
$6.48. She gives the clerk $10.00.
How much change does she get?

    A. $4.68
    B. $16.48
    C. $3.52
    D. not here

14. On Saturday 15,627 people
attended the football game. On
Sunday 9,708 people attended the
game. How many people attended
the game during this weekend?

    A. 25,335
    B. 26,325
    C. 5,919
    D. not here

15. There are 36 boxes of spaghetti in a
carton. How many boxes are in 28
cartons?

    A. 352
    B. 1,238
    C. 1,008
    D. not here

16. Mr. Jones's car averages 14
kilometers per liter of gasoline. How
many liters does he use on a
1,022-kilometer trip?

    A. 14,308
    B. 73
    C. 67
    D. not here

17. Alice works as an auto mechanic.
On Saturday she worked $6\frac{3}{4}$ hours.
On Monday she worked $7\frac{1}{2}$ hours.
How many more hours did she work
on Monday than on Saturday?

    A. 2
    B. $\frac{3}{4}$
    C. $1\frac{3}{4}$
    D. not here

18. Neil rides his bicycle 2.4 kilometers
to school. He then rides 0.54
kilometers to the library and
3.6 kilometers home. How far does
he ride in all?

    A. 6.54 km
    B. 11.4 km
    C. 7.46 km
    D. not here

19. Ellen buys a coat for $92.00. There
is a sales tax of 7%. What is the
total cost of the coat?

    A. $7.36
    B. $73.44
    C. $98.44
    D. not here

20. There are 140 bicycles at John's
Bike Store. 60% of the bicycles are
racers. How many bicycles are
racers?

    A. 76
    B. 82
    C. 84
    D. not here

Extra Practice

Set 1 (pages 2–7)

Write the expanded forms.

1. 256   2. 918   3. 4,771   4. 1,307   5. 8,095   6. 2,640

What number does each blue digit name?

7. 491   8. 7,526   9. 80,379   10. 462,183   11. 514,070   12. 733,992

In what place is each blue digit?

13. 120   14. 25,437   15. 8,986   16. 603,751   17. 915,348   18. 370,059

Use all the digits in each exercise. Write the greatest number and the least
number possible.

★19. 1, 6, 5, and 4   ★ 20. 8, 7, 0, 3, and 6   ★ 21. 4, 4, 0, 1, 2, and 3

Write the digits that are in the millions period.

22. 57,414,320   23. 981,662,583   24. 7,205,964,318

Write the digits that are in the billions period.

25. 46,151,207,599   26. 320,888,145,676   27. 1,007,623,805

Set 2 (pages 8–13)

Write >, <, or =.   1. 5,976 ⬤ 6,821   2. 36,464 ⬤ 36,464   3. 90,542 ⬤ 90,572

Write in order from least to greatest.

4. 481; 563; 425   5. 1,790; 1,709; 1,097   6. 52,341; 51,243; 54,132; 53,412

Round to the nearest ten.   7. 48   8. 283   9. 1,725
Round to the nearest hundred.   10. 4,591   11. 8,148   12. 60,263
Round to the nearest thousand.   13. 2,399   14. 15,545   15. 372,860
Round to the nearest ten thousand.   16. 77,059   17. 115,822
Round to the nearest hundred thousand. 18. 249,786   19. 7,878,650
Round to the nearest million.   20. 2,754,318   21. 37,358,642
Round to the nearest billion.   ★ 22. 1,678,054,239   ★ 23. 58,223,409,187

Write the exponent forms.

24. $4 \times 4 \times 4 \times 4 \times 4$ 25. $5 \times 5 \times 5$ 26. $2 \times 2 \times 2 \times 2$

Write the numbers.

27. 3^4 28. 9^2 29. 10^5 30. 7×10^2 31. 4×10^4 32. 2×10^3

Problem Solving for Chapter 1   (pages 14–15)

Use the table on page 14 to answer the questions.
1. Which state has a population between 7 million and 10 million?
2. Which state has a population of 4 million when rounded to the nearest million?
3. Which state has the smaller population, Texas or New York?

Extra Practice

Set 3 (pages 24–31)

Add.

1. 3
$+8$

2. 7
$+7$

3. 6
$+1$

4. 4
$+9$

5. 5
$+0$

6. 8
$+6$

7. 9
$+7$

8. $2 + 5 = \underline{\ ?\ }$

9. $0 + 9 = \underline{\ ?\ }$

10. $7 + 8 = \underline{\ ?\ }$

Find the missing numbers.

11. $6 + \underline{\ ?\ } = 13$

12. $\underline{\ ?\ } + 2 = 11$

13. $4 + \underline{\ ?\ } = 10$

When parentheses are used with addition and subtraction, do the operation
inside the parentheses first.

★**14.** $(8 + 4) + 3 = \underline{\ ?\ }$

★**15.** $15 - (9 - 2) = \underline{\ ?\ }$

★**16.** $(11 - 5) - 1 = \underline{\ ?\ }$

Estimate. Round to the nearest hundred, thousand, or hundred thousand.

17. 462
$+315$

18. 837
-184

19. 578
$+691$

20. 7,150
$-2,678$

21. 6,162
$-1,982$

★**22.** 409,567
$+382,009$

Add.

23. $4,593 + 828 = \underline{\ ?\ }$

24. $57 + 75 + 88 + 4 = \underline{\ ?\ }$

25. $395 + 67 + 904 = \underline{\ ?\ }$

26. 37
$+88$

27. 244
$+569$

28. 4,453
$+\ 197$

29. 1,821
6,556
$+\ \ 478$

30. 13,770
8,514
382,657
$+\ \ \ \ \ 835$

31. 714,908
250,133
17,664
$+162,785$

Set 4 (pages 32–35, 38–39)

Subtract.

1. 65
-37

2. 423
$-\ 85$

3. 9,044
$-7,787$

4. 51,225
$-49,531$

5. 210,630
$-\ 72,653$

6. 762,403
$-308,511$

7. $40,000 - 32,134 = \underline{\ ?\ }$

8. $612,093 - 608,196 = \underline{\ ?\ }$

★**9.** $90,000,000 - 127,548 = \underline{\ ?\ }$

Write the missing digits.

10. 7 □ 4
$-\ \ \ 6$ □
$\overline{\square\ 5\ 7}$

★**11.** □ , 1 0 □
$-\ \ \ \ \ \square\ 3\ 9$
$\overline{5 , 7\ \square\ 6}$

★**12.** 3 □ , 1 □ 6
$-\square\ 8 , 0\ 7\ \square$
$\overline{1\ 7 , \square\ 9\ 7}$

Write >, <, or =. **13.** $53 + 27$ ● 78 **14.** $262 + 59$ ● 321 **15.** $700 - 182$ ● 618

Problem Solving for Chapter 2 (pages 36–37, 40–41)

1. Mary bought a coat for $45.79. How much change did she receive from $60.00?

Write the equation. Then solve.

★**2.** There are 9 birds on a wire. First 5 more birds land on the wire. Later there
are only 8 birds on the wire. How many birds flew away?

Extra Practice

Set 5   (pages 50–55)

Multiply.

1.	2	2.	5	3.	0	4.	4	5.	8	6.	7	7.	9
	$\times 6$		$\times 5$		$\times 9$		$\times 3$		$\times 6$		$\times 7$		$\times 5$

8. $6 \times 4 = \underline{?}$ 9. $3 \times 9 = \underline{?}$ 10. $7 \times 5 = \underline{?}$

11. $1 \times (4 \times 2) = \underline{?}$ 12. $(5 \times 1) \times 0 = \underline{?}$ 13. $(3 \times 3) \times 6 = \underline{?}$

Find the missing factors.   14. $8 \times \underline{?} = 40$ 15. $\underline{?} \times 9 = 36$ 16. $6 \times \underline{?} = 42$

Complete. Multiply within the parentheses first.

★ 17. $(4 \times 5) + 3 = \underline{?}$ ★ 18. $7 + (8 \times 6) = \underline{?}$ ★ 19. $(9 \times 9) - 17 = \underline{?}$

Multiply.

20.	87	21.	613	22.	2,508	23.	78,118	24.	245,767	25.	538,954
	$\times\ 4$		$\times\ 9$		$\times\quad 7$		$\times\quad 3$		$\times\qquad 2$		$\times\qquad 8$

Write >, <, or =.   26. $5 \times 98 \bullet 512$ 27. $7 \times 643 \bullet 4,499$ 28. $3 \times 2,715 \bullet 5 \times 1,629$

Multiply.

29.	57	30.	349	31.	86	32.	691	33.	48	34.	270
	$\times 20$		$\times\ 60$		$\times 400$		$\times 500$		$\times 3,000$		$\times 8,000$

35. $6 \times 7,175 = \underline{?}$ 36. $70 \times 607 = \underline{?}$ 37. $6,000 \times 28 = \underline{?}$ 38. $5,000 \times 366 = \underline{?}$

Set 6   (pages 56–57, 60–61)

Multiply.

1.	47	2.	83	3.	154	4.	9,166	5.	43,087
	$\times 56$		$\times 29$		$\times\ 95$		$\times\quad 27$		$\times\qquad 54$

6.	604,167	7.	538	8.	9,024	9.	27,569	10.	$68.87
	$\times\qquad 64$		$\times 243$		$\times\quad 537$		$\times\quad 924$		$\times\quad 209$

11.	$506.94	12.	$932.18	★ 13.	480,197	★ 14.	175,866	★ 15.	829,071
	$\times\qquad 317$		$\times\qquad 456$		$\times\qquad 730$		$\times\qquad 194$		$\times\qquad 583$

16. $96 \times 19 = \underline{?}$ 17. $729 \times 36 = \underline{?}$ 18. $3,508 \times 74 = \underline{?}$ 19. $40,309 \times 97 = \underline{?}$

20. $735,094 \times 28 = \underline{?}$ 21. $729 \times 415 = \underline{?}$ 22. $8,075 \times 512 = \underline{?}$ 23. $69,403 \times 806 = \underline{?}$

Problem Solving for Chapter 3   (pages 58–59, 62–63)

1. A bag of sunflower seeds costs $1.39. A grocer orders 45 bags. How much does he pay in all?

Do you have enough money? Answer YES or NO.

2. You have $60.00. You want to buy 8 record albums. Each album costs $6.79.

Extra Practice

chapter 4

Set 7 (pages 72–83)

Divide.

1. $8\overline{)42}$ 2. $5\overline{)34}$ 3. $7\overline{)63}$ 4. $6\overline{)213}$ 5. $2\overline{)151}$ 6. $8\overline{)487}$ 7. $5\overline{)260}$ 8. $6\overline{)4,786}$

9. $9\overline{)6,543}$ 10. $7\overline{)3,060}$ 11. $8\overline{)34,277}$ 12. $5\overline{)7,502}$ 13. $3\overline{)17,571}$

14. $6\overline{)51,893}$ ★15. $9\overline{)114,381}$ ★16. $7\overline{)84,021}$ ★17. $3\overline{)604,227}$ ★18. $5\overline{)1,854,035}$

19. $17 \div 3 = \underline{\ ?\ }$ 20. $208 \div 8 = \underline{\ ?\ }$ 21. $75 \div 4 = \underline{\ ?\ }$ 22. $539 \div 6 = \underline{\ ?\ }$

23. $778 \div 2 = \underline{\ ?\ }$ 24. $1,253 \div 9 = \underline{\ ?\ }$ 25. $4,906 \div 7 = \underline{\ ?\ }$ 26. $13,540 \div 5 = \underline{\ ?\ }$

27. $9,200 \div 3 = \underline{\ ?\ }$ ★28. $46,688 \div 8 = \underline{\ ?\ }$ ★29. $271,733 \div 4 = \underline{\ ?\ }$ ★30. $87,793 \div 7 = \underline{\ ?\ }$

Do the operation inside the parentheses first.

★31. $252 \div (9 - 2) = \underline{\ ?\ }$ ★32. $366 - (8 \times 7) = \underline{\ ?\ }$ ★33. $(415 + 557) \div 9 = \underline{\ ?\ }$

★34. $(171 \div 3) \times 5 = \underline{\ ?\ }$ ★35. $810 \div (30 \div 6) = \underline{\ ?\ }$ ★36. $(97 \times 4) - 299 = \underline{\ ?\ }$

Find the averages.

37. 100, 91, 94, 86, 87, 68, 85, 93

38. 95, 96, 100, 81, 94, 88, 96, 98, 80

Set 8 (pages 84–91, 94–95)

Divide.

1. $86\overline{)472}$ 2. $67\overline{)505}$ 3. $92\overline{)1,081}$ 4. $59\overline{)4,639}$ 5. $78\overline{)2,886}$

6. $49\overline{)62,857}$ 7. $25\overline{)87,175}$ ★8. $55\overline{)860,722}$ 9. $464\overline{)3,810}$ 10. $257\overline{)9,429}$

11. $112\overline{)50,065}$ 12. $585\overline{)91,277}$ 13. $430\overline{)897,155}$ 14. $821\overline{)985,200}$ 15. $266\overline{)713,138}$

16. $767 \div 85 = \underline{\ ?\ }$ 17. $400 \div 61 = \underline{\ ?\ }$ 18. $532 \div 77 = \underline{\ ?\ }$

★19. $313 \div \underline{\ ?\ } = 52 \text{ r} \underline{\ ?\ }$ ★20. $683 \div \underline{\ ?\ } = 97 \text{ r} \underline{\ ?\ }$ 21. $1,794 \div 53 = \underline{\ ?\ }$

22. $3,040 \div 49 = \underline{\ ?\ }$ 23. $29,441 \div 85 = \underline{\ ?\ }$ 24. $86,507 \div 24 = \underline{\ ?\ }$

★25. $69,199 \div 18 = \underline{\ ?\ }$ ★26. $373,946 \div 8,000 = \underline{\ ?\ }$ ★27. $612,775 \div 3,000 = \underline{\ ?\ }$

Problem Solving for Chapter 4 (pages 92–93, 96–97)

1. A crate of 24 mangos costs $13.92. How much does each mango cost?

2. There are 260 guests at a wedding. Each table in the banquet hall seats 14 people. How many tables are needed? If 10 more guests are invited, will another table be needed?

Extra Practice

Set 9 (pages 106–111)

Use the line graph below to answer questions 1 through 5.

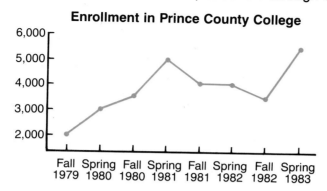

Enrollment in Prince County College

1. During which semester was the enrollment highest? lowest?

When was the enrollment lower,

2. fall 1980 or fall 1981? spring 1981 or spring 1982? spring 1981 or fall 1981?

3. During which semesters was enrollment more than 4,000 students? less than 3,500 students?

4. In which semesters did enrollment increase? decrease?

★ 5. In which semester did enrollment change the most?

Set 10 (pages 112–115)

Use the grid to answer questions 1 through 11.

What letter is at each point?

1. (5, 1)   2. (2, 4)   3. (4, 3)   4. (3, 1)   5. (0, 3)

What ordered pair tells the location of each point?

6. V   7. O   8. P   9. Y   10. C   11. F

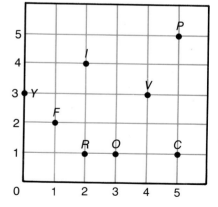

Problem Solving for Chapter 5 (pages 116–117)

Which operation would you use? Write ADD, SUBTRACT, MULTIPLY, or DIVIDE. Then solve.

1. In January, 11 inches of snow fell. In February, 18 inches fell. How much more snow fell in February?

2. There are 182 seats in a theater. They are arranged in 14 rows. How many seats are in each row?

Extra Practice

Set 11 (pages 126–135)

Find all the factors for each number. List them in order.

1. 20   **2.** 48   **3.** 85   **4.** 66   **5.** 54

6. 82   **7.** 70   **8.** 105   **9.** 126   **10.** 156

Write PRIME or COMPOSITE.

11. 29   **12.** 57   **13.** 65   **14.** 103   **15.** 113

Write the prime factorization of each number. Use a factor tree. Write the factors in order from least to greatest.

16. 30   **17.** 84   **18.** 75   **19.** 36   **20.** 56

21. 68   **22.** 49   **23.** 99   ★ **24.** 120   ★ **25.** 400

Find the greatest common factor for each pair.

26. 9, 12   **27.** 24, 20   **28.** 14, 49   ★ **29.** 8, 12, 20   ★ **30.** 9, 15, 24

Find the least common multiple for each pair.

31. 5, 7   **32.** 6, 18   **33.** 9, 15   ★ **34.** 6, 18, 30   ★ **35.** 4, 5, 6

Set 12 (pages 138–149)

Complete.   **1.** $\frac{3}{8} = \frac{?}{16}$ **2.** $\frac{12}{15} = \frac{4}{?}$ **3.** $\frac{2}{3} = \frac{10}{?}$ **4.** $\frac{4}{28} = \frac{?}{7}$ **5.** $\frac{5}{6} = \frac{15}{?}$

Write each fraction in lowest terms.   **6.** $\frac{15}{25}$ **7.** $\frac{18}{27}$ **8.** $\frac{22}{33}$ ★ **9.** $\frac{77}{91}$ ★ **10.** $\frac{54}{84}$

Find the least common denominator for each pair. Write equivalent fractions.

11. $\frac{2}{3}, \frac{1}{4}$ **12.** $\frac{3}{5}, \frac{5}{6}$ **13.** $\frac{1}{8}, \frac{1}{10}$ **14.** $\frac{2}{5}, \frac{7}{15}$ **15.** $\frac{4}{9}, \frac{1}{2}$

Complete.   **16.** $2 = \frac{?}{3}$ **17.** $5 = \frac{?}{4}$ **18.** $8 = \frac{?}{2}$ **19.** $6 = \frac{?}{6}$ **20.** $4 = \frac{?}{9}$

Write as fractions.   **21.** $1\frac{2}{3}$ **22.** $4\frac{1}{5}$ **23.** $7\frac{3}{4}$ **24.** $6\frac{7}{8}$ **25.** $5\frac{7}{10}$

Write >, <, or =.   ★ **26.** $5\frac{4}{5} \bigcirc 5\frac{3}{4}$ ★ **27.** $3\frac{3}{10} \bigcirc 4\frac{3}{10}$ ★ **28.** $6\frac{1}{3} \bigcirc 6\frac{4}{12}$

Problem Solving for Chapter 6   (pages 136–137, 150–151)

Decide what steps you must take to solve the problem. Then solve.

1. A small container holds 2 quarts, and a large container holds 3 quarts. Tillie fills 6 small containers and 5 large containers with soup. Hw many quarts of soup does Tillie use?

Use the schedule on page 150 to answer the question.

★ **2.** Mr. Welch leaves Dobbs Ferry on the 9:31 A.M. train. He gets off at Greystone and stays there for two hours. He then catches the next train to New York. At what time does Mr. Welch arrive in New York?

Extra Practice

Set 13 (pages 160–165)

Add. Write the answers in lowest terms.

1. $4\frac{1}{6}$
    $+4\frac{2}{6}$

2. $3\frac{7}{10}$
    $+6\frac{1}{10}$

3. $7\frac{1}{12}$
    $+8\frac{7}{12}$

4. $8\frac{2}{5}$
    $+4\frac{1}{10}$

5. $3\frac{9}{40}$
    $2\frac{13}{40}$
    $+7\frac{3}{40}$

6. $10\frac{7}{32}$
    $8\frac{9}{32}$
    $+\,6\frac{8}{32}$

7. $\frac{5}{8}$
    $+\frac{1}{6}$

8. $\frac{2}{3}$
    $+\frac{3}{5}$

9. $\frac{4}{9}$
    $+\frac{5}{6}$

10. $6\frac{4}{5}$
     $+2\frac{7}{10}$

11. $8\frac{2}{3}$
     $+\,\frac{5}{6}$

12. $4\frac{3}{5}$
     $+5\frac{1}{2}$

13. $10\frac{8}{9}$
     $+\,6\frac{1}{6}$

14. $5\frac{7}{12}$
     $+7\frac{3}{4}$

15. $9\frac{11}{15}$
     $+4\frac{7}{10}$

16. $2\frac{7}{8}$
     $+8\frac{1}{3}$

17. $6\frac{13}{16}$
     $+9\frac{3}{8}$

18. $12\frac{9}{10}$
     $+\,3\frac{18}{25}$

19. $\frac{1}{8} + \frac{3}{8} = \underline{?}$

20. $\frac{3}{11} + \frac{7}{11} = \underline{?}$

21. $\frac{21}{50} + \frac{9}{50} = \underline{?}\frac{3}{5}$

22. $2\frac{5}{7} + 1\frac{9}{14} = \underline{?}$

23. $5\frac{2}{3} + 3\frac{3}{4} = \underline{?}$

24. $6\frac{11}{12} + 4\frac{1}{3} = \underline{?}$

25. $13\frac{1}{4} + 5\frac{17}{20} = \underline{?}$

★26. $7\frac{1}{12} + 8\frac{1}{3} + 2\frac{1}{4} = \underline{?}$

★27. $3\frac{3}{8} + 9\frac{1}{6} + 6\frac{1}{12} = \underline{?}$

★28. $4\frac{1}{4} + 2\frac{1}{5} + 10\frac{1}{3} = \underline{?}$

Set 14 (pages 166–173)

Subtract. Write the answers in lowest terms.

1. $7\frac{8}{9}$
    $-1\frac{2}{9}$

2. $10\frac{5}{6}$
    $-\,3\frac{1}{6}$

3. $16\frac{4}{5}$
    $-\,8\frac{2}{5}$

★4. $326\frac{13}{16}$
    $-112\frac{3}{16}$

★5. $847\frac{9}{25}$
    $-431\frac{4}{25}$

6. $\frac{11}{12}$
    $-\,\frac{3}{4}$

7. $\frac{7}{8}$
    $-\frac{1}{3}$

8. $7\frac{4}{9}$
    $-2\frac{2}{6}$

9. $9\frac{4}{5}$
    $-3\frac{3}{4}$

10. $13\frac{9}{10}$
     $-\,4\frac{11}{15}$

11. $6\frac{5}{12}$
     $-5\frac{11}{12}$

12. 9
     $-2\frac{2}{5}$

13. $\frac{8}{11} - \frac{2}{11} = \underline{?}$

14. $\frac{9}{20} - \frac{3}{20} = \underline{?}$

15. $6\frac{7}{8} - 3\frac{3}{4} = \underline{?}$

16. $5\frac{13}{15} - 4\frac{1}{5} = \underline{?}$

17. $6\frac{3}{7} - 2\frac{4}{7} = \underline{?}$

18. $10 - 3\frac{7}{8} = \underline{?}$

19. $7\frac{3}{10} - 4\frac{9}{10} = \underline{?}$

20. $8\frac{1}{2} - 5\frac{7}{8} = \underline{?}$

21. $3\frac{1}{9} - \frac{1}{6} = \underline{?}$

22. $2\frac{2}{5} - 1\frac{11}{15} = \underline{?}$

23. $17\frac{7}{10} - 6\frac{22}{25} = \underline{?}$

Problem Solving for Chapter 7 (pages 174–175)

What other information do you need to solve each?

1. It takes Tomás 6 hours to wash and wax his car. How many hours does he need to wax the car?

2. One-fifth of the city budget is used for education. How much money is used for education?

Extra Practice

Set 15 (pages 184–189)

Multiply. Write the answers in lowest terms.

1. $\frac{1}{3} \times \frac{9}{10} = \underline{?}$ **2.** $\frac{2}{5} \times \frac{5}{7} = \underline{?}$ **3.** $\frac{3}{4} \times \frac{3}{8} = \underline{?}$ **4.** $\frac{1}{6} \times \frac{3}{5} = \underline{?}$ **5.** $\frac{1}{2} \times \frac{7}{9} = \underline{?}$

6. $\frac{3}{10} \times \frac{1}{6} = \underline{?}$ **7.** $\frac{7}{8} \times \frac{3}{14} = \underline{?}$ ★ **8.** $\frac{3}{5} \times \frac{5}{7} \times \frac{1}{2} = \underline{?}$ ★ **9.** $\frac{1}{3} \times \frac{2}{5} \times \frac{3}{8} = \underline{?}$

10. $15 \times \frac{9}{10} = \underline{?}$ **11.** $\frac{3}{4} \times 11 = \underline{?}$ **12.** $9 \times \frac{13}{20} = \underline{?}$ **13.** $\frac{5}{8} \times 12 = \underline{?}$

14. $14 \times \frac{1}{14} = \underline{?}$ ★ **15.** $\frac{2}{3} \times \frac{5}{9} \times 6 = \underline{?}$ ★ **16.** $\frac{1}{4} \times 9 \times \frac{5}{6} = \underline{?}$ ★ **17.** $7 \times \frac{3}{7} \times \frac{4}{5} = \underline{?}$

18. $5\frac{2}{5} \times 3\frac{1}{3} = \underline{?}$ **19.** $4\frac{1}{2} \times 2\frac{5}{9} = \underline{?}$ **20.** $7 \times 2\frac{3}{4} = \underline{?}$ **21.** $1\frac{5}{6} \times 9 = \underline{?}$

★ **22.** $2\frac{1}{3} \times 2\frac{1}{2} \times \frac{3}{10} = \underline{?}$ ★ **23.** $3\frac{3}{4} \times 6 \times 1\frac{2}{5} = \underline{?}$ ★ **24.** $3 \times \frac{5}{8} \times 2\frac{2}{3} = \underline{?}$

Set 16 (pages 190–197)

Find the reciprocals.

1. $\frac{4}{5}$ **2.** $2\frac{1}{3}$ **3.** 8 **4.** $\frac{13}{7}$ **5.** $5\frac{7}{8}$

Find the missing factors. If an answer is greater than 1, write it as a mixed number.

6. $\frac{3}{10} \times \underline{?} = 1$ **7.** $\underline{?} \times 2\frac{1}{2} = 1$ **8.** $4 \times \underline{?} = 1$ **9.** $\underline{?} \times \frac{7}{16} = 1$ ★ **10.** $\frac{5}{8} \times \underline{?} = 6$

Divide. Write the answers in lowest terms.

11. $\frac{2}{3} \div \frac{5}{6} = \underline{?}$ **12.** $\frac{1}{8} \div \frac{1}{4} = \underline{?}\frac{1}{2}$ **13.** $\frac{3}{5} \div \frac{4}{5} = \underline{?}$ **14.** $\frac{7}{2} \div \frac{2}{7} = \underline{?}$ **15.** $\frac{9}{4} \div \frac{3}{8} = \underline{?}$

16. $\frac{7}{9} \div \frac{4}{3} = \underline{?}$ **17.** $\frac{2}{5} \div \frac{1}{6} = \underline{?}$ ★ **18.** $\left(2 + \frac{1}{3}\right) \div \frac{7}{4} = \underline{?}$

★ **19.** $\left(\frac{1}{2} + 1\frac{3}{4}\right) \div \frac{6}{5} = \underline{?}$ ★ **20.** $\left(\frac{5}{3} \times \frac{7}{6}\right) \div \frac{5}{12} = \underline{?}$ **21.** $\frac{3}{8} \div 3 = \underline{?}$

22. $\frac{12}{11} \div 4 = \underline{?}$ **23.** $6 \div \frac{1}{4} = \underline{?}$ **24.** $\frac{7}{10} \div 14 = \underline{?}$

★ **25.** $\left(\frac{5}{6} \div 2\right) \div \frac{5}{3} = \underline{?}$ ★ **26.** $\frac{5}{6} \div \left(2 \div \frac{5}{3}\right) = \underline{?}$ ★ **27.** $\left(8 \div \frac{3}{2}\right) \div 4 = \underline{?}$

Problem Solving for Chapter 8 (pages 198–199)

Answer the questions. Use only the facts you need.

1. *How many hours of music does radio station WXYZ play in one day?*
WXYZ is on the air for 20 hours each day. Each day there is a $1\frac{1}{2}$ hour news show on WXYZ. WXYZ gives a weather report once every hour. WXYZ plays music for $\frac{3}{5}$ of the time it is on the air.

2. *How many of the students in Mr. Burkhardt's class passed their exam?*
There are 30 students in Mr. Burkhardt's class. $\frac{1}{10}$ of the students are absent on the day of the exam. $\frac{2}{9}$ of the students who take the exam do not pass. Eight of the students receive a grade of B on the exam.

Extra Practice

Set 17 (pages 208–215)

Write the decimals.

1. $54\frac{3}{100}$
2. $11\frac{1}{10}$
3. $608\frac{29}{100}$
4. $89\frac{69}{1,000}$
5. $2,731\frac{3}{1,000}$
6. $400\frac{992}{1,000}$

7. seventy-two hundredths
8. eighty-one and nine-thousandths
9. three thousand ten and two-tenths
10. thirty thousand nine and six-hundredths

In what place is each blue digit?

11. 36.417 12. 609.5 13. 1.6882 14. 375.44 15. 1,060.43 16. 921.474

What number does each blue digit name?

17. 572.4 18. 26.003 19. 4,816.9 20. 7.2428 21. 90.385 22. 4,510.57

Write decimals that name the same number.

23. $4.9 = \underline{?} = \underline{?}$
★ 24. $3.21 = \underline{?} = \underline{?}$
★ 25. $\underline{?} = 9.070 = \underline{?}$

Write >, <, or =.   26. 26.7 ● 27.6   27. 55.545 ● 55.455   28. 63.700 ● 63.7

Write in order from least to greatest.   ★ 29. 89.889, 88.989, 88.998, 8.9898, 8.8998

Set 18 (pages 216–219, 222–223)
Round to the nearest whole number.   1. 17.86   2. 8.417   3. 400.93
Round to the nearest tenth.   4. 6.24   5. 81.55   ★ 6. 852.97
Round to the nearest hundredth.   7. 7.873   8. 9.225   ★ 9. 389.798
Round to the nearest thousandth.   10. 0.02391 11. 5.4777 12. 48.3696

Add or subtract.

13.   56.093   14. 8.118   15. 215.5   16. 9.054   17. 684.7
    +275.18   4.275   69.48   −5.879   − 6.847
                    +3.566   553.829
                                +   4.137

18. $5.3 + 7.92 = \underline{?}$ 19. $36.41 + 8.79 = \underline{?}$ 20. $7.85 + 78.5 + 6.307 = \underline{?}$

21. $62.89 - 17.92 = \underline{?}$ 22. $306 - 26.17 = \underline{?}$ 23. $780.1 - 594.23 = \underline{?}$

Write >, <, or =.

★ 24. 3.83 + 7.59 ● 10.42   ★ 25. 56.014 + 7.987 ● 64.001   ★ 26. 23.11 − 14.88 ● 8.33

Problem Solving for Chapter 9 (pages 220–221, 224–225)

Read the problems. Then tell what you need to know before you can solve them.

1. Garo can read 20 pages of a book per hour. Krikor can read 25 pages per hour. How much longer does it take Garo to finish the book?

★ 2. The New York Aces have won 9 of their softball games. The Boston Barons have won 7 of their games. Which team has the better record?

Extra Practice

Set 19 (pages 234–239, 242–243)

Estimate to place the decimal point in the answers.

1. 92	**2.** 257	**3.** 8.6	**4.** 40.8	**5.** 71.5	**6.** 9.43
×2.3	× 1.4	×5.9	× 3.7	×6.28	×8.52
2116	3598	5074	15096	449020	803436

Multiply or divide.

7. 3.61	**8.** 75	**9.** 2.49	**10.** 206.07	**11.** 0.223	**12.** 0.548
× 24	×1.8	× 5.6	× 0.182	× 0.4	×0.129

13. $365 \times 0.807 = \underline{?}$ **14.** $19.8 \times 1.32 = \underline{?}$ **15.** $4.06 \times 9.75 = \underline{?}$

16. $6\overline{)32.4}$ **17.** $3\overline{)17.58}$ **18.** $8\overline{)90.64}$ **19.** $91\overline{)0.7553}$ **20.** $9\overline{)1.1187}$

21. $137.64 \div 74 = \underline{?}$ **22.** $20.631 \div 39 = \underline{?}$ **23.** $0.1360 \div 85 = \underline{?}$

Set 20 (pages 244–253)

Divide until the remainder is 0.

1. $5\overline{)2.4}$ **2.** $2\overline{)5.3}$ **3.** $4\overline{)11.8}$ **4.** $6\overline{)50.7}$ **5.** $8\overline{)7.8}$ **6.** $4\overline{)0.93}$

7. $0.081 \div 45 = \underline{?}$ ★**8.** $26.8 \div 32 = \underline{?}$ ★ **9.** $800.1 \div 144 = \underline{?}$

Multiply or divide.

10. $10 \times 3.46 = \underline{?}$ **11.** $1,000 \times 0.298 = \underline{?}$ ★ **12.** $10,000 \times 21.667 = \underline{?}$

★ **13.** $9,301 \div 10,000 = \underline{?}$ ★ **14.** $37.71 \div 0.036 = \underline{?}$ ★ **15.** $0.0076 \div 0.32 = \underline{?}$

16. $0.7\overline{)1.54}$ **17.** $0.15\overline{)0.0645}$ **18.** $0.003\overline{)0.00132}$ **19.** $47.9\overline{)24.429}$ **20.** $0.72\overline{)0.4572}$

Find the decimals. Divide until the remainder is 0.

21. $\frac{4}{5}$ **22.** $\frac{9}{40}$ **23.** $\frac{5}{8}$ **24.** $\frac{11}{16}$ **25.** $\frac{31}{25}$ **26.** $\frac{67}{20}$

Find the decimals to the nearest hundredth.

27. $\frac{1}{12}$ **28.** $\frac{7}{9}$ **29.** $\frac{6}{11}$ **30.** $\frac{17}{24}$ **31.** $\frac{19}{13}$ **32.** $\frac{92}{29}$

Problem Solving for Chapter 10 (pages 240–241, 254–255)

★ **1.** Assad earns $9.50 an hour on weekdays and $14.25 an hour on weekends. Last week he worked 24 hours during the week and 12 hours on the weekend. How much did Assad earn last week?

Solve. Estimate to make sure that your answer makes sense.

2. It costs $11.50 per square foot to waterproof a basement. Mr. Cavendish needs to waterproof 37.25 square feet. What is the total cost of the job?

Extra Practice

Set 21 (pages 264–279)

Complete.

1. 3 m = $\underline{?}$ km
2. 5 km = $\underline{?}$ m
3. 12 m = $\underline{?}$ cm
4. $\underline{?}$ m = 900 cm

5. 29 mm = $\underline{?}$ m
6. $\underline{?}$ mm = 16 m
7. $\underline{?}$ cm = 0.063 m

8. $\underline{?}$ m = 0.0715 km
★9. 9.75 dm = $\underline{?}$ mm
★10. $\underline{?}$ cm = 2.16 hm

The length and the width are given. Find the area of each rectangle.

11. $l = 8$ m
$w = 7$ m
12. $l = 14$ cm
$w = 9$ cm
13. $l = 56.1$ mm
$w = 23.9$ mm
14. $l = 38.4$ km
$w = 38.4$ km
★15. $l = 760$ mm
$w = 32$ m

The base and the height are given. Find the area of each parallelogram.

16. $b = 9$ cm
$h = 5$ cm
17. $b = 8$ km
$h = 17$ km
18. $b = 24$ m
$h = 11$ m
19. $b = 13$ mm
$h = 13$ mm
★20. $b = 5.1$ km
$h = 107$ m

The base and the height are given. Find the area of each triangle.

21. $b = 4$ km
$h = 6$ km
22. $b = 16$ m
$h = 9$ m
23. $b = 12$ cm
$h = 7$ cm
24. $b = 10$ mm
$h = 11$ mm
★25. $b = 56$ mm
$h = 7.3$ cm

Set 22 (pages 280–295)

Find the volume of each figure.

1.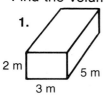
2.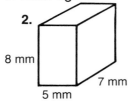
3.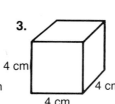
4.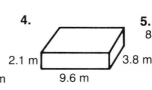
5.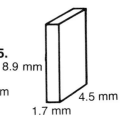

Complete.

6. 62 L = $\underline{?}$ mL
7. $\underline{?}$ L = 8,932 mL
★8. 4.3 kL = $\underline{?}$ mL
9. 47 g = $\underline{?}$ mg

10. $\underline{?}$ kg = 705 g
11. 7,040 yd = $\underline{?}$ mi
★12. $2\frac{2}{3}$ yd = $\underline{?}$ ft
★13. $\frac{5}{12}$ mi = $\underline{?}$ ft

Complete.

14. 13 fl. oz = $\underline{?}$ tbsp
15. 7 gal = $\underline{?}$ qt
16. 8 qt = $\underline{?}$ c
17. 2 c 7 fl. oz = $\underline{?}$ fl. oz

★18. $1\frac{3}{8}$ gal = $\underline{?}$ pt
19. 48 oz = $\underline{?}$ lb
20. 6 lb = $\underline{?}$ oz
21. 14 T = $\underline{?}$ lb

Problem Solving for Chapter 11 (pages 296–297)

1. Mrs. Shisado buys two turkeys for her holiday dinner. One turkey weighs 9 pounds 11 ounces, and the other weighs 10 pounds 9 ounces. How much do the two turkeys weigh in all?

★2. There are 100 feet on a roll of plastic. A customer buys 2 pieces, each one 13 feet 5 inches, and another piece that is 16 feet 8 inches. How much plastic is left on the roll?

Extra Practice

Set 23 (pages 306–313)

Use a protractor to draw the angles.

1. ∠*PQR*: 45° **2.** ∠*GHI*: 140°

3. ∠*WXY*: 70° **4.** ∠*CDE*: 105° **5.** ∠*LMN*: 170° **6.** ∠*TUV*: 15°

Measure each angle. Then use your protractor to draw a congruent angle for each.

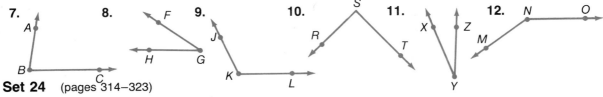

7. **8.** **9.** **10.** **11.** **12.**

Set 24 (pages 314–323)

Triangles *ABC* and *DEF* are congruent. Name the corresponding parts.

1. $\overline{AB} \leftrightarrow \underline{?}$ **2.** ∠*B* ↔ $\underline{?}$∠ **3.** $\overline{BC} \leftrightarrow \underline{?}$ **4.** ∠*C* ↔ $\underline{?}$∠ **5.** $\overline{AC} \leftrightarrow \underline{?}$ **6.** ∠*A* ↔ $\underline{?}$∠

7. Name the circle.

8. Name four radii.

9. Name four chords.

10. Name two diameters.

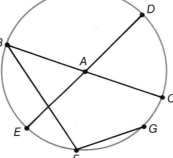

11. If $\overline{AB}$ measures 3 cm, how long is $\overline{BC}$?

★ **12.** If $\overline{DE}$ measures 78.6 mm, how long is $\overline{AC}$?

Trace the figures. Draw the lines of symmetry.

13. **14.** ★ **15.**

Problem Solving for Chapter 12 (pages 324–325)

Make a drawing to help you solve the problem.

1. A store display of cans is arranged in 6 rows. There are 10 cans on the bottom row. Each row has one less can than the row below it. How many cans are in the display in all?

★ **2.** A bingo card has 5 rows with 5 squares in each row. There are white markers on all of the squares on the border. There are red markers on the inner squares that form the letter X. The remaining squares have blue markers. How many blue markers are there in all?

Extra Practice

Set 25 (pages 334–347)

Complete.

1. $\dfrac{3}{8} = \dfrac{?}{24}$ **2.** $\dfrac{2}{7} = \dfrac{10}{?}$ **3.** $\dfrac{5}{12} = \dfrac{?}{72}$ **4.** $\dfrac{16}{?} = \dfrac{64}{100}$ ★**5.** $\dfrac{?}{20} = \dfrac{0.7}{35}$ ★**6.** $\dfrac{?}{10} = \dfrac{8.1}{45}$

Is the proportion true? Compare the cross products. Then write YES or NO.

7. $\dfrac{5}{9} = \dfrac{6}{11}$ **8.** $\dfrac{7}{1} = \dfrac{42}{6}$ **9.** $\dfrac{16}{26} = \dfrac{8}{13}$ **10.** $\dfrac{30}{12} = \dfrac{20}{9}$

Write = or ≠.

★**11.** $\dfrac{0.4}{15}$ ● $\dfrac{0.9}{32}$ ★**12.** $\dfrac{21}{3.5}$ ● $\dfrac{30}{5}$

Solve the proportions.

13. $\dfrac{9}{12} = \dfrac{12}{?}$ **14.** $\dfrac{14}{5} = \dfrac{?}{20}$ **15.** $\dfrac{6}{18} = \dfrac{5}{?}$ **16.** $\dfrac{39}{26} = \dfrac{?}{2}$ ★**17.** $\dfrac{0.75}{16} = \dfrac{8.25}{?}$ ★**18.** $\dfrac{8.4}{12.6} = \dfrac{?}{9}$

Find the missing measures.

19. $\overline{AB}$ = 6 mm
$\overline{AD}$ = 4 mm
$\overline{EF}$ = 3 mm
$\overline{EH}$ = ? mm

20. $\overline{AB}$ = 18 cm
$\overline{AD}$ = 12 cm
$\overline{EF}$ = 12 cm
$\overline{EH}$ = ? cm

21. $\overline{AB}$ = 30 mm
$\overline{AD}$ = 21 mm
$\overline{EF}$ = 20 mm
$\overline{EH}$ = ? mm

★**22.** $\overline{AB}$ = 7.5 cm
$\overline{AD}$ = 4.5 cm
$\overline{EF}$ = 6.5 cm
$\overline{EH}$ = ? cm

Set 26 (pages 348–359)

Write the percents for the ratios.

1. 29 out of 100 **2.** 86 out of 100 **3.** 73 per 100 **4.** 41 per 100 **5.** $\dfrac{54}{100}$ **6.** $\dfrac{97}{100}$

Write the percents for the decimals.

7. 0.12 **8.** 0.65 **9.** 0.38 **10.** 0.06 ★**11.** 0.8 ★**12.** 0.2

Write the fractions for the percents. Write the answers in lowest terms.

13. 83% **14.** 16% **15.** 35% **16.** 77% **17.** 40% **18.** 29%

Find the answers.

19. 60% of 65 = ? **20.** 75% of 84 = ? **21.** 22% of 105 = ? **22.** 6% of 450 = ?

23. 41% of 296 = ? **24.** 98% of 525 = ? ★**25.** ?% of 40 = 16 ★**26.** ?% of 96 = 64

Find the total cost.

27. price: $9.50
sales tax: 4%

28. price: $46.25
sales tax: 6%

29. price: $417.85
sales tax: 7%

30. price: $832.99
sales tax: 5%

Problem Solving for Chapter 13 (pages 360–361)

Use the map on page 360 to answer the questions.

1. About how far is it from (690) to (5) along (297) ?

2. In which direction would you go to travel from Syracuse to Binghamton?

Extra Practice

chapter 14

Set 27 (pages 370–377)

Name the opposite numbers.

1. $^-6$ 2. $^+13$ 3. $^-37$ 4. $^-91$ 5. $^-706$ 6. $^+511$

Name the opposite integers.

7. $^+20$ 8. $^-8$ 9. $^+17$ 10. $^-35$ 11. $^-52$ 12. $^+89$

Which is greater?

13. $^+3, ^+5$ 14. $^-7, ^-6$ 15. $^+11, ^-11$ 16. $^-4, ^+2$ 17. $^-8, ^+9$ 18. $^-10, ^+1$

Write > or <.   19. $^+4$ ⬤ $^+8$ 20. $^+3$ ⬤ $^-3$ 21. $^-24$ ⬤ $^-16$

Add.

22. $^+5 + ^+2 = \underline{?}$ 23. $^-3 + ^-3 = \underline{?}$ 24. $^-4 + 0 = \underline{?}$

25. $^-7 + ^-8 = \underline{?}$ 26. $^+9 + ^+4 = \underline{?}$ 27. $^+2 + ^+8 = \underline{?}$

★ 28. $^-6 + \underline{?} = ^-11$ ★ 29. $0 + \underline{?} = ^+9$ ★ 30. $\underline{?} + ^-3 = ^-10$

31. $^+3 + ^-12 = \underline{?}$ 32. $^+14 + ^-8 = \underline{?}$ 33. $^-10 + ^+2 = \underline{?}$

★ 34. $^+4 + ^+7 + ^+5 = \underline{?}$ ★ 35. $^-3 + ^-9 + ^+8 = \underline{?}$ ★ 36. $^-2 + ^+1 + ^-6 = \underline{?}$

Set 28 (pages 378–383)

Subtract.

1. $^+6 - ^+4 = \underline{?}$ 2. $^-7 - ^-2 = \underline{?}$ 3. $^+3 - ^+8 = \underline{?}$

4. $^+5 - ^+5 = \underline{?}$ 5. $^-1 - ^-10 = \underline{?}$ 6. $^-6 - ^-3 = \underline{?}$

★ 7. $^+2 - \underline{?} = ^+2$ ★ 8. $\underline{?} - ^-4 = ^+4$ ★ 9. $^-1 - \underline{?} = ^-3$

What letter is at the point?

10. $(^+3, ^+3)$ 11. $(^-4, ^-1)$ 12. $(^+4, ^+1)$

13. $(0, ^-4)$ 14. $(^+5, ^-2)$ 15. $(^+2, 0)$

16. $(^+1, ^+5)$ 17. $(^+3, ^-6)$ 18. $(^-6, ^+6)$

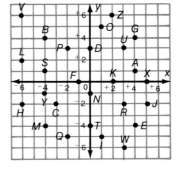

Problem Solving for Chapter 14 (pages 384–385)

Make up one question that can be answered using the information given on page 384.

1. The balance in Richard's account at the end of 1982 was $305.49. One year later his balance was $333.29.

2. Richard made three withdrawals from his account between September 2, 1982, and March 9, 1984. The withdrawals were $75.00, $100.00, and $167.58.

TABLE OF MEASURES

Metric	**United States Customary**

Length

10 millimeters (mm) = 1 centimeter (cm)
10 centimeters = 1 decimeter (dm)
10 decimeters = 1 meter (m)
1,000 meters = 1 kilometer (km)

12 inches (in.) = 1 foot (ft)
$\left.\begin{array}{r}36 \text{ inches} \\ 3 \text{ feet}\end{array}\right\}$ = 1 yard (yd)
$\left.\begin{array}{r}5,280 \text{ feet} \\ 1,760 \text{ yards}\end{array}\right\}$ = 1 mile (mi)

Area

100 square millimeters (mm^2) = 1 square centimeter (cm^2)
10,000 square centimeters = 1 square meter (m^2)

144 square inches (in.^{2}) = 1 square foot (ft^2)
9 square feet = 1 square yard (yd^2)

Volume

1,000 cubic millimeters (mm^3) = 1 cubic centimeter (cm^3)
1,000,000 cubic centimeters = 1 cubic meter (m^3)

1,728 cubic inches (in.^{3}) = 1 cubic foot (ft^3)
27 cubic feet = 1 cubic yard (yd^3)

Capacity

1,000 milliliters (mL) = 1 liter (L)
1,000 liters = 1 kiloliter (kL)

1 cup (c) = 8 fluid ounces (fl. oz)
2 cups = 1 pint (pt)
2 pints = 1 quart (qt)
4 quarts = 1 gallon (gal)

Mass/Weight

1,000 milligrams (mg) = 1 gram (g)
1,000 grams = 1 kilogram (kg)

16 ounces (oz) = 1 pound (lb)
2,000 pounds = 1 ton (T)

Time

60 seconds (s) = 1 minute (min)
60 minutes = 1 hour (h)
24 hours = 1 day (d)
7 days = 1 week (wk)
28 to 31 days = 1 month (mo)
$\left.\begin{array}{r}12 \text{ months} \\ 52 \text{ weeks}\end{array}\right\}$ = 1 year (yr)
100 years = 1 century (cen)

TABLE OF SYMBOLS

$+$	plus
$-$	minus
$\times$	times
$\div$	divided by
$=$	equals or is equal to
$\neq$	is not equal to
$>$	is greater than
$<$	is less than
$\approx$	is approximately equal to
$\sim$	is similar to
$\cong$	is congruent to
...	pattern continues without end
7 r4	seven remainder four
14.3	decimal point: fourteen and three-tenths
$0.\overline{27}$	repeating decimal: 0.272727...
30%	percent: thirty percent
4:3	ratio: four to three
8^2	eight to the second power or eight squared
$\sqrt{64}$	square root: square root of sixty-four
$+3$	positive three
-3	negative three
(1,4)	ordered pair: ($x = 1$, $y = 4$)
$\llcorner$	right angle
$\angle ABC$	angle ABC
$\circ$	degree (angle or temperature)
$.A$	point A
$\overline{AB}$	line segment with endpoints A and B
$\overrightarrow{AB}$	ray AB with endpoint A
$\overleftrightarrow{AB}$	line through points A and B
$\parallel$	is parallel to
$\perp$	is perpendicular to
$\triangle ABC$	triangle ABC
π	pi (approximately 3.14 or $\frac{22}{7}$)
P(E)	probability of event E

GLOSSARY

Acute angle   An angle whose measure is greater than 0° and less than 90°. (p. 308)

Addend   A number that is added. (p. 24)
Example: 8 + 7 = 15   The addends are 8 and 7.

Addition (+)   An operation on two numbers resulting in their sum. (p. 24)
Example: 9 + 8 = 17   9 and 8 are addends. 17 is the sum.

Angle   Two rays with the same endpoint. The endpoint is the vertex of the angle. (p. 308)
Example:

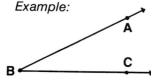

Point B is the vertex of ∠ABC.

Area   The number of square units needed to cover a surface. (p. 272)
Examples: Some formulas to find area are;
rectangle $A = \ell \times 2$
parallelogram $A = b \times h$
triangle $A = \frac{1}{2} \times b \times h$
circle $A = \pi \times r^2$

Associative property of addition   The way in which addends are grouped does not change the sum. (p. 24)
Example: (7 + 5) + 6 = 7 + (5 + 6).

Associative property of multiplication   The way in which factors are grouped does not change the product. (p. 50)
Example: (3 × 4) × 5 = 3 × (4 × 5)

Average (mean)   The quotient found by dividing a sum by the number of addends. (p. 80)
Example: The average of 2, 3, and 7 is 4 because 2 + 3 + 7 = 12 and 12 ÷ 3 = 4.

Bar graph   A graph with bars (rectangles) of different heights to show and compare information. (p. 108)

Capacity   The amount a container will hold when filled. (p. 282)

Chord   A line segment with endpoints on a circle. (p. 318)

Circle   A closed curve with all points an equal distance from a center point. (p. 318)

Circumference   The distance around a circle. (p. 270)

Common denominator   A common multiple of the denominators of two or more fractions. (p. 144)
Example: 18 is a common denominator for $\frac{5}{6}$ and $\frac{2}{3}$.

Common factor   A factor of two or more numbers. (p. 132)
Example: 1, 2, 3, and 6 are the common factors of 6 and 12.

Commutative property of addition   The order in which addends are added does not change the sum. (p. 24)
Example: 6 + 4 = 4 + 6

Commutative property of multiplication   The order in which factors are multiplied does not change the product. (p. 50)
Example: 5 × 7 = 7 × 5

Composite number   A whole number greater than 1 that has more than two factors. (p. 128)
Example: 8 is a composite number since its factors are 1, 2, 4, 8.

Cone A solid with one circular face and one vertex. (p. 322)

Congruent Angles Angles that have the same measure. (p. 311)

Congruent polygons Polygons that have the same size and shape. (p. 316)

Coordinate graph A drawing of numbered lines that cross at right angles and are used to name the positions of points. (p. 382)

Cube A rectangular prism with six congruent square faces. (p. 322)
Example:

Customary measurement system A measurement system that uses inches, feet, yards, and miles as units of length; cups, pints, quarts, and gallons for liquid capacity; ounces, pounds, and tons as units of weight; and degrees Fahrenheit as units of temperature. (p. 290)

Cylinder A solid with two bases that are congruent circles. (p. 322)

Decagon A polygon with ten sides. (p. 314)

Decimal A number that uses place value and a decimal point to show tenths, hundredths, thousandths, and so on. (p. 208)
Example: 3.85 Read as three and eighty-five hundredths.

Degree (°) A standard unit for measuring angles. (p. 308)

Degree Celsius (°C) A standard unit for measuring temperature in the metric system. (p. 286)
Example: Water freezes at 0°C and boils at 100°C.

Degree Fahrenheit (°F) A standard unit for measuring temperature in the customary measurement system. (p. 299)

Example: Water freezes at 32°F and boils at 212°F.

Denominator The number below the bar in a fraction. (p. 138)
Example: $\frac{3}{4}$ The denominator is 4.

Diameter A line segment through the center of a circle with endpoints on the circle. (p. 318)

Difference The answer to a subtraction problem. (p. 26)
Example: $14 - 9 = 5$ The difference is 5.

Digit Any one of the ten symbols 0, 1, 2, 3, 4, 5, 6, 7, 8, or 9. (p. 2)

Distributive property of multiplication over addition The product of a number and the sum of two numbers equals the sum of the two products. (p. 52)
Example: $3 \times (4 + 2) = (3 \times 4) + (3 \times 2)$

Dividend The number that is divided in a division problem. (p. 72)
Example: $12 \div 4$ 12 is the dividend.

Divisible A number is divisible by another number if the quotient is a whole number and the remainder is 0. (p. 126)
Example: 18 is divisible by 6.

Division ($\overline{)}$ or $\div$) An operation on two numbers that results in a quotient and a remainder. (p. 72)

Divisor The number by which the dividend is divided. (p. 72)
Example: $7\overline{)45}$ with 6r3 The divisor is 7.

Edge The line segment where two faces of a solid meet. (p. 320)
Example:

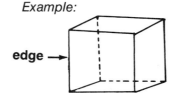

edge →

410

Endpoint A point at the end of a line segment or ray. (p. 306)

Equation A number sentence that uses the symbol = . (p. 40)
Examples: $5 \times 4 = 20$; $8 + N = 13$

Equilateral triangle A triangle with three equal sides. Each angle measures 60°. (p. 314)

Equivalent fractions Fractions that name the same number. (p. 140)
Example: $\frac{3}{4}$ and $\frac{6}{8}$ are equivalent.

Equivalent ratios Ratios that show the same comparison. (p. 336)
Example: $\frac{1}{3}$, $\frac{2}{6}$, and $\frac{3}{9}$ are equivalent ratios.

Even number A whole number that is a multiple of 2. An even number has 0, 2, 4, 6, or 8 in the ones place. (p. 126)
Examples: 4, 16, 28, 120 are even numbers.

Expanded form A way to show a number as a sum of multiples of ten. (p. 2)
Example: $387 = 3 \times 100 + 8 \times 10 + 7 \times 1$.

Exponent A number that tells how many times the base is used as a factor. (p. 12)

$$\overset{\text{exponent}}{3^2} = 3 \times 3 \text{ or } 9.$$
base

Face A flat surface of a solid. (p. 322)

Factor A factor of a number is a whole number that divides it exactly. (p. 128)
Example: 1, 2, 3, and 6 are factors of 6.

Factor tree The prime factors of a number can be found by making a factor tree. (p. 130)
Example:

```
        20
       /  \
      2  ×  10
     /    /   \
    2  ×  2  ×  5
```

$20 = 2^2 \times 5$

Flow chart A diagram that shows the steps used from start to end. (p. 331)

Fraction The quotient of two whole numbers: $a \div b = \frac{a}{b}$. In the fraction $\frac{a}{b}$, a is called the numerator and b is called the denominator. (p. 138)

Graph A drawing used to show and compare information. Some types of graphs are bar graphs, circle graphs, line graphs, and picture graphs. (p. 106)

Greatest common factor (GCF) The greatest factor that two or more numbers have in common. (p. 132)
Example: 7 is the GCF of 14 and 21.

Heptagon A polygon with seven sides. (p. 312)

Hexagon A polygon with six sides. (p. 314)

Integers The whole numbers and their opposites.
$\ldots, -3, -2, -1, 0, +1, +2, +3, \ldots$
-2 is a negative integer. $+2$ or 2 is a positive integer. (p. 370)

Intersecting lines Lines that meet or cross. Intersecting lines have only one point in common. (p. 312)

Inverse operations Operations that undo each other. Addition and subtraction as well as multiplication and division are inverse operations. (p. 26)
Examples:
$29 - 13 = 16$ and $16 + 13 = 29$
$15 \div 3 = 5$ and $5 \times 3 = 15$.

Isosceles triangle A triangle with two equal sides and two equal angles. (p. 312)

Least common denominator (LCD) The least common multiple of the denominators of two or more fractions. (p. 144)
Example: 12 is the LCD for $\frac{1}{4}$ and $\frac{5}{6}$.

Least common multiple (LCM)   The smallest nonzero multiple that two or more numbers have in common. (p. 134)
   Example: The LCM of 6 and 9 is 18.

Line   A straight path extending in both directions with no endpoints. (p. 306)

Line graph   A graph in which a line is used to show a change. (p. 110)

Line of symmetry   A line that divides a figure into two congruent parts. (p. 320)

Line segment   Part of a line with two endpoints. (p. 306)

Lowest terms   A fraction is in lowest terms when the numerator and the denominator have no common factor greater than one. (p. 142)

Magic square   The sum of the numbers in each row, column, and diagonal is the same. (p. 227)

Example:

4	3	8
9	5	1
2	7	6

Median   The middle score in a distribution. (p. 101)

Metric system   A measurement system that uses centimeters, meters, and kilometers as units of length; milliliters and liters as units of capacity; grams and kilograms as units of mass; and degrees Celsius as units of temperature. (p. 264)

Mixed number   The sum of a whole number and a fraction. (p. 146)
   Example: $3\frac{1}{2} = 3 + \frac{1}{2}$.

Mode   The score with the highest frequency in a group of scores. (p. 101)
   Example: 3 is the mode of 2, 3, 3, 4, 5.

Multiple   A number that is the product of a given number and a whole number. (p. 134)
   Example: Multiples of 3: 3, 6, 9, 12, 15, . . .

Multiplication ($\times$)   An operation on two numbers, called factors, which results in a product. (p. 50)
   Example: $8 \times 9 = 72$ 8 and 9 are factors and 72 is the product.

Negative number   A number less than zero. (p. 370)

Number line   A line with equally spaced points named by numbers. (p. 376)
   Example:

$$-3 \quad -2 \quad -1 \quad 0 \quad 1 \quad 2 \quad 3$$

Numerator   The number above the bar in a fraction. (p. 138)
   Example: $\frac{2}{5}$ The numerator is 2.

Obtuse angle   An angle whose measure is greater than 90° and less than 180°. (p. 308)

Octagon   A polygon with eight sides. (p. 314)

Odd number   A whole number that is not a multiple of 2. An odd number ends in 1, 3, 5, 7, or 9. (p. 126)
   Examples: 3, 17, 29, 235 are odd numbers.

Opposite numbers   Two numbers whose points on the number line are the same distance from 0, but in opposite directions. (p. 370)
   Examples: 4 and −4 are opposites.
   $-\frac{2}{3}$ and $\frac{2}{3}$ are opposites.

Ordered pair   A pair of numbers, (x, y), arranged in order so that x is first and y is second. (p. 114)

Outcome   Each possible result in a probability experiment. (p. 346).

Parallel lines   Lines in the same plane that do not intersect. Parallel lines have no points in common. (p. 312)

Parallelogram   A quadrilateral with opposite sides parallel and congruent. (p. 314)

Pentagon   A polygon with five sides. (p. 314)

Percent (%)   Percent means per hundred.
$P\% = \frac{P}{100}$. (p. 346)
Example: $\frac{2}{5} = \frac{40}{100} = 40\%$

Perimeter   The sum of the lengths of the
sides of a polygon. (p. 268)
Examples: Some formulas to find
perimeter are:
rectangle $P = 2 \times (\ell + w)$
square $P = 4 \times s$

Period   A group of three digits set off by a
comma in a number. (p. 6)
Example: Three million, four hundred
twenty thousand, seventy-one is written:
3,420,071.

Perpendicular lines   Two lines that intersect
to form right angles. (p. 312)

Pi (π)   The number that is the ratio of the
circumference of any circle to the length of
a diameter of that circle. Approximations for
π are 3.14 and $\frac{22}{7}$. (p. 270)

Pictograph   A visual representation used to
make comparisons. A key always appears
at the bottom of a pictograph or picture
graph showing how many each object
represents. (p. 106)

Place value   In a decimal number, each
place for a digit has a value ten times the
value of the place at its right. (p. 4)
Example: $8,763 = 8 \times 1,000 + 7 \times 100$
$+ 6 \times 10 + 3 \times 1$.

Point   An exact location. A dot is often drawn
to represent a point. (p. 306)

Polygon   A closed plane figure formed by
three or more line segments joined at the
endpoints. (p. 314)

Positive number   A number that is greater
than zero. (p. 370)

Prime factorization   Any composite number
can be factored as a product of primes. This
product is called the prime factorization of
that number. (p. 130)

Examples: $24 = 2 \times 2 \times 2 \times 3$ or $2^3 \times 3$.
$45 = 3 \times 3 \times 5$ or $3^2 \times 5$.
$60 = 2 \times 2 \times 3 \times 5$ or $2^2 \times 3$
$\times 5$.

Prime number   A whole number greater than
1 that has only two factors, 1 and itself.
(p. 128)
Examples: 2, 3, 5, 7, 11, 13, 17, 19 are
all prime numbers.

Probability   A number from 0 to 1 that tells
how likely it is that an event will take place.
(p. 546)

Product   The answer to a multiplication
problem. (p. 12)

Property of one for multiplication   When
one of the two factors is 1, the product
equals the other factor. (p. 50)
Examples: $a \times 1 = a$; $6 \times 1 = 6$.

Proportion   An equality of two ratios. The
terms in a proportion are called the means
and extremes. If $\frac{a}{b} = \frac{c}{d}$ then $a \times d = b \times c$.
(p. 338)
Example: $\frac{5}{8} = \frac{15}{24}$ since $5 \times 24 = 8 \times 15$.

Protractor   An instrument used to measure
angles. (p. 310)

Pyramid   A solid with one fact that is a
polygon and three or more faces that are
triangles with a common vertex. (p. 322)
Example:

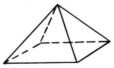

Quadrilateral   A polygon with four sides. (p.
314)

Quotient   The answer to a division problem.
(p. 72)

Radius (pl. radii)   A line segment with one
endpoint at the center of a circle and the
other endpoint on the circle. All radii of a
circle are equal. (p. 318)

Ratio   A comparison of two numbers. (p. 334)

   Example: The ratio of two to five can be written as 2 to 5, 2:5, or $\frac{2}{5}$.

Ray   A part of a line that has one endpoint and extends on and on in only one direction. (p. 306)

Reciprocals   Two numbers whose product is 1. (p. 190)

   Examples: $\frac{3}{5}$ and $\frac{5}{3}$ are reciprocals.

   8 and $\frac{1}{8}$ are reciprocals.

Rectangle   A parallelogram with four right angles. (p. 314)

Remainder   The number left over in a division problem. The remainder must be less than the divisor. (p. 72)

   Example:

   $\frac{9r3}{4)\overline{39}}$ The remainder is 3.

Rhombus   A parallelogram with four congruent sides. (p. 314)

Right angle   An angle that measures 90°. (p. 308)

Right triangle   A triangle with one right angle. (p. 312)

Roman numerals   Symbols used by the Romans to name numbers. Roman numeration does not use place value. (p. 17)

   Examples:

I	V	X	L	C	D	M
1	5	10	50	100	500	1,000

Rounding   Expressing a number to the nearest thousandth, hundredth, tenth, one, ten, hundred, thousand. (p. 10)

   Example: 37.85 rounded to the nearest tenth is 37.9.

Scale drawing   A drawing that is the same shape as an actual object, but not the same size. The scale gives the ratio of the size in the drawing to the size of the actual object. (p. 340)

Scalene triangle   A triangle with three unequal sides. (p. 314)

Scientific notation   Writing a number as the product of two factors. The first factor is between 1 and 10. The second factor is a power of 10. (p. 259)

   Example: $32,000 = 3.2 \times 10^4$

   $0.035 = 3.5 \times 10^{-2}$

Similar polygons   Polygons that have the same shape. Corresponding sides of similar polygons are in proportion. Corresponding angles are congruent. (p. 344)

Sphere   A solid with all points an equal distance from the center. (p. 320)

Square   A rectangle with 4 congruent sides. (p. 314)

Square number   The product of a number and itself. (p. 389)

   Example: $5^2 = 5 \times 5 = 25$ The square of 5 is 25.

Square root   One of the two equal factors of a number. (p. 389)

   Example: $\sqrt{25} = 5$ because $5^2 = 25$

Straight angle   An angle that measures 180°. (p. 306)

Subtraction $(-)$ An operation on two numbers resulting in a difference. (p. 26)

   Example:

25	minuend
− 8	subtrahend
17	difference

Sum   The answer to an addition problem. (p. 24)

Surface area   The sum of the areas of all the surfaces of a solid. (p. 278)

Symmetry (line)   A figure has line symmetry if it can be folded about a line so that the two halves of the figure are congruent. The fold line is the line of symmetry. (p. 318)

Time line   A number line showing dates. (p. 19)

Trapezoid   A quadrilateral with one pair of parallel sides. (p. 314)

   Example:

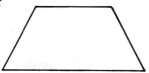

Triangle   A polygon with three sides. (p. 314)

Unit price   The ratio of the total cost to the number of units. (p. 257)

Unlike fractions   Fractions with different denominators. (p. 162)

   Example: $\frac{2}{3}$ and $\frac{3}{4}$ are unlike fractions.

Vertex (pl. vertices)   The point at which two rays of an angle, two sides of a polygon, or three or more edges of a solid meet. (p. 308)

Volume   The number of cubic units needed to fill a solid. (p. 280)

   Example: Volume of a rectangular solid is $V = \ell \times w \times h$.

Zero property for addition   When 0 is added to any addend, the sum equals the addend. (p. 24)

   Examples: $9 + 0 = 9$; $0 + 12 = 12$.

Zero property for multiplication   If 0 is a factor, the product is always 0. (p. 50)

   Examples: $13 \times 0 = 0$; $0 \times 7 = 0$.

Zero property for subtraction   When 0 is subtracted from a number, the answer is the number. (p. 24)

   Example: $8 - 0 = 8$.

A 4
B 5
C 6
D 7
E 8
F 9
G 0
H 1
I 2
J 3